——————— NATIONALIST VOICES IN JORDAN ———————

NATIONALIST VOICES IN JORDAN

The Street and the State

BETTY S. ANDERSON

UNIVERSITY OF TEXAS PRESS

AUSTIN

First edition, 2005

Requests for permission to reproduce material from this work
should be sent to Permissions, University of Texas Press, Box 7819,
Austin, TX 78713-7819.

⊗The paper used in this book meets the minimum requirements
of ANSI/NISO z39.48-1992 (R1997) (Permanence of Paper).

Library of Congress Cataloging-in-Publication Data
Anderson, Betty S. (Betty Signe) 1965–
Nationalist voices in Jordan : the street and the state / Betty S.
Anderson.— 1st ed.
    p.   cm.
Includes bibliographical references and index.

ISBN 0-292-70625-1 (pbk. : alk. paper)
1. Jordan—Politics and government—20th century.
2. National characteristics, Jordanian. 3. Arab nationalism—Jordan.
4. Opposition (Political science) —Jordan. I. Title.
JQ1833.A58A53 2005
320.54′095695—dc22

2004021549

For my parents,
Joyce and Elroy Anderson

CONTENTS

ACKNOWLEDGMENTS

To do the research that I needed to complete my book, I received financial support from a Fulbright grant, American Center for Oriental Research/United States Information Agency grants, and a UCLA History Department research grant. With these grants, I was able to live in Jordan for two years and then return there for additional summers of research.

I would like to express my gratitude to the many people who helped me research and write this book. My first thanks go to Professor Afaf Marsot for guiding me and advising me through the years of graduate school. She forced me to look at the many possible angles each historical event presented and to take a pragmatic view of the realities of life in the Middle East. Professor Nancy Gallagher articulated and focused my ideas at a time when I needed just that kind of encouragement and support. Later, when I revised the manuscript, Ellen Lust-Okar and Michael Fischbach willingly stepped forward to provide constructive advice. The quality of this book increased immeasurably because of their efforts.

In Jordan, my project would not have been possible without the generous support of many people. Time after time, people opened their homes and allowed me to read their books and conduct interviews with them. These men did so because they wanted their story told and because they had come to trust me with it. I would like to thank all of my interviewees, without whose insights I would never have been able to complete this project. I hope this book provides a new understanding about their lives and their work. Having said that, I take sole responsibility for the information contained within this book.

I want to extend a special note of thanks to Moraiwid al-Tell for selflessly extending his help to me. He organized most of my interviews and then regaled me with stories of Jordanian history while we drove to and from them. He, Ruth, Miranda, and Tariq opened their wonderful home to me and made me feel like a member of the family.

Barbara Bernstein made my years at UCLA so much easier because of her constant help. Shauna Mulvihill, Wendy Wright, Amy Schmidt, Louise Cainkar, Fida Adely, Aimen Haddad, Jennifer Lindsay, Kurt Zamora, and Rebecca Mello have, at all times, stood by me to give encouragement and practical advice whenever my spirits began to fail. To all of my friends, I give a heartfelt thank you for all of your help.

Finally, I wish to thank my parents for their absolute and unconditional support for all of my endeavors. My mother died before I entered graduate school, but those years when she stood behind me as a relentless cheerleader for all of my projects strengthened me, and I knew, as she always said, that I would "hang in there" until I saw this book in press. My father provided the emotional and physical anchor I required as my life became increasingly nomadic and unpredictable. I always knew, no matter where I had landed, figuratively or literally, that he would be on the other end of the telephone line to hand out advice and reassurances. Because of their help, I dedicate this book to Joyce and Elroy Anderson, with all of my love.

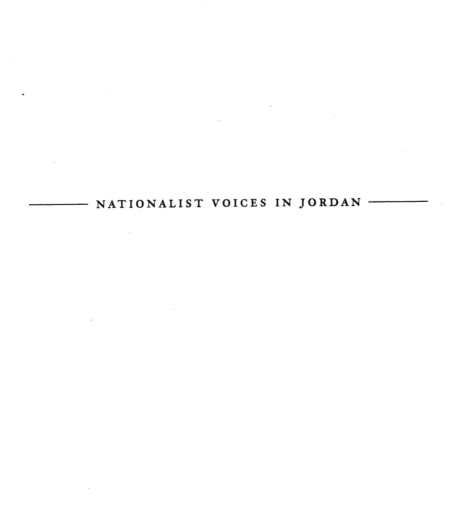

NATIONALIST VOICES IN JORDAN

ONE

THE WRITING
OF A NATIONAL NARRATIVE

*We have struggled and we have fought from the beginning, and on
behalf of a message, just as our fathers and grandfathers fought
beforehand, in defense of their message, the message of unity, the message
of freedom, the message of strength, the message of building, the message
of protecting our sacred things and our sacred land, and the message of
protecting the land of the Arabs for the unity of the Arabs.*

KING HUSAYN[1]

King Husayn holds the "hearts of the people."[2]

AL-TARIKH AL-ʿARABI AL-HADITH, *MODERN ARAB HISTORY*

The quotes above come from history textbooks published by the Hashemite Kingdom of Jordan in 1959 and 1975, respectively. The theme of these quotes and of the textbooks as a whole is: The Hashemites are Jordan; Jordan is the Hashemite family. A sample sentence says, "The Arabs in Jordan welcomed Emir ʿAbdullah bin Husayn with a great fervor, and they gave to him the title of savior of Syria. In April 1921, the Emir established a government for his Emirate."[3] Subsequently, the subject of sentence after sentence is the reigning Hashemite king and the state he controls. The citizens of the country have no faces and no names. The British creators of the state are merely a force to be fought by the Hashemite kings.

His Majesty King ʿAbdullah continued until the end of the Second World War to struggle to end the British Mandate in Jordan. In spring 1946, His

I

Majesty went to London to demand independence for his country, and for his patience and his political wisdom, he signed with Britain a new treaty abrogating the Mandate over Jordan.[4]

Regardless of the fact that the Hashemites themselves were foreigners to Jordan, the lesson to be learned is that Jordan could not exist without the Hashemites. To succeed in their transformation from Hijazis to Jordanians, the Hashemites had literally to "imagine" the state because no such entity called Jordan existed before the establishment of its boundaries and administrative structures in 1921.[5] They then had to manufacture institutions and a narrative inextricably connecting Jordanians to a state ruled by them. Concomitantly, the Hashemites expropriated, as part and parcel of Hashemite lore and biography, events that had taken place throughout history, yet were now bounded by the borders of twentieth-century Jordan.[6]

These textbooks instruct students to look to Kings 'Abdullah and Husayn as the generators of state largesse; to thank 'Abdullah and Husayn for protecting the rights of the Palestinians; and to reward 'Abdullah and Husayn with their loyalty.

> His Majesty Emir 'Abdullah attached importance to opening schools and spreading education among all levels of the society, just as he was concerned with the army and with improving the economy of the country and in organizing the administrative apparatus. There hastened to Transjordan many of the Arabs of Palestine and Syria to live under the protection of a just, democratic Arab government and to enjoy what Transjordan had to offer in terms of security and prosperity.[7]

The overall message conveyed is that students should express their gratitude to the Hashemites.

As for the faceless residents of this new state, the textbooks discuss them only in relation to the places where they live: in "urban," "rural," and "nomadic" areas.[8] The textbooks provide only simple recitations of their lifestyles and the type of schooling required for each group. For example, urban residents have a decreasing appreciation for the customs and traditions existing in the villages. Discussion of the rural areas highlights the need to reconfigure education to focus on the particular concerns of agriculture. In both areas, the biggest problem is the need for more social and recreational centers to give people direction in their free time. In discussions of the bedouin areas, subdivided into nomadic, semi-nomadic, and settled categories, the texts stress the people's reliance on their own laws and the problems peculiar to nomadic lifestyles. In some of the texts, the Palestinian refugees represent yet a fourth category of inhabitants, who, if God wills, will be returned to their usurped paradise. The people of Jordan have no right to act on behalf of the nation; they must only react to the dictates of the Hashemites.

In these texts, the Hashemites are constructing a history that grounds their leadership in Jordan over a designated timeline. The writing and "recovery" of such a linear narrative became a primary goal of the new nation-states of the nineteenth and twentieth centuries, in Europe and then the colonial world. The point behind this project was to show that a primordial nation existed on a given piece of land, that regardless of who ruled, or who colonized the area, something intrinsically unique about these people and this land could be identified. Implicit in this process is the idea that the nationalist liberation movement or the new state government served as the inevitable culmination point of that narrative. The process of compiling and constructing a national history has often proved problematic for new states, however, because of the many different definitions of identity used by the people living within and outside their boundaries. In the case of Jordan, the Hashemites had to find ways to accommodate the larger Arab nationalist narrative that served as the accepted historical, ethnic, and linguistic bond in the region prior to World War I and the subsequent division of the region into Arab nation-states. To avoid a conflict between the existence of the Jordanian nation and "the message of protecting the land of the Arabs for the unity of the Arabs," the Hashemites placed Jordan into the continuum of Arab history, and then as a logical extension of it. The Hashemites proclaimed themselves the personal bridge connecting the two narratives. As the leaders of the Arab Revolt in World War I, they took on the mantle of Arab nationalist leadership, laying claim to the leadership of the whole Arab nationalism movement from that point forward.[9] Jordan was not just a separate state, under its Hashemite rule. It stood at the epicenter of a potential reunion of the divided Arab states, precisely because of that Hashemite leadership.

While it is understandable that the Hashemite kings would place themselves at the center of the Jordanian historical narrative, most scholars writing about Jordan over the last twenty years have failed to question the basic premise of these texts. They add to the Hashemite narrative primarily by showing that a small oligarchy of politicians—the "King's men"—and a series of British advisors augmented the work of the Hashemite family.[10] The basic question they all try to answer is: How did the Hashemites and the "King's men" stay in power? They ask this question because the Hashemites faced a powerful opposition movement in the 1950s, working under the title of the Jordanian National Movement (JNM). The leftist political parties—the Ba'th, Communist, and National Socialist Parties, and the Movement of Arab Nationalists—became so influential by October 1956 that King Husayn granted the leader of the National Socialist Party (NSP)—Sulayman al-Nabulsi—the right to serve as prime minister of a leftist-nationalist government. However, in April 1957, the King and the "King's men" fought against their subsequent exile from the political stage and completely destroyed the JNM.

In study after study, including those by Uriel Dann, Clinton Bailey, Benjamin Shwadran, Amnon Cohen, and Kamal Salibi, to name just a few, the debate about how the Hashemites stayed in power has focused on this battle between the state and the leftist political parties that emerged in the 1950s. These authors wrote about the opposition, led by the Jordanian National Movement, but describe it as merely a weak attempt by disgruntled Palestinians and a few rogue Jordanians, aided by "outsiders," to upset the Hashemite balance of power. They implicitly accept the narrative of the Hashemite father-shaykh of the new Jordanian nation-tribe presented in the textbooks. They take as a given that the Hashemites were the legitimate, historical rulers over the country.

These scholars pinpoint the Palestinians as a primary catalyst for opposition because their politicization under the British Mandate and their distrust of the Hashemite regime made them particularly susceptible to the messages of Arab unity, anti-imperialism, and political liberalization voiced by the National Movement.[11] The decade of the 1950s saw the Palestinians organizing their forces to pressure the government to increase their level of participation. These forces proved so numerous that, as Amnon Cohen writes, "their numerical strength (and perhaps even the resultant emphasis on the Palestinian problem) make it possible to view the parties [of the JNM] as primarily belonging to the West Bank."[12] The problem with this scenario is that, by highlighting Palestinian grievances toward the Hashemites, these scholars negate the possibility that "true" Jordanian natives held similar views.[13]

To explain the fact that Jordanians did enter the political parties of the JNM and did protest in enormous numbers against the regime in the 1950s, these scholars look outside the country for their motivators. The most influential person they found was Gamal Abdel Nasser, the president of Egypt and self-proclaimed leader of the leftist movement throughout the Arab world in the 1950s and 1960s. Benjamin Shwadran, for example, speaks of Nasser's influence when he wrote that King Husayn, when the pressure became too heavy in the mid-1950s,

4

capitulated to Nasser, hoping that perhaps he could fit into the Nasser scheme. He dismissed Glubb, renounced the Anglo-Jordanian treaty, and lost the British subsidy. But when he realized that Nasser meant to eliminate him completely, especially after the parliamentary elections which brought Nabulsi to power, he had no alternative but to return to the West.[14]

Uriel Dann voices a complementary opinion when he states that the king remained in power because Nasser lacked the resolve to take the final steps to dethrone him. "It is as good as certain that Abdel Nasser never gave the lead, as distinct from, at most, his presumed blessing or his generalized knowledge of plots in the offing. His underlings went much further, but nothing could replace his own active involvement."[15] As this narrative evolved, those who fought against the regime did so under the guidance—and often the pay—of Nasser. The Jordanians and their political parties do not appear as the operative actors.

The overall viewpoint of these diplomats and scholars is summarized by Robert Satloff's statement that,

> In sum, after 1957, the contours of Hussein's monarchy bore a strong resemblance to the regime built up by Abdullah, Kirkbride, and Glubb in the years before the 1948 war. There were, of course, important differences, the two most glaring of which were the departure of a permanent British military presence in August 1957 and the emergence of the emotive call for a "Palestinian entity," in March 1959. But the two eras of Hashemite history, pre-1948 and post-1957, were built on similar foundations and sustained on similar principles. What connected them were the politics and personalities of the "king's men."[16]

For these scholars of Jordan, the tumultuous period of the 1950s served merely to solidify the strength and legitimacy of the Hashemite leadership. The Hashemites maintained their position despite the work and desires of the "outsiders" and the rogue elements in the society. No societal changes impinged upon this balance of power.

These scholars are absolutely correct in their analyses of the power of the Hashemite family and the state constructed around it. The Hashemites successfully destroyed the JNM in 1957 because they were able to garner support from key components of the society—the "King's men," the bedouin tribesmen in the army, the peasants in the villages, and the merchants in the cities—and the opposition, in the end, could not gather as much support from their own, disenfranchised urban communities. The more interesting question, which is not addressed by any of these scholars, is *why* those elements in the society chose to support the Hashemites, given that the Hashemites were foreigners to the area themselves and came to power on the wings of British colonialism. On the other side of the coin: Who supported the Jordanian National Movement, and why did they do so? Were they merely duped into doing so by men like Nasser, or did they have their own rationales for opposing the Hashemite state?

Partha Chatterjee has said of the interplay between colonialism and nationalism that, "In the beginning, nationalism's task is to overcome the subordination of the colonized middle class, that is, to challenge the 'rule of colonial difference' in the domain of the state."[17] He reminds us that the colonial state was "destined never to fulfill the normalizing mission of the modern state because the premise of its power was a rule of colonial difference, namely, the preservation of the alienness of the ruling group."[18] How, then, did the Hashemites successfully "fulfill the normalizing mission of the modern state"? How did they convince this population that Jordan had a legitimate right to exist and that they deserved this population's allegiance? Why did the JNM fail to overcome the "alienness of the ruling group"?

Recent scholarship has begun to address some of these questions by focusing on the relationship between the Hashemite state and its citizenry. Andrew Shryock, Michael Fischbach, and Joseph Massad have all examined the relationship between the Hashemite state and different social groups living within its borders.[19] The general theme presented in all of these works is that the Hashemite leaders successfully managed to garner support for their national project because they supplied services never seen before, they provided a national narrative with resonance in the society, and they co-opted into their national project many of the symbols of the nation, tribe, family, and history so central to the area. These works have given three-dimensional life to the "bedouin" and "rural" inhabitants and begun the process of examining the most influential agencies for change in these arenas. The new emerging narrative highlights the fact that the people of Jordan did not follow the Hashemite state blindly but did so because of a burgeoning reciprocal relationship between them.

This study will focus on the far more neglected "urban" areas and the institutions most influential in generating the feelings of national identity that existed there. The urban areas are key to understanding the societal transformation and subsequent political conflict Jordan witnessed, precisely because the cities witnessed the largest expansion of institutions, services, and populations in the entire country. This means that the bulk of the bureaucratic offices, schools, and media outlets opened in the cities, influencing the largest number of rural migrants and job seekers. Out of these new institutions—these agencies of change and socialization—emerged both the supporters of the state and its opposition. Both groups contributed to the national history of the Hashemite Kingdom of Jordan; the Hashemite kings did not work alone or merely with the "King's men." The national narrative, left out of the textbooks and the earlier scholarship of Jordan, needs to include the work of the elite politicians *and* the Jordanians and Palestinians who worked with and fought against the regime and its colonial overseer. In the case of Jordan, societal change wrought political conflict. The urban areas served as the focal points for these clashes because demonstrations, strikes, and party activities exploded in them month after month throughout the 1950s. The Hashemites had to recognize the demands of their changing society in order to survive in power; they did not work in a vacuum, as earlier studies and their own textbooks have suggested.

This struggle to survive grew particularly difficult throughout the 1950s as those Palestinians already politicized by years of opposition to the British Mandate came together with the Jordanians who had questioned the rule of the Hashemites. They formed the political parties of the Jordanian National Movement, and, under the umbrella of Arab nationalism, the two groups spent the 1950s opposing the Hashemite monopoly over the institutions of power and definitions of national identity. In the beginning, their goal was to make the governmental structure in Jordan more inclusive and representative, and, over the long term, to unite Jordan with one or more of the Arab countries. By utilizing this pan-national umbrella, the leaders of the JNM proposed that a reorganization of the political boundaries of the region would simultaneously solve the country's political, social, and economic problems. Arab nationalism symbolized for the leaders and participants in the JNM not just a regional political movement but also a call for revolutionary change at the domestic level. This study will illustrate that the rallying call was for the youth—the "new"—to replace the "old" politicians of the Hashemite regime. Demands for social and economic justice merged naturally with those for independence from colonial rule. The "new" would eliminate the colonialism of the "old." Thousands flocked to join the parties of the JNM, their demonstrations, and their strikes, because Arab nationalism held resonance for a society in flux.

In the 1950s, the struggle was fought most visibly on the streets of the country's cities and in the halls of government, but beneath the surface an ideological debate fueled it, fought out in the schools, the clubs, and the media. Even though the JNM ultimately failed on the political level and was destroyed in 1957, the Hashemites had to recognize that the country's socioeconomic framework had changed dramatically in the course of the 1950s, with new strata and new demands threatening their position. To succeed, the state had to adapt itself to the new conditions in the society by co-opting many of the new urban strata into its ranks and by expanding state services to many more. Thus, Jordan represents a case study about the institutions and agencies vital for the successful establishment of a new state; the interplay between changing societal conditions and political activity; and the simultaneous writing of a historical narrative defining and delineating national identity.

As this review has shown, the history of Jordan that has emerged—in scholarly works and the histories produced by the Hashemites themselves—has until recently examined only a small cadre of actors. In that story, the "Arab street" plays no role in the development of the country or the analyses of its policies through history. However, it is precisely this "Arab street" that holds a key to understanding not only developments in Jordan in the twentieth century, but the Fertile Crescent as a whole. An examination of the Jordanian National Movement will provide a window onto a society in flux, one beginning to function within a new array of national institutions. Memoirs of the Jordanian and Palestinian leaders of and participants in the Movement, newspaper accounts of the day, transcripts of radio broadcasts, and minutes of the parliamentary debates will be used to answer that question of why Jordanians and Palestinians chose to participate in an opposition movement. They will also show which agencies proved to be the most influential in disseminating ideas about national identity and political activity.

In essence, the story of the Jordanian National Movement is a personal story of the men and women who led the Movement and participated in its activities in the 1950s. Interviews with and memoirs of its leaders and participants provide an invaluable insight into the influences they felt were particularly important in their lives. Working with such sources always presents problems for the researcher, and those of the Jordanian opposition movement are no exception. For example, the fact that these people wrote these memoirs at the end of their lives, after years of political activism, clearly influences the tone. They wanted to go back in their history to locate the events that had particularly affected them. Historical memory often distorts such events. Also, only a small number of the leaders of the Movement recorded their memoirs or discussed their experiences in interviews. As a result, the work of those who did record their activities takes on added importance vis-à-vis those who did not. In a glaring example, the memoir of Sulayman al-Nabulsi, one of the most important, if not the most important, leader of the day, is inaccessible to the researcher.[20] That fact does not negate the depth of his participation. In the Palestinian case, 'Abdullah al-Rimawi of Ramallah and 'Abdullah Na'was of Jerusalem neglected to compile memoirs before their deaths.[21]

Despite such limitations, these memoirs and interviews still represent a microcosm of the experiences and influences young people were undergoing in the first half of the twentieth century in both Jordan and Palestine. In their own voices, these Jordanians and Palestinians bring to life the reasons why they chose to struggle on behalf of their political goals and to lead lives which condemned them to jail or exile for months and even years at a time. At the same time, their lives reflect the changing sets of opportunities available to Jordanians and Palestinians of very different economic classes, both because of the state's constructions and their own initiatives. New kinds of schools, an urbanizing population, better means of transportation, and new occupations all connected people within the state and the region in new kinds of ways. People like those who led the JNM served in the vanguard for these transformations and, accordingly, played an important role in helping others to make the transition. As a consequence, the stories of the leaders and members of the Jordanian National Movement highlight many of the socioeconomic changes Jordan and Palestine experienced in the Mandate and early independence periods. These memoirs provide the names and the lives behind the faceless Jordanians and Palestinians of the Hashemite texts. They also illustrate the fact that the history of Jordan and Palestine should not be bifurcated, as is the case in so many earlier studies; their histories merge for a period in the mid-twentieth century.

What comes through the memoirs most clearly is a personal, collective fervor to initiate political change. Ba'th Party member Jamal al-Sha'ir has said of the nationalism of these opposition members that it should be considered "patriotic," in the very emotional sense of the word.

> We call ourselves patriotic; not like saying the national health service in England. No, patriotic. We are patriotic. We are the ones who love our country.... Actually, if we want to translate the name of the Hizb al-Watani al-Ishtiraki, it should not be the National Socialist Party, it should be the Patriotic Socialist Party. This is what they meant when they say, watani: "I love my country. You don't love my country like I do."[22]

This may be an overly idealistic and naïve perception on the part of these activists, but it is still important to keep in mind, particularly since the histories of Jordan so often negate the passion of the participants, especially of the opposition. The most learned people in the society—Jordanian and Palestinian—came out in opposition to the Hashemite state and put forward clear policies for solving its problems. These people were not radicals inherently opposed to the government; they wanted to free their country of European control and the limitations presented by the existence of a colonial proxy government. While some people joined the progressive and Arab nationalist parties in a bid to gain power for themselves, the majority did not. They wanted to find new avenues for gaining access to governmental power so they could initiate the programs they felt would solve the problems surrounding them. They expressed a multiplicity of opinions about the possible solutions. Their passions and ideologies led them to form the parties, write for the newspapers, and lead the demonstrations that demanded these changes in the regime throughout the 1950s. The leaders who emerged in the early 1950s took on the task of mobilizing the next generation. The politicization process, thus, became self-perpetuating.

By explaining why and how the JNM proved so successful in garnering support from the urban populations, these memoirs simultaneously highlight the role the schools, clubs, media, Boy Scout troops, and national militaries, to name some of the most influential institutions, played in forming political and national loyalties. States and national liberation and political opposition movements all use different kinds of institutions to disseminate their messages. Looking solely at the actions of the elite political actors neglects the political nature of these institutions. It is not only the diplomatic and political maneuvering taking place at the elite level that activates people; local institutions play a similar if not more influential role in explaining and defining political events for the general populace. Participation in these institutions provides a framework for involvement in the national political sphere because, in them, the new political roles people need to play are identified. For a study of national development, these institutions are key because most of them were newly adapted or newly formed within the societies of the colonial and post-colonial worlds of the twentieth century. These institutions provide an insight into the mechanisms for developing and spreading new ideas and new national consciousnesses. The importance of memoirs and interviews in this analysis stems from the fact that these institutions do not have the same kinds of documents government agencies typically produce. Lists of lectures given at a specific club, archives of newspaper editions, and syllabi at local schools can be analyzed by the researcher, but only memoirs can truly articulate the influence these institutions had on the populace. Granted, these analyses are subjective and may be distorted by time; nonetheless, these memoirs provide the best information about how local and state institutions activate people on a national level. National consciousness and political symbolism certainly emanate from the political elite, but they infiltrate the population through these local institutions, these agencies of change and socialization.

The first section of this study will examine the interwar period, when the Jordanian and Palestinian leaders worked to establish their legitimacy on their respective lands. The study will focus particularly on the agencies of socialization—the schools, the clubs, and the governmental offices—to analyze how identity became an arena of contention in both Jordan and Palestine. The second half of the study will focus on the 1950s, when the new professional intelligentsia, made up of Jordanians and Palestinians, working with the burgeoning urban strata, threatened the very existence and identity of the Hashemite Kingdom of Jordan.[23] This part of the story examines the leftist political parties these men established and incorporated under the title of the Jordanian National Movement. Struggles took place over Jordan's entrance into the Baghdad Pact, Arabization of the army, the formation of a nationalist government between October 1956 and April 1957, and the very borders of the state. Throughout the decade, the opposition influenced government decision-making from outside, via street politics, and then from inside the halls of government itself. In the end, the Hashemite state succeeded in physically destroying this national opposition movement but could not negate its influence. In reaction, in the 1960s, the state broadened its base of support to make its institutions far more inclusive. The social safety net, as well as the instruments of Hashemite socialization, became more extensive and more influential in generating a Jordanian national identity.

In illustrating this story of nation-building via the media of memoirs and interviews, this study will not provide a recitation of political events; that story of Jordan and Palestine has already been told in earlier works and in the Hashemites' own histories. Instead, this study focuses more on the reactions people had to given events and the influences people found the most useful in their own route toward national identification, whether Jordanian, Palestinian, or Arab. The political catalysts will be discussed rather than the play-by-play of political exchange.

TWO

THE "DOMAINS"
OF NATIONAL IDENTITY

O Sister of Rumm!! How is Rumm?
And how are Bani Atiyyah?
Are their highlands still proud and lofty?
And is their land still healthy and wholesome?
Are the hillocks of Wadi al-Yitim still smiling?
And is its soil still fertile?
Are Shihan lower slopes still gorgeous,
Abounding in luxurious plants?
When Franks had no sway in our land
And when foreigners had no posts erected in your desert?

MUSTAFA WAHBAH AL-TELL, 'ARAR[1]

All poetry, books, volumes [speak] about the Arab nation. It's rooted in
the mind that there is one nation, called [the] Arab nation.

HAMAD AL-FARHAN[2]

These nationalist songs and others implanted in the souls of our
generation a spirit of freedom and nationalism.

BAHJAT ABU GHARBIYAH[3]

The history of Jordan and Palestine illustrates that ideology does matter; that debates about national identity can alter day-to-day events and relationships. In Partha Chatterjee's terms, the "domains" of national identity give structure and meaning to new state institutions and feelings of shared experiences.[4] In Jordan and Palestine, the debates about the "inner" and "outer" domains played out on the ground in the twentieth century because political activity came hand in hand with nationalist discourse. Nationalism became a passion for political activists of all stripes, whether for those in Palestine fighting against the British, or for others in Jordan fighting against the Hashemites, because nationalism became equated with political freedom. Everywhere, people sang nationalist songs and recited poetry extolling past Arab glories, expressing sentiments evident in the passage from Bahjat Abu Gharbiyah quoted at the beginning of the chapter. The story of the Jordanian National Movement (JNM) can only be told within this context. The actors within the Movement continually placed their activities within the context of nationalism, and the Hashemites used their own defined nationality to counteract Movement influence.

Given this reality, of course, the parameters of the "nation" were hotly contested. To construct their national identity, the Hashemites and the Palestinians looked inward, from the boundaries that "limited"[5] their lives. Institutions constructed by the British, the Hashemites, and the Palestinians began slowly to define the two nations. However, many Jordanians, and the Palestinians who joined them in the JNM in the 1950s, also began to widen the parameters of their national consciousness. For them, Arab nationalism supplied the answers not only to the political divisions within the region, but also to the economic and social problems they deemed inextricably connected to them. The loss of most of Palestine to Israel exacerbated this view. Throughout the 1950s, a nationalized solution to these problems would be put forward by the leaders of the JNM.

The proponents of these different national forces—the Hashemites, the Jordanians, and the Palestinians—had to initiate the process whereby, as Homi Bhabha says, "the scraps, patches and rags of daily life must be repeatedly turned into the signs of a coherent national culture, while the very act of the narrative performance interpellates a growing circle of national subjects."[6] To facilitate this process, Fatma Müge Göçek believes that

nationalism is constructed through a similar process of social closure whereby a social group assumes the cloak of the "nation" to contest, negotiate, and determine which groups, meanings, and practices ought to define the imagined community of the nation. As this group identifies certain shared characteristics of what comprises a nation, as it creates common myths, employs specific cultural symbols, passes particular laws, it concomitantly starts to form social boundaries around the imagined community that include some elements and exclude others.[7]

In Jordan and Palestine, the competing territorial and Arab nationalisms found the defining symbols and myths differed depending on their national parameters and their constituencies. Each of the "social groups" chose the "scraps, patches and rags of daily life" that conformed to its particular national narrative and its need to increase its "growing circle of national subjects." In this realm, the schools, social and literary clubs, the media, the political parties, the streets of the cities, as well as the halls of government, came to be creative arenas for nationalist growth and the dissemination of new ideas. For as Göçek says of the Ottoman Empire in general,

> The transformations through war, commerce, and reform certainly set the parameters within which nationalism emerged. Yet it was the new interpretations offered by historical visions, literary interpretations, and educational innovations that endowed the structural transformations with meaning. As history and religion created new visions of the future, as literature and linguistics generated new realms of meanings, and as education and the print media reproduced sets of alternate images of society, the Greek, Armenian, Turkish, and Arab nationalisms acquired a boundless spirit that recaptured the past, present, and future.[8]

It is here, in the many agencies for social change, that the most vitriolic debates about national identity took place. It is also here where the national narratives of the opposing forces in Jordan's political arena took center stage. The battle between the state and the opposition in the 1950s would certainly be about political power, but would always be articulated within the framework of differing national solutions to Jordan and Palestine's myriad problems. Thus, nationalism in the Jordanian and Palestinian situations served as a focus for the passions of the political sphere. An understanding of the political conflicts and the socioeconomic changes that took place in Jordan and Palestine in the twentieth century requires that the discussion begin with an examination of the different national positions put forward by the Hashemites, the Palestinians, and the Arab nationalists.

HASHEMITE-JORDANIAN NATIONALISM

Before the British installed 'Abdullah as the head of the new government of Transjordan in April 1921, the area had been divided by socioeconomic, geographical, and political interests and did not in any way represent a united nation. No national movement emerged before or during World War I calling for the establishment of a nation on that land. This does not mean, however, that no state structure existed beforehand or that the land was a completely blank national slate for those living on the land. But nothing called "Transjordan" had existed, and the people who would eventually be defined as "Transjordanian" could never have envisioned the form the Anglo-Hashemite state took after 1921. The northern inhabitants looked to the Syrian and Palestinian towns of Damascus and Nablus for their political and economic interactions, while the south looked more toward the Hijaz and southern Palestine. Transjordan's importance to the Middle East as a whole lay with its location as a route for the Hajj [Pilgrimage] caravan to Mecca. The Arabs traveling from Mecca called the area masharif al-Sham [approaches to Syria], and those going in the other direction designated it as masharif al-Hijaz [approaches to the Hijaz].[9] The late nineteenth century saw the reimposition of Ottoman rule on the region, with the reorganization of administrative centers and the integration, often for the first time, of the inhabitants of what would become Transjordan into the Ottoman state and the world economic trading system. These administrative divisions, however, did not unite the people of the future Transjordan into the political entity in which they would find themselves after 1921. Only when the Ottoman Empire fell at the end of World War I did the inhabitants of this region begin to think in broader, more nationalistic, terms. They demanded of the British government that a national council and an Arab prince be appointed to lead the area, but only vaguely defined the boundaries and the identity of the inhabitants to be included. The borders the European colonialists subsequently drew in the Middle East after World War I gradually began to serve as the parameters for people's national imaginations. Jordan was no different. The issue here, however, is what kind of state and nation would be constructed. In this debate, the primary actors in the process—the original inhabitants, 'Abdullah, the British officials assigned to the Jordanian Mandate, and the first officials in its government—all had different and conflicting ideas about what this new nation would ultimately become.

The very first step toward the construction of the new Transjordanian nation, taken in 1922, was to cut the Palestine Mandate into two, roughly along the Jordan River, creating the Emirate of Transjordan on the eastern shore. In the next few years, British officials and the Transjordanian government drew the lines between British Transjordan and French Syria, and then the Hijaz and Transjordan. With these acts, residents of the region were arbitrarily brought into or excluded from the new state, based not on their own desires but regional strategic issues. Implicitly and explicitly, those who came within the boundaries of the Jordanian state became potential citizens of the nation it represented; no other uniquely Hashemite-Jordanian commonality united them in this early stage. These boundaries formed the framework through which all subsequent political discussions have taken place throughout the entire Fertile Crescent. It is within these boundaries that the Europeans and their indigenous clients established the institutions identified with the new states. Thus, maps and nationhood became integrally related in the nineteenth and twentieth centuries as the red pens of the European politicians and mapmakers drew the outlines of the colonial world.

These red pens did more than just delineate what existed on the ground; they helped produce nations out of disparate religions and ethnicities, uniting these groups as citizens within them. As Thongchai Winichakul has asked, ". . . how could a nation resist being found if a nineteenth-century map had predicted it?"[10] In much of the colonized world in the nineteenth and twentieth centuries, those lines pre-dated the nations; people on the ground in Africa, the Middle East, or Asia did not get invited to the Berlin Conference in 1884 or to the San Remo Conference after World War I, nor did the European representatives at these talks fully understand the lands they were dividing. For example, Alec Kirkbride reports that the politicians in Paris in 1930 who worked on a map to demarcate the border between Syria and Jordan had never even been to either area, and the maps with which they worked were inaccurate.[11] Regardless, the lines on a map drawn in Paris and in other such arenas had become the boundaries of people's national imaginations, had become the walls between "us" and the "others" left outside. As Thongchai theorizes for Thailand,

> Boundary lines are indispensable for a map of a nation to exist—or, to put it another way, a map of a nation presupposes the existence of boundary lines. Logically this inevitably means that boundary lines must exist before a map, since a medium simply records and refers to an existing reality. But in this case the reality was a reversal of that logic. It is the concept of a nation in the modern geographical sense that requires the necessity of

having boundary lines clearly demarcated. A map may not just function as a medium; it could well be the creator of the supposed.[12]

In much of the colonized world, the lines created the "supposed" "reality"; the maps served as conduits for regional political strategies, not indigenous national desires.

In many ways, the shifting of boundaries in the Jordanian state puts a lie, again, to the role of mapmaking in the process of depicting the "supposed." Thongchai says that "a map claims to have a mimetic relationship with reality. A map is able to operate as long as one postulates that a map is the non-interfering medium between spatial reality and human perception—that reality is the source and the referent of the relationship."[13] Yet no ethnic, linguistic, religious, or historical context for the Hashemite-Jordanian nation existed. Instead, the Anglo-Hashemite leaders defined the nation based initially on those boundary lines. Presented with an empty shell, with no institutions existing under the rubric of "Jordan," the British and 'Abdullah took on the task of reformulating the institutions that had already been established there and, more importantly, building from scratch those that would be irrevocably related to the new state in the eyes of its inhabitants.

Those affiliated with these state structures gained the right to "assume the cloak of the 'nation'" and define its history, its boundaries, and its peoples. In Iraq, Lebanon, and Syria, as in Jordan, the French and British established systems of indirect political rule in which the populations of these areas participated in elections of national parliaments and obtained jobs in the colonial bureaucracies and militaries. Despite the fact that these systems granted Jordanians, Iraqis, Lebanese, and Syrians little real political power, they did serve as magnets enabling the establishment of territorially based nationalisms. Vested interests emerged, attached to these institutions. Just as these institutions of imperialism "limited" the scope of action under which these men could function, they also provided them with an arena in which they held a certain degree of power.

Throughout the Fertile Crescent, notable families and tribal and village leaders all gained positions within the new colonial structures and thus became beholden to the states' continued existence. They joined the proxy governments and signed contracts to supply them with goods, thereby forming the first pillars of their states. They are the ones who initially benefited from the very existence of the states and the European role in their construction. They held a stake in the continuation of those borders and governments, not only in their own states but in the surrounding ones. If a boundary came down between two states in the region, the domino effect could bring down even more, thus destroying the power base each group had created in its individual arena. A member of the Movement of Arab Nationalists, Hamad al-Farhan, has said of the governments of the Arab world, "every government became supported by 20 other governments, defending the same thing" in their regimes.[14] Inevitably, many of these government officials and clients began to identify themselves nationally as "Syrians" or "Jordanians," as defined by the borders and the governmental institutions dictating the limits of their lives.

To make this transformation work, leaders like the Hashemites had to gain the loyalty of the new inhabitants of the state; they had to convince them that they had the legitimate right to rule over them, that they were the true nationalist leaders, despite the artificiality of the borders and the governmental institutions. Even more importantly, the Hashemites had to convince the populace that they were not foreigners, and thus had the right to define who the "true" Jordanians were. In the Hashemite case, a multipronged approach provided the answer to these dilemmas. Governmental institutions supplied services the diverse population demanded, and the national narrative disseminated by the state presented a plausible story connecting the past to the present via the agency of the new state and the royal family. In the process, vested interests became beholden to the continued existence of this Hashemite state.

The support the Hashemites and the British gained in the country via the new state institutions they built—the bureaucracy, the army, the schools, and the clubs—as well as the many services supplied, such as electricity and improved transportation, garnered a great deal of support from among the inhabitants. These structures, starting with the establishment of the Emirate in 1921, served to produce a centrifugal force radiating out from 'Abdullah and the capital, Amman. The expanded government created new jobs for those fortunate enough to attend the few schools in the country, doled out funds for development, established a new military culture for the bedouin, and dictated the legal terms under which Transjordanians now needed to identify themselves, to use one of Joseph Massad's theories of state construction in the Emirate.[15] Politicians, shaykhs, office seekers, and the like now had to turn to the government for answers to their requests. Pertinent to the state's founding is John Roberts's theorizing about a later period: "The Hashemite state did . . . embark upon an ambitious modernization program in the hope of creating a sense of Jordanian nationalism while improving the country's ability to prosper."[16] The goal of this project was to consistently make the connection between that prosperity and the existence of the Hashemite state. Roberts adds that "Modernization policy assisted in the weaving together of a Jordanian civil society whose focus remained on Amman and whose consciousness of the means of political action was inextricably tied to Hashemite institutions."[17] The boundaries drawn by the British and the governmental structures established by 'Abdullah provided the framework under which Transjordanians now had to live and work. Through government services, couched in the language of Hashemite patronage, the people living in this new state began to collect benefits they had never received before. For example, Michael Fischbach has identified a reciprocal relationship between the peasants and the state via the agency of land reform. He says that "In the process, both the shape of state-societal discourse and the conceptualizations of 'property' and of 'Jordan' itself were defined by the state, which was in turn constrained, however, by its commitment to safeguarding the cultivators' land."[18] In this instance, protection begat a degree of loyalty to the regime.

In other words, when the state "worked"[19] to improve people's lives, the ethos of Hashemite leadership perpetuated itself. Fewer and fewer people found the need to "overcome the subordination of the colonized masses,"[20] to use Partha Chatterjee's terms, as they began to reap benefits from the state. In specifically discussing the peasant majority in the country, Fischbach has found,

> the fact is that Jordan's overall stability and the contentment of its populace with the regime can be traced not to a naive popular appreciation for British rule nor even admiration of the Hashemites, although they have in fact been widely hailed, especially during the reign of 'Abdullah's grandson King Husayn (1953–99). Rather, this stability stems directly from the state's perceived ability to secure and protect the interests of the country's peasant majority throughout the 1930s–1950s.[21]

Through similar methods, the Hashemites slowly garnered support from bedouin tribesmen and the expanding merchant class in the cities.

Once governmental institutions have been established, states like those of the Hashemites use school systems to provide a forum for the physical reformulation of relationships within the new entity. Benedict Anderson has compared the educational trajectory under imperialism to a pilgrimage, not to a religious site, but toward jobs in a colonial bureaucracy.[22] Along these routes, students meet "travelling companions," as Anderson describes them, and acquire a belief in a shared experience, culture, and history, albeit within the artificial boundaries drawn by the colonial rulers.[23] The move out of the village, to the regional capital, and on to the colonial center alters students' frames of reference and sense of national identity as they move away from their local concerns and find like-minded companions from regions spread throughout the colony. Along the Jordanian educational route, the Hashemite regime decreed that students must recite the pledge of allegiance and sing songs extolling the nation-state. These acts constantly reminded the students that they owed obedience to the regime and its leading family. Through these schools, students followed Anderson's "pilgrimages" to government office.

In most colonial areas, over time, "nationalists" typically emerge from the schools and the administrations to overthrow the power structures of the colonial state. These institutions provide them with the vocabulary and the expertise to serve in such a vanguard position. These "nationalists" rarely question the boundaries limiting their lives; they question the power structure in the state. Thus, the state structure produced by the colonialists and the "colonized middle class" becomes the focus for national opposition and agitation. National liberation movements, coups, and revolutions frequently act as the catalysts for overthrowing the vestiges of these colonial regimes. In Jordan, however, the Hashemites successfully preempted the national movement by taking on that position themselves. They gave themselves the sole right to "fulfill the normalizing mission of the modern state"[24] by completely dismissing the role of the British in the creation of their state.

In Jordan, the act of writing this particular nationalist historical narrative contains an element of conquest over the people of Jordan. The Hashemites came from the outside, supported by another outside power, the British, yet claimed to have the right to rule the land because of their leadership over the Arab Revolt during World War I and their descent from the Prophet. On the date of Transjordan's provisional independence in 1923, King ʿAbdullah made that connection explicit by saying,

> You know how the Abbasids lost all that the Arabs had acquired, so that our race remained backward until the war of 1914–18, which took place at a time when we had awakened and were endeavouring to recover our past glory. The Arab movement was led by King Husain, the man whom God had chosen. He called his people to the right way, awakened those who were asleep and opened the eyes of those who were blind.[25]

Along with Faysal's brief kingship over Syria, these events allowed the Hashemites to claim for themselves the overlordship of the Arab nationalist movement from that point forward. The Hashemites used this history to superimpose their own narrative over those of the people of Jordan. In this narrative, the Hashemites were not foreigners, but Arab commanders leading Jordan and the region toward unity.

Yet Jordan was not a blank slate on which to write as the Hashemite leadership wished. Histories and lives existed there and fought against their submission into this new identity. This problem harks back to 'Arar's poem of this chapter's opening page.[26] For him, the people and the landscape represent Jordan, and he bemoans the fact that "Franks" and unidentified "foreigners" have conquered and destroyed its essence. The Hashemite state is inimical to his definition of Jordan. Yet the Hashemites not only destroyed alternative visions of the Jordanian nation as a threat to their position, but often did so by co-opting those elements they felt supported their cause. For example, 'Arar's poetry would become, by the second half of the twentieth century, required reading in the state's own school curricula.

In the same way, the Hashemite state initially acknowledged the many tribes' historical narratives on the land. In his study of the Balqa' tribes, Andrew Shryock has found that "each tribe has its own territory (its *bilad* or *dura*), its own history, and its own set of genealogies that link it both to the past and to the physical space it now occupies."[27] The state recognized these histories at the beginning of its tenure and even incorporated this concept into the national mapmaking process. Shryock found that

> The maps of Amman, Kerak, and Ma'an printed in 1949 by the Department of Lands and Surveys of Jordan bore dozens of tribal names, as if to suggest that tribes, like rivers, mountains, and cities, were objects on the natural landscape. The likelihood of tribal names appearing on such maps today is close to nil. Indeed, the removal of tribes from abstract space goes hand in hand with their removal from electoral politics. In the Balga, specific tribes are not recognized as electoral districts—how could they be if they are unmappable?[28]

Tribes as subcomponents of the nation-state were literally erased from the maps of the Hashemite state. While tribesmen would come to serve as the cornerstone of the country's military forces, tribes, in and of themselves, no longer formed the framework of the nation. Only the Hashemite state, henceforth, had the right to determine which aspects of tribal life constituted an element of nationalism. The symbols of the tribes' lives would be exploited by the Hashemite national project.

To be successful in co-opting and negating these alternative narratives, the Hashemites needed to locate the precise formula for gaining and maintaining power, based on both new and old modes of leadership. For example, Andrew Shryock found that even though the 'Adwan were once a powerful tribe in the Balqa', in the words of Muhammad Hamdan al-'Adwan, "then dominance was taken by the government, and we all became, as they say, one family. King Husayn is the father of that big family. *Today there is only respect and exchange.*"[29] Along with this view, Shryock has found that "The etiquette of respect and exchange is the manner 'sons' (the Jordanian tribes) should adopt in the presence of their 'father' (the Hashemite monarch), and the observance of this etiquette turns certain historical topics and modes of expression into evidence of disrespect."[30] The myth of the Hashemite state is precisely structured on the ability of the population to transfer their allegiance from the "fathers" of yore to the "kings" of the present.[31]

By these acts, the Hashemites successfully established in the minds of the population now living within Jordan that Jordan had a right to exist as a separate nation-state. As early as the 1920s, even those who opposed the specific project the Hashemites were undertaking did not question the existence of Jordan. Then, during the course of the Mandate period and in the first years after independence, fewer and fewer members of the population continued to question the reality of the Hashemite leadership of that state. A top-down approach to national construction worked in the case of Jordan.

PALESTINIAN NATIONALISM

In their search for national identity, the Palestinians used schools, the media, and the clubs as the most creative outlets for their initial pursuits. The idea of Palestine—as a nation—spread from the urban to the rural areas via the agency of these organizations. As Rashid Khalidi has shown, the Palestinian national cause built upon the religious attachment to the holy sites of Palestine, the Ottoman administrative boundaries of this land, awareness of the European interest in its history, and "a powerful local attachment to place" among the predominantly agriculture-based population.[32] From that point, in the early twentieth century, the Palestinians formed the institutions at the grassroots and elite level that should have, in most cases, worked to form a nascent national government. The political parties, the women's organizations, the schools, the poetry circles, and the scout troops all should have gradually formed the basis for an incipient nation-state. However, the Palestinian trajectory was truncated by the movement's own internal divisions, and even more so by the national desires of the Zionists. A tripartite battle ensued as two separate national sentiments emerged within those boundaries to alternately fight each other and their British colonizers. The British did not allow the formation of a clear-cut "colonized middle class" because by doing so they would have recognized one community over another or, alternatively, have established unity between the two communities in a cohesive national body. The Zionists came closer to establishing a pseudogovernmental structure through both British help and their own initiatives. As Khalidi has stated, "The Mandate reprised the wording of the Balfour Declaration in speaking of a 'Jewish people' with a right to a 'national home,' and recognized the Zionist movement, under the name of the Jewish Agency, as a 'public body for the purpose of advising and cooperating with the Administration' in order to establish this home."[33] The Palestinians had no such national or state recognition, so had to articulate and disseminate their national idea through a broader array of civil society organizations than their Jordanian neighbors. In so doing, the Palestinians had to overcome the British denial of their national rights and concomitant British support for the Jewish immigrants laying national claim to the land. Internally, they had to overcome the historic differences existing between the urban and rural areas, and the competing families.

Signs of Palestinian dissatisfaction with these conflicts appeared throughout the 1930s. As 'Arif al-'Arif, the Palestinian judge, has stated, "the atmosphere was electrified" by 1935 because of the failed promises of the British regime, the increasing numbers of Jewish immigrants flooding into the country, and the politicization process so many Palestinians were undergoing.[34] As a result, Ylana Miller theorizes, "by 1936 Palestinian Arabs knew that their lives had changed irrevocably; their rage at British failure to recognize this fact now became impossible to deny."[35] Aiding these developments, the mass of the Palestinian population had become literate enough in the nationalized political vocabulary of the urban elite politicians that many understood the extent of the threat and the means by which the threat needed to be combated. Agencies of change had proliferated throughout the Palestinian areas, providing forums for the dissemination of nationalist ideas and the discussion of events rapidly changing Palestinian society. A clear sense of Palestinian identity resulted by 1948 from these urban and rural organizing efforts.

ARAB NATIONALISM

Throughout the 1950s, "in that feverish period of modern Arab history," as the Jordanian historian Sulayman Musa identifies it,[36] the question about national identity in Jordan became even more complex when Palestinians teamed up with their Jordanian colleagues to form the Jordanian National Movement (JNM). When the people of the East and West Banks voted to unite within the Hashemite state in 1950, Jordanians and Palestinians who opposed the type of government led by the Hashemites found an oppositional ideology in Arab nationalism. Palestinians naturally gravitated toward it because of their opposition to Hashemite rule; the Jordanians favored the activism inherent in the newly energized Arab nationalism of the post–World War II period. The leaders of the Jordanian National Movement learned about the tenets of Arab nationalism from schools and universities around the Arab world. They then spread them to the increasingly urbanized and politicized populations on both banks of the Jordan River. Throughout the 1950s, the calls for Arab nationalism would be the most potent motivators bringing people out into the streets in protest against the Hashemite regime.

By the time Jordanians and Palestinians tapped into its message in the twentieth century, Arab nationalism had witnessed a long cultural and political history throughout the Fertile Crescent. In the words of George Antonius, in the nineteenth century,

> the national movement, the Arab national movement, began as a cultural movement, which had nothing to do with politics in its early days or with any of the concepts of nationalism which had begun to appear in Europe. It began entirely independently, as a cultural revival, and it was not until a generation or two after that the first signs appeared of this cultural movement turning to politics and developing into a movement for national independence.[37]

Assuredly, politics played a role, as the Arabs used the vocabulary of nationalism emanating from the more powerful European states. They consciously or subconsciously integrated the political structure they found so powerful in the West into their efforts to strengthen their own positions. Nonetheless, Antonius is correct in saying that political organizations emerged only later, in reaction to Ottoman and European attempts to maintain and then take control over the Arab world. Secret societies and literary clubs of the nineteenth century gradually gave way in the last years before World War I to nascent political parties throughout the

Fertile Crescent. The main work of all these groupings was to locate the genesis of Arab cultural and national feeling.

In all of these arenas, the Arab language provided the continuity between the "Golden Age" of the medieval Arab-Islamic empires and the present period. For Ngugi wa Thiong'o, "language, any language, has a dual character: it is both a means of communication and a carrier of culture."[38]

> But there is more to it: communication between human beings is also the basis and process of evolving culture. In doing similar kinds of things and actions over and over again under similar circumstances, similar even in their mutability, certain patterns, moves, rhythms, habits, attitudes, experiences and knowledge emerge. Those experiences are handed over to the next generation and become the inherited basis for their future actions on nature and on themselves. There is a gradual accumulation of values which in time become almost self-evident truths governing their conception of what is right and wrong, good and bad, beautiful and ugly, courageous and cowardly, generous and mean in their internal and external relations. Over time this becomes a way of life distinguishable from other ways of life. They develop a distinctive culture and history. Culture embodies those moral, ethical and aesthetic values, the set of spiritual eyeglasses, through which they come to view themselves and their place in the universe. Values are the basis of a people's identity, their sense of particularity as members of the human race. All this is carried by language. Language as culture is the collective memory bank of a people's experience in history.[39]

The Arab nationalists of the late nineteenth and early twentieth centuries used this linguistic "memory bank" to construct an historical and cultural narrative for the Arab peoples. As Hamad al-Farhan said in the quote on this chapter's first page, "it's rooted in the mind that there is one nation, called [the] Arab nation." Language, in this case the Arabic language, transmitted the cultural artifacts from one generation to the next. Antonius described the Arab-Muslim expansion of the Middle Ages to the Royal (Peel) Commission in 1937, saying that

> The Arabs came, their language displaced those former languages and, when Arab power itself had disappeared and been succeeded by another power with another language, the Arabic language with its extraordinary hold on the minds of the people remained. That may seem to you a digression, but it is important for the light it throws on the powerful hold the Arabic language and the Arabic culture have on the Arab mind; hence the

fierceness with which Arabs seem sometimes to hold and cling to their language and their culture.[40]

Ngugi further illustrates this powerful connection by saying that "The verbal signposts both reflect and aid communication or the relations established between human beings in the production of their means of life. Language as a system of verbal signposts makes that production possible. The spoken word is to relations between human beings what the hand is to relations between human beings and nature."[41] In the same way, the Arabic language connects the Arabs to Arab culture and history. That language takes the Arabs on a journey from their pre-Islamic roots to the glories of the 'Abbasid era, to the pressing need to reform in the modern period. Thus, the rootedness of the Arabic language and culture provides "signposts" for national identity. While differences certainly exist between the written, classical Arabic and the various dialects, the connection does survive. What does not exist is a unique connection between language and the Jordanian state or culture and the Syrian state.

When the European powers established the Mandates and divided the Arab world within separate national borders, state governments and leadership structures then constructed institutions geared to keeping people inside of them. Arab nationalism reemerged in different guise during the interwar and postindependence years. For example, many Arab nationalists worked toward the reunification of Greater Syria—Syria, Lebanon, Jordan, and Palestine—as a stated goal. By the 1950s, Gamal Abdel Nasser's self-proclaimed leadership over the Arab nationalist movement meant that Egypt presented itself as an Arab nation ready to unite with its fellow Arabs. Through all these transformations, Arab nationalism stood as an independence movement against not only the Europeans but also the regional proxy governments. Consequently, a conflict arose between the narratives presented by the new kind of territorial nationalism, *wataniyah*, and those of pan-nationalism, *qawmiyah*, that had begun to reemerge in the region after World War I. Political parties and organizations emerged in the interwar periods to further the goals of each.

ARAB NATIONALISM AND
THE JORDANIAN-PALESTINIAN
POLITICAL OPPOSITION MOVEMENT

While the pre–World War I variety of Arab nationalism had involved only a small cadre of elite intellectuals, by the outbreak of World War

II, it had become a more mass-based movement throughout the region. Increasing numbers of students at the region's universities formed and joined new kinds of political parties, like the Ba'th, while Arab cultural and political connections remained ever-present within the population. Refugees from the Druze Revolt in Syria and the Palestinian battle against Zionism told their stories throughout the region, to all who would listen. Teachers moved from job to job throughout the Arab world, passing on the messages of Arab nationalism they had imbibed on their own educational pilgrimages. Because of this atmosphere, throughout the interwar years, the many bonds of the Arabs could not be ignored, despite the best efforts of the new state structures to build loyalty for their separate national projects. By the 1940s and 1950s, Arab nationalism was not just a movement of the elite, but had succeeded in mobilizing populist opinion in rural and urban areas throughout the region. Proponents of this latest manifestation of Arab nationalism claimed for themselves the vanguard of the anticolonial and progressive movement.

Schools in all the countries served as training grounds for this new, more activist Arab identity. As Gregory Starrett has found for Egypt, "Educational systems thus have a direct political role in creating the intellectual and institutional technologies that generate distinctly new social groups, not just an indirect role diagnostic of a standing distribution of power."[42] Schools supply such a service because, while they can successfully train their young charges for the new roles assigned to them by the state and its appended agencies, by so doing they also provide students with the vocabulary they need to question the very agencies they are supposed to be supporting.

Despite the best efforts by the states, like the Hashemite one in the interwar years, the narrative of Arab nationalism could not be harnessed for their territorial national projects.[43] The work of the Hashemites during World War I became part of Arab nationalist history, but many Jordanians still did not fully accept them as the bridge between the Arab narrative and the new Jordanian one being written in front of them. Historical textbooks published in cities such as Beirut, Damascus, and Jerusalem in the interwar period accentuated this identity formation. Included in these texts is an inherent recognition of the Arab unit as a whole, one undivided by boundaries. In them, a common theme identifies the invasion of Egypt by Napoleon in 1798 as a pivotal moment in the awakening of the Arabs to the sciences and ideas of Europe.[44] From that starting point, the common narrative follows that a nationalist sensibility resulted from, for example, the reforms of Muhammad Ali in Egypt, the Arab Revolt of World War I, and the overall neglect of the Arabs by the Ottoman

Empire.[45] According to a number of texts, the Arab ba'th, or rebirth, ultimately occurred first in Syria because of its people's innate intelligence, their own desire to learn, the establishment of foreign-controlled schools there, and, most importantly, the opportunities provided by the promulgation of the Ottoman constitution.[46] In these books, the interconnectedness of Arab history, language, and ethnicity is confirmed. Loyalty to a larger Arab collective superseded loyalties toward the new, far less legitimate, states now emerging around these students.

Students emerged from their "national" educational systems having been forced to acknowledge the existence of their new states but having also acquired a consciousness of the wider Arab world. The latter bond was enhanced by a dearth of opportunities available for entering higher education. Accordingly, pilgrimages took a select number of students down an increasingly narrow path toward educational advancement and, for many, political activism. Many went through the halls of the American University of Beirut (AUB), the American University of Cairo (AUC), and Damascus University. In these venues, the students found a larger "imagined community" of students from throughout the region and learned about their separate struggles against imperial control. In *this* "community," the European-drawn boundaries did not exist; they ran counter to all the experiences these young men were having. As a result, though these Arab students were structurally contained within new national borders, they found collegial ties with people outside their new frontiers. Thus, *wataniyah* and *qawmiyah* served as the guideposts for these students as they entered political life in the 1950s and 1960s, forcing them to work on the nation-state stage on behalf of more broadly based regional goals.

They emerged into that realm having been trained primarily as a new urban professional intelligentsia—doctors, lawyers, engineers, journalists, civil servants, and teachers. After graduation, the members of this stratum primarily chose not to return to their small villages but to work within larger urban settings. From an economic point of view, their new occupations necessitated this move, while from a social standpoint, these professionals wanted to be in areas with larger concentrations of like-minded members of the same stratum. Peter Gubser provides an example of this development in his discussion of professional men's activities in Karak, Jordan, during the early 1970s.

The educated men have formed a very definite mutual identity and a measure of corporateness through a few formal and informal sub-groups. Although family and tribal associations certainly retain importance for these men, the bonds have weakened to varying degrees, allowing other relationships to gain a strong hold. First, it should be noted that these men have been brought up considerably differently from former generations. They have associated much more intensively over protracted periods of time with people who are not members of their family, tribe, or village. This new pattern started in the schools, especially in secondary school, for the pupils have to leave their villages and live in Al-Karak town. . . . Secondly, for the vast majority, their mature lives are spent in the town, where they live next to members of other tribes, work with men of all segments of the society. . . . Consequently, the nature of their lives calls for association with individuals not of their traditional social groups. Further, their occupations and social desires throw them with members of their own stratum. Thus, the sustained contact, extensive social intercourse, and similar shared values and approaches to life have created among them a sense of common identity.[47]

This long quote illustrates the connections forged within this stratum and the loose definition that can be used to identify it. Men with both university and secondary degrees belonged and sought each other out as they worked their way through the bureaucracy or opened private offices, trying to maintain the collegiality established on their educational pilgrimages. This collegiality meant not only the continuation of new professional and social relationships but also the perpetuation and dissemination of new political ideologies and new outlooks on government and national identity. The resulting multiplicity of ideas generated debates within the stratum about the solutions they felt would solve the country's problems. As this new stratum no longer favored the identities posited by their national governments, many of its members had to find new, broader-based, and more revolutionary ones to encompass their new ideologies and relationships.

This professional stratum found itself at the forefront of national political discourse throughout the region by the late 1940s because of its educational experiences and its unique position within a changing socioeconomic milieu.[48] As a new stratum in Jordanian and Palestinian society, this group had to—albeit often unconsciously—forge a new relationship with its new and old communities. Its opposition to the status quo became both a revolutionary and a nationalizing tactic in opposition to the "normalizing mission" of the Hashemite state and the British Mandate. The stories of its members thus illustrate how new educational opportunities and new analyses about national identity can politicize a population and alter political outlooks. As Starrett found for Egypt,

> For the new Egyptian elites created by the schools, educational institutions eventually became centers of nationalist resistance to imperial goals, as they struggled both with the British and with the traditional Turco-Circassian elite of the Palace for control over the benefits of schooling as an engine of agricultural productivity, a tool of social control, and later as a basis for mass mobilization.[49]

A similar phenomenon took place in the Jordanian and Palestinian schools, as these students and their teachers felt they must fight against the entrenched interests of the Hashemites, the British, and often the elite Palestinian politicians as well. To combat them, this new stratum generated new pan-national ideas about the makeup of its society. Thus, a generational and ideological clash became a national one as each side not only recruited people within new types of institutions but did so under the rubric of different national infrastructures.

As part and parcel of this transformation, these new professionals also stepped into new kinds of leadership positions. For example, as the old urban networks, led by religious figures and guild leaders, began to dissolve in the twentieth century, urban professionals gradually took on their leadership roles. As Guilain Denoeux theorizes, "More importantly, these groups, whose lives revolved around universities, high schools, factories, and modern offices, did not usually engage in politics through the old networks built around the mosques, the quarters, and the crafts and trades. Instead they were attracted to better organized, more recently established, and modern-looking entities, such as political parties, trade unions, and syndicates."[50] For these new urban leaders, responses came through different types of collective action, including mass demonstrations, strikes, and boycotts.[51] As doctors, they treated the sick; as opposition leaders, they organized the street theater.

Thus, just as the new states of the Fertile Crescent came into independence in the 1930s and the 1940s, armed with their own constituencies and definitions of identity, proponents of Arab nationalism emerged from the colonial period armed with an activist agenda. As Israel Gershoni has theorized, "the professional intelligentsia sought a new ideology and political strategy to pursue its interests. They found it in Arab nationalism and the idea of Arab unity. The new professional intelligentsia did not receive and assimilate Arab nationalism passively, however, but rather imbued it with a far more radical, populist, and politicized line."[52] This new urban professional intelligentsia emerged from the new educational systems, graduated from universities like AUB, and returned to their countries trained not only for professional positions but as political activists. "In the Arab case, the professional intelligentsia's struggle against these various obstacles entailed fashioning a political counterculture based on populist nationalism combined with socialist elements as an alternative to the established conservative political culture with its constitutional parliamentary orientation and its links with the West."[53] As a result, many of them formed and participated in the political parties designed to overthrow and alter regime after regime, primarily in the name of Arab nationalism and social and economic justice. Young military officers joined in the work of these civilian professionals because they could not remain immune from the socioeconomic and ideological currents of the day. Many had attended the same schools as their civilian counterparts and had participated in some of the same political events. For both the military and the civilian components of the new Arab movement, the nationalized message of Arab nationalism meant replacing the "old" with the "new." The "old" states of the European colonizers would be replaced with the "new" unity of the Arab world. In the words of Sulayman Musa, to be "radical" meant to be a "nationalist."[54]

By the 1930s and 1940s, the vocabulary of Arab nationalism also took as a core component Palestine's central position within the Arab world. In the national narrative emerging throughout the Arab world, an historic, legitimate Arab claim to the land of Palestine was detailed. Textbooks published throughout the Fertile Crescent in the interwar period started with a glorification of the "Arab Canaanites" who brought prosperity and civilization to the region. Then, the timeline of history followed the brief Jewish reign on the land, but quickly reverted back to the history of its Arab owners. Thus, Arab culture, so essential to binding the Arabs together, also granted legitimacy to the Palestinian claim to the land. The insecurities wrought by British Mandate rule over Palestine necessitated the iteration of a stronger claim to that land. Arab and Palestinian nationalists found themselves natural allies because of this need.

CONCLUSION

The revolutionary implications of Arab nationalism came to represent for the younger generation emerging from the schools and universities at the end of the interwar period a viable alternative to the European-constructed nation-states. This generation nationalized its ideals and goals to forge an Arab nationalist rebirth, more activist than the nationalist movement that had emerged in Damascus prior to World War I. In Jordan, Hashemite-Jordanian national identity symbolized for these young people colonial control and, thus, implicitly, an obstacle to real development and growth. For the Palestinians, specifically, it meant continued frustration of their national aspirations. For these Jordanian and Palestinian party leaders, the first step in restructuring a new society was to eradicate colonialism and all its attributes. The next step was to bring a new kind of relationship to the social and economic situation in the Middle East, to better balance the different strata emerging. A study of the leaders, members, and activities of the Jordanian National Movement in the twentieth century illuminates the debates about national identity and socioeconomic change that so altered the Jordanian and Palestinian political and urban landscapes. This clash of nationalisms symbolizes also a clash of societal, economic, and political goals.

THREE

CONCEIVING TRANSJORDAN
1921–1948

O, Jordanian women! If I happen to die outside my home town,
Please weave my shrouds with your own hands
And say to my friends: "Inter some of his bones
At Irbid's Tal (hill) or at the bottom of Mount Shihan.
Hopefully a damsel with kohl-embellished eyes, passing by some day,
May recite a short text of the Quran over his grave."

'ARAR[1]

They say: those in charge of affairs in Amman are angered
At my frankness and, therefore, they have excommunicated me!!

They say those wielding influence in Amman have got fed up
With my behavior because I have befriended a wanton gang.

Amman's magnates have severely censured
My hastening to gypsies' tents with my friends and drinking buddies.

How true this would have been had Amman ever known
Since its foundation any person of consequence!

'ARAR[2]

As 'Abdullah took over the governance of the new Emirate of Transjordan in 1921, the most immediate problems involved subduing the tribes and extending the reach of governmental power to all corners of the state. Yet underlying these more practical concerns was a key question about the long-term survivability of the Hashemite leadership over this fragile new state. As Richard Taylor has asked, "By virtue of Jordan's status as a country, the rise of nationalism was inevitable. But what form was such nationalism to take?"[3] The 1920s and 1930s witnessed the Hashemite attempt to answer this question. To succeed at his new task, 'Abdullah had to, first, convince his new subjects that Transjordan had a legitimate right to exist within its borders. Second, 'Abdullah had to inextricably connect the Hashemite family to that state of Transjordan. The interwar years saw the successful completion of the first goal, with Transjordanians coming increasingly to accept the political existence of the Emirate of Transjordan because of the explicit connection made between the services provided and the state initiating them. This period saw slower movement toward the second goal, as military and political movements came out in opposition to the Hashemite type of government and the definition of the nation it proffered. The Hashemite historical narrative had not been fully established yet, but its bases had been laid.

TRANSJORDAN BEFORE
THE HASHEMITE STATE

As Eugene Rogan has shown, "It was the Ottomans who introduced the registers of a modern bureaucracy, a regular system of taxation, a codified system of law, and a communications infrastructure to the southern extremities of their Syrian province which came to be known as Transjordan. The modern state was introduced in Transjordan by the Ottomans in the nineteenth century, not the British or the Hashemites after the First World War."[4] Socially and economically, the Ottomans increased the numbers and types of settlements, settled some of the bedouin tribes, and founded some of the country's important cities, while allowing for an increase in economic relations between the areas under Ottoman control.[5] The steps the Ottomans undertook in the second half of the nineteenth century prepared the people to accept the later imposition of the Hashemite state on their lives, because they understood the benefits that could accrue from the existence of such a state. As Rogan has shown, the Ottoman Tanzimat state did not move into the region in a solely repressive capacity but brought with it institutions that changed the social fabric, often for the better. Also, by individualizing people's relationship to the state, through such acts as the 1858 Land Law, the Ottomans germinated the concept of citizenship and a recognition of the reciprocal relationship between the state and the population.

During World War I, the area of Transjordan came under occupation from both British forces and the army of the Arab Revolt, organized by Sharif Husayn of Mecca and led by his son, Faysal. Rogan has found that "Turkish intelligence reported that the Hashemites won tribesmen to their cause through a combination of propaganda and gold, and so the Ottomans responded in kind. Cemal *Pasha* sought to gain tribal loyalty by suspending taxes and bestowing state honors on key tribal *shaykhs.*"[6] As the Ottomans were more successful in their efforts, "For the duration of the war, most of the tribes of Transjordan remained deaf to the appeal of Arab Revolt."[7] Thus the people of Transjordan were not natural allies for the Hashemites, who would later come to rule them. When the Ottoman sultan surrendered, the Allies placed Transjordan within Occupied Enemy Territory Administration (OETA) East, which extended from Aqaba to Aleppo, and fell under Emir Faysal's rule in Damascus. Faysal's government, however, completely failed to extend its authority over Transjordan because his officials lacked the military power necessary to enforce their rule. As it became clear that the French intended to take over the interior of Syria, Faysal's position grew even more unstable. On July 24, 1920, French forces under General Henri Gouraud forced Faysal to flee Damascus, thus ending the brief Arab kingdom based there, and leaving the area of Transjordan in an uneasy position, poised between the French and the British.

In this situation, British officials assigned to the region and different Transjordanian tribal and merchant leaders vied for political influence. As part of this process, both groups met in Salt on August 21, 1920, and in Umm Qais on September 2, 1920, to work out a governmental plan for the region. In Salt, the British High Commissioner for Palestine, Sir Herbert Samuel, met with about six hundred Transjordanian notables and clearly stated that the British government had decided to keep the administration of Transjordan separate from that of Palestine and that local governments would be created throughout the area with the aid of British advisors. To help facilitate economic growth, free trade would exist with Palestine, and the British government would initiate efforts to provide Transjordan with the goods it would need. In the second meeting, in Umm Qais, Major F. R. Somerset acted as the British representative. The Transjordanian participants handed Somerset a list of their demands instead of, as in the previous meeting in Salt, waiting for the British offer. They wanted an independent Arab government in Transjordan, led by an Arab prince, an emir. To rule with this emir would be a majlis, a legislative body, representing the people of the country and with the power to enact legislation and administer the affairs of the country.

Jewish immigration to Transjordan would be strictly forbidden, as would the sale of land in Transjordan to Jews. To protect the people of Transjordan, a national army would be formed, and the British government would supply the arms and ammunition the army required. On the economic front, the participants in the meeting called for free trade between Transjordan and its Arab neighbors.

The vocabulary of the nation and its state boundaries had clearly infiltrated the consciousness of the Transjordanian leadership. The representatives at both Salt and Umm Qais put forward demands for unity and independence, predicated on the establishment of a modern nation-state. No borders were specifically demarcated, as symbolized by the fact that they declared that British mandatory power should be extended to include all of Greater Syria. The participants at these meetings hoped this political arrangement would facilitate Syrian unity after independence. Certainly these men attended these meetings to protect their own positions vis-à-vis their rivals, but it is interesting to note that they voiced their demands within a wider, nationalized framework.

However, a unified state did not emerge from these conferences, as the men requested; instead, six British officers arrived in Transjordan to organize separate local governments. However, all the governments failed to control even the small amounts of territory assigned to them. Samuel reported, "It cannot be claimed that the system of administration so set up was satisfactory. The authority of the councils was flouted by large sections of the population; taxes were collected with difficulty; the funds at the disposal of the local authorities were insufficient to ensure the maintenance of order, still less to defray the cost of roads, schools, hospitals, or other improvements for the benefit of the people."[8] Tribal and village competition precluded the opportunity for compromise and cooperation. As a result, the governments were essentially based on the old tribal and family hierarchies that had always existed in the area and not on the blossoming sense of national unity displayed in Salt and Umm Qais.

THE HASHEMITES AND THE EMIRATE OF TRANSJORDAN

While these governments floundered, yet another group emerged on the scene to alter the national debate still further. The Arab Revolt had left a physical legacy in Transjordan as soldiers in its army and as officers in Faysal's short-lived Syrian government flocked to Transjordan seeking refuge from French attacks. The al-Istiqlal Party [Independence Party], which had emerged out of the al-Fatat [Young (Arab)] movement that originated first in Paris and then moved to Syria, stood as the largest and most influential grouping at the time. Its ultimate aim was the formation of an independent Arab government, combining all the Arabs who had once lived under Ottoman rule. Because so many Istiqlalists and refugees from Faysal's government arrived in Amman after Faysal's fall, it became the temporary capital for the propagation of Arab nationalism. With their arrival on Transjordanian soil, just as Transjordanians themselves were starting to articulate a national identity, the question about nationhood and the boundaries surrounding them came up for debate. These refugees called on Transjordanians to help their fellow Arab brethren in the reconquest of Syria, rejecting the notion that Transjordan deserved to stand alone as an independent nation. Their call found resonance in Transjordan because even those men who stood in Salt and Umm Qais calling for an independent Arab state in Transjordan had not fully divorced themselves from other allegiances in the region. Both groups coalesced around the idea of inviting an Arab emir to lead them, and both also included Syria, Palestine, and Transjordan—or Greater Syria—within the area to be designated for his rule. According to Sulayman Musa, Sa'id al-Mufti, a leader of the Circassian community, remembers that, "After the French occupation of Syria, Transjordan lived in chaos. It was not long before we sent to King Husayn bin Ali a telegram demanding in it that he send one of his sons to the country to deliver it from chaos."[9]

When Emir 'Abdullah subsequently arrived in Ma'an from Mecca in November 1920, under the self-proclaimed title of the Vice-King of Syria, he stated that his goal was to retake Syria on behalf of the Arabs.[10] On his arrival, many Syrian expatriates, Arab nationalists, and Transjordanian leaders rallied around him. Since national identity was in flux in the region soon to be named Transjordan, 'Abdullah capitalized on it. The Arab nationalism of the Arab Revolt appealed to those political figures scrambling to define their positions amidst the division of the Arab world by the European powers. For them, the tenets of Arab nationalism meant, most immediately, the uniting of Greater Syria under an Arab emir. 'Abdullah's message of the time was one of pan-Arabism and anti-imperialism, not yet of Transjordanian unity or nationalism, because the region of Transjordan existed as merely a province of Syria. 'Abdullah claimed to be organizing the resistance to French rule in Syria, not lobbying for a position as leader of Transjordan. Transjordanians, Syrians, and Hijazis rallied to his side because of this call. Reflecting this sentiment, the region's first newspaper, *al-Haq Ya'lu*, appeared at this time, published under the slogan of 'Arabiyah Thawriyah [Revolutionary Arabism].

When 'Abdullah began to move north, toward Amman, he gained supporters because of both the ultimate success of the Hashemite-led Arab Revolt and the popularity of his brother Faysal. By then, the Syrian refugees from Faysal's government and the participants in the failed local governments of the British were looking for a new kind of leader. 'Abdullah, himself, was an unknown quantity to the vast majority of those who came to his court, but his family name preceded him and allowed people of all different political ideologies to rally around him in large numbers. They transferred their particular desires onto his shoulders.

'Abdullah's increasing support among the inhabitants of Transjordan required that the British accept his rule or use military force to oust him. Since the latter option could not be undertaken in an era of British military cutbacks and public dissatisfaction with military endeavors, Winston Churchill, the British colonial secretary, met with 'Abdullah in Jerusalem in late March 1921 and proposed that he form his own government in Amman for a six-month trial period. As part of the bargain, Britain agreed to give 'Abdullah a financial subsidy and appoint a British resident to advise him on administrative matters. 'Abdullah acceded to this position and agreed to Britain's conditions that he work to prevent attacks against the French from Transjordanian soil and accept their policy in Palestine, which implied an acceptance of the Balfour Declaration and Jewish immigration into the region.

This was a major shift in national identity on the part of 'Abdullah, a literal redrawing of the boundaries, as 'Abdullah's immediate ambitions focused not on the Arab world, or even the territory of Greater Syria, but just on Transjordan. Those people living in the new state would now be called, first and foremost, Transjordanians, as a result of that meeting held in Jerusalem. Back in Transjordan, this new shift caused a great deal of resentment among the politically active members of the population, both Syrian and Transjordanian. As Taylor has summarized,

> A certain bewilderment on the part of Prince Abdullah's constituents was understandable. They had pledged allegiance to his father's dream of a free united Arabia. The general understanding was that this was to be achieved by expelling all foreigners from the region. Prince Abdullah's agreement with Churchill had created a second conflict of loyalty. To be loyal to Jordan was to curtail one's loyalty to the original cause of the Arab revolt.[11]

For the Syrians and Transjordanians who had initially supported 'Abdullah, based on the Hashemite role in the Arab Revolt, "Appeal to a dream

of a Greater Syria was now to be relegated to the status of historical ro-
mance, a dream that never quite fades but hovers in the imagination like
an elusive mirage." [12]

Arab political unity under his control would remain a hallmark of
'Abdullah's goals, but henceforth it would also be harnessed to legitimate
Hashemite rule over Transjordan. Helping the Palestinians, in 1936 or
1948, became an act of Hashemite-Arab nationalism. The rising movement of Arab nationalism among Jordanians in the 1950s could be countered with celebrations and reminiscences about the Hashemite role in
the Arab Revolt. Through this imagery, 'Abdullah could simultaneously
claim the apparently contradictory right to leadership of a nation-state
and a regionwide, pan-national entity. As a result, 'Abdullah never completely abandoned his regional ambitions. On the contrary, in the interwar and post–World War II periods, he proposed scheme after scheme
to unite various parts of Greater Syria under his rule. All failed, because
of opposition not only from the British and the French, but also from
many of the Arabs living in the different areas of Greater Syria. The only
"success" he could claim would come in 1950, when Jordan conquered
the West Bank and East Jerusalem. What this reorientation meant in reality was that 'Abdullah could harness Arab nationalism in support of his
more important and ultimately more successful project: solidifying his
control over Transjordan. He could continually call for a reunification
of the Arabs of Syria and keep his reputation as an Arab nationalist while
he solidified his position at home. Hashemite rule over Jordan would be
characterized by this dichotomy, throughout the twentieth century, of an
Arab nationalist monarch ruling over a territorial nation-state.

To attain this position, 'Abdullah's first goal was to strengthen his position within Transjordan. Situating the capital in Amman, and away from
the more established city of Salt, served part of that purpose. When the
British divided the Palestine Mandate and ultimately created the Emirate
of Transjordan east of the Jordan River, they needed to establish an administrative center that, contrary to Salt, had few historical ties with the
Palestinian region. [13] This move transferred people's focus to a new political and economic center, befitting the creation of a new state structure
in their lives. Since Amman contained almost no infrastructure, every institution henceforth constructed in the city would symbolize the growth
and substance of Hashemite rule.

However, that construction came slowly, as 'Abdullah and the British
had little money to spend. The bulk of the budget went toward creating a
new military force, not a government. In the interwar years, a hospital, a

prison, and 'Abdullah's palace, Raghadan, were built, among other buildings, but little effort was put into the physical architecture of government: a house of parliament or a court of justice.[14] Without these symbols of national power, the British and 'Abdullah had to rely on symbolic acts to remind the new citizenry that they held the bulk of the power in the country and that the country itself would not disappear as the earlier governments had. As Rogan reports, the British and the Hashemites relied on inexpensive ceremonies to perpetuate their existence in people's minds. For example, 'Abdullah would process from his palace, through the center of town, to attend Friday prayers in the 'Umari Mosque.[15] When raids against the regime, either from indigenous sources or from the Saudi border, made the regime appear weak, military drills through King Faysal Street and the elaborate awarding of medals indicated for the population of the city that the regime was capable of defending itself.[16] These spectacles demonstrated for the soldiers and their witnesses that these people did not fight on behalf of their tribes or their families alone, but also to protect the Transjordanian national body. 'Abdullah, handing out those medals, served as both the modern leader of the new Transjordanian state, with its sophisticated weaponry, and as the father, the shaykh of the tribe, rewarding his sons for their loyalty. When these methods did not work, the British military forcibly repressed all subsequent insurrections.

At the end of the six-month trial period, British policy-makers determined that 'Abdullah, despite some of his weaknesses, stood as the only viable leader of a Transjordan administered by the British. 'Abdullah's temporary position in Transjordan became a permanent one on May 25, 1923, when Britain declared Transjordan a provisionally independent state under his rule. This new status, however, came with conditions, as the British government strengthened its control over 'Abdullah's expenses and his decision-making power. Thus, 'Abdullah agreed to another bargain that limited his national goals.

To set the limits of this new state, the British gradually set out to demarcate its borders, shifting people inside and outside the Transjordanian "nation." Michael Fischbach theorizes that maps are a vital component of how people identify themselves vis-à-vis their nation and those of the surrounding region when he says,

> Much as ideas are given concrete form through words, the notion of a Transjordan separate from the rest of Greater Syria became tangible after the population could locate its new country concretely on a map. The first two generations of Jordanians probably did not come in much contact with

maps. But the reality remains the same, for by the 1980s the outline of Jordan was a common feature on Jordanian television and the reality of a Jordan mapped in space was real. The physical outline of the country was drawn by survey maps. . . . Transjordan's land department thus literally put the country on the map.[17]

Alec Kirkbride and a French-Transjordanian-Syrian team officially demarcated the line between Syria and Transjordan in 1932. After repeated battles among the tribes living in the desert between Transjordan and the Hijaz, then ruled by the Saud-Wahhabi alliance, the border between the two was established in 1925, with the loss of Wadi Sirhan to the Hijaz and the annexation of Ma'an and Aqaba to Transjordan. The Transjordanian Nationality Law of 1928 declared that all people living in the country prior to 1924 were citizens. However, as Joseph Massad points out,

> Following this Orwellian move, the cities of Ma'an and Aqaba and the area between them (previously part of the kingdom of the Hijaz), which were annexed in June 1925, are identified by the 1928 law as having been Transjordanian in 1923, which is the originary moment of the law's application, and their populations are thus defined as having lived in the territory of Transjordan when at that time they were in fact Hijazis living in Hijazi territory.[18]

Boundaries, politics, and strategies defined Transjordan's citizenry, not the activities of the inhabitants. The lines had now been drawn between the "us" inside Transjordan and "them" outside.

Maps can also reconfigure relationships inside the nation, as the state takes control over defining land ownership rights. For, as Fischbach has noted, "Property by the 1950s was no longer defined merely by conceptualizations of a share of the village's land but by state-issued maps and deeds. The state entered forcefully into the equation. In surveying land and registering land rights systematically, the state was reconceptualizing the spatial dimensions of the country as well."[19] The new concepts of land rights and land use were reconfiguring people's relationships to each other and to the state. The primary actor in this respect was the Hashemite state, and this fact came home to the new citizenry in dozens of ways, as Hashemite officials mapped out the land and as Hashemite officials collected the taxes. "These processes were done in consultation with the villagers, but their result was that the villages conceived of their socio-economic space in terms of reference created by the state along Western lines."[20] Westernized versions of land ownership transformed people's relationship with the land from a vertical relationship, where different people had rights to work different aspects of a given piece of land, to a horizontal one, where individual ownership spread across a spatial grid. As Thongchai Winichakul has theorized, "In a premodern map, there was no inference that a spatial unit depicted was part of a spatial wholeness. There was no indication of the position of that unit on the earth's surface."[21] A "modern" nation-state map does just the opposite, as it differentiates one nation or village from another and implicitly recognizes a certain parallelness of construction among these states and these villages, if not a complete equality between them. By drawing maps around states and then regions within each state, governments take control over the spatial relationship among the now differently defined groups. Transjordanian citizens had a new identity vis-à-vis the people living in another part of the map, whether in Transjordan or the country next door. "The reality of 'Transjordan,' and later 'Jordan,' as a distinct entity separate from 'Syria,' 'Palestine,' 'Hijaz,' and the 'Ottoman Empire,' became a concrete reality for villagers because of the survey maps, the land registration documents, and the land tax lists drawn up by the land department."[22]

"TRANSJORDAN FOR THE TRANSJORDANIANS," PART I

As the superstructure of the state began to materialize, Transjordan's first opposition movement emerged, because Transjordanians actually received little benefit from the new state supposedly established in their name. The question was not so much over the right of Transjordan to exist, but over who had the right to administer and define it. The Salt and Umm Qais meetings had presaged the creation of a state; the bulk of the demands made at these meetings were ignored, however. No indigenous Transjordanian organizations arose from the demands and articulations of the people; the Hashemite definition of the state superseded theirs. Thus, the call that rang out throughout the 1920s from the new opposition movement was "Transjordan for the Transjordanians."

In the first years, under British supervision, non-Transjordanians, from Syria, Palestine, and the Hijaz, held the few positions of power available to Arabs. For example, 'Abdullah, a foreigner himself, formed his first government on April 11, 1921. While the bulk of the cabinet members were from Syria and the Hijaz, only one member of the first government,

Ali Khulqi al-Sharayri, was a native Transjordanian. He had participated in the Arab Revolt in 1917 and then was initially appointed as the chief of police in Transjordan in 1921. From 1921 to 1923, Syrians and, to a lesser extent, Palestinian, Iraqi, and Hijazi immigrants filled the majority of the governmental and bureaucratic posts. In all, only two Transjordanians served as cabinet members from 1921 to 1929.

Even the army did not employ natives in its ranks in the first few years because Transjordanians were reluctant to join and the British questioned their abilities. Lt. Col. Frederick Peake served as the commander of the army from its inception in 1921 until his retirement in 1939. He initially employed ex-Ottoman Arab officers, Hijazi soldiers, and Syrian refugees, until 1924, when volunteers from Palestine and then the towns of Transjordan replaced the Syrians. This force became the Arab Legion on October 1, 1923, and, from 1926 until 1940, served primarily as an internal police and gendarmerie force, designed to subdue the bedouin tribes and any other domestic military opposition. It did not fight outside the borders of Transjordan until 1941. In 1926, the British formed the Transjordanian Frontier Force (TJFF), equipped and manned by the Palestine Mandate government, to protect Transjordan's borders and to stop excursions against the French. Initially these forces remained weak and ineffectual against threats to the regime; only in the 1930s did the armed forces acquire enough manpower and experience to sufficiently control the country.

Because 'Abdullah and the British chose non-Transjordanians to administer the government and the army, 'Abdullah's initial popularity in the country dropped dramatically.[23] The traditional bedouin and village shaykhs who had welcomed 'Abdullah soon came to resent him because of their exclusion from the highest posts in the government. 'Abdullah had now become a known quantity, and, for different reasons, many Transjordanians found they did not want the man to lead them. Transjordanians retaliated against their exclusion from positions of political power by beginning to loosely unify their forces against their two common enemies: the new state and its imperial benefactor. The goal of these protests was not to overthrow the government, but to make it more representative of the population.[24] Tribal leaders, merchants, and members of the growing bureaucratic strata formed coalitions to synthesize military might with political demands. The vocabulary of nationalism and popular sovereignty framed their demands, as a sign that they recognized the legitimacy of the new state now forming around them. To show their opposition to the government, many of the region's indigenous leaders

fought back by refusing to pay taxes, by ignoring governmental authority, and, most importantly, by engaging in tribal raids against the new
government. Political demands for the incorporation of Transjordanians
into the administration, the promulgation of a constitution, and the election of a representative assembly accompanied each of these protests, but
'Abdullah used Britain's superior military power to repress these efforts.

In May 1921, the people of al-Kura, an area within the district of
Ajlun, refused to pay their taxes and came out in revolt against the government. With the inauguration of the Transjordanian government,
Kulayb al-Sharayda, the paramount leader of the al-Kura area, had requested that the area become a separate district. Instead, the new government incorporated al-Kura into the district of Ajlun, headed by Ali Khulqi
al-Sharayri, the Jordanian cabinet member and al-Sharayda's enemy. To
put down the subsequent rebellion, the British Royal Air Force (RAF)
bombed the town of Tibna, al-Sharayda's stronghold. Al-Sharayda and
other members of his tribe were then sentenced to prison. Following the
al-Kura rebellion, a wave of small revolts took place over the next two
years in Wadi Musa, Karak, Tafilah, Ajlun, and Balqa', but British forces
quickly suppressed them.

The next major rebellion occurred in August 1923, when the 'Adwan
tribe grew increasingly resentful of 'Abdullah's favoritism toward the
Bani Sakhr. 'Abdullah had extended this favor because the Bani Sakhr
had stood on the front line against Saudi-Wahhabi attacks from the Najd,
time and time again.[25] To put forward his case, Sultan al-'Adwan marched
seven hundred of his men to the outskirts of Amman in September 1923,
presenting 'Abdullah with a petition demanding the immediate promulgation of a constitution and the election of a Transjordanian parliament.
The Royal Air Force crushed this rebellion as quickly as it had the previous ones. Sultan al-'Adwan and his followers were arrested and accused
of conspiracy against the state. Before sentencing, Sultan al-'Adwan and
his sons escaped and fled to Jebel Druze in Syria. Others were captured
and taken to Ma'an and then on to Jiddah, where they came under the
supervision of 'Abdullah's father, Sharif Husayn. As Andrew Shryock has
found,

> The power to break the state and smash its minions came to a decisive end
> in 1923, the year of the ill-fated 'Adwan revolt against the new, British-
> backed regime of the Amir 'Abdullah. The state of Transjordan was a po-
> litical configuration quite unlike anything the Balga tribes had seen before.
> It combined the moral authority of the Hashemites—proponents of Arab
> nationalism and descendants of the Prophet—with the military brawn of

Christian Europe. The Balga tribes were unable, and many of them were unwilling, to resist this new ideological and coercive partnership.[26]

Henceforth, the tribes would slowly be subsumed into the Hashemite project through repression and co-optation. Tribes would serve as instruments of the state, not as initiators in their own right.

To further guarantee their loyalty, 'Abdullah garnered political support from important Transjordanian tribal leaders. In one such move, he offered land grants to them. Mithqal al-Fayiz, paramount shaykh of the Bani Sakhr tribe, received the lands of Zizya village, and Atawi al-Majali, a notable of Karak, 70,000 dunams in his region.[27] 'Abdullah presented cars and chauffeurs to Mithqal al-Fayiz and Rufayfan al-Majali and offered tax relief to a number of others. 'Abdullah paid out cash subsidies to leaders of the tribes, a traditional way of gaining support, and continued to do so into the 1930s, even when forced to do so from his own funds.

When military opposition failed to alter the tenets of the Hashemite regime, a broader-based opposition force emerged from the educated cadres of the population, including the urban merchants and new civil servants. Mustafa Wahbah al-Tell, known by his pen name, 'Arar, can be considered an example of this phase of the opposition, as he joined many of the shifting political alliances formed throughout the decade. Joseph Massad even credits him with coining the phrase "Jordan for the Jordanians."[28] In his work, he used poetry to articulate the positions voiced by the opposition. While few of his colleagues chose this specific route, among Jordanians, "he is held up as a pioneer in Jordanian patriotism at a time when Jordan, as a political entity, was too recently established to hold significant meaning in the hearts of its people."[29] His depictions of life under Hashemite rule can serve as examples of how his colleagues felt about the regime arising around them. For example, he called the "independence" that had been achieved in 1923 a "cardboard box," led by a "fortune teller government," and reacted by organizing a group of primarily educated Jordanians to oppose the measure.[30]

In his poetry, to show his opposition to the Anglo-Hashemite project, 'Arar differentiated between "the present as illustrated by the intrusion of imperialism and the control it exercised over Jordan" and "the past, i.e., the days of the revolution and the ability to make decisions without dependence on any body [sic] else."[31] For him, the "Franks" and the "foreigners" had desecrated the sanctity of the land and people of Jordan. His country had "suffered all types of humiliation, / My fold has been ravaged and wolves have taken possession of my flocks," while delight has given way to suspicion.[32] In pinpointing the focus of his anger, 'Arar frequently singled out particular British officials for special opprobrium, as "'Arar's triumvirate of evil, the Urizenic sons of perfidious Albion, consisted of Peake, Cox and Hober [*sic*]."[33] The first founded the Arab Legion, the second served as High Commissioner in the 1920s and 1930s, and the third worked as the British Advisor to the Ministry of Justice. "The 'law of Cox and Hober [*sic*],' as 'Arar expressed it, disrupted Jordanian traditions and altered the relationship of man to man and man to the land."[34] Tapping into his dislike for the military regime established by the British, he criticized John Bagot Glubb, the later commander of the Arab Legion, by asking a woman, "Did you, lass, think me one of Abu Hnayk's troops? And so you looked askance at me, giving me no chance to greet you?"[35]

But his undefined "foreigner" clearly encompasses the Hashemites as well, not just their British overseers. His criticism of 'Abdullah and his regime came most frequently in the form of an attack against the city of Amman. The city represented, for 'Arar, the destruction of the natural beauty of Jordan and the imposition of foreign rule over its people. No "person of any consequence" had ever ruled over the city, in a direct attack against the Hashemite regime.

> Amman has got tired of me and I have come to you,
> Seeking to fulfill (my) hopes in Madaba.
>
> (It sounds) As if Amman did not know any pleasure seeker
> And tavern visitor except me.
>
> But for love, I would not shed tears on ruins
> Or yearn for the ruins of Amman.
>
> And after Amman there are people whom blessings never quit,
> Thanks to the graces bestowed on them by the Sovereign living in
> Raghadan.[36]

The sarcasm displayed toward Emir 'Abdullah comes through clearly, as 'Arar expresses his belief that both Amman and the people that it serves have clearly destroyed the country. "Amman" is not worthy of devotion or loyalty; the real Jordan is.

In opposition to this foreign-ruled government, 'Arar glorifies the many periods of time he found himself in exile, by order of that same regime. "Mustafa defied the new colonists just as he had done with those who preceded them and declared his affiliation to his home country to a degree that was tantamount to sanctification. He also championed the rights and entitlement of his people to freedom, independence and [a] decent life. He tried to rouse them against their oppressors and urged them to ask fervently for their rights and liberty."[37] For him, "Madaba," instead of an exile, served as a respite from the world of "Amman." He took refuge in gypsy tents whenever life oppressed him, finding in it a return to an older way of life and a rootedness in the natural world. The gypsies could be said to represent the Jordanian people, alienated from the nation-state now being constructed around their heads. Just as the gypsies had no real home, so the Jordanians lacked one. As Taylor has said, "He was sent to prison and exile to learn respect: instead, his contempt grew. Condemned to live among outcasts, he became their spokesman."[38]

Not only did he write in opposition to the state, he also produced positive images of what it meant to be Transjordanian, presaging the emergence of an emotional patriotic tie to this state in which the people now found themselves living. For 'Arar, each locale had a distinctive character; for example, "mountains and plateaus in 'Arar's poetry . . . are inextricably linked with the causes of freedom and resistance and rejection of imperialism or colonialism."[39] He so reveres the Jordanian scene that he questions the existence of beauty elsewhere. "Why should I drink from unpalatable Zamzam Spring? Please give me a gulf of Hasban water instead."[40] Expressing yet another such sentiment, 'Arar writes,

> I am not interested in Damascus; for Dahl is not located in its Ghutah
> Nor are its mountain tops as lofty as those of Jordanian highlands.
> My eyes have not felt any affinity with any of its maids,
> Nor did they find any beauty in any of its fair ladies.
> In fact my heart enjoys more a barren plot
> Of Irbid even if it were deprived of grass and water.
> The eyes that enjoy the sight of Hazim al-Zaybi
> Are not attracted (even) by your luxuriant gardens (O·Damascus!).[41]

This Jordan has no national borders, per se, but 'Arar delineated the "us" of national identity as encompassing the family and tribal relationships so integral to society in the area, as well as the reliance of almost the entire population—whether bedouin or settled—on the land for its sustenance. To further articulate this point, he typically used localisms in his poetry, foregoing the classical vocabulary and rhythm so connected to Arab poetry until that point. As Taylor relates, "His use of dialect, idiom, proverb and other oral formulae helped delineate Jordanian Arabic as a vehicle for literary expression."[42] His Jordan is not one of metanarratives, of nation-alist discourses, but of the beauty, joy, and struggle of daily life.

Why spend so much time on 'Arar, a poet "ahead of his time"?[43] Despite the small size of the literate public, 'Arar's poetry reached an enormous proportion of the population. As Taylor has theorized,

> The story of Arar is largely the story of the personal relationship between himself and Prince (later King) Abdullah. Both men were poets, probably the leading Jordanian poets of their day. Within their time and culture poetry held an importance it has not held in the West since the days of the Elizabethans. Poetry was frequently memorized and recited; poetry fulfilled the function of history text, newspaper and political speech. It was, in short, the major vehicle for formulating cultural identity in response to historical events. As leading Jordanian poets of their time, Prince Abdullah and Arar could have been considered responsible for formulating alterna-tive visions of their country's identity and future.[44]

To give some idea about the complexity of this relationship between 'Arar and Emir 'Abdullah, the Acting British Resident reported in July 1930, "Mustapha Wahbi, a politically minded youth who had been sen-tenced to reside at Aqaba for a year on account of his attack in the Press on the Amir, was released by the Amir as a reward for a poem composed in memory of King Hussein."[45] People throughout the new country read and heard 'Arar's poems, so he had an influence far beyond the small lit-erate class living in the expanding towns and cities. He was in tune with the national narratives already resonating in Jordan, irrespective of the actions of the Hashemites themselves. He also articulated the political demands of at least the educated and urbanized population, who included Transjordanian civil servants, merchants, and some tribal leaders, as well as many of the Syrian émigrés.[46]

The political opposition that men such as 'Arar waged against the re-gime can most vividly be seen in the events surrounding the signing of the 1928 Anglo-Transjordanian Agreement and the subsequent drafting of Transjordan's first constitution in the same year. Lord Plumer, the Brit-ish High Commissioner for Palestine, and Hasan Khalid Abu'l-Huda, the Chief Minister, signed the Agreement in Jerusalem on February 20, 1928. In it, Transjordan rose from a region within the Palestine Mandate to an independent emirate, subject to British control over foreign affairs, defense, and finance. Militarily, Britain received the right to organize and mobilize Transjordan's forces as it wished, while, at the same time, stationing its own troops at bases within Transjordan. Britain also had the right to exploit the natural resources of the country. In return for these rights, Britain promised to give the Transjordanian government an annual subsidy for the maintenance of the armed forces. Transjordan, however, was required to pay the expenses of the British Resident and his staff. 'Abdullah was bound by the Agreement to refrain from issuing any decree or sanctioning any piece of legislation that hampered the fulfillment of Britain's international obligations and policies.

This agreement angered the residents of Transjordan because of Britain's dominance over the government in the financial, military, and administrative realms. *The Near East and India*, considered the mouthpiece of the British Colonial Office,[47] reported that

> some of the conditions of the late Treaty with Great Britain were most unpopular, notably that which charges Trans-Jordan with some of the cost of the British forces stationed here, and of the Trans-Jordan Frontier Force. A further grievance is the occupation by Muslims of neighbouring countries of posts in the Government, more especially when these posts are those of highly paid officials. The recent bad season has caused great poverty and consequent discontent, and these combined causes have produced a threat completely to boycott the elections.[48]

With the solidification of the state, judicially and administratively, independence appeared no closer and Transjordanians were becoming weaker vis-à-vis the Anglo-Hashemite leadership.

The government promulgated the Organic Law, complementing the Anglo-Transjordanian Treaty, in April 1928. It recognized 'Abdullah as the head of state with hereditary rights and dictated that a new government be composed of Executive and Legislative Councils, with the former serving as the cabinet and the latter as the legislative body for the nation.[49] 'Abdullah had the right to appoint and dismiss the members of the Executive Council, who were directly responsible to him rather than the Legislative Council. Non-Transjordanians were prohibited from sitting in the Legislative Council; 'Abdullah retained the right to convene, dismiss, prorogue, and dissolve it, with few restrictions. Only the Chief Minister or the head of a department could initiate legislation, which the Legislative Council would then debate. In the case of a major disturbance in the country, or even the indication that one was arising, 'Abdullah had the right to declare martial law throughout the country and to suspend the ordinary laws of the state.

Opposition forces came out against this law because they believed it derived from the spirit of the Anglo-Transjordanian Agreement and not the people.[50] Transjordanians and their Syrian allies protested against the fact that the Legislative Council held only advisory powers, as no law passed by the Legislative Council could be implemented unless 'Abdullah and the British Resident accepted it. Because of these restrictions, the Council served primarily as a debating society, allowed to rubber-stamp decisions made ultimately by British colonial officials and secondarily by 'Abdullah. Protests and demonstrations broke out throughout the country as the ramifications of these documents became clear.

> Strikes of various lengths occurred in the cities. In Irbid the bazaar closed in protest on April 12, 1928 for a week. In al-Salt work was abandoned for three days. Telegrams and messages were directed to Abdullah who was either hailed as the leader or condemned as the traitor of his people. The Foreign Office also received messages expressing the violent rejection of the preferred agreement by the people of Transjordan.[51]

In Salt, schoolboys threw onions at 'Abdullah, while in Amman a student demonstration forced 'Abdullah to give the final oral exams that year himself, passing and failing students according to their political loyalty.[52] A delegation of forty notables from Ajlun presented a petition to the Emir protesting the Agreement. Although 'Abdullah promised the delegation he would consider the recommendations, Hasan Khalid Abu'l-Huda, the Chief Minister, on April 16, 1928, asked Frederick Peake to arrest Ali Khulqi al-Sharayri, now in opposition, Rashid al-Khiza'i, Sulayman al-Sudi, 'Abd al-Qadir al-Tell, Najib al-Sharayda, and Mustafa Wahbah al-Tell ('Arar), the Transjordanians who had led the petition drive.[53] The Amman newspaper Sada al-'Arab [Echo of the Arabs] protested against the agreements and "denounced 'Abdullah as a traitor and alienator of the freedom of his people."[54] 'Abdullah fought back by suspending the paper's publication and expelling the editor, a Syrian, from the country.

To organize the nascent protest movement and to attempt to fight the governmental and colonial apparatus, a number of men, ranging from the traditional tribal leaders to the urban merchant class, to new Syrian and Palestinian immigrants, resolved to plan their opposition strategy. The first move in this regard occurred on July 25, 1928, when about 150 "notables, shaykhs and intellectuals"[55] met in the Hamdan Coffee House in Amman at 3:00 P.M. The conferees elected Husayn al-Tarawneh of Karak as president at the first meeting, and he remained in this post until the fifth and last National Conference meeting in 1933. The main goals of the Conferences included the reduction of 'Abdullah's powers and the adoption of a truly constitutional and representative regime under his rule. As Massad reports, "Thus, the Congress confirmed the juridical creation of the nation-state by the British and the Hashemites. It questioned only the governing arrangement of the new nation-state and not its modality."[56]

As a part of their program, the participants of the first National Conference drafted a National Pact, calling on the League of Nations to recognize the doctrine of self-determination in Transjordan. The Pact contained eleven points, essentially demanding the establishment of a constitutional monarchy under 'Abdullah's rule. The Pact required that this government be responsible to a justly elected legislative assembly. To elect just such an assembly, the Pact called for the repeal of the Electoral Law[57] and its replacement by direct elections and representation determined by population. As an indication of the continuing objection to the employment of non-Transjordanians in the government, the Pact called for the hiring of only Transjordanians in the administrative affairs of the country. It also called for complete independence from foreign rule, meaning Britain would have no sovereign control over Transjordan. Four annual National Conferences followed the first and all issued similar petitions opposing the Anglo-Transjordanian Agreement.

Despite a strong boycott effort on behalf of this opposition group, the government went ahead with the elections in early 1929, and a large number of demonstrations erupted, with participants often clashing with police. "The elections to the Council were held in February, but not without strong opposition, for there was considerable expression of discontent with the form of Government proposed and a demand that the Government should be fully responsible to the electorate."[58] Students protested until the directors of the schools announced that all participants would be expelled. When newspapers came out in opposition to the government's actions, they faced closure, as *al-Sharia* did in September 1927, *Sada al-'Arab* in 1928, and *al-Urdun [Jordan]* in November 1928. The government seized the first edition of 'Arar's newspaper, *al-Anba' [The News]*, in April 1928, and someone bought up all the copies of the first edition of *al-Mithaq [The Pact]* and burned them in reaction to the stories printed. The final tally showed that only about 3 percent of the population voted.

Regardless of the call for a boycott, five signers of the National Pact ran in the elections and succeeded in gaining seats. Even with such a small opposition bloc, the newly elected Legislative Assembly came into conflict with 'Abdullah and his British advisors almost immediately. In the first debate, the members argued so forcibly during the session concerning ratification of the Anglo-Transjordanian Agreement that the

Chief Minister arbitrarily closed it. Four members of the opposition then withdrew. Once the opposition members left the chamber, a majority of the remaining representatives ratified the Agreement. A larger crisis arose between the government and the Legislative Assembly over the ratification of the 1931 budget. The Assembly initially accepted the estimated budget but then refused to vote on amendments that the colonial officials later made. In a more specific complaint, the members disagreed with a British request to fund a Desert Mobile Force under the leadership of the British officer John Bagot Glubb. In the larger sphere of Anglo-Transjordanian relations, the Assembly rejected British control over the budget process and, by implication, subordination of the Transjordanian governmental process to colonial desires. When it became apparent that the majority of the members refused to accept the budget for these reasons, Britain successfully pressured 'Abdullah into dissolving the Assembly.

All five of the Legislative Assemblies elected after 1931 proved docile because of British and governmental manipulation of the election results, co-optation of some members of the opposition, and repression of others. More than half of the fifty legislators who occupied the eighty seats from 1929 to 1947 were land-owning tribal chiefs. All of the members elected to the Legislative Assemblies after 1931 were from thirty-six prominent families. The success of Husayn al-Tarawneh and the Syrian émigré 'Adil al-'Azamah in gaining seats in the second Legislative Assembly furnished the only opposition voices there, and in their case only until 1934. Thereafter, the opposition movement disintegrated, with some of its leaders opting for work with the government, others seeking refuge outside the country, and still others choosing to leave political life.

THE ANGLO-HASHEMITE
NATIONAL PROJECT

Once it became clear that the "Transjordan for the Transjordanians" opposition movement had failed to gain enough power to influence government policy, the Hashemites and the British then had more leeway to start building the infrastructure of the new state. By so doing, they gradually brought members of the population into their circle, as political allies and as loyal supporters. The pillars of the state—the bedouin, the peasants, and the merchants—established their positions during the Mandate period as they found themselves drawn into the state structure in myriad ways. Even 'Arar and his colleagues, initially in opposition to the state's policies, found themselves accepting them over time; they provided the necessary cadres of civil servants and teachers the state required to build the country.

On the governmental level, 'Abdullah and the British continued to expand the state structures in order to solidify their leadership positions. In a dramatic change at the very top, the Syrian reign over the Hashemite government proved to be short-lived because the Syrians, themselves, became disillusioned with 'Abdullah's focus on Transjordan and their repeated campaigns against the French threatened 'Abdullah's hold over Transjordan. An early 1925 report from the Chief British Resident in Amman stated, "I fear that the Amir will never become reconciled to the presence of Rikabi Pasha in Trans-Jordan as Chief Minister. He loses no opportunity of intriguing against him and uses as his tools some of the worst men in the country."[59] Because of the Syrians' anti-French actions, the British and 'Abdullah expelled them from Transjordan, while the British personally directed the purge of the non-Transjordanians from the armed forces. 'Abdullah supported this policy because once he chose to concentrate his attention on Transjordan, the Syrians held little value for him. Those Syrians who had not held the highest posts in the government, like 'Azamah, stayed in Transjordan and continued to work with the political opposition.

With Britain's guidance, 'Abdullah then relied on Palestinian officials to run his government. Starting in 1933, the post of Chief Minister rotated primarily among three men, Tawfiq Abu'l-Huda, Samir al-Rifa'i, and Ibrahim Hashim, all Palestinians. Between April 11, 1921, and May 25, 1946, eight men headed eighteen cabinets, but not one of them was a Transjordanian. This fact is important, because it meant that the Chief Minister was always dependent on 'Abdullah and the British, and not on the Transjordanian population, for his power base. These men came to be known as the "King's men" and not only ran the government in Transjordan in the 1920s but continued to do so for years, most outlasting 'Abdullah himself.

To run this new government, the British and 'Abdullah established advisory institutions at the executive level and a bureaucracy to carry out the laws. Alongside this administrative structure came a legal regime that further dictated the parameters of national life.[60] With every law passed, the people recognized as citizens of the new state found the apparatus of that state increasingly penetrating their daily lives. In the 1930s, 'Abdullah gradually began to incorporate Transjordanians into the administration. Of the 683 employees in the civil administration in 1936, 465 were Transjordanian, while 215 were Palestinian, Iraqi, Syrian, or Egyptian. Three were Europeans and the remainder were British.[61] Thus, a few of the Transjordanian leaders found positions in the new regime, while the larger governmental demands of the "Transjordan for the Transjordanians" movement had failed to materialize. Non-Transjordanians, primarily Englishmen and Palestinians, continued to hold the most influential positions.

In addition to the construction of a national government, 'Abdullah and the British began to construct the infrastructure necessary to extend their control throughout the country. Britain financed the building and improvement of roads because this policy enabled the army to move more easily to stop rebellions. Simultaneously, their extension made economic unity within Transjordan more possible. Post and telegraph offices, as well as telephones, operated in eleven towns and villages by 1925. In 1927, a passport office opened under the direction of the Arab Legion. In 1925, forty-six government boys' schools and six government girls' schools existed.[62] Only the secondary school in Salt provided a full, four-year university preparatory degree throughout the Mandate period, although the school in Irbid briefly provided that service from 1928 to 1930.[63] The numbers of schools increased steadily throughout the Mandate period, but saw more change at the elementary than the secondary level. To build up the body of teachers, the Department of Education sent a few students to Jerusalem and the American University of Beirut (AUB) in the interwar and immediate post–World War II years. The government placed them under contract to teach in public schools after their graduation.[64] These teachers and these schools produced the new cadres of civil servants and professionals, many of them supportive of the state. Still others, as the formation of the Jordanian National Movement illustrates, came through this new educational experience primed to oppose the Hashemite regime. On May 28, 1923, the official newspaper, *al-Sharq al-'Arabi [The Arab East]*, opened under the editorship of Muhammad al-Sharqi. In 1926, it changed its name to *al-Jaridah al-Rasmiyah lil Hukumah Sharq al-Urdun [Official Gazette for the Government of Transjordan]* and published only laws, statutes, and official announcements.

All of these institutions extended Transjordanian governmental control over a wider area of the society and simultaneously placed the Hashemite imprint on all such activities. Transjordanians were starting to feel the influence of the state's institutions in their daily lives. As they traded across borders, they understood the nationalization process of the separate legal regimes; as they attended the few schools they found "traveling companions" from the farthest reaches of the country; and as they traveled on new roads, they recognized the protective power of the nation's army.

Culturally, the new Hashemite state made efforts to develop a national heritage attached to its name. To this end, Emir 'Abdullah established a series of cultural associations throughout the country. In Hani al-Amad's analysis,

> the Emir's Association is bound to figure prominently in any history of the cultural movement in Jordan. Its numerous congresses, devoted to literary and intellectual questions, were largely responsible for the nation's cultural awakening. There was scarcely a writer in the region east of the Jordan during the Emir's reign who did not participate in these congresses and benefit from the Emir's personal attention and care.[65]

Clubs were opened throughout the country, including the Arab Catholic Youth League in Madaba (1922), the Okaz Club in Ajlun (1929), and the Jordan Club (1941), among others, to serve as forums for lectures on literature and science.[66] Clearly, the Hashemite state hoped to use this association and its affiliates as a means for disseminating a Hashemite-Transjordanian cultural ethos. The question arises as to how effective and how correct al-Amad's assessment proved to be in the interwar years. It is more likely that these clubs, formed by the Hashemites, or at least claimed as part of the Hashemite largesse, provided forums for both political and literary discussions, for both the opposition and those in support of the government. They are important because any such club would provide a forum for the rising professionals, the new civil servants, and some of the traditional leaders to discuss the situation in their new country. These clubs must have generated debates that aided both the state and the opposition to formulate policies and national identities.

Just as 'Arar serves as an example of the literary and political opposition to the state, his story also illustrates how interdependent the state and the emerging educated professional middle class were becoming. 'Arar spent the bulk of his adulthood working for the very government he excoriated in his poetry. From the late 1920s to the early 1940s, 'Arar vacillated between teaching jobs and work for the government and many later periods spent in exile for his political activities. He ended his government career as, first, the chief of protocol at Emir 'Abdullah's court and then as the governor of the Balqa' District. In the last years before his death in 1949, he retired to a private law practice. As the chief clerk and executive official of the Irbid law court, he wrote,

> Time, and I can't call it my time
> Has thrown me amidst post stamps and fees
> And has turned my joys into a calculating clerk's concerns,
> Raving in multiplying three by eight.
>
> See how drinking companions have dispersed
> After me and how dust covered my wine vessels,
>
> And how trifling my poetry has become,
> How eloquent diction has failed me,
>
> How my sweet wishes are being unfairly treated
> As humiliated slaves by the scourge of punishment.
>
> For throes of death resulting from Hober's [sic] law
> Have precluded composition of poetry and any eloquent words.[67]

Despite this view, 'Arar and his compatriots could not ignore the burgeoning state structure around them. As a member of the very class in the society that had been educated in more Westernized methods, 'Arar had a duty to work with the state to improve people's lives. 'Arar, himself, attended elementary school in his hometown of Irbid and then completed his secondary work at the al-Anbar School in Damascus and the Sultaniyah School of Aleppo. In 1921, when Transjordan was established, 'Arar was one of only a small number of teachers serving a population of approximately 250,000 people. The new administration provided him and his colleagues with new avenues for utilizing their skills. They could see themselves building the very infrastructure of the state to which they now belonged. Alternatively, the state was reliant upon them, particularly as the initial group of Syrians who ran the government became disillusioned with 'Abdullah's quest to keep his throne in Jordan. "Even though Arar was a thorn in the government's side, his skills as an educator and administrator were indispensable, and after every session of imprisonment, he was restored to some post of responsibility."[68] The small cadre of educated men like 'Arar thus became intertwined with the state, even as many, like 'Arar, spent periods of time in opposition to it. The Hashemite state could import clerks and politicians from the surrounding areas, but to gain a foothold in the country, it needed to rely upon indigenous skills.

Anderson's "bureaucratic pilgrimages" can be detected in this process, as more and more Jordanians found themselves educated by the new state

and then employed in its offices after graduation. In the case of the Emirate of Transjordan, this educated group did not represent a large proportion of the population, but the nation-state had slowly begun to generate
an awareness of permanence, if not yet a sense of nationalism and loyalty,
among its pilgrims. The state had become the entrenched power for an
increasing percentage of the population. In the eyes of many, Hashemite
"nationalism's task" was not to "overcome the subordination of the colonized middle class" but to bring more people into this national project.

Increasingly, the bedouin, too, came to represent a component of the
nation-state. As the tribal leaders started to support 'Abdullah's government, the primary institution the government used to co-opt the rank-
and-file members of the tribes was the military. John Bagot Glubb, a British army officer transferred from Iraq, arrived in Transjordan in 1930,
assigned to create a Desert Mobile Force of bedouins. The goal of the
force was to subdue the tribes and stabilize the desert areas. As Kirkbride
theorized, "The purpose behind this plan was not to set a thief to catch
a thief but to secure the co-operation of the beduin by convincing them
that the 'government' was not always an enemy. Such co-operation could
only appeal to the beduin mentality by way of other men of the same
background."[69]

Glubb arrived at a time when the economic status of the bedouin was
deteriorating markedly. The technological age, symbolized by the increase in the number of trains, trucks, and cars, reduced the need for cam-
els. Droughts in the late 1920s and early 1930s decreased the value of land
and decimated the livestock population. Employment in the armed forces
became an attractive, and then necessary, option for bedouin tribesmen.

> Having arrived in Transjordan when hunger stalked the desert and the
> prestige of the government was at its nadir, [Glubb] had forged a new or-
> der, which bound the tribes to the Mandatory regime. A welfare system
> centred on the Desert Patrol now tided the bedouin over bad years, and
> patches of grain west of the Hijaz Railway—well within the state's span
> of control—supplemented the yield of their diminished flocks. Soldiering,
> subsidies and relief work had replaced the claims on clan and shaykh that
> had guaranteed survival in the past.[70]

Over the years, tribesmen came to form a basic pillar of the Hashemite
monarchy. As Massad has theorized,

> By incorporating the Bedouins into the repressive state apparatus par excel-
> lence, Glubb ensured that not only would their internecine and interna-

tional raiding be stopped, but also their group loyalty would be transferred to the nation-state, guaranteeing that the Bedouins would protect that state against all threats, especially so due to their contempt for city-folk from which anti-state threats might arise. Also, due to their kinship ties across the new national borders and their tribal affiliation, the Bedouins were seen as a threat to the nation-state. Nationalizing them, therefore, through territorialization, was part of nation-building.[71]

As part of the process of incorporating the bedouin into the state structure, the government set up schools for them. "In Arab Legion schools, every effort was made to teach the boys a straightforward open creed—service to king and country, duty, sacrifice, and religion."[72] Through this policy, the army simultaneously nationalized a large proportion of the population to the Hashemite national ethos and provided a repressive institution for use against those who opposed the project.

Land reform policies initiated by the British and carried out by the new Hashemite state also helped transform the economic, and thus the national, landscape. Starting with the Ottoman Tanzimat period, Western definitions of land ownership had been brought to the area via the Land Reform Law of 1858. The British and the Hashemites continued the process of land registration, and, as Fischbach theorizes, "In no other colonial setting in the Middle East did the state so thoroughly intervene in and restructure land matters by the 1940s, and the introduction of European concepts of land ownership and exploitation went far toward contributing to the development not only of the country's economy but of its identity and self-conceptualization as well."[73] From the perspective of the state, land registration meant the systemization of tax collection. On the other side, the process of land registration not only benefited small farmers economically by giving them clear individual rights to the land they worked, but also reinforced in their minds the connection between the Hashemite state and those land rights. "Maps, land deeds, and land tax receipts bore the name 'Emirate of Transjordan,' reinforcing the concept among landowners that their property, their homes, and thus their identities, were constructs of the state handed to them via the land department."[74] At the same time, the farmers and the village leaders themselves participated in the project and found a receptive audience for their views on land ownership. This process allowed the peasants to become familiar with state officials and with the very concept of the new state's intervention into their affairs.[75] The state would not have succeeded in garnering this loyalty if it had not provided benefits. Small farmers could see the advantages accruing to them by the Hashemite-led land reform program.

"The result would be the most massive state intrusion ever conducted into the socio-economic details of Transjordanian cultivators' lives, a state intrusion that not only would change the way land was owned, registered, and taxed but also one that would solidify the very definitions of what 'Transjordan'—and by extension, 'Jordan'—meant."[76]

British and Hashemite economic policy also helped to generate support for the regime from the merchant class, particularly by the 1940s. The land reform program made the country more stable economically by clarifying land ownership and by creating procedures for the transfer of land and property. Merchants thus benefited from the program as they bought shops and invested in rural property.[77] Workshops for mining, repair, mechanics, brick-making, and carpentry specifically opened because of the British and government need for these services.[78] The annual subsidy paid by the British brought a steady stream of money into an economy that, only a few years before, had relied heavily on barter.[79] This process accelerated in World War II as the merchant class benefited from the increased British need for goods and transportation facilities in the area.[80] "The populace did not merely support 'Abdullah and his successors because of the regime's strength (which initially was not very strong at all) or the Hashemites' descent from the Prophet Muhammad. A major explanation for the longevity of the regime stems from the fact that the country's peasant majority and its merchants overall appreciated the government's land program and felt that it served their interests."[81] Thus, merchants and peasants began to appreciate the existence and the work of the Hashemite state as they saw tangible benefits accruing from their participation in it.

CONCLUSION

With the repression, co-optation, or exile of so many of the early Transjordanian opposition leaders, the Hashemite-generated narrative had the opportunity to spread its national ethos without a clear-cut opposition. The leadership exploited the family's role as the giver of the largesse people were now slowly starting to receive. The "King's men" solidified their leadership positions in the government, tribal shaykhs gained land and administrative appointments, bedouin tribesmen received guaranteed jobs in the military regime, and peasants found services creeping in their direction. Even 'Arar and his colleagues found themselves dependent upon the state for their new livelihoods. Thus, the most important act the Anglo-Hashemite project could complete in the interwar years was to force the inhabitants of Transjordan to accept the existence of the state in their lives. This "supposed" "reality" is important because the state did not have the resources to extend its reach into every village and provide new kinds of benefits to every one of its new citizens. In fact, very little change would come to the average village until well into the 1950s, as evidenced by the large amount of out-migration to the cities in that decade. Yet that reach was being extended, through land reform, electrification, and school construction, to name just a few agencies. Those people left out of the new system of largesse clamored to enter, by implication granting the new state the legitimate right to rule over them. Thus, a top-down approach to nation-building began to succeed in the Jordanian example as institutions gradually supplied people with connections to their new state. People openly declared themselves "Transjordanian" early in the Mandate period, despite the apparent artificiality of the state's construction. Yet the very institutions established by the Hashemite state also began to produce the very strata that would come to lead the most threatening opposition movement the Hashemite state had faced in its short history: the Jordanian National Movement (JNM).

FOUR

HASHEMITES AND JORDANIANS

1921–1948

Oh, all Arab countries are home to me, from Sham toBaghdan.

NATIONALIST SONG SUNG AT THE MADRASSA AL-KARAK[1]

*Our minds were opened, but not only by reading books and articles.
This was a cultured air . . . [and the encouragement of] participation
in all elements of life, things not obtainable in the classroom alone.
There was an air of discussion, in all possible discussions, and in all
world topics. What we understood and what we did not understand, the
interchange between all types of study and specialties and the interchange
between students from most areas of the eastern Arab world, with some
inoculation of foreign students. . . . All of that left in myself a new
influence. It took my life and ideas and my mind into a new direction,
similar to what happened to many of the other students.*

MUNIF AL-RAZZAZ, DESCRIBING
THE AMERICAN UNIVERSITY OF BEIRUT (AUB)[2]

As the concept of Transjordanian statehood and nationality came to be
accepted in people's minds, any who opposed the process needed to rally
around an alternative national identity. Arab nationalism came to serve
that purpose because its broad goals and definitions allowed its proponents to work on the domestic political stage in Transjordan and on the
regional stage in the Fertile Crescent simultaneously. By World War II,
Arab nationalism meant revolutionary change regardless of its arena.
It also brought to the forefront of political discourse new social strata,
primarily of the urban areas, led by the burgeoning professional intelligentsia. Early opposition leaders like 'Arar faded from the political spot-

light, to be replaced by new leaders in the post–World War II era. In the 1950s, this movement would be mobilized within the Jordanian National Movement (JNM); it would be started in discussions in living rooms and schools throughout the Mandate period. The future leaders of the JNM would be politicized by these discussions and the events they witnessed taking place around them during these early years. As they traveled on their "pilgrimages" to political opposition, they realized that the very institutions the Hashemite state used to socialize new citizens became the breeding ground for a broader national identity. An analysis of the JNM must begin with this formative period, because the participants themselves followed the same chronological trajectory in their own memoirs; their voices trace the path they took toward Arab nationalism and political opposition. The JNM did not appear out of a vacuum in the 1950s but arose from a series of political influences the leaders encountered during their childhood and school and university years. The stories of their lives, as related in memoirs and interviews, bring to life the students and professionals who came to lead the opposition force.

THE LEADERS OF THE JORDANIAN NATIONAL MOVEMENT (JNM)

The men whose voices have been recorded in different media include Yaʿqub Ziyadin and ʿIsa Madanat, Christian Transjordanians from the Karak area, who later came to be leaders of the Jordanian Communist Party; Nabih Irsheidat, a Transjordanian from Irbid and a member of the Communist Party; Hamad al-Farhan, a Transjordanian leader of the Movement of Arab Nationalists; and Ali Abu Nuwar, another Transjordanian from Salt who later became the leader of the Arab Legion and alleged head of the 1957 coup attempt against the king. Abd al-Rahman Shuqayr and Munif al-Razzaz, both later leaders of the National Front and the Baʿth Party in Jordan, moved from Syria at a young age. Shuqayr and his mother fled Damascus to escape the fighting during the 1925 Syrian Revolt against the French, while al-Razzaz's family moved to Amman after the French suspected his father, a veterinarian, of collaboration with the rebels. The stories of these men have been intermingled with memoirs from activists of the next generation who were influenced by their work. This second generation sat in the classrooms and political salons of the leaders of the JNM and imbibed the message of political mobilization disseminated by them. All these stories highlight the fact that Jordan's history is certainly not just one of the Hashemite family; it is a history of how people absorbed and reacted to the many new challenges confronting them in the new state structure and under continued colonial rule.

On their road to political activism, the Transjordanian members of the future movement, and the Syrian émigrés who joined them, followed a political trajectory that took them from experiences and discussions in their homes to schools throughout Transjordan, then to the universities of Beirut, Damascus, Cairo, and Baghdad, and back to Transjordan in the 1940s. At home, in their early years, they listened to influential family members and neighbors speak about the political struggles waged in Transjordan against the regime, in Syria against the French, and in Palestine against the British and the Zionists. The future opposition leaders then took a step toward political work when they went to the only full-fledged, four-year secondary school in Transjordan, the one in Salt, where the teachers, mostly graduates from the American University of Beirut (AUB), instilled in the students a sense of Arab nationalism and anti-imperialism. Daily, they sang patriotic Arab songs and heard about the brave exploits of their Arab ancestors. All participated in strikes against events such as the Jewish Agency's attempts to buy land in Transjordan and demonstrations in support of the 1936 Arab Revolt in Palestine. Later, they attended universities throughout the Arab world, where their "minds were opened" to myriad political ideologies and, just as importantly, to the skills required for political organization. Because of their experiences, these young men returned to Jordan in the mid-to-late 1940s ready to initiate these activities at home.

All of the new leaders came from families, both rural and urban, that had the resources to put together enough money to send at least one of their sons to secondary school and then to the university. In a period where barter served as a primary means of exchange in Transjordan, this entailed an enormous sacrifice on the part of the families. Because few of these families were truly wealthy, most had to find creative ways to put that cash together. For example, 'Isa Madanat received a loan from the Jordanian Ministry of Education; after his father's death, Munif al-Razzaz temporarily left his medical studies in Syria to teach back in Amman.

At the same time, the leaders of the national movement were predominantly not members of important families within Transjordan, families that had begun to wield influence or had garnered political posts as part of their alliance with the king. Shuqayr and al-Razzaz emigrated from Syria, so lacked a power base within Transjordanian society; Ziyadin and Madanat, as Christians, remained alienated from the majority of the powerful posts within the regime. Education proved to be the most valuable tool these men could acquire because of their minority status. Al-Nabulsi, as a native of Salt, grew up in a more powerful family but also amidst a large number of political activists. The city of Salt had served as an important center for political activities during the life of the first opposition movement in the 1920s, and many of the Salti families encouraged political activism on the part of their sons because of this.

As for the most important political influences these men experienced during their lives, their memoirs emphasize the value of discussions at school and in family settings about the political events taking place throughout the region. A number of studies have been conducted to determine how important nonpolitical influences and political events are in the socialization of children. As one would imagine, the family and primary school have proved to be the most influential of these processes in the years leading up through adolescence. In addition, peer groups, clubs, and the mass media play a role in the politicization of the young.[3] The level of education attained by a person also affects later political involvement. With education often come the skills required for political participation; schools also bring together people with similar educational abilities and political proclivities.[4] The political subjects discussed in school also have an influence on students' later political ideologies because they define the vocabulary necessary to question and/or accept the political tenets disseminated by the state. In a situation like Jordan's, where the state was so very new and the focus of loyalty so fluid, schools provide a powerful means for regrouping and redefining the identities of students. Many of the messages imparted highlight the need for obedience to the new state structure, while the underlying goal of education, to provide new types of information to the students, has the potential to undermine those very same messages.

These memoirs clearly indicate that these young men considered themselves in a unique position. Obviously, new skills created new avenues for social mobility, so personal fulfillment played a role in their desire for education. However, experiences at school and an awareness of the political events taking place around them also instilled in these young men a desire to work on behalf of the larger society. For some, this meant entering government service to work from the inside. For others, political opposition proved to be a more attractive option. Regardless of the venue these men ultimately chose, it is safe to say that these first schools mobilized them to work for wider societal causes. As a result, a feeling of a "brave new world" comes through these memoirs because these men were handed the keys to open new doors.

The memoirs and interviews reveal a number of instances when the young boys came into contact with the main political actors of the day. Shuqayr mentions living in Amman and bringing food to Syrian refugees from the 1925 Revolt. 'Adil al-'Azamah, a leader of the first Transjordanian opposition movement and an émigré from Damascus, opened an office in downtown Amman, in front of the Husayni Mosque, to organize activities against the French during the Revolt. His office became a pilgrimage site for nationalists and political leaders of many areas, including Transjordanians, Syrians, and Palestinians.[5] Ali Abu Nuwar recounts listening to a large number of discussions amongst his father and relatives about the events and ramifications of the Arab Revolt, the Balfour Declaration, and the fall of Faysal's government in Syria.[6]

Nabih Irsheidat lived for years in exile from his hometown of Irbid because of his father's participation in the Syrian Conference which appointed Faysal king, and for his continued activities on behalf of the Syrian Arab nationalists thereafter.[7] While 'Abdullah initially supported such activities, when he chose to concentrate primarily on the Transjordanian nation-state, these activists became an obstacle to him. At the age of about five, Irsheidat saw his house surrounded by police and his father interrogated about his political connections to Rikabi Pasha. Irsheidat considers this his "first shock," because he became aware of the aggressiveness of the government.[8] When his father explained that the government was acting in accordance with British wishes, Irsheidat felt even more anger.[9] His father was then exiled to Karak, and in later years to Tafillah, Ma'an, and Madaba as well. During this period, Irsheidat frequently overheard discussions about the dangers of the Anglo-Transjordanian Treaty and watched as important opposition figures like Husayn al-Tarawneh visited his home to discuss political events. On the day of the first Legislative Assembly elections in 1929, Irsheidat personally walked the streets shouting his support for al-Tarawneh, in opposition to Rafiqan al-Majali, who welcomed the treaty. In addition to these discussions about Syria and the Transjordanian government, Irsheidat felt that the struggle of the Palestinians further awakened the national and political consciousness of the people. For him, their struggle said that "they had announced with loud voices that Palestine was Arab."[10] When a British official, "Ball," was due to arrive in Karak in 1936 to discuss the Palestinian Revolt, Irsheidat and his friend Muhammad Bajis al-Majali initially wanted to pour sulfuric acid on the delegation's cars.[11] After searching fruitlessly throughout the school for the acid, they decided to hold a demonstration instead. As they marched through the streets of Karak, they shouted out slogans, against British imperialism and for the fall of Zionism.

SCHOOLS AND NATIONAL IDENTITY

Throughout the Fertile Crescent, both the state and the different opposition forces pressed their national messages on the impressionable students entering the school systems. Simultaneously, these states and their borders were so new and so tainted by colonial enterprise that stories of Arab heroes throughout history held more resonance for the students than those about leaders like Emir ʿAbdullah, who received his pay from the British and commanded his British-officered army. In Transjordan, images of the Arab Revolt could represent both Hashemite ascendance or pan-nationalism, depending on the producer of the particular image. Each side used these kinds of images and messages, assuming the "cloak of the 'nation,'" to work to nationalize the students according to its particular identity. The memoirs emphasize the students' desire to learn and, more importantly, to use that knowledge to improve the political and economic situation around them.

The fact that the Hashemite budget allowed for the construction of more schools enabled the state to spread its national message to an ever increasing group of students. The numbers of Jordanian students who traveled the educational path remained small up until the 1950s, but the numbers did grow steadily. For example, by the 1945–1946 academic year, 28 percent of children were enrolled in the kingdom's seventy-three schools.[12] In these schools, the Hashemites tried to generate among the student body loyalty for their national narrative. As the text of the Law of Education of 1964 states, the goal of the Jordanian education system was to prepare the "child to develop into a good citizen who believes in: God, Country and King."[13] While this statement appears later than the period being discussed in this chapter, it reflects Hashemite planning from the earliest days.

To succeed at its task, the state had to supervise the school activities as closely as possible. Obedience and allegiance to the Hashemite national story and leadership structure stood at the top of the priority list. Abd al-Rahman Munif, the future author of *Cities of Salt*, recounts the fact that at al-ʿAbdaliyah School in Amman in the 1940s, he and his fellow students had to line up in the southern yard to sing "Long live the Amir" every morning.[14] Irsheidat recalls celebrating the Great Arab Revolt annually on the 9th of Shaʿban. Before starting any of the speeches, a teacher would be called upon to read an Arab poem or a piece of literature glorifying the Arabs and their history. The speeches then attacked the treachery of the British and the French.[15] In this case, the celebration of the Arab Revolt came via the agency of the Hashemite state, so the narrative of the primordial Arab nation led inevitably from the greatness of Arab civilization to the anticolonial battle waged by the Hashemites. Thus, each year, the students and the community were reminded of the pivotal role the Hashemite family had played in not only the Arab Revolt but, by implication, all of Arab history.

The Hashemite state gradually began to generate a feeling of "Transjordanianness" among the students on this trajectory. No matter what the particular ideology they eventually professed, these young men became part of an "imagined community" of Transjordanian travelers because of the pilgrimages they undertook and the uniqueness of their positions within a country where few people attended any school at all.[16] They traveled from their villages and met companions from around the country, from different tribal groupings, and from all occupational sectors. The reality of the Hashemite-Jordanian state influenced these educational pilgrimages as the students became aware of the boundaries of their political lives and the connections among them and their new colleagues. The fact that many of them formed and joined specifically Jordanian political clubs while at universities in the surrounding areas is an indication of the power of national identification, even amidst the continuing influence of Arab nationalism.

Yet as Gregory Starrett found in his study in Egyptian state schools, "As sociologists of education have shown us, students are neither the passive pawns of educational organization and ideology, nor are educators their absolute masters. The belief held by cultural elites that 'modern' education is the most effective machine of social pacification has acted to stunt their own recognition of its ambiguous and unpredictable influence."[17] By providing students with the tools to build their societies, the states actually handed them the means by which to tear down the same belief systems. In fact, "If schools, universities, the press, and the military barracks act as centers of revolt, it is because the spread of their unique disciplinary practices across the whole of society is accompanied by the spread of the distinctly new techniques and potentials for revolt associated with them."[18] The mere fact that schools ask that their students question much of what they had come to accept means that the process of debate has potentially no limit. According to the memoirs of the Jordanian students, this rebellion involved a strong desire to improve the situation around them. Their education gave them a call to arms, so to speak, because they graduated with a strong desire to activate change.

While the Hashemites tried to control the national image disseminated in the schools, they could not cover all possible bases. For example, no Jordanian history textbooks appeared until the mid-1950s, and the state did not have an apparatus sufficient to supervise all the teachers in all the classrooms. With little threat of retribution, teachers could bring their own political positions into the classroom and to the extracurricular events after school.[19] That political position often meant support for Arab nationalism, not Transjordanian exclusivity. Accordingly, Transjordanian students were constantly reminded that Jordan remained within a larger Arab "community" and that the ultimate political configuration for the Arab world had not necessarily been decided by the European colonialists. Ya'qub Ziyadin recalls singing songs such as "Suriya, ya dhat al-majd" ["Syria, Oh, You Glorious One"] and watching students be severely reprimanded by the teachers when they did not participate.[20] Hamad al-Farhan has stated that the feelings of Arab nationalism were culturally based in the people of the region; "So, it didn't start by an idea, [an] admission of Arab nationalism. It's back in the children's poetry."[21] The history textbooks used in the schools came from places like Damascus and Beirut and emphasized Arab national history over any of the new territorial narratives then being constructed by leaders like the Hashemites. Transjordan became a reality of the students' identity but failed to wipe out the larger cultural affiliation symbolized by Arab history, language, and literature. The problems for the students were: Which national identity holds resonance in these students' lives? To which "community" did they belong?

Questions and answers became more complex when, coming from various towns and cities in Transjordan, these boys all congregated at the secondary school in Salt to continue their political socialization. Before the establishment of the Emirate of Transjordan, Salt had served as the chief trading center for the region. It contained a number of old, established merchant and landowning families who resented their exclusion from power when the British and 'Abdullah arrived and hired non-Transjordanians to administer their new government. The tensions between Amman and Salt increased as Amman became the political, social, and economic center of the new country, relegating Salt to the status of a second-class town. After the French occupation of Syria, refugees came to Salt in large numbers and cooperated with the various nationalist and opposition leaders of the area, increasing the opportunities for political activity.[22]

The boys at the secondary school could not remain immune to the political currents flowing through their new home. In one instance, Bahjat al-Salibi, a political activist in Salt, invited a group of students to his home to vote on holding a demonstration against the proposed arrival the next day of Jewish Agency representatives. The rumor had spread that they planned to buy land in the area. To protest this attempt, Shuqayr and his colleagues went the next day to stake out a position along the Amman-Salt road. When a car drove by carrying men in "felt hats," the boys threw onions at the car and fled back to Salt.[23] The mutassarif of Salt briefly detained them as punishment and then let the boys go home. In another incident, boys at the school staged demonstrations in support of the Palestinian Arab Revolt of 1936. As the British Resident, C. H. F. Cox reports, Emir 'Abdullah tried to speak to the ringleaders in order to convince them to stop: "All this, however, has proved of no avail as the boys are badly infected by what they have seen going on in other countries and action has now been taken by closing the 9th and 10th Classes of the Secondary School at Es-Salt on the 27th [of June], by shutting the Arts and Crafts School in Amman as from the 31st, and by expelling the ring leaders."[24] Cox, however, warned that these punishments would not stop the students for very long. "These measures have successfully neutralized the school boy nuisance but there is likely to be trouble from a youth club, which has recently been formed, whose members dress themselves in black shirts with green neck cloths."[25]

In this atmosphere, the teachers played a pivotal role in politicizing their young charges and in galvanizing them to action. Ngugi wa Thiong'o describes the reverence that such teachers were granted in his village in Kenya, a feeling akin to that which comes through these Jordanian memoirs.

> When I was growing up, the teacher was a most important figure in the village. It was not simply a matter of his being better paid than the surrounding population of labourers. He could have gone barefooted. He could have worn patches. But he was a teacher, *mwalimu* as he was invariably called. Even pupil-teachers were venerated. Education became a communal ideal and success, a communal achievement.[26]

While this quote comes from the African experience, it is relevant for the Arab one as well. These teachers represented a new kind of knowledge, a new kind of stratum in the society. The young men sitting in their classes felt, as reflected in their memoirs, immense admiration for their teachers' work. At the same time, the relationship between the teachers and the students was not a purely vertical one, but had horizontal components, as the teachers wanted to bring the students along the same path they had trod. A mentoring relationship thus merged into more of a partnership among like-minded individuals, people who were entering and leading a new kind of world. The young boys craved the information these teachers could provide, and the state had to let these teachers remain, regardless of how subversive their message might be. In Transjordan, their message was often subversive to the Hashemite national narrative, as they disseminated the contrary narrative of an Arab greatness divorced from Hashemite action. The state could only monitor the activities of these teachers on a part-time basis, because it did not have the resources, in the interwar years, to initiate closer supervision. Teachers, as seen with ʿArar, were also aware of their singular position, so knew they could transgress the curriculum or the dictates from Amman without severe punishment. The memoirs clearly indicate that, for these teachers, political activism was a duty they felt they had to perform. The state could not co-opt their ideas regardless of the fact that it paid their salaries.

Sulayman al-Nabulsi, after graduating from AUB, served briefly as a teacher at the school in Karak. Sulayman Musa explains that al-Nabulsi walked into the class his first morning and asked the students, in English, to identify the importance of that day.[27] When no student could answer the question, al-Nabulsi repeated the question a number of times to no effect. Finally, al-Nabulsi revealed that it was November 2, the anniversary of the Balfour Declaration. After describing the history of the document, he then led the students in a demonstration against it. Hazzaʿ al-Majali feels this might possibly have been the first demonstration ever held in Karak.[28] Irsheidat reports that he remembers those events even today and recalls how influential they were because they generated a "feeling of the Arab brotherhood which we were growing in the school."[29] The government quickly transferred al-Nabulsi to the secondary school in Salt. The politicization of the students in Karak continued, however. For example, when Irsheidat's brother, Mamduh, graduated from AUB and briefly taught at the school in Karak, he waged a campaign to get the Christian boys to change their names to Arabic-sounding ones. Irsheidat feels that, while this might sound like a simple change, it had a positive influence on the students' conception of their national heritage, "and ancient Arab names spread thereafter among the Christians of Kerak."[30]

Asher Susser reports that Wasfi al-Tell, beginning his study at the school in Salt in 1936, was encouraged by the history teacher, Saʿid al-Dura, "who inspired them in a powerful sense of identification with the Arab nationalist cause."[31] When al-Tell himself worked as a teacher at the school after graduating from AUB in 1941, he often drifted into political sessions with his students on the threat of Zionism and the need for Arab unity.[32] Ziyadin traces his interest in Marxist ideas to Husni Fariz. The teacher did not instruct his students on the tenets of Communism;

he merely discussed in brief the Russian Revolution of 1917. The mere fact that a Socialist revolution had taken place came as an "electric shock" to him.[33] The same Husni Fariz influenced Irsheidat when he taught nationalist songs in Karak. Ali Abu Nuwar recalls that the teachers at the school in Salt reminded the students that "our Arab Ummah [Nation] was colonized and enslaved and fragmented and that it was on the shoulders of our generation to take responsibility for freedom and unity."[34] The teachers also organized the boys into informal clubs and discussion groups, outside of class, to debate political issues. One such club, the Jalad Sports Club, later renamed the Nadi al-Ittihad [Union Club], opened in the 1930s. Thus, these teachers imparted to their students the "three R's" but did so as they activated them to initiate programs for change.

Abd al-Rahman Munif reports that these activities galvanized students throughout Jordan to seek out more information about the events and ideologies swirling around them. As Amman did not have many libraries or bookshops in the 1940s, young men brought books back after visits to surrounding Arab countries, especially Egypt. Once in Jordan, these books circulated around to everyone in a particular group, leading to not only a dissemination of ideas but also a politicization of the student body.[35] Hence, the educational system and the crises in the region politicized the student body in Jordan by the end of the 1940s. As Munif said, "If we move to a wider context, we find that Amman in particular and Jordan in general were passing through a phase of emotion and inquiry. Banned, dangerous questions that had been suppressed became everyday questions. Why? How? What now?"[36]

When these Jordanian and Syrian students graduated from Salt, they asked just these kinds of questions in their quest for more knowledge. They clearly enunciate, in their memoirs, a progression from those childhood discussions at home to the schooling, both formal and informal, which they had received from their teachers, to the political work they later undertook. When they arrived at universities throughout the Middle East, they transformed this knowledge into the skills needed to organize to fight for their political goals. Education gave these young men a sense of power, a possibly naïve sense of the efficacy of political activism. The opportunities for change seemed endless to them; the university experience enhanced this view. In an April 1938 report, the British High Commissioner analyzed the effect he felt these schools were having on the young men of Transjordan. "There are as well 76 boys and young men receiving secondary or university education abroad and these become imbued with strong political ideas which cannot be controlled as well as in the schools in Trans-Jordan."[37] Clearly, British officials were not aware of the politicization process taking place in these latter schools simultaneously.

The university experience exposed these young men to the opportunities they had heard about while in school back in Transjordan. As al-Razzaz said in this chapter's opening page, "Our minds were opened." The experiences of these men placed them in a special category within their society because so few friends and relatives had been able to take advantage of these new opportunities. As Philip Altbach has theorized, "Third World university students constitute an incipient elite and have, in many countries, a consciousness that they are somehow special."[38] These Transjordanian students understood the new place they had carved for themselves in the society; the biggest question concerned what kind of society they wanted to build. Altbach concurs by saying, "in many countries, the subculture of the university (and of intellectuals generally) is frequently an 'oppositional' subculture, which examines carefully and critically the society of which it is a part. The professorate [sic] often adds to the sense of intellectual ferment by encouraging students to ask difficult questions and, in some instances, by displaying oppositional political and social views."[39] The activism of Arab nationalism of the 1940s and 1950s emerged, for many, from this indoctrination in the university. Professors like Constantine Zurayq and Antun Sa'adah of AUB encouraged their students to participate in as many different political currents as possible and to find the one most applicable to their national circumstances.

When these young men arrived in Damascus, Beirut, Cairo, Baghdad, and other places to continue their studies, they encountered a number of different ideological movements fighting against European colonialism. Syria and Lebanon remained in political turmoil from the end of 1935 until independence in 1945, as demonstrations and strikes wracked both countries. Cairo and Baghdad continued to oppose British control and the increasing corruption of their proxy regimes. As a result, competing territorial and pan-national ideas and institutions played out in the larger realm of anticolonial opposition.

In Syria, the initially influential National Bloc began to lose its monopoly over political power, and a number of other movements emerged in the 1930s.[40] The 'Usbat al-'Amal al-Qawmi [League of National Action] emphasized supranational [qawmi] Arab unity over the more limited Syrian nationalism [wataniyah] favored by the National Bloc. In its goal of achieving Arab unity, the League stressed the need for economic development and integration to successfully fight to oust the French from Syrian soil.[41] The League was forced underground during World War II and gradually disintegrated as other pan-Arab movements were established. The Nadi al-ʿArab [Arab Club] was founded in February 1937 on a platform of Arab social, economic, and political unity. During World War II, this group worked to increase German influence in Syria.

The Arab Baʿth Party was established in Syria in 1943 by Michel Aflaq and Salah al-Bitar and, ten years later, merged with the Arab Socialist Party, led by Akram Haurani, to form the Arab Socialist Baʿth Party. The major tenets of the party focused on Arab unity, liberty, and socialism, and, as an indication, the constitution of the party begins with the lines "The Arabs form one nation. This nation has the natural right to live in a single state and to be free to direct its own destiny."[42] Aflaq laid out the emotional appeal of nationalism by saying, "the prime mover for the Arabs in the present phase of their life is nationalism (al-qawmiyah), the secret word which is capable of moving the strings of their hearts, and penetrating to the depths of their souls. It reflects their basic needs."[43] Aflaq preached the need for *inqilab* [upheaval] to transform the Arab spirit and revolutionize society. Consequently, the basic ideas of the Baʿth Party called for a new, nationalized solution to the endemic problems of the divided body politic. Socialism would pave the way for a more equitable distribution of wealth within it.

In Lebanon, al-Hizb al-Qawmi al-Suri [the Syrian National Party] and the Communist Party grew in popularity in the 1930s. Al-Hizb al-Qawmi al-Suri, founded in 1932, began open, above-ground activities in 1935. Founded by Antun Saʿadah, of AUB, it stated as its goal the unification of Greater Syria as a single nation within its natural borders. The party foundered by late 1938 because of government repression and the imprisonment of many of its members. The Communist Party had been founded in 1930 in Beirut by Armenians but gradually came to be dominated by Arabs. In the late 1930s, it proved successful in organizing demonstrations and getting its message disseminated, through organs such as the *Sawt al-Shaʿab [Voice of the People]* newspaper, published after 1937. The party quickly found supporters throughout Syria and Lebanon.

Demonstrations and strikes heated up as World War II began and as the two countries demanded complete independence from France. In 1943, the Free French forces granted both Syria and Lebanon autonomy but made it clear that the Mandates would remain intact. When the Lebanese government tried to write a new constitution, eliminating all vestiges of Mandate rule, French troops attacked the homes of the government leaders, suspended the constitution, and dissolved the parliament. The British, militarily in control of both Lebanon and Syria, forced the French to accept Lebanon's new constitution and a similar one written by the Syrians. By May 1945, these tensions had degenerated into violent clashes between the Syrians and French troops. The French bombarded Damascus while Syrians attacked French facilities. The British finally moved their troops into Damascus and forced the French to withdraw. Both countries became independent in 1945.

Into this political turmoil, the Transjordanian students arrived. For those who attended the University of Damascus, the events in the city proved particularly fruitful for political organizing. A key figure for these students was Subhi Abu Ghunaymah, a Transjordanian exile living in Damascus. He had been a leader of the early Transjordanian opposition movement who had fled the country in the 1930s, refusing to be co-opted by the Hashemite state. In Syria, he organized political discussion groups among the students and exhorted them toward political activism. One vehicle he used for this was al-Hizb al-Watani al-Urduni [Jordanian National Party], established after he and some of his colleagues had moved to Damascus. Jordanian students studying in the city joined the party and spread its ideas. Fearing he would incite a rebellion during World War II, the British successfully pressured the French into imprisoning Abu Ghunaymah.[44] Once released, he and his students formed the Jami'ah al-Shabbat al-Ahrar al-Urduniyin [Jordanian Free Youth Association] in 1946 to fight for Jordan's complete independence, political liberalization within Jordan, and Arab unity. He grew so popular, King 'Abdullah even contemplated having Abu Ghunaymah serve as prime minister of a postindependence government; in the end, the different sides could not work out their political differences.[45] The students' participation in these parties serves as evidence of the Jordanian shared feeling that emerged among the students by the 1930s. They organized on behalf of both the wider Arab and the more narrow Jordanian goals simultaneously.

While studying in Damascus, Shuqayr relates demonstrating a number of times in 1936 in favor of the National Bloc, with some of the events ending in clashes with French police. When these activities culminated in a six-week nationwide strike, Shuqayr traveled to Transjordan to successfully collect donations to sustain it. In other periods, Shuqayr became actively involved in a number of political activities at school, including lectures, anti-illiteracy campaigns, and programs for the dissemination of nationalist ideas. Nabih Irsheidat participated in many cultural and educational activities while in Damascus, centered around events at such venues as the Orthodoxy Club and poetry readings in coffeehouses.[46] He exposed himself to the ideas of both the Communist Party and the Syrian Qawmiyyun but preferred the former because the latter accepted a division of the Arab world.[47] He slowly began working for the Syrian and Lebanese Communist Party, entering into lengthy discussions with its members, selling the party's newspaper, and distributing its leaflets.

In Lebanon, the American University of Beirut (AUB) provided an arena for politicization for thousands of Arab students in the first half of the twentieth century. Granting it a charter in 1863 as the Syrian Protestant College, the American Board of Commissioners for Foreign Missions, representing the Congregational and Presbyterian Churches, stated as its initial goal: "[T]o aid the natives of Syria and other countries speaking the Arabic language, in obtaining in such college or educational institution a literary, scientific, or professional education."[48] By initially instructing the students in Arabic, the school took advantage of the shared language of the region to educate young men from many of the surrounding countries. Even after the school changed its policy and used English as the language of instruction, the school became a magnet for students of all political allegiances because Arabs from throughout the region flocked to the school. In addition, the professors not only disseminated contemporary political ideologies but also galvanized students to participate in national and regional affairs.

Sulayman al-Nabulsi in the early 1930s attended AUB, where, as described by Husni Fariz, "Most of [our] companions were insatiably reading the Arabic newspapers and journals, with profound interest in understanding their role in the Arab world."[49] Standing foremost among these "companions" stood al-Nabulsi, for, as Fariz reports, he considered political work more important than his studies.[50] His house served as the gathering point for all his friends and acquaintances, to the point where the house came to be called "the Inn."[51] Al-Razzaz entered the American University of Beirut in 1937, after having spent a brief period studying in Cairo. Al-Razzaz and his colleagues, members of al-'Urwah al-Wuthqa [Indissoluble Bond], were firmly entrenched in the al-'Arab al-Qawmiyyun [Arab Nationalist] current, which worked toward complete Arab unity. Guiding the members of this organization were the ideas and influence of Constantine Zurayq, a Christian Arab from Damascus and professor at the school. Writing in 1939, Zurayq bemoaned the lack of national consciousness among the Arabs and called on them to rally around the cause of Arab nationalism. Zurayq advocated the unity and independence of the Arab state, run by a government whose tenets would be based on the ideas of Anglo-Saxon liberalism and European social reform.[52] The Arab Nationalist organization acted underground but used as its front organization the 'Usbat al-'Amal al-Qawmi [League of National Action].

75

Ziyadin entered medical school at al-Jamiʿat al-Yasoʿyah [the Jesuit College] in Beirut in the 1940s and soon began to hear about Communist ideas. Because these ideas piqued his interest, he frequently visited the Communist Party office, reading works by Stalin and Lenin, as well as the Beirut newspaper *Sawt al-Shaʿab*. Once he convinced himself that Communism answered his questions about politics, he began distributing *Sawt al-Shaʿab* himself, later spreading the message to other students, especially his Jordanian companions. Within a few months, he had joined a Communist Party cell, which met to discuss political issues. Upon graduating, he moved to Jerusalem in 1950 to work at Augusta-Victoria Hospital.

Cairo and Baghdad proved just as influential for those Transjordanian students studying in their universities. At the American University of Cairo (AUC), by 1936, student demonstrations had become a way of life. Donald Malcolm Reid reports that "Students spearheaded demonstrations for independence, skirmished on behalf of the fractured national parties, and protested policies which threatened their academic success or future job prospects."[53] ʿIsa Madanat, as a student there, organized a demonstration in opposition to the United Nations plan for the partition of Palestine in 1947. Madanat says that he got involved in politics after writing a paper about Marx and Engels for a university class.[54] Wahdan Oweis, a future member of the Baʿth Party, was exposed to both Communism and Baʿthism in Baghdad.[55] While he liked the Communist idea of equality and redistribution of wealth, he disagreed with the atheism associated with its tenets. He preferred Baʿthism instead because it covered the essential needs of the Arab people: unity, freedom, and Arab socialism. He did not join the party while studying in Iraq; he joined back in Jordan in 1954 or 1955.[56]

For these young graduates the field of Arab nationalism had become, in Partha Chatterjee's words, where "nationalism launches its most powerful, creative, and historically significant project."[57] These individual stories bring to life the questions and debates posed by a slowly increasing segment of the population in the Fertile Crescent. They show the anger wrought by the arbitrary division of the Arab world and offer the nationalized solution the new strata saw as the only answer to the socioeconomic problems thus created. Henceforth, calls for independence from colonial rule of all kinds were paired with those for social and economic justice. These young men had the skills and the ideological foundation to believe they had the power and the right to change their societies. Boundary lines may have structurally divided their political lives, but a cohesiveness was forged by the university experience and then maintained afterward through clubs and professional organizations. These men forged their own "imagined community" of like-minded professionals and fellow Arabs, ignoring at least on one level the European divisions. The fact that the few universities that existed serviced the regional community fostered the emergence of this regional national identity. The proponents of this identity stood at the forefront of changes that would come to yet more strata in the society in the postindependence periods of the 1950s and 1960s.

These men and their colleagues graduated with degrees in law, medicine, education, and engineering, thus joining forces as part of a new urban professional intelligentsia. Most of these professions allowed them to work autonomously, outside of governmental control. However, only one of the memoirs specifically mentions a desire for such an independent profession, specifically with the hope of undertaking political activities. Nabih Irsheidat reports that he took Dr. Subhi Abu Ghunaymah as his role model, a man who was able, as a doctor, to work without dependence on any government.[58] Even though the other memoir writers do not specifically state their preference for this kind of independence, the mobility their professions afforded them had to have become a factor during their political lives. They often set up their offices and clinics in different towns and in different countries when sent into exile by the Hashemite regime. Others of this educated class chose to work within the government structures but did not allow that work to impede their opposition activities. Taking government positions, as in the schools or the Ministry of the Economy, two prime posts for political opposition figures in the 1950s in Jordan, did not in any way compromise their political values. Hamad al-Farhan and 'Isa Madanat worked as teachers in the government schools before joining the Ministry of the Economy. Munif al-Razzaz worked as a teacher before entering other professions, while Sulayman al-Nabulsi served in a number of cabinet and government positions throughout his career. King 'Abdullah even granted him the honorific title of "Pasha" as he entered the government of Samir al-Rifa'i in December 1950.[59] Muhammad Bajis al-Majali worked for the government in Amman in the 1950s and subsequently held seventeen different positions; he was fired repeatedly for causing trouble but always hired back soon thereafter.[60] It was natural for these men to work for the very government they opposed during their extracurricular activities, just as 'Arar and his colleagues had done earlier. They held their positions while working in political opposition because they needed the jobs and the state needed their services. In many cases, only the state provided the positions commensurate with their new skills. Also, little differentiation existed between most of the government employees and the opposition forces; their shared social stratum typically outweighed their ideological differences. Thus, as Musallam Bseiso, a Palestinian journalist of the 1950s, reports, "the whole day everyone is in his work; in the evenings we are at the coffeehouse together. You find the Communists, the Baʿthists, the Nationalists, the under-secretary of the government. Only some people, who were the instruments of the government," who the people knew, stayed away.[61]

When the future leaders of the JNM returned from university in the mid-1940s, their offices served as focal points for political activities throughout the country as people flocked to informal salons in clinics, pharmacies, and lawyers' offices. Munif reports that the medical clinics of Abd al-Rahman Shuqayr and Munif al-Razzaz in Amman received the sick, the poor, and the politically active all at once.[62] Nabih Irsheidat created the same atmosphere in his clinic, and in the 1950s even published from it a Communist Party paper, al-Jabha [The Front], with the Palestinian Fayiq Warrad.[63] The doctors proved particularly popular because they treated the sick at low prices. Political clubs in Amman, such as the Arab Club, run by the Baʿth Party, and the Literary Club, led by the Communists, served as the meeting places and dissemination points for men engaged in these political activities and professions. Even in the smaller towns, such as Karak, men met at the clubs to play cards and backgammon, but also to maintain cohesion as a social stratum.[64] These meeting places served to protect the collegiality these men experienced on their educational pilgrimages and, from a practical point of view, provided places for political organization and the dissemination of political ideas.

"TRANSJORDAN FOR THE TRANSJORDANIANS," PART II

In the mid-to-late 1940s, these clubs and offices served as the organizing centers for a new political opposition force in Jordan. Its proponents organized, at this time, not around the larger goals of Arab nationalism, influenced by their activities at school and university, but on the smaller Jordanian plane temporarily. This act was not a diminution of their larger goals but rather a recognition of the political divisions in the Fertile Crescent. The political activism learned in universities around the region provided them with an incentive to immediately organize an opposition movement once they got home. The most pressing goals of the late 1940s were more akin to the earlier "Transjordan for the Transjordanians" phase of the opposition struggle than to the Arab nationalist one that would emerge after 1948. However, even with these narrow goals, they initially proved as ineffectual as the first movement had been because they failed to dramatically alter government policy. To become more powerful, they would need the influx of the Palestinian population in 1948 and the participation of a more politicized Jordanian one, organized under the umbrella of Arab nationalism.

Two key political events occurred that required the immediate attention of these new activists: the Rashid Ali coup in Iraq and the 1946 declaration of Jordanian independence. To influence government policy in these instances, the new leaders formed political parties and led protest demonstrations. The first event, the Rashid Ali coup in Iraq, forced Transjordanian troops to fight alongside British forces in Iraq and proved to this new opposition movement that both the British and their own government worked against their interests. The coup generated a great deal of sympathy within Transjordan and particularly among the emerging opposition leaders. The inclusion of the Transjordanian Arab Legion in the force that eventually destroyed the movement sparked demonstrations in Amman. Alec Kirkbride, the British Resident, eventually calmed the city but took a relatively long time to do so because the majority of the country's troops had been posted to Iraq.

The second event, the granting of Jordanian independence on May 25, 1946, did little but confirm that British control remained, although under a new guise. Accompanying this declaration came a new Anglo-Jordanian Treaty, signed on March 22, 1946. The basic system of control remained intact, as the British agreed to continue their annual subsidy to support the Arab Legion, British troops stayed in their bases in Amman and Mafraq, and 'Abdullah agreed to consult Britain on matters of foreign policy "which might affect their common interest."[65] The name of the country was changed to the Hashemite Kingdom of Jordan, a fact confirmed in the constitution of February 1947, and 'Abdullah took the title of king. Alec Kirkbride became Britain's first ambassador to Jordan. As evidence of Jordan's weakness as a state, the Soviet Union refused to recognize Jordan's independence, as it felt Jordan stood as a bulwark of Western imperialism in the Middle East and as a base for the British military.[66] Because of this opinion, the Soviet Union blocked Jordan's admission into the United Nations in August 1946 and continued to do so until December 1955.

The new state issued a constitution on February 1, 1947, which replaced the Organic Law of 1928. It created a Majlis al-Ummah [Parliament] composed of two houses, the Majlis al-Nuwwab [Chamber of

Deputies] and the Majlis al-A'yan [Chamber of Notables], to oversee the legislative branch of the government. The lower house contained twenty members, allotted by both district population and confessional and ethnic group. Twelve seats went to Muslims, four to Christians, two to the bedouin, two to the Circassians, and two for the Chechen. All but the bedouin deputies were elected by universal manhood suffrage for four-year terms. By so doing, the state disproportionately allotted seats in the majlis to the populations deemed loyal to the regime. Like its predecessor, the Legislative Assembly, this new majlis held little power within the government and served primarily as a debating society. The cabinet and the king retained the right to ratify the budget, even without the acceptance of the deputies, and the cabinet could issue provisional laws in the absence of the Majlis al-Nuwwab. The upper house contained ten appointed members, serving for eight-year terms. All power lay with the king, so the government was not required to obtain a vote of confidence from the majlis.

To elect the Majlis al-Nuwwab, a new Electoral Law was passed on April 5, 1947.[67] This expanded the number of electoral districts, giving, according to Mary Wilson, "the impression of a more precise system of representation, but in fact shifting electoral weight away from the towns, rapidly growing in population and in political sophistication, to the countryside where Abdullah had his most loyal and least politicized constituency."[68] Indirect elections were abolished, as every voter received the right to directly elect his representative.

The new opposition forces protested against this arrangement because, as Shuqayr said, independence was an illusion.[69] Activities included demonstrations in Amman, the creation of political parties, and the publication of new newspapers and journals. A group calling itself the "Jami'ah al-Shabab al-Ahrar al-Urduniyin" [Group of Jordanian Liberals] issued a series of broadsheets at the end of 1946 demanding specific reforms to the governmental structure. In a February 13, 1947, broadsheet, this group summarized its political demands by calling for a true constitutional government, a democratic government responsible to the Majlis al-Ummah, free elections to the majlis, amendment of the Anglo-Jordanian Treaty to end foreign control over the country, expulsion of the foreign army from Jordanian soil, and cancellation of the economic concessions granted during the Mandate period.[70] Shuqayr organized political activities out of his medical clinic in Amman, where he wrote a number of articles for the Palestinian press critical of the Jordanian government and British policies. By the beginning of 1947, his activities had become known to the government, so police raided his clinic in search of incriminating articles. Once they found the articles they wanted, the officers took him to the Amman jail for the first time. While this stay lasted only three days, another one, three months later, lasted two weeks and resulted in Shuqayr's exile from Jordan, on the pretext of his continued Syrian citizenship. As a sign of the mobility afforded by his medical career, Shuqayr immediately set up a clinic in Damascus and waited for the Jordanian government to allow him to return. 'Abdullah granted Shuqayr and other exiles permission to return a few months later because rumors were spreading that Ibn Saud, 'Abdullah's enemy across the border, was trying to effect an alliance with them.

Sulayman al-Nabulsi, having vacillated between governmental and nongovernment jobs since returning to Amman in 1932, was first arrested in 1945 for agitating in Jerusalem against a Jordanian government decision to grant a mineral concession to a Jewish company.[71] Upon his return to the East Bank, he was arrested at Allenby Bridge and exiled for three months to the southern town of Shobeck. Typical of this era, his opposition activities did not hinder his political career. For example, from 1946 to 1947, al-Nabulsi served as Minister of Finance and Economics. At the same time, government work did not end his opposition activities. He spent nine months in Amman Prison for publishing an article opposed to the 1948 Anglo-Jordanian Treaty.[72] His particular focus during the late 1940s and early 1950s was the removal of Tawfiq Abu'l-Huda from positions of power.

The first elections in independent Jordan took place in October 1947. The majority of winners were the tribal leaders, landowners, and wealthy businessmen who had won seats in the Legislative Assembly since 1931. Two government-supported political parties were licensed in anticipation of the elections, al-Hizb al-Nahda al-'Arabiyah [the Arab Rebirth Party] and al-Hizb al-Sha'ab al-Urduni [the Jordanian People's Party]. Both pledged to work on behalf of the country, economically, politically, and culturally; only the former participated in the elections, winning four seats. The government dissolved the latter party when it started to gain popularity. One opposition party formed, al-Hizb al-'Arabi al-Urduni [Jordanian Arab Party], with Subhi Abu Ghunaymah as the elected president. Its platform paralleled that of the National Pact of 1928, calling for the democratization of the system, supported by the separation of powers; a freely elected parliament; a government responsible to the people; protection of civil liberties; and modification of the 1946 Anglo-Jordanian Treaty to accord the country true independence.[73] Party adherents were not allowed to run in the elections under party aegis, but two of its members, Shafiq Irsheidat and Abd al-Halim al-Nimr, were elected to this parliament as independents.

As a result of the protests against the status of the Anglo-Jordanian relationship, the two countries concluded a new treaty on March 15, 1948, which reduced British prerogatives but basically retained Jordan's dependent position. The British and Jordanian governments did this because they wanted to make the former's patronage responsibilities over the country less obvious.[74] Britain retained the right to use airstrips in Amman and Mafraq and to keep a small garrison in Aqaba. In return, Jordan was granted additional military aid.

To protest the new treaty, a number of lawyers and doctors went to the Majlis al-Nuwwab on November 6, 1948, to deliver a petition to the government. This petition stated that the government had failed to fulfill its ministerial program and requested the creation of a national charter and a new constitution, and the nullification of exceptional laws and the Anglo-Jordanian Treaty. It also demanded that government repression of the people's natural rights cease. Prime Minister Tawfiq Abu'l-Huda arrested a number of the signers, under the terms of the Defense Law, claiming they were Communists. In opposition to this act, Shafiq Irsheidat accused the government of using the Defense Law and its power in an abusive way. Abd al-Halim al-Nimr declared that putting forward a petition was not sufficient grounds for imprisoning citizens.[75]

This second movement ultimately failed to radically transform 'Abdullah's policies. The government made alterations to the Anglo-Jordanian Treaty but did not overturn its basic tenets. The fact that 'Abdullah's government needed British goodwill at this point more than the support of its own population helped account for the early movement's failure. Also, the nascent opposition movement still proved too weak to oppose this balance of power. To be successful, the movement required an infusion of new voices and outlets for its activities. The message of revolutionary change and Arab nationalism had to find resonance in a sufficient percentage of the population. The enthusiasm of the leaders needed to be matched by a population fully immersed in the same sorts of socialization processes they had undergone. Overall, for a truly powerful movement to emerge, a larger proportion of the population would have to be nationalized away from the story of the Hashemite state and toward the goals attached to Arab nationalism. The 1950s would witness the emergence of just that kind of movement, favored by the population and able to influence government decision-making.

CONCLUSION

The political socialization period for the leaders of the Jordanian National Movement (JNM) illustrates a number of elements of Transjordanian life under the Hashemite state, elements that must be understood to analyze both the state and the opposition later in the 1950s and 1960s. As the memoirs illustrate, the state itself facilitated the growth of a new stratum in the society, the urban professional intelligentsia, because it required these men to literally build its country. Many chose that route and worked within the different government agencies then emerging. However, these very same institutions, particularly the schools, forced these young men to question the messages the state disseminated. They could see around them the economic inequities the state perpetuated, and they wanted a new kind of regime to resolve these problems. They found "traveling companions" amongst their Jordanian citizenry, but their experiences took them outside those confines, those boundaries, and put them into a larger Arab group that asked the same questions they were asking at home. For a brief period in the 1950s, the Hashemite national narrative could not compete with the power of Arab nationalism. To become strong, the Jordanian proponents of this new revolutionary ideology had to find allies in the Palestinian community that entered the Jordanian stage in 1950, already armed with a national awareness of its place within the larger Arab world.

FIVE

HASHEMITES
AND PALESTINIANS
1921–1948

Palestine, the blessed land, is the land of Bani Ya'rub [Sons of the Arabs].

A POEM THAT APPEARED ON THE WALL
OF AL-RASHIDIYAH SCHOOL IN 1918[1]

*The Arabs are the real and original people of this country. They have
owned and possessed this country for centuries without any interruption.
Their connection with this land without any interruption dates back
for a period of thirteen hundred years.*

EVIDENCE OF IZZAT DARWAZAH
TO THE ROYAL (PEEL) COMMISSION IN 1937[2]

*I recalled in more than one conversation the Frankenstein monster
raised by Zaghlul in Egypt, where the whole system of Government was
undermined by students' demonstrations; and quoted the true story of
the daughter of an Egyptian Minister, leading into his office a delegation
of school girls, who threatened her father's life unless his Government
instantly yielded to their demands.*

HUMPHREY BOWMAN, CAUTIONING PALESTINIAN
ARAB LEADERS TO KEEP POLITICS OUT OF THE CLASSROOM[3]

The Hashemite state had used the interwar period to establish its top-down approach to nation-building, "working" to establish for itself a legitimate place in the population's eyes. When the initial indigenous opposition movement disintegrated, governmental and nongovernmental agencies served to acclimatize the population to the existence of the new state that emerged. However, national identity became an arena for conflict in the new agencies of socialization because the Hashemite leadership and its national identity did not hold resonance for the new social stratum emerging in them. In Palestine, in contrast, legitimacy and national identity were not so much in question; the problems there were those inherent in a situation where two peoples claimed nationhood on the same piece of land. The Balfour Declaration of November 1917 encouraged the establishment of a Jewish homeland in Palestine, but conditioned it on the guarantee of civil rights for the "non-Jewish majority." This set up a basic contradiction within the very Mandate structure. As a result, the British never allowed a clearly defined national governmental structure to emerge, one that would lead toward a clearly defined independent nation for one or both of the communities. By the very terms of the Mandate, Jewish rights were more clearly articulated than those of the "non-Jewish majority." As a result, the Jewish community of Palestine stood in a position more analogous to that of the Hashemites next door, working to form a national governmental structure within a colonial framework.[4] To counteract their ambiguous position and to make their claim for national legitimacy, the Palestinians generated at the elite and grassroots levels those agencies for change pivotal to the spread of national identity and political activism, bringing into the national project much of the population by 1948. Yet they were continually stymied in their goals for the future. As Rashid Khalidi has stated, "This absence of sovereignty through history has denied the Palestinians full control over the state mechanisms—education, museums, archaeology, postage stamps and coins, and the media, especially radio and television—which myriad examples show is essential for disseminating and imposing uniform 'national' criteria of identity."[5] Thus, the realities of the Mandate structure meant that the Palestinian leadership could not create that centrifugal force around governmental and national symbols that the neighboring Arab states and the Zionists could at the same time.

As a result of these obstacles, the Palestinians had fewer resources at their disposal to eliminate the differences present between the urban and rural areas of the country, to present a more uniform whole to their many enemies. Elite urban families controlled the political process in the Ottoman era and then continued this role into the Mandate period. Contacts between the urban and rural areas were fragmentary at best because of the poor quality of roads and the different social and economic structures dividing them. More importantly, the Palestinians did not have access to national governmental structures established in their name. "For the Yishuv and for the other Arab countries under the mandate system, such a forum proved invaluable for the polity to coalesce around or compete for, or as a focus for its action, even if complete control over it was denied by the colonial power."[6] Connections between rural and urban areas had to occur in more informal arenas because the government could not serve that unifying function; no force provided the cohesion encompassing, for example, the people of Jordan. Issa Khalaf concurs when he says, "More fundamentally than self-governing institutions, the lack of effective power over the state meant that the Palestinian Arab notability which headed the national government would be unable to use the resources of the state to centralize power in its hands and thereby develop into a cohesive stratum."[7]

Despite these obstacles, in the late Ottoman and then early Mandate periods it did appear that this cohesion was starting to form, as better roads, more schools, and generally more opportunities for interaction developed between these urban and rural areas. In some cases, urban notables specifically went out into the countryside to educate the population about national issues and the threats posed by Zionism. For example, even prior to World War I, Khalidi reports, "We can see that many of those in the cities who warned against the dangers of Zionism made a conscious effort to build this shared sense of destiny between city and countryside, city-dweller and *fellah*."[8] In one such example, "The editors of *Filastin* sent free copies of their paper to the *mukhtar* [chief] of every village in the Jaffa district with more than 100 inhabitants. The objective, they wrote in an editorial, was to 'acquaint the *fellah* with what is happening in the country, and to teach him his rights, in order to prevent those who do not fear God and his prophets from dominating him and stealing his goods.'"[9] When an increasing number of students obtained access to the secondary schools in the cities, they served as conduits for information between the two areas. Newspapers and radio reports supplemented their work. Through such avenues, a creeping sense of national identity moved out of the cities and into the rural areas throughout the Mandate period because, along with the expansion of new agencies of change, a new nationalized vocabulary followed.

The message henceforth disseminated was that the Palestinians could claim the Arab primordial inheritance to the land as their national birthright. Izzat Darwazah's assertion at the beginning of the chapter, that "the Arabs are the real and original people of this country," summarizes the basic view gaining acceptance by the Mandate period. Textbooks, articles, and testimonies to British Mandate committees consistently negated the Zionist historical claim to the land. Instead, the glories of the "Arab Canaanites" were extolled, and the history presented was one of a continuous Arab presence on the land. As the Mandate period progressed and Jewish immigration to Palestine increased, the message also included a call for the neighboring Arabs to protect this inheritance. Palestine was then depicted as the heart of the Arab world because of the Holy Sites located there and the need to fight the threat coming to its shores. Thus, Palestinian nationalism, from its first manifestation in the years leading up to World War I, always had both territorial and pan-national components, connecting it to the past, the present, and the future.

Despite the recognition of a shared threat and a shared identity, differences persisted between the urban and rural areas because of the fragmentation at the elite political level and the dearth of cohesive national institutions. As a result, the urban and rural areas often participated in different kinds of nationalist activities, reflecting different social, political, and economic concerns. Rosemary Sayigh reports that

> The socio-cultural distance between the educated urban middle class and the mainly illiterate peasants grew wider under the impact of "modernization", a distance reflected in politics by the only slight participation of the middle class in the national struggle, and the dangerous underdevelopment of the rural areas. With the majority of the educated classes as non-militant and "moderate" in their stance towards the British, resistance was deprived of organizational and ideological development, and remained coloured with religious fundamentalism.[10]

While urban elites formed political parties around their family alliances, rural partisans supported military bands led by religious leaders like Izz al-Din al-Qassam.

Even with this fragmentation and differentiation in tasks, the overall result of these activities was to politicize the bulk of the population by 1948. Both the urban and rural populations learned the vocabulary of nationalism while participating in myriad agencies disseminating these ideas. Memoirs of the day highlight the fact that urban areas saw the most fervent debate about the ideas and institutions of nationalism, with the rural areas slowly drawn into the process. As an example of the experiences young people were having, this chapter will focus on Bahjat Abu Gharbiyah, a future leader of the Ba'th Party in Jordan, and the only Palestinian leader of the Jordanian National Movement (JNM) to record his memoirs. To provide images of life under the British Mandate, this chapter will refer to the stories reported about the village of Bethany by Saïd K. Aburish; and memoirs, testimonies, and interviews by, among others, George Antonius, member of the Education Department in the 1920s;

Khalil Sakakini, headmaster of the Arab College in Jerusalem and Inspector of Education for the British Mandate; Khalil Totah, headmaster of the Arab College in Jerusalem and the Friends' School in Ramallah; Husni Ayesh, resident of Tulkarm and future teacher; Musallam Bseiso, resident of Beersheba and a future journalist; Tal'at Harb, resident of Haifa and future member of the Communist Party; Amin al-Khatib, resident of Jerusalem and future member of the Ba'th Party; Hatim Kamal, resident of Nablus; Ghada Karmi, resident of Jerusalem; Hala Sakakini, a resident of Jerusalem and daughter of Khalil Sakakini; Yusrah Salah, resident of Nablus; and Mahmoud Zeitoun, resident of Hebron and future member of the Ba'th Party.

SCHOOLS, SCOUTS, AND THE URBAN AREAS[11]

In the urban areas, the Palestinian political trajectory followed the Transjordanian one in that it took young Palestinian men and women from political discussions in their homes to the more formal settings of schools. Simultaneously, the Palestinians participated in the strikes, demonstrations, and, finally, armed resistance waged to combat British occupation and Zionist expansion. Even for those who did not actively join some kind of political organization or event, British actions served to collectivize people's awareness of their shared suffering. The myriad number of curfews alone brought home to Palestinians in all areas of the country the threat posed by the colonial power and the new settlers. Even young children realized that it was not just their families or their neighborhoods or even their cities experiencing these events, but a larger group of people known as the Palestinians. For Jordanians, discussions at home and experiences in school provided the most influential means for politicizing youth; in Palestine, a larger array of civil society institutions, such as festivals, scout troops, and military bands, complemented the work being done in the homes and schools.

Eids [festivals] became particularly important because they often turned from religious and historical celebrations into collective, nationalized political events. The most important such eid, the one commemorating the prophet Musa, became an annual opportunity to decry the actions of the British and the Zionists.[12] From Jerusalem, "A great procession made up of groups from the various regions of Palestine would move slowly through the streets of the city towards St. Stephen's Gate on their way to Nabi Musa, which lies northeast of Jerusalem."[13] When the procession returned to Jerusalem a few days later, people gathered along the Jericho road to watch the Mufti of Jerusalem, Hajj Amin al-Husayni, ride his horse from the eastern edge of the city to Damascus Gate.[14] Taking several days, the celebration involved thousands of demonstrators marching down the streets of Jerusalem, dancing the dabka and singing nationalist songs and anthems. Protests against the Mandate rang out, with calls for independence and freedom. "The red flag of Jerusalem, the green flag of Hebron, the violet flag of Nablus and the flags of the al-Aqsa mosque and the prophets, David and Musa, flew throughout the crowd."[15] Participants sacrificed sheep and goats all along the route. Hala Sakakini recalls the one time she attended the events in Jerusalem, highlighting the importance of this event in the lives of Palestinians.

> We sat on a high spot on the slope north of St. Stephen's Gate. The place was densely crowded. Everywhere you could see the Arab flag with its green, red, white and black colours fluttering high above the heads. The scene filled us with enthusiasm and national pride. Every now and then strong young men would link their arms together and, forming circles, would start dancing the '*dabkeh*' and singing. It was thrilling to watch and wonderful for the spirit. Although the *Nabi Musa* feast was supposed to be a religious occasion, it was in fact a national day in which all the Arabs of Palestine, Christians and Moslems alike, shared.[16]

A number of other celebrations also turned into political opportunities because they highlighted the glories of the Arab-Islamic past. "Religious occasions, like the birthday of the Prophet Mohammed, the New Year's Day of the Hijirah Moslem calendar and the first day of the holy month, Ramadan, were usually celebrated by a festival which began with an address showing the importance of such occasions for past Arab greatness."[17] Celebrations such as these gave cohesion to a community just beginning to nationalize its demands and its identities. The glories of the past could be re-created in the present; these events tied the present Palestinian experience to the Muslim and Arab primordial past on that land.

Rituals such as these play a strong role in the political socialization and nationalization of a population. Christel Lane states that "ritual . . . relate[s] the individual to the collective. Ritual provides ready-made channels which allow the individual to express his feelings while at the same time funneling them into a socially accepted direction."[18] These events are a mixture of spontaneous desire and conscious and systematic preparation.[19] They intermingle political ideas with traditional religious and historical celebrations and, by so doing, attempt to spread new political values. According to Lane, processions and demonstrations in the French Revolution provided this necessary combination of national, historical, and religious symbols to produce new political ideas and demands. "The main form of ritual was the massed procession, ending in a climactic gathering on one of the places closely associated with the Revolution. Often the procession would progress from station to station, halting in various symbolic places (e.g. the Mars Field)."[20] In each place, speeches would be made highlighting the religious or political significance of the demonstration and the demands of the crowd. These events physically connected the contemporary population to a romanticized and coherent historical past.

As with the Nabi Musa procession, other Middle Eastern religious rituals were transformed just as easily into a new means for organizing and nationalizing populations. For example, in Egypt, Gregory Starrett has found that "The conscious invention of public ceremonies became an important part of the state's mass mobilization program, and schools began to capitalize on public events like the Prophet's Birthday, Unity Day, and Mother's Day to clothe nationalist values like unity, cooperation and brotherhood with the appearance of important religious principles."[21] Emir 'Abdullah understood this point when he processed down the streets of Amman on his way to the mosque on Fridays. He provided the new Transjordanian citizenry with a ritual to call their own, while simultaneously nationalizing the leadership role of the royal family. Palestinian leaders may or may not have engineered the transformation from religious to political ritual in the case of celebrations like the Nabi Musa commemoration. Yet they must have understood the political benefit they would accrue as they brought out the flags of the "nation" in celebration of both religion and nationhood. By transforming beloved religious rituals into political events, the leaders successfully recruited into their national project those people who might have been disconnected from the new agencies of socialization. The enemies of the people became the enemies of the nation; leaders of the families and tribes became the leaders of the national citizenry.

As with the work of 'Arar, Palestinian poets provided an emotional context for such events in the interwar period. Adnan Abu-Ghazaleh theorizes that "The economic development of the country and the growth of schools and literary clubs simultaneously provided a sizeable audience for the work of these writers, which illustrated the increasing concern of Palestinians for their country's future."[22] A perfect example of this development is the poetry of Ibrahim Tuqan (1905–1941). He incorporated classical Arab poetic meter with new nationalist imagery. "Tuqan's poetry was primarily concerned with national considerations; it was a call to his compatriots to rebel against the British authorities and to liberate their homeland from foreign rule."[23] Salma Khadra Jayyusi feels that he was particularly energized during his university studies, for "It was during his studies at the American University of Beirut, where he met other poets and participated in the active literary life of the university, that his talent began to sparkle."[24] Like his compatriots in the professions, he returned to Palestine after graduation "strongly armed with the spirit of one who felt responsible for awakening his countrymen to their predicament."[25] As an example of the themes he covered, he called out to Lord Balfour, the author of the Balfour Declaration: "Balfour! that in your glass is not wine but the martyrs' blood."[26]

Poems like this one provided an emotional, creative complement to the political process of nationalization taking place among the Palestinians. As Ghada Karmi relates, writing of Jerusalem, "I remember my father talking about the poetry readings at the Arab Orthodox Club in Baq'a where my uncle Salma and his fellow poet Ibrahim Tuqan read their nationalist verses. This kind of poetry was new to Palestine, since it concerned itself with political subjects and expressed opposition and resistance to what was happening in the country with a passion which drew enormous sympathy from the audience."[27] As with 'Arar, poetry served as the national news service, articulating people's passions and patriotisms, just as it defined the creative parameters of the nation. Nationalist poems, read and memorized in the schools, added an emotional weight to the messages the teachers were disseminating.

Events taking place throughout the country also highlighted the very real connections still existing between the Palestinians and the surrounding Arabs in yet a larger national collective. Hala Sakakini relates an event that took place in the summer of 1934 that not only highlighted this connection but placed Palestine into a special position within the Arab world. The event was the Arab Exhibition, held in the Awqaf building on St. Julian's Way in Jerusalem.

A large variety of goods from different Arab countries was on display—exquisite brocades from Syria; thick, woolen blankets from Iraq; leatherware from Egypt; perfumes and confectionery from Lebanon; heavy camelhair *abayas* and light black ones from Iraq. Then there were the local products of which we were very proud: the colourful, sweet-smelling balls of soap produced in Nablus; the mother-of-pearl goods from Bethlehem; the rough, handwoven woolen mats from Beersheba and Gaza; the handwoven towels from Majdal; the olive wood articles made in Jerusalem. Leisurely winding

our way through the throngs in the large halls, we would feast our eyes on
the many articles everywhere on view. There was enthusiasm, and a strong
feeling of patriotism, in the air. Everybody seemed elated. Even as children
[my sister] Dumia and I were keenly aware of this. Now I know why people
felt the way they did at the time. It was the joy and pride of belonging to the
Arab nation. For them the Exhibition had a symbolic value. It was material
evidence that Palestine was an integral part of the Arab world.[28]

The collective national space included not just the newly identified
Palestinian nation but the larger Arab world. The tenets of Palestinian
and Arab nationalism had become intertwined, with the former serving
as the heart of the latter, the latter granting additional legitimacy to the
former.

Throughout the Mandate period, young children absorbed these messages as they sat listening to their parents and their elders discuss events
of the day. Amin al-Khatib remembers sitting many times, as a child,
with the men of his family in Jerusalem's Old City, listening to discussions about the English occupation and the means for resisting it.[29] When
his father bought a radio in the 1930s, with the spread of electricity to
their quarter, yet more people gathered in his house to listen to the news.
As a result of these experiences, "from the earliest [days] of our youth,
we hated the foreign occupation and we opposed it, and the atmosphere
which we were living in prepared us for that. Hajj Amin al-Husayni, our
neighbors, and the children of my uncle were with us always and our
relatives were keeping busy with work and the majority of their events
revolved around the nation and the occupation."[30] Friday prayers in the
1930s became opportunities for political discussions, both in the sermons
and in the informal discussions that took place in small groups around the
Haram al-Sharif in Jerusalem afterward.[31]

Bahjat Abu Gharbiyah came to be an activist in Palestine and then one
of the leaders of the Ba'th Party in Jordan during the 1950s. He was born
in Khan Yunis in 1916, but he and his family relocated to Hebron after
Khan Yunis fell to British forces in World War I. They remained in the
town until the end of the war and then moved to Jerusalem. At home,
Abu Gharbiyah experienced a number of influences that later affected
his political actions. For example, his mother frequently told him stories
of Arab historical heroes who had fought against oppression, and, when
clashes took place outside their door, she encouraged him to participate.
In discussions around him, "All I heard about was the dark British occupation, and about the Balfour Declaration and Zionism, and about the
support of the British for the Zionist movement and their promise to

them to establish the Jewish homeland. . . . I and the sons of my generation noticed, with clarity, the increased number of Jews in Jerusalem."[32]
Later, during the 1933 demonstrations in Jerusalem, Abu Gharbiyah saw
British policemen kill a number of the participants. "During that time a
deep hatred for the English was created in my chest."[33] He then began to
actively oppose British rule.

From these discussions and scenes, these children moved to the more
formal settings supplied by the expanding private and public school systems. As in Transjordan, Palestinian schools proved pivotal in spreading
the nationalist message—both Arab and Palestinian—to an increasing
percentage of young people. In an attempt to forestall this politicization
process, British officials completely monopolized their leadership and
their decision-making positions.[34] Thus, the British Director of Education "introduced and piloted all educational legislation; all direction
and control of education [were] primarily in his hands; he appointed and
dismissed teachers; and he controlled all school curricula; and said the
final word in all professional matters."[35] The government's reports on the
educational situation in Palestine were not even published in Arabic.[36]

While the British discouraged the solidification of nationalist sentiment, they undertook a much larger school building program than the
Hashemites next door. In 1914, at the start of World War I, Palestine had
95 elementary schools and 3 secondary schools, with a total of 234 teachers and 8,248 pupils, of whom 1,840 were girls.[37] In addition to these
Ottoman state schools, 379 private Muslim schools were also functioning
during World War I, although most were of the kuttab type and were
situated within village mosques.[38] When the British occupied the area
during the war, they took charge of the state educational system and, by
reopening schools closed during the war, accounted for 311 by 1922.[39]
From that point forward, new schools did open but at a much slower
pace. As of the 1946–1947 academic year, only 57 percent of Arab boys
and 23 percent of Arab girls attended the full school program of five to
fourteen years, but 74 percent of boys and 27 percent of girls attended
for a period of about five years.[40] As Matta Akrawi and Roderic Matthews
reported, even as of 1949,

> the supply of educational facilities continues to fall short of the ever-
> increasing demand motivated by the new Arab awakening. Recent years
> have witnessed a growing measure of participation in the educational effort
> by both local municipalities and the Arab populace in general. This par-
> ticipation manifests itself in the vigorous school-building activity carried
> on largely at the expense of the local authorities and supported by contri-

93

butions from the people, in the collection of education taxes by a number of municipalities, and in the willingness of local authorities to finance new schools and pay additional teachers.[41]

Even with this additional aid, by the end of the Mandate period about half the eight hundred Arab villages had no schools at all.[42] According to A. L. Tibawi, for Arabs, "briefly described[,] the system was nothing more than a limited elementary education of four–five years, and a restricted and highly selective intermediate (two years) and secondary (four to six years) education, chiefly designed to supply teachers."[43] The vast majority of students attended village schools for a short period, with a small number of particularly gifted students traveling to the larger towns to continue their studies.

For those privileged few, the Men's Training College, renamed the Arab College in 1927, and the Women's Training College, both in Jerusalem, served as the state's first secondary schools. Both of these schools, by 1926, provided students with a full four-year program and the ability to take the Palestine matriculation examination in preparation for university work.[44] Al-Rashidiyah College in Jerusalem was originally a day elementary-secondary school for boys and served as one of the few Turkish secondary schools to survive the transfer to British control.[45] In 1939, the fourth secondary class was added, which allowed the students to take the matriculation examination.[46]

Since no Palestinian textbooks existed in the early Mandate period, almost all the textbooks used in the government schools came from Egypt, Lebanon, and Syria. In particular, history, geography, and science books were lacking at first, so teachers had to improvise in the classroom.[47] Most of the texts that did exist consistently avoided the Palestinian issue as a national issue, commensurate with the British desire to leave ambiguous the national basis for the governmental structure. In the first three years of study, as laid out in the government syllabus of 1925, Arab and Palestinian history was illustrated through the lives of "great men."[48] The situation did not improve in the early secondary years either, as nationalists complained that Arab history remained too fragmentary.[49] Tibawi reports that critics of the system felt, regarding the history and geography syllabus, that "While it contained features of the geography and history of the Arab countries, . . . it insisted in its content and tone on the international rather than the national character of Palestine."[50] A Jaffa textbook of 1946 provides an example of the internationalization of Palestinian history.

Palestine had a special place in the heart of the ancient world, between the continents of Asia, Africa and Europe, and it was a natural route uniting the Nile Valley and Tigris and Euphrates Valley, and, considering its small size, it was a more important center for culture and economics and war than most of the countries of the world mentioned in history, matchless for the prophets and messengers and the incidence in it of wars and civil strife, and so it was during the dawn of history a battleground for wars of division between the east and west.[51]

The goal of all national narratives is to connect the past and the present, the people living on a given piece of land, within a stated boundary, over time immemorial. The British, consciously or unconsciously, refused to allow such a narrative to exist, for a national narrative, provided by the Palestine government's school textbooks, would have given official sanction to the Palestinian historical claim to the land. British policy consistently refused to recognize such a claim. According to Khalil Totah, Arabs frequently criticized this British-run educational system precisely because it was hostile to their national political aspirations and was designed "to bring up a generation which is to be docile and subservient to imperialism and its chief attendant evil, Zionism."[52]

Reports from the ground highlight the very real absence of the concept of the Palestinian nation in these textbooks. Husni Ayesh, going to school in Tulkarm in the 1940s, remembers that all of his textbooks came from Egypt and that he never read about Palestinian history in any of them, as the Mandate government would not have allowed books of that kind.[53] Concurring, Amin Hafez Dajani reports that the textbooks were written by Egyptians and contained almost no information about the Arab world, focusing instead on the ancient history of Greece.[54] In his view, the students left school with a much better grasp of English history and literature than those of the Arabs.[55] To offset this deficiency, nationalist activists in Palestine called for an "exclusively Arab history as the main interest in the lower elementary cycles and world history studied in relation to Arab and Palestine history in the upper cycle."[56] Like those of their Arab neighbors, this syllabus would have extolled the breadth and glories of Arab history, leading in a direct line to Palestinian national history. Provided with a disconnected narrative, students came away without the necessary context for their own history.

To curtail this process, the Department of Education censored all books potentially available for use in the classroom. For example, Khalil Totah informed the Palestine Royal (Peel) Commission on January 18,

1937, that "I was co-author of a book, the History of Palestine in Arabic for schools, and Sir Herbert Samuel the then High Commissioner banned the book, the Government banned the book, because it had a very inoffensive reference to Zionism. You could not write a history of Palestine up to date without making some reference to it. It was not rabid, it was not a violent attack on it. It is there for everyone to read, but the book was banned, and is still banned."[57] In step with their own unwillingness to clarify their role in Palestine, the British tried to discourage and forbid the Palestinians from doing so independently.

By the 1940s, Arabs in the surrounding states were starting to publish textbooks on historical subjects. Particularly by the end of World War II, the texts that appeared highlight an Arab historical stability on the land, explicitly granting Palestinians the right to its legacy. By so doing, the texts deny any Zionist national claim to this same land. In an Egyptian text of 1946, for example, the Palestinian historical opposition to foreign control is extolled. "The Arab residents of Palestine are of the most modern, and when the Arab Muslims conquered it, the language of the Quran spread in it as the pure Arabic. The Europeans attacked it long ago and governed a great part of it for several (200) years, but the Muslims expelled them from it, because it was an Arab country and the Arabs were not satisfied with being governed by a foreign nation."[58] Texts such as this one, although used only sparingly in the Palestinian school system, started the process of delineating a Palestinian national narrative as the logical extension of the Arab primordial claim to the land. The Palestinians, in this narrative, were the modern inheritors of that earlier, Arab, legacy.

Palestinians also complained against the suppression of their cultural traditions within the school structure. As Totah asked of the Royal (Peel) Commission on January 18, 1937, "Why do not the Arabs have a chance to control the education of their children in equality with the Jews in Palestine, with the Trans-Jordanians and the Iraqis and every civilised community?"[59] As he further theorized, Jewish education was geared toward establishing a National Home, but Arab education, as designed by the British, had no such aim.

> Take Arab music. There has been no serious attempt by the Government or the Department of Education to revive or to encourage Arab music or music of any kind in the schools, singing. Of course, the favourite theme of children's songs in this country is nationalism, they are national songs, always national. Nothing had been done to give them anything in the way of good music or good singing. The same thing applies to Arab art in the

form of embroidery and all these native things, native dancing, story telling, poetry competitions as the Arabs used to do and love to do.[60]

Palestinian schoolteachers and schoolmasters held poetry contests and dance recitals on their own, but, as Totah explained, the Department of Education and the government did not encourage these pursuits, as the neighboring states were doing with their students. Without support, these events could only be solitary events, not national contests or collective actions performed by the students to better understand their nation and the people and cultures living within it.

Despite Britain's best efforts, Palestinian schools became key agencies for the dissemination of nationalist ideas because of the activities of the teachers themselves and the undeniable recognition by the students that they lived within a Palestinian nation. Even though the British Mandate refused to clarify the goals of its administration over Palestine, the very existence of this administration, the boundaries surrounding it, and the expansion of the school system meant that Palestinian students traveled an educational "pilgrimage" to national awareness. In addition, the teachers in the government schools throughout Palestine were generally graduates of universities abroad or of the Arab College; most worked to spread nationalist ideas. The vocabulary of nationhood and independence came into the area from the West; the Palestinian teachers and their students filled these words with meaning. Khalil Sakakini, as inspector for the British public school system in Palestine, exhorted the teachers to mobilize their students. For example, in a meeting in Nablus on December 6, 1934, he said, "If each of us is a nationalist and he tried to struggle to spread nationalist spirit to his students, we will mobilize for the country a free, courageous, honorable, and educated army."[61] Khalil Totah told the Royal (Peel) Commission on January 18, 1937, that education in Palestine was also influenced by the political situation, for "one feels in Palestine schools that there is something hanging over their head, the atmosphere is charged."[62] In explanation, he added that the students "hear their parents talking politics, they read newspapers everywhere, they read of dissatisfaction with the present system and on the 2nd November, Balfour Day, we schoolmasters always expect a day's strike. It is like a festival: you expect it and prepare for it. It is very rare when the 2nd November comes that there is not a general strike, with demonstrations and the boys running out into the streets and creating some kind of excitement."[63]

One solution to the complaints registered by the Palestinians against the British-run system was to open private secondary schools outside foreign control.

Hence there gradually developed during the thirties and forties a new type of private national schools which were attended by Muslim and Christian children, but were in fact neither Muslim nor Christian in the usual sense. The general tone, if not always the curriculum, was distinctly national. . . . Unlike the foreign schools, all the national schools taught through the principal medium of Arabic and exceeded the Government schools in the amount of time they devoted to Arab history and current Arab affairs.[64]

As of 1926, Palestinians alone had opened forty-five private schools.[65] The most important of these were the Orthodox College in Jaffa, managed by the Orthodox National Society, the boys' and girls' schools conducted by the National Committee of Bir Zeit, al-Nahda College in Jerusalem, and Gaza College in Gaza. After World War I, a local committee in Nablus opened the Najah School, which developed as a boarding institution with a full elementary and secondary course.[66]

Its Board of Trustees defined its goals as: first, providing a suitable atmosphere for adolescence and bringing out the student's potential for responding to his society; second, forming character and breeding love of work; third, strengthening the national consciousness of the student and planting in him devotion and respect for the Arabs' cultural heritage and awareness of the inseparable bonds of the Arab nation in the various Arab countries. In view of the conditions in Palestine at that time the third goal overshadowed the first two in the curricula of the college.[67]

Private and public schools quickly became hotbeds of nationalist agitation during the Mandate period because the teachers used their classrooms as forums for political discussions. The teachers at schools like the Arab College instilled in their students, despite the restrictions placed upon them by the British, the history of their nation, their umma, and the policy of the British Mandatory government.[68] The Royal (Peel) Commission of 1937 found, "The fact, therefore, must be faced that every year some thousands of young Arabs emerge from a school-system which has inevitably fostered their nascent patriotism."[69] Besides imposing their censorship rules, British officials tried to forestall this eventuality by restricting the activities of the teachers. For example, Karmi's uncle, 'Abd al-Karim Karmi (Abu Salma), was dismissed from his job as a teacher with the education department for publishing a poem, entitled "Jabal al-Mukabbir" ["al-Mukabbir Mountain"], describing the place where Muslim troops saw Jerusalem for the first time in 638. In the Mandate period, the British High Commissioner's house stood on the spot. "Using a mixture of allegory and symbol, the poem vowed that no Palestinian would rest until he had brought the British citadel of power in Palestine crashing down."[70] Despite this example, Tibawi has found that

> In general, the teachers—even those with modest cultural attainments—were so fired by the claims of nationalism that they found no difficulty in circumventing the restrictions in the classroom. There was no power able to control all their activities all the time in this sphere of their work. While they conformed to the letter of the officially published syllabus, they lost no chance to give it a national spirit of their own.[71]

In Humphrey Bowman's view, regarding those in the government schools,

> everyone of these, whether teacher or pupil, was a supporter of the Arab cause; every one an ardent anti-Zionist. Following Zaghlulist policy in Egypt, the Arab leaders in Palestine did their utmost to make the schools the nucleus of nationalist inspiration. Their aim was to embarrass the Government by giving the schools a nuisance value; and, at the same time, to inculcate in the Arab youth a passionate nationalism which would show itself in overt acts whenever an opportunity served. To achieve this end, they tried by every means in their power to persuade the children to strike; to influence the teachers to suborn their pupils, and to force the parents by threats to support them.[72]

As Ylana Miller concurs, "Differences between an impersonal, imported definition of appropriate behavior and the priority of nationalist claims became particularly evident in the field of education. The rank and file of teachers were entering a professional stratum for the first time in the history of their families. In many cases they found themselves torn between official directives, often articulated by Arab inspectors of a higher class, and emotional commitments to open opposition."[73] The British definition of public service involved a certain degree of impartiality, a professionalism that called for a separation between the official and the governed. However, the "Frankenstein" monster could not be kept in the laboratory as the British had hoped. As with Transjordan, teachers knew they served as mentors to and partners with their students; they wanted to bring these students along the political path with them.

As part of this process, myriad discussions took place, with the teachers, with political leaders, and among the students themselves, about politics and ideology.[74] In discussing the Arab College, Tibawi has said that

This College had been considered by the Arab national leaders as an excellent field for their operations. Several members of the staff, notably the history lecturer, were ardent nationalists actively in contact with those leaders. The literary society in the College was a clearing-house for all studies in national history and Arabic literature. The weekly evening meetings at which speeches were given by students and lecturers were as national in tone as any delivered elsewhere in the country. Small wonder then that this College soon assumed the leadership of other secondary schools in national agitation.[75]

For example, the students of the school held a demonstration in 1925 to protest Lord Balfour's visit to Jerusalem to inaugurate Hebrew University. According to a report by the British District Governor of the Jerusalem-Jaffa District, almost all the stores in the Christian and Muslim quarters of the Old City shut in protest, and "the flying of black flags was a new feature in Jerusalem, chiefly to be observed in the Moslem quarters round Herod's Gate, in the Mesrara and Sheikh Jarrah Quarters, and in the Old City."[76] In addition, "The Arab press appeared with their front pages heavily outlined in black and with leading articles in English."[77] Once the students started demonstrating with Arab flags and national songs, the government closed down the Arab College temporarily and sent the students home under police escort.[78] In addition to work in the class periods, the teacher Nicola Ziyadeh supervised the activities of the Arab College's cultural society and "encouraged students to invite persons known for their national devotion to speak at its weekly meetings."[79] Abu-Ghazaleh personally remembers the influence Ziyadeh had on his own political awakening later at al-Rashidiyah School.[80]

Amin al-Khatib, as a student at the Arab College in the 1930s, began to get involved in political work, alongside a majority of his classmates. "The professors pushed me and my friends to think about the development of our struggles. . . . We began to make contact with some of the revolutionaries existing in the holy Haram al-Sharif and we offered to them our services, especially the smuggling of weapons to them inside the Old City."[81] He also participated in demonstrations against the British, walking from the school to the Old City, and in posting homemade leaflets about current events. Dajani feels that schools like al-Rashidiyah School spread consciousness and knowledge, and, as a result, the students and the teachers became the primary enemy of the colonialists.[82] "Although no mention [of it] was ever made in any declaration of such strikes," annually, on the anniversary of the Balfour Declaration, schools of all grades became involved and general or partial strikes by pupils were observed. In the case of young children in elementary schools their absence on a strike day may be taken as either safety precautions on the part of their parents, or fear of bullying by senior pupils. Senior pupils, specially boys, went on strike deliberately with quite sufficient understanding of its significance.[83]

At Najah College in Nablus, the students sponsored semiannual lectures at the Literary Club in the school. Leading personalities spoke to them about the events taking place around them. In addition, the students held an annual festival where "they usually produced a stage performance that reflected some of the memorable episodes in the history of the Arabs."[84] Hatim Kamal reports that "the professors of al-Najah and especially the martyred poet Abd al-Rahim Mahmud, [as well as] Asaf Kamal and Mamduh al-Sukhun and others, filled us, always, with love of the nation, and the need to oppose the British occupation."[85] A recognition of their shared experiences translated, in this atmosphere, into a nationalized message collectivizing the larger "community." Arabism and Palestinian nationalism served as their ideological and emotional guideposts, especially by the 1930s. In Gaza and Beersheba, Musallam Bseiso reports, the teachers "were nationalists ... who told us really how to struggle and they were organizing us, really, in one way or another. Not as parties, but to mobilize us, to get informed in the demonstrations."[86] He believes that the teachers felt it was their duty to impart this information to their students, and students, as young as eight or nine, started to get involved in the many demonstrations as a result.

When student strikes grew more numerous by the end of World War II, the British closed a number of the schools, and then "the daily papers published inflammatory articles repeating the usual accusations that the Government was deliberately keeping the Arab population in a state of ignorance and stifling the national feeling of the rising generation."[87] They complained specifically about the attempt by the British to stop this nationalization process. In Bowman's words, "In the neighbouring country of Egypt, school strikes and demonstrations had had a disastrous effect on discipline, and had seriously reacted on educational progress. Once this virus entered the schools of Palestine, I knew we were doomed: and from the first I resolutely set my face against allowing the Department to be affected by politics, in so far as this was humanly possible."[88] Both the Arab College and al-Rashidiyah School were closed for periods of time in the Mandate period because of the activities of the students and the teachers. British collectivized punishments such as these confirmed for the students the messages disseminated by their teachers. A united action required a united response.

Complementing the work of the schools, scout troops of different kinds and origins proved influential in politicizing schoolboys. In association with the public school system, the Baden-Powell Boy Scout organization set up scout troops throughout the country. Cognizant of the political situation arising in Palestine, British Mandate officials must have seen the scout movement as an opportunity for garnering obedience to British rule. As a sign of the different administrative strategies on the two sides of the Jordan River, no such scout movement emerged in Transjordan in the interwar years. While students east of the river were clearly displaying oppositional tendencies by the 1930s, the British must not have felt as insecure as they did in the Palestine setting. However,

> the attempt to impose British standards on Arab children failed most miserably in the case of the scouting movement. The first training camp of the Palestine branch of the Baden-Powell Scouts was set up by Bowman, as County Commissioner for Palestine, in 1922. But from 1928 the Arab Scouts became increasingly politicized, marching in processions organized by nationalist movements like the Istiqlal party, or parading with Islamic, anti-imperialist slogans at the Nabi Musa and other religious festivals, the "Scouts" (many of them adult men) carrying staves and daggers.[89]

By 1923, the Baden-Powell Association had eighteen troops throughout Palestine, containing 650 Muslim and Christian boys and run by government teachers, increasing to fifty-three troops and 1,304 scouts by 1927.[90] The Palestinians themselves understood the value of such work, so established their own scout troops for military and nature training. As Miller analyzes,

> The organization of youth was an important aspect of many political movements in these years, and in this respect Palestine was no different from many other countries. In Palestine, however, the scouts reflected two processes specific to the Arab community and its relationship to the mandatory government. First, the development among youth of a new organizational political base with national characteristics was part of an evolving social tendency to form societies and clubs as voluntary forms of association. Second, the history of scouting indicated the limits of government control over educational institutions and their student bodies.[91]

Scouting thus provided yet another conduit for the national picture disseminated in the schools and homes around Palestine. Just as the schools were doing, scout troops physically removed the boys from their village and urban settings and showed them the breadth and extent of the nation they claimed as their own. They forged new relationships as they traveled. As the Royal (Peel) Commission reported in 1937, scouts had specific jobs to perform in the national cause. "It offers them opportunities of active service in the national cause as 'Scouts'—and these 'Scouts' do actually and usefully scout—or as patrols to enforce a 'strike' or 'boycott,' or even, it is suspected, as assassins."[92] In the case of the scout troops, the addition of military training added a new component to this educational pilgrimage because members were being taught how to fight against the regime opposing their national aspirations.

As with many boys his age, Abu Gharbiyah joined a scout troop in the early 1930s. He learned valuable information about living outdoors, a skill that came in handy when he and his friends decided to form their own military band in 1934. They named this band "al-Hurriyah" for freedom. The members purchased weapons and trained in the countryside outside Jerusalem, setting as their goal the complete independence of Palestine. This group fought in both the 1936–1939 Arab Revolt and the 1948 Arab-Israeli War. "In the town of Tulkarm and the nearby village of al Tayyiba, local Scouts troops set up their own fighting units. They played an active role in the Arab Revolt, and from then on the police appealed to the government to disband them."[93] Musallam Bseiso ran a scout troop as a teacher in Gaza in 1947. "We built the scouts movement in the college itself and we started to select good and qualified students to be trained on arms. And even we trained them to shoot at a tank, or whatever."[94]

After this period of politicization, many of the Palestinian graduates of the secondary schools in Palestine went on, as their Transjordanian counterparts did, to universities throughout the Arab world. As the threat to Palestine increased with each year, culminating in the 1948 defeat, political organizations around the Fertile Crescent increasingly focused their energies on the place of Palestine in Arab history and life. Amin al-Khatib worked for the Arab Nationalist movement while studying medicine at the University of Damascus. He participated in demonstrations opposing the UN Partition Plan and organized work camps in Palestine during his summer vacations. For others, the American University of Beirut (AUB) proved pivotal, as they, in Munif al-Razzaz's words, felt that "their minds were opened" to the many political streams operating at the school. As the interwar years progressed, Palestine became an important rallying point for the students studying at the school. Hala Sakakini, a student at AUB from 1944 to 1946, says of the experience,

> As travelling to Europe or America was at the time virtually impossible, the University was crowded with students from all over the Middle East. Young men and women from Egypt, Sudan, Iraq, Syria, Lebanon, Palestine, Saudi Arabia, formed the student body. You could hear many different Arabic dialects on the campus. For Dumia and me it was always thrilling to see all these types of Arabs mixing together so easily and naturally. Most of them enthusiastically shared the same political aspiration—Arab Unity. Discussions concerning the future form of Arab unity seemed neverending. In clubs and societies, in private rooms and in student lounges, smaller and larger groups of students were constantly debating the merits of this system of government and that, whether a federation or a confederation would be more suitable, how to prepare for that day in the future, what our part as educated men and women should be.[95]

As those young people pledged to work for change, Sakakini witnessed a real camaraderie among them.

> I shall never forget the thrill I felt as we were walking home towards the Women's Hostel late one night after attending a political debate of this nature. All the way we could hear, coming from different directions (as students in groups were dispersing to the lodges and dormitories on the campus and outside it) the strong, young voices of the students filling the air with a patriotic song which was very popular at the time: "*Nahnu shabab lana'l ghadu*" (to us young people belongs the future).[96]

Here youth meant working to bring in the "new" independence and to throw out the "old" colonial past. Palestine, a focus of the "new," played a particularly important role in uniting these students, as a direct threat still hung over the area. Most of the other Arab countries were heading toward at least a degree of independence, but Palestine seemed to be falling more firmly under British control. Sakakini reports that

> Whenever November 2, the date of the Balfour Declaration, came round, the whole student body would cut classes and go out in immense demonstrations through the streets of Ras Beirut shouting slogans against that notorious declaration and carrying large placards to the same effect. On that day you knew beyond any doubt that every Arab student at the Uni-

versity, no matter what country he came from, belonged to one and the same nation—the Arab nation. Even more, on that day every Arab became a Palestinian.[97]

Palestinians found, during these events, that not only did they consider themselves the heart of the Arab world, but their Arab colleagues concurred with them. The power generated by this unity encouraged the Palestinians and their Arab neighbors to go back home to work for change, just as their Jordanian counterparts were doing.

Integral to this process, the graduates of these schools were starting to form into a new professional intelligentsia. As in Jordan, the numbers were small but pivotal in the changes taking place throughout the country; they served as the conduit between the new agencies and the bulk of the population. As Tibawi has theorized,

> The influence of this *elite* class was out of all proportion to the small number of its members. Apart from their contributions in bringing to bear the fruits of intelligence and liberal education on their daily tasks, they associated themselves directly or indirectly with all socialist and liberal movements. Chiefly by forming social or cultural clubs, or by sponsoring periodicals and contributing articles, they disseminated their ideas among less educated and socially conscious associates, with remarkable patience and skill.[98]

As their compatriots were doing across the river and in the new countries of the Middle East, these Palestinian professionals took on the role of educators, providing a bridge between different societies and different kinds of political identities.

Of the thirty or so clubs that emerged during the Mandate period, some involved as many as three thousand people, as was the case with the Arab Club of Nablus, or as few as a hundred, in the case of the Literary Arabic Club of Beersheba.[99] The clubs collected books and daily newspapers discussing aspects of Palestinian and Arab political events and the few literary and historical books published by Palestinian Arabs.[100] The major political contribution of these clubs was to hold lectures on political topics relevant to the Palestinian and Arab experience.

> Certain anniversaries became occasions for lectures and discussions in all the clubs: that of the issuance of the Balfour Declaration, in which the condemnation of Britain and Zionist designs were favourite topics; of the first shot fired by Hussein ibn Ali, of the Hashemite family, declaring the be-

ginning of the Arab revolt against the Ottomans; of the execution of the three "heroes" of Hebron; and of the beginning of the three year revolt of 1936.[101]

Karmi reports that Khalil Sakakini frequently gave lectures at the Orthodox Club in Jerusalem, while other "such people," the Palestinian intellectual class, traveled to clubs in Jaffa, Haifa, Nablus, and Gaza to present similar lectures.[102] Because these clubs served both as dissemination points for information and as gathering points for activists, they proved influential in the larger nationalist movement. They maintained the camaraderie the urban professional intelligentsia had found on their educational "pilgrimages," specifically organized on a national basis.

Tal'at Harb relates how these kinds of clubs helped him become politically conscious.

> In the city of Acre my eyes and my ideas were opened to the nationalist movement, and the political developments in Palestine, and my age did not exceed 16. I awoke to the importance of liberation movements and their followers in all areas of the world, among them the Arab peoples, and the progressive forces among other countries and other movements, especially after the end of the Second World War. The people were striving for freedom and independence, and at its head were the Palestinian people.[103]

He attended the many lectures on current events given throughout the city. When he felt he understood the lessons sufficiently, he joined the Communist-aligned League of National Liberation in its move to organize workers and to spread political ideas. Harb's experience highlights the fact that these clubs provided political newcomers the historical information and the political vocabulary required to recognize the national body politic.

THE 1936–1939 ARAB
REVOLT AND THE RURAL AREAS

The 1936 to 1939 Palestinian strike and revolt[104] provide examples of how widespread the concept of nationalism had become by that point, illustrating how its ideas had expanded into the rural areas. The revolt started first as a countrywide strike in reaction to the escalation of violence between Arabs and Jews and the subsequent British repression against the

Arabs. It ended as a rural military revolt against the British, the Jews, and, to a certain extent, the Palestinian urban elites. On one level, Palestinians organized themselves into a series of national committees, designed to provide supplies, funds, and an organizational apparatus for the functioning of the strike. These committees included groups to monitor the road-traffic strike, national guard units, boy scouts, and women's organizations. On another level, military bands roamed throughout the country attacking Jewish and British personnel and installations.

In the summer of 1938, at the height of the revolt, Palestinian bands took over a majority of rural Palestine. In the villages they controlled, the bands organized courts, administrative offices, and intelligence centers. In the fall of that year, these bands even took over the Old City of Jerusalem. However, within a short period of time the divisiveness present among the various military bands in the country, the enormous economic loss experienced by the Palestinians since 1936, and the massive British military reaction finally destroyed both the strike and the revolt. While experiencing initial success, the Palestinian forces could not sustain the revolt for long against the superior economic and military power of the British forces. The British succeeded in killing and arresting a large number of the Palestinian leaders, destroying the organizational basis for the revolt in the process. The revolt disintegrated by 1939.

In the midst of the revolt, the British High Commissioner reported that all classes in Palestinian society had come out in support and that "While there are still a number of foreign volunteers it is no longer the fact that the majority of the armed men are foreigners; on the contrary they are 'locals' and moreover there have been several instances of villagers turning out *en masse* to assist a gang which is engaged with Government forces."[105] In this case, cultural, religious, and governmental symbols were intertwined to create that national ethos. A British observer of October 1938 stated that

> Practically all Arabs, Christians and Moslem, have assumed at the behest of the rebel "high command" the headdress of the kaffiyeh and 'agal . . . ; women are wearing the veil more and more; edicts have been issued by the rebels calling on all Arabs to come to their courts to settle their complaints rather than go to the King's courts; other decrees forbid strong language and loose morals and invite the wives of faithless husbands to seek redress in the rebel courts. All these facts indicate that the Arab movement has recently become more of a national one, and that it is directed as much against the Mandatory Power as against the Jews.[106]

For, as the Royal (Peel) Commission reported in 1937, "The story of the last seventeen years is proof that this Arab nationalism with its anti-Jewish spearhead is not a new or transient phenomenon. It was there at the beginning: its strength and range have steadily increased; and it seems evident to us from what we saw and heard that it has not yet reached its climax." [107] The authors of the report believed that two key internal factors had facilitated the growth and solidification of the movement. As they found, "First, the movement is now sustained by a far more efficient and comprehensive political machine than existed in earlier years." [108] The authors of the report particularly mentioned the cohesive role of the Arab Higher Committee and the existence of National Committees in every Arab town. "The second internal factor in the growth of Arab nationalism is education." [109]

Hala Sakakini remembers that feeling of excitement and patriotism she felt, even as a child, hearing, along with her older sister, about the sacrifices Palestinians were making on behalf of their nation during the 1936 general strike.

> The period of the strike was an exciting time for Dumia and me. I remember how eagerly we used to wait for the news every day. As soon as we received the newspaper in the morning, Mother would read to us. There was a guerrilla warfare going on all over Palestine. Our men fought heroically against the well-trained and well-equipped divisions of the British army. Soon heroes' names were on everybody's lips and we used to speak of their exploits with great pride. Remote, obscure villages in Palestine became famous throughout the bloody, fierce battles that took place in their neighbourhoods. [110]

People gathered in homes, in coffeehouses, on the streets, to talk about the progress of the strike and the political ramifications.

> Whenever we went visiting with Mother and Aunt Melia, and there was a gathering of ladies, the subject of conversation was the same: the foolish demands of the Zionists, the heroic fighting of our men, the traitors. The news of the day was repeated again and again, and every version of it was slightly different. [111]

Yusrah Salah reports revolutionaries knocking on people's doors during the 1936 revolt to ask for donations. [112] The British government reported that in the early months of the revolt, "Practically all the town schools were compelled to close owing to the non-attendance of pupils. In the

villages, conditions were not uniform. In the early stages of the disturbances about 77 per cent. [*sic*] village schools remained open, chiefly in
the districts of Galilee and Samaria, while later on the percentage fell to
52.4 per cent."[113] In al-Khatib's recollection, "With the beginning of
the six-month strike of 1936, there was not for us any event except the
revolution and the events surrounding it. We gave aid to the revolutionaries by transporting their weapons inside the Old City where their major
center was."[114] Children were picked for this job because British soldiers
did not search them as they passed through the checkpoints. Musallam
Bseiso also felt that as a child he had a special role to play in the 1936
revolt. In addition to bringing weapons to the revolutionaries hidden in
the area, he and his friends also threw nails on the streets to blockade
British traffic and to stop anyone smuggling goods out of the area during the six-month strike.[115] Many of these young people also witnessed
battles literally in their front yards during this period. Tal'at Harb reports
that British troops fought with local revolutionaries in his area during the
revolt of 1936. Musallam Bseiso saw a young friend of his, maybe ten or
eleven years old, shot down by British troops during a 1936 demonstration in Beersheba.[116]

People joined military bands and political organizations in such large
numbers because, by the 1930s, people saw the threat come into their
villages; absentee Arab landowners and impoverished Palestinians sold
land to the Jewish Agency, and many others subsequently lost jobs to the
newcomers. British collective punishments affected all socioeconomic
classes. As Miller summarizes, "During the twenties the task of explaining the mandate and its implications was left to the traditional leadership
of the nationalist movement. By the early thirties villagers were coming
to experience the impact of Jewish presence and British government in
more complex ways."[117] The British Mandate, by its very existence, had
brought rapid change to Palestine, in the leadership structure and in the
ways people began to identify themselves. Palestinians, particularly the
teachers and the urban political leadership, then took the reins of change
themselves as they spread new ideas throughout the country. Rural villagers embraced the national message coming out of the cities because it
addressed the very real threat to their livelihoods they recognized in their
daily lives.

During the Mandate period, the Palestinian economy was predominantly agricultural, with 25 percent of the peasants living below the subsistence level.[118] According to the Government of Palestine Census of
1931, 66 percent of the Muslim population participated in agricultural
production. The agricultural unit, the village, was semifeudal in char-

acter. It satisfied its own needs, the exchange of goods was limited, and the use of money equally restricted.[119] Farming methods remained outdated.

The Mandate's administration forced this means of production to enter the capitalist system, and money became the principal means of exchange. Article 18 of the Mandate document stated that Palestine could not impose discriminatory tariffs against a member of the League of Nations. This left Palestine's market open to foreign competition and hampered expansion of local enterprises. Inflation of land prices increased the rents paid by tenants, often up to as much as 50 percent of a tenant's income.[120] The fellah was at the mercy of his creditors, who often charged 30 percent interest on annual loans. The price of wheat decreased from £Palestinian 15.875 per ton in 1924–1925 to £P 7.500 per ton in 1930.[121] These economic problems were exacerbated by the fact that Jews owned approximately 5 percent of the land by 1930, alienating Arab workers from most of it.[122] At the same time, as British government investigators found,

> Evidence from every possible source tends to support the conclusion that the Arab fellah cultivator is in a desperate position. He has no capital for his farm. He is, on the contrary, heavily in debt. His rent is rising, he has to pay very heavy taxes, and the rate of interest of his loans is incredibly high.[123]

The Johnson-Crosbie Committee of 1930 calculated that 91.8 percent of the Arab landowners controlled less than 100 dunams each (a dunam being approximately a quarter of an acre), with most owning less than 50 dunams.[124] The Hope-Simpson Report of 1930 estimated that the "Lot viable" varied by region, but fell roughly between 130 and 240 dunams.[125] As quoted by Kenneth Stein, a February 16, 1934, article in al-Jami'ah al-Islamiyah summed up the position of the Palestinian fellah. "[He] seeks employment but can not find it; he has no work because the Jews took over all the work; the fellaheen are driven from the land because the Jews bought it from the rich landlords. The fellaheen are drawn to the towns to seek jobs which they do not get."[126] The British Commission on the Palestine Disturbances of August 1929 concurred, saying that "There is no alternative land to which persons evicted can remove. In consequence a landless and discontented class is being created."[127] As a result, it reported, "Both in evidence which was submitted to us in Jerusalem and in the speeches which were addressed to us by the spokesmen of the many deputations which we received in every part of the country, the fears of the Arabs that the success of the Zionist policy meant their expropriation from the land were repeatedly emphasised."[128]

With these rising threats in the countryside now moving into the urban areas, the historical differences between the two regions began to lessen for the first time. Schools provided new arenas for urban and rural children to interact on an equal basis, and the improvements in transportation systems throughout the Mandate allowed for more mobility.[129] Urban political leaders began to come into the countryside to interact with their neighbors, while rural residents sought the advice of the reportedly more knowledgeable urban residents. Saïd K. Aburish states that his grandfather, Khalil, in Bethany, sought out one of those urban intellectuals when the Jewish Agency first came to buy his land in 1928. He spoke to 'Arif al-'Arif, a Palestinian judge, because "Al-'Arif, unlike Aburish, belonged to an educated city bourgeoisie who saw Palestine as a country, a national entity which belonged to its Arab inhabitants. He even viewed Palestine as part of a larger Arab world, perhaps a single state in a huge federation incorporating all the Arab countries."[130] Al-'Arif cautioned him not to sell because the Jews wanted to colonize the land, not just farm it in companionship with their Palestinian neighbors as earlier immigrants had done. When Aburish subsequently refused the Jewish Agency offer, its representatives moved on to another landowner; when that man wavered, Aburish burned down the man's orchard, as a sign of his power.[131] The concept of national unity had spread to at least the Aburish family because of these experiences and their new nationalized knowledge. Despite the fact that villages like Bethany were cut off from so many agencies of social change, opposition to British and Zionist plans in Palestine was spreading.

On these and other issues, Bethany can also serve as a prototypical village, gradually drawn into the political experience of Palestinian nationalism. For example, the people of Bethany witnessed a dramatic change throughout the late 1920s and 1930s, as more people became aware of the political threats around them and as more political stimuli influenced them. To Khalil Aburish, initially

the idea of Arabs running their own country was still alien . . . , as no one had ever tried to arouse any national sentiment in him. Unavoidably, this issue came to occupy a central place in his last days. The first Arab political daily papers came into being in 1929, about the time when the Jews were becoming more open about their eventual plans, and when the elder Aburish children were developing a sense of political awareness. The bourgeoisie's discovery of vehicles to reach the villages coincided with the emergence of a new generation of relatively educated Arabs, whose ambitions were moulded neither by Turkey's legacy nor Britain's largesse.[132]

Even though much of Bethany remained ignorant of the larger events taking place outside its doors, "the ideas [the newspapers] were disseminating took hold, because nationalism was being preached in schools to the educated elite and in mosques to the ignorant faithful. Advocates of an independent Arab Palestine began to pay attention to villages the size of Bethany through special representatives who sought to generate a religious and nationalist fervour against the British and the Jews."[133] The man the Arab Higher Committee assigned to Bethany was Shaykh Mousa Shahine, a judge of the High Islamic Court and a member of the Committee. Khalil's son, Muhammad, married Shahine's daughter.

> At the suggestion of his father-in-law, Mohammad would roll into Bethany in one of his taxis in time for the all-important 6.00 P.M. radio news. As the taxi was equipped with a radio, one of the three in the whole of Bethany, he would turn it on with the doors of the car open so that the villagers could gather to hear news about Palestine, Hitler and Mussolini. This surpassed [Uncle] Ibrahim's [earlier] readings of the newspaper in the local coffee house which were irregular, less dramatic, unreliable and in any case reached a smaller audience. Ten, fifteen, occasionally twenty people would gather around the black Plymouth as night descended, then disperse into smaller groups to discuss what they had heard.[134]

Since by the mid-1930s, no less than 30 percent of Bethany's boys were attending schools, Saïd Aburish feels clear connections existed between the expansion of the school systems, the message they disseminated, and acceptance of the concept of nationalism among Bethany's villagers. They followed educational pilgrimages to national awakening.

Just like the residents of Bethany, villagers throughout Palestine were rethinking their identities and their places within a larger nation, just as the threat to their livelihoods became greater. "The picture of life in Bethany in the early 1940s was a microcosm of Palestine, particularly the villages, which still accounted for over fifty per cent of the population. People were forced into a sudden acquaintance with the outside world. Heetar (Hitler), Mussorini, Dunkirk, Hawaii and Crete became household names."[135] Young people imbibed the new ideas in the schools in the village and in the secondary schools in the cities and then brought these ideas back home with them. They often carried newspapers and radios with them as they followed their teachers' advice to organize to fight the occupation. They teamed up with many of the traditional leaders, like Khalil Aburish, who had come to the realization that they had to alter their leadership style to fit the new realities. They encountered people angry at British transgressions and Zionist encroachments onto their land.

1948 WAR

Many of the writers of these memoirs—both those living in urban and those in rural areas—also participated in the fighting of 1947 and 1948, as a natural progression from the politicization process they had already undergone. Bahjat Abu Gharbiyah served as a military commander in Jerusalem. Amin al-Khatib worked as a medic in the Old City, despite the fact that he had very little medical training.[136] At the beginning of the fighting, Musallam Bseiso left Gaza with a group of fifteen or so students and friends, in search of a military band they could join. They traveled to Jaffa, then to Ramleh and Ramallah, and then on to Jerusalem, but faced a similar problem in each area: no one had enough weapons for the men volunteering to fight.[137] In the end, Bseiso worked as a war correspondent for a number of Western and Arab news services. The Palestinian leadership commissioned Ibrahim, one of Khalil Aburish's sons, to form a militia unit in Bethany.

> The local militia, which Ibrahim headed with obvious and considerable glee, was known throughout Palestine as the Holy Strugglers (al-Jihad al-Mukades). Their insignia, which they wore on their chosen headdress, whether beret, forage cap or an Arab *egal* (head band), was a badge incorporating reproductions of Muslim and Christian holy places—the Dome of the Rock and the Church of the Holy Sepulchre. This was a clever attempt by the Mufti to foster Muslim and Christian unity against "Jewish intruders". In that regard he was totally successful and Muslim and Christian Arabs were at one in their opposition to the Jews, and in their desire to create an independent Palestine governed by its indigenous population.[138]

Later, the Mufti of Jerusalem sent from Cairo ill-fitting, secondhand uniforms and rusty arms left over from the North African desert during World War II. The Mufti also succeeded in sending a small amount of cash to Ibrahim, who then dispersed it to his troops. The money did not amount to much, but in an economy at a standstill, represented all that most men could bring home to their families.

Between November 1947 and early 1949, they and others, along with the armies of the surrounding Arab states, failed to achieve the nationalist ambitions of the Palestinian people. As a result of the war, Israel established its state on 78 percent of Mandate Palestine, and Egypt took control over the Gaza Strip. The bulk of the Palestinians then came under the management of the Jordanian army, in the West Bank and East Jerusalem. Hundreds of thousands of others fled as refugees to Lebanon, Syria, and Egypt. The solution to the conundrum of the British Mandate over Palestine had been determined on the battlefield, and the Palestinians had failed in their national efforts. The limitations placed upon their national aspirations by the British colonial officials, their own political fragmentation, and the power of the opposing "other" on the ground proved far too strong. Instead, the bulk of the Palestinians had to live under Hashemite leadership from 1948 until 1967. However, they did not acquiesce to this political change without working to improve their positions within it. Many of them chose to continue their political opposition, but now doing so within the boundaries of the Hashemite state and under the rubric of Arab nationalism.

UNION WITH JORDAN

Soon after the fighting ended in the 1948 War, the West Bank, East Jerusalem, and the Hashemite Kingdom of Jordan united. The first step in this regard took place in Jericho on December 1, 1948, when Palestinians gathered to vote on unity with Jordan.[139] After some debate, the conference agreed to unite the West Bank and East Jerusalem with Jordan; the conferees saw no other viable alternative.[140] The Arab Legion occupied the whole area and stood as the only force capable of stopping the Israelis from advancing farther into Palestinian land. Many of them also hoped union with Jordan would constitute the first step toward the reunification of the Arab world. By now, explicitly and implicitly, support for Arab nationalism also automatically meant working to recapture Palestine. Palestine was no longer just the emotional heart of the Arab world, but the centerpiece of a new, more militant national movement.

To promote goodwill with his new Palestinian population, King 'Abdullah enacted a number of measures to incorporate them into the system. He dismissed the government and appointed a new one under

Tawfiq Abu'l-Huda. His new cabinet included three Palestinians, with a fourth added a few months later. In February 1949, Palestinians received Jordanian citizenship, in contrast to the Palestinians living in the other Arab host states, which refused to do so for fear that Palestinians would forfeit their rights to Palestine. 'Abdullah also promulgated a new Election Law, which doubled the size of the Majlis al-Nuwwab, from twenty to forty. Because Palestinians formed the majority of the population, they were actually misrepresented by the even division of seats between the two banks. In addition, the Jordanian government doubled the number of seats in the appointed Majlis al-A'yan to twenty, but 'Abdullah was not required to appoint ten Palestinians to it.

Elections for the new Majlis al-Nuwwab took place in April 1950, involving both banks of the Jordan for the first time. For the forty seats, 125 candidates competed, with 60 from the East Bank and 65 from the West Bank.[141] Estimates of voting ranged from 70 to 75 percent of the electorate.[142] Five unofficial political parties emerged as the elections neared. Despite the fact that these parties remained illegal during the campaign, party-affiliated candidates succeeded in winning seats, with the Ba'th, Communist, and leftist supporters winning fourteen and the pro-regime parties, the al-Hizb al-'Arabi al-Dusturi [Arab Constitutional Party] and the Hizb al-Ummah [Party of the Nation], winning ten.[143] The East Bank returned primarily supporters of the government, just as it had since 1929. The Palestinians, on the other hand, elected mostly highly educated professionals, lawyers, civil servants, teachers, journalists, and doctors, reflecting their leadership roles in the community.[144] 'Abdullah al-Rimawi and 'Abdullah Na'was, both future leaders of the Ba'th Party, were elected and formed the core of a new parliamentary opposition bloc. The first act of this new parliament was to officially ratify the union agreement on April 24, 1950, accompanied in Amman by a twenty-one-gun salute.

CONCLUSION

As Miller has summarized, "The history of the Palestinian Arab community under the mandate is one of search in all dimensions, of the attempt to preserve cultural integrity while absorbing new situations, of the need to balance new ideas with old values."[145] The memoirs illustrate that, throughout the Mandate period, people of all social classes were searching for a nationalized solution to the problems surrounding them and for the hopes they held for the future. The Palestinians who came under

Jordanian control in 1948 arrived in Jordan having experienced thirty years of searching for this national identity.[146] As Samih Farsoun describes it, "By the time in 1948 that Palestine was shattered as a society, partitioned as a country, and destroyed as a nation, modern Palestinian identity was consolidated."[147] The proliferation of agencies of social change had catalyzed an increasing number of Palestinians to demand yet more change, and to do so within a nationalized vocabulary. The historical narrative of the Palestinian experience was being written in the schools, in the clubs, and in the media, bridging the gap between the urban and rural areas. As this narrative shows, the 1930s had witnessed a movement from politics from above, led by the traditionally powerful Palestinian families, to organization from below, where "youth, labor, scouts, and middle-class groups pressured the elite to act more militarily."[148] During this time, Palestinians not only learned the glories of their past and recognized the indignities of the present, but learned how to struggle against them.[149] For these newly politicized Palestinians their obvious allies were the Jordanian urban professionals beginning to form the Arab nationalist and progressive political parties in opposition to Hashemite rule. Both groups had been socialized to an Arab nationalist message during impressionable periods in their lives. As Sulayman Musa theorizes, "Whatever the case may be, the unity of the two banks after the war of 1948 created a new awakening on behalf of the workers in the Jordanian political field, since the problem of the existence of the Israeli state in the greater part of Palestine became a shared Arab problem and especially as it pertained to the countries surrounding Palestine."[150] Palestinians of all socioeconomic classes and Jordanian urban migrants subsequently formed the bulk of all the demonstrations and the rank-and-file membership of the political parties because of their previous political experiences and because of their demands for more socioeconomic change. Jordanians sought the realization of the goals of Arab nationalism as a counter to the Hashemite-Jordanian national narrative; the Palestinians did so hoping to achieve their national desires.

SIX

FORGING THE JORDANIAN
NATIONAL MOVEMENT (JNM)

*[T]here is a strong and widespread nationalist spirit which pervades all
the educated classes of society and is by no means confined to extremists
or unbalanced students.*

CHARLES DUKE, BRITISH AMBASSADOR TO JORDAN, 1954[1]

Everybody belonged to a party in the 1950s.

PHRASE HEARD REPEATEDLY DURING FIELD STUDY

The Mandate period in Transjordan and Palestine had seen key groups in
both populations turn into political activists. Agencies for change, meant
to bring people into the respective national projects, succeeded to a certain extent in Transjordan, as more people came to support the Hashemite
state. Some, for example, would channel this support through the agency
of the Muslim Brotherhood, patronized by King 'Abdullah from its first
days in 1945, and by taking government jobs. Still other Jordanians
emerged from this politicization process opposed to the state—for both
its governmental policies and its unique status as a nation-state—and activated to work for reform of the administration and a reconfiguration of
the region's boundary lines. Palestinians became increasingly politicized
as the failures of their national aspirations became apparent. Urban and rural, territorial and pan-national agencies for change worked together and
in parallel to politicize the population around both Palestinian and Arab
national goals. In 1950, with unification of the two banks, the nascent
Jordanian opposition movement of the immediate post–World War II
period merged with the Palestinian–Arab nationalist movement cata-

lyzed by the failures of the British Mandate and the success of the Zionist project. The two groups found common ground and a shared national vocabulary under the umbrella of Arab nationalism. In it, Jordanian and Palestinian activists formed the progressive and Arab nationalist political parties of the Jordanian National Movement (JNM), designed to garner support for revolutionizing the Hashemite governmental structure. The urban professional stratum of both communities led the parties and mobilized the increasingly urbanized population. Agencies of change proliferated in both rural and urban areas in the 1950s, so succeeded in disseminating to these areas the messages of revolutionary Arab nationalism coming out of the JNM. Educational expansion supplied the Movement with its activist cadres, economic growth pushed the population into the cities, where people could be easily organized, and the expanded media spread the messages of the Movement. The JNM represented the "new" going up against the "old" Hashemite national structure, promising socioeconomic justice, political reform, Arab unity, and a return of Palestine. The calls of Arab nationalism—whether for Hashemite political reform or Arab unity—brought people out into the streets in the thousands throughout the decade. This national call held resonance for a population—both Jordanian and Palestinian—witnessing rapid socioeconomic change.

Jordanians and Palestinians worked together at all levels of the Movement to initiate changes to the Jordanian political structure, attacking the Hashemite national narrative from all sides. The goals of Arab nationalism provided the needed umbrella for the Jordanian National Movement because they proved broad enough and sufficiently revolutionary for many different political strands to coalesce. Under this umbrella, Palestinians could work toward recovering their homeland, Jordanians could lobby for more liberal political rights, and Communists could struggle to create a socialist state, to name just a few trends. Thus, the discourse and organizational structures resulting from calls for Arab nationalism allowed political activists to work on the domestic level for goals specific to their lives, with the recognized reality that they worked, in the long term, for Arab unity. As the quote above states, "everybody belonged to a political party in the 1950s," because it was completely natural to do so, given the political atmosphere of the day. "Everybody" rallied around the JNM because it provided the largest umbrella for opposition activities; no other Jordanian or specifically Palestinian opposition existed on this political stage. This diversity of opinion allowed for growth while the JNM stood outside the halls of government; it would prove problematic once the JNM entered government and worked to put its policies into practical effect.

SUPPORT FOR THE JORDANIAN NATIONAL MOVEMENT (JNM)

The Jordanian National Movement was composed initially of urban professionals, including physicians, lawyers, journalists, and teachers from both banks of the river. Also mobilized were a large number of Arab officers in the lower ranks of the armed forces, angry that British officers held the most important posts. These groups made up the leadership and activist elements of the political parties. The leaders of the parties, once they were founded, then appealed for support from students and the urban masses. The same agencies of change which had produced the JNM's leadership allowed that very leadership to recruit new members. The same focus on mobilization catalyzed a new generation in the 1950s.

Educational influences continued to be particularly important for Jordanians and Palestinians after Jordan united with the West Bank in 1950. The Movement took advantage of the fact that the state undertook a massive school expansion program in the 1950s which increased the school enrollment figures by 113 percent between 1951 and 1961, with the number of teachers rising by 209 percent simultaneously.[2] The Movement's leadership set up party cells throughout the school system to recruit student activists and future party members. As a result, students and teachers comprised the largest group of demonstration participants and party members. Thus, the experiences of the Mandate period carried over to the early independence years. In other words, the students of the earlier period had been mobilized to initiate change. Their social uniqueness had been instilled in them and used as a mobilizing tool. Once they, themselves, became teachers or formed their own political parties, they naturally turned to the next generation of students for support. Education was equated with action; many decided to funnel that action into oppositional politics.

As it had under the Emirate, the government tried to control the curricula and the choice of teachers for the schools after independence. However, this attempt did not guarantee that all decisions made in Amman or in the district offices would be put into practice in the country's school system. Throughout the 1950s many of the teachers continued to graduate from universities in the surrounding Arab countries and preach the revolutionary slogans of Arab nationalism they had learned there. Munif al-Razzaz reports that he was able to discuss political issues with his students while teaching science at a public school in Amman. To accomplish this, he brought together a group of about forty-five senior students for a study group that focused mostly on scientific subjects, but, as al-Razzaz points out, "I did not leave out a place for nationalism and culture and ethics. . . . I occasionally read to them from literary journals and occasionally I took the opportunity to teach anthems that had the spirit of nationalism. All of that was outside the classroom."[3] Mahmoud Zeitoun, a Ba'thist mathematics teacher in Hebron, reports that while he taught the government-approved syllabus during class hours, he often talked to students about political affairs at clubs after school.[4] Teachers fulfilled the same function throughout the country. Because of the continuing shortage of teachers throughout the 1950s, the government lacked the ability to control all the teachers who strayed from the stated curriculum. In a situation where teachers could not be replaced easily, the Ministry of Education still had to accept those who deviated from its plans.

With the help of the political parties, students in the urban areas on both banks of the river began to organize. Since no university existed in the country until 1962, with the founding of the University of Jordan, the activists in this movement were secondary school students at home and university students studying abroad. The first indigenous movement of Jordanian students can be dated to 1951.[5] In that year, students from three secondary schools in Amman held a meeting to discuss student issues. A number of Ba'thist and Communist-affiliated students won election to the executive committee, with a Ba'thist serving as president at every subsequent annual conference. Out of the conference came a document stating the plans of the new organization: to form a Jordanian Student Union; to establish a national university; to achieve a reduction in the fees to study in the private schools; and to highlight the importance of Arab culture and heritage.[6] These party-affiliated students then proved pivotal in spreading the parties' ideas to yet more students. To do so, they set up secret meetings of students all over the country to explain the goals of the new organization, under the protection and support of the Ba'th and Communist Parties and the Movement of Arab Nationalists.[7] Before long, student committees were set up in schools in Amman, Salt, Irbid, Karak, and Tafillah on the East Bank; Jerusalem, Nablus, and Hebron on the West Bank. The first official conference of the Jordanian students met in August 1953 in the Kulliyah al-'Alamiyah building in Amman, although that conference and all subsequent ones were held in secret because the government prohibited them. Conferences continued to meet each year during the early 1950s, with three to four hundred students attending the one in 1956.[8]

Between conferences, students organized political lectures in their schools, and a number wrote for the Jordanian and Arab newspapers, voicing their political concerns. The most effective means of disseminating information and announcing events was through the use of broadsheets, distributed to the different schools and student groups. These broadsheets put forward opinions about the political events of the day and influenced students' ideas about them.[9] Students also came out in large numbers for all the major demonstrations that took place throughout the decade. In summary, as Samir Khrainou reports, "The Jordanian students inside the country always helped the nationalist issue. They sang the nationalist songs for Algeria in the schools during the revolution and they supported, during the 1950s and 1960s, the establishment of political relations with the Arab organizations which believed in the idea of unity and with the socialist camp, as a strategic alliance to oppose Zionism and the West."[10]

While many people came to support the JNM via this route of educational expansion, still others found the Movement a viable alternative to the state in a period of economic change. In the late 1940s and early 1950s, both Jordan and Palestine had economies that were largely agricultural, with few technological advances, barely able to sustain the large numbers living there. That status began to change slowly during the 1950s with increased investment in business and industry by state and private contractors. The state also moved into the job sector by maintaining a relatively large army and by expanding its bureaucracy. This meant that many people—bedouin and peasant—moved off the land in order to collect the guaranteed salaries paid by the government.[11] Foreign aid contributed to the initiation of a number of infrastructure projects employing large numbers of citizens. As a result, employment directly attributable to government and foreign projects accounted for almost one-quarter of the gross national product (GNP) in 1954.[12] In fact, the economy grew throughout the decade, averaging about 7 percent a year between 1952 and 1966,[13] but not at a rate sufficient to employ the expanding population.

Agriculture saw only incremental improvements and forced many to move to the urban areas for new opportunities. Jordan's agricultural land was divided into small plots, with the average family owning only fifteen acres, an amount insufficient for sustenance, particularly in the many drought years.[14] As Michael Fischbach explains further, "These statistics clearly demonstrate a trend that was underway by the 1950s: population growth, combined with the results of land settlement, led to an increasing number of persons owning a finite amount of land with the result that plot sizes began shrinking."[15] For example, 'Ajluni villages increased in population from 2,769 persons in 1934 to 4,966 in 1954, but controlled the same amount of territory.[16] Fragmentation of land had come as a result of the state land reform program, when collectively controlled land had been subdivided and registered to individuals. In the interwar years, "The Department of Lands and Survey estimated that the average size of landholdings in villages that had been settled in 'Ajlun from 1933–1937 had shrunk a full 22 percent within ten years of settlement."[17] This fragmentation contributed to the inefficiency of cultivation and the lack of funds available for investment in new resources. In cases where the land was too small for profitable cultivation, the owners typically leased it out to sharecroppers and then moved into the cities.[18] Short-term tenants did not have the capital or the desire to initiate improvements on the land. Although irrigation projects were undertaken throughout the 1950s, they did not alter Jordan's agricultural economy in a meaningful way before construction began on the East Ghor Canal in 1958. Michael Mazur reports that, even with some improvements in the 1950s, "domestic food production was able to do little more than keep up with the growth in the domestic demand for food."[19] The result of all this was that many of the fellaheen chose to leave the land and move into the cities to find work.

This move into the city exacerbated rather than solved the unemployment problem. Jordan's population, in the 1952 census, stood at 1,360,000 people, which was about triple the population living in the country before 1948.[20] Unemployment stayed very high, with Palestinian jobs and farmlands lost to the state of Israel and Jordanian seasonal labor there eliminated. A World Bank mission to Jordan in 1955 estimated that unemployment stood at 16.5 percent and that another 11 percent of the population was only partially employed.[21] Unemployment hurt a disproportionate number of people in Jordan because of the high degree of dependency of the nonproductive population on each worker. In other words, in 1961, only 23 percent of the total population held jobs, while the remainder, including the 45 percent of the population under the age of fourteen, relied on a small number of people for sustenance.[22] Palestinian refugees, as would be expected, formed the largest proportion of the unemployed, with studies showing in 1954 that only about 10 percent of the refugees held full-time positions.[23]

In sum, the changing socioeconomic situation in Jordan in the 1950s contributed to the National Movement's efforts to recruit Jordanian and Palestinian supporters because the Hashemite state appeared to be failing in a number of fields. The Jordanians found difficulties in the rural areas, but were unable to find sufficient jobs in urban industry. The increasing numbers of civil service positions mitigated this problem somewhat but did not employ enough of the job seekers. This gap left a large segment of the population alienated from the regime and ready to fight against its policies. The gap between rich and poor Jordanians widened, as only a few benefited from housing and goods while the vast majority lived at a subsistence level. The Palestinians, by and large, remained outside the realm of government largesse, for few civil service positions opened for them. While some Palestinian professionals and those with money to invest in industry did benefit from contracts with the government and were able to invest capital in new businesses, such as construction, the majority remained in refugee camps and urban areas, with the necessary goods and services beyond their reach.

To try to improve this situation, the Ministry of the Economy served as a center for nationalist work throughout the 1950s. In his own words, Hamad al-Farhan said that he told the minister of the economy when he was first hired in 1951, "Look here. I can't just be the undersecretary of the economy, undersecretary of economy and just this part and take salary. We must change the order to become self-reliant."[24] Al-Farhan and his colleagues wanted the government and outside agencies to fund projects specifically designed to build a strong domestic economy for the country, one that would not be so dependent upon outsiders for support. Even though the minister agreed with his goals, the rest of the cabinet ministers, in that cabinet and in the subsequent cabinets of the 1950s, understood very little about economics, so did not see the validity of al-Farhan's argument. Al-Farhan and his colleagues also tried to convince private investors to work with the government to open new industries. While some mixed public and private investment was initiated, the government did not support the Ministry's efforts wholeheartedly, as seen in the fact that the government did not enact sufficient supplementary legislation to entice and support investors.

Al-Farhan and his colleagues also fought against foreign control over the economy and demanded that large-scale, government-led development programs be enacted to thoroughly transform the Jordanian economy.[25] U.S. and British aid agencies ignored these requests and initiated programs they deemed more suitable for Jordan's weak economy. Britain concentrated on a gradual development program, aimed at building up Jordan's institutional capacity, particularly in agriculture.[26] Jordanians in the Ministry of the Economy criticized these measures, including the Village Loan Scheme, saying they were not comprehensive enough and were focused too heavily on Jordan's agricultural sector.[27] The United States, on the other hand, concentrated on bringing technology into Jordan, technology that required the construction of a large administrative apparatus to support it.[28] Over the long run, the American plan saddled the Jordanian government with high costs and the problem of incorporating the technology into its economic scene. While industry did expand through these domestic and foreign efforts, too many obstacles to national self-sufficiency hindered further development. Jordan's dearth of national resources requires a well-coordinated industrial plan, but the efforts by al-Farhan and the economic nationalists generally came to naught because of lack of support, domestically and internationally.

A direct result of these economic problems was the rapid rate of urbanization that Jordan experienced in the 1950s, with Palestinian refugees and Jordanian fellaheen seeking increased economic opportunities in the cities. Urban crowding had already arisen in the 1920s and 1930s when poor harvest and drought conditions forced a large number Transjordanians to move off the land and into the cities or out of the country to places like Palestine.[29] After the 1948 War, even more of that labor force, which was not absorbed by Jordan's expanding army,[30] moved into Jordan's cities. Hamad al-Farhan, when asked why people moved into the cities in the 1950s, replied, "It was [because] facilities in the big towns became available and nice. We didn't have enough facilities in the rural areas. We didn't have electricity. We didn't have telephones. We didn't have good communication."[31] Thus, the push out of the countryside was met by the expectation that city life would be better. A survey conducted in 1958 confirmed this finding when it reported that approximately 75 percent of migrant heads of households claimed to have been seeking a better job or were displaced persons.[32] As an indication of the rising expectations of these migrants, entire families typically moved into the cities, not just the heads of households.[33] The 1961 census shows that 43.9 percent of the population lived in urban areas, with 50.6 percent living in rural areas, and a remaining 5.6 percent still residing in scattered tents.[34] Many of these migrants found jobs in the government or in private industry, but a large proportion still remained without steady work.

The expectations of a better life went largely unrealized by the urban migrants as people remained unemployed or underemployed and as cities soon became overcrowded. A Pilot Survey conducted in Amman in the 1950s showed that five people to a room was commonplace.[35] Rents stayed unnaturally high throughout the 1950s because of the imbalance between supply and demand. Sewage, water supply, and electricity to the majority of the urban areas remained inadequate. Jane Hacker found in

1958 that, "by whatever means the monthly earnings are supplemented to raise the standard of living, the fact remains that *the average worker does not earn enough money from his daily job to keep him and his dependents at a minimum level of health and comfort.*"[36] Hacker stated that in her survey nine out of every ten residents in Amman were dissatisfied by the poverty in which they found themselves.[37] Palestinians and Jordanians flooded the cities, heading particularly toward Amman, but found when they arrived that the numbers and types of jobs were insufficient for their skills and their financial needs.

In Jordan, high unemployment, urbanization, and dissatisfaction with government services contributed two elements to the growth of the National Movement. First, it produced a population disenchanted with the state, unable to benefit from most of the largesse it offered. Jamal al-Sha'ir reports that Sulayman al-Nabulsi said to him that he could not remember any demonstration taking place in Jordan that specifically demanded the lowering of bread prices, but, nonetheless, prices always played a role in the national call for unity and independence.[38] Al-Farhan put forward a similar analysis when he said that the "demonstrations in the '50s were mainly from three sides, three parties. They were caused either by a very big accident, an Arab accident, outside Jordan or a problem with Palestine, the Zionist movement, or a local crisis like prices, food, unemployment, sometimes."[39] Second, the growth in the urbanized areas made a large proportion of the population available for the massive party demonstrations and strikes. While the majority of the urban masses did not become party activists or even official members, the parties used their rising anger as ammunition against government policies. Workers, rural migrants, and the unemployed all came out in protest whenever the parties led the way.

Urban populations such as these have the ability to destabilize the power structures in traditional societies because of the flow of new ideas and the proliferation of new social strata. Lucian Pye has theorized that "the spread of popular politics in traditional societies has meant a constant increase in the number of participants and the types of organizations involved in the political process. This development has been stimulated by the extraordinary rise in the urban population, which has greatly increased the number of people who have some understanding about, and feeling for, politics at the national level."[40] Moshe Ma'oz, in his study of the West Bank political leadership in the 1950s, found that in towns with growing populations, such as Nablus and Jerusalem, where many villagers and refugees poured in looking for work, the traditional leadership struggled to maintain its influence.[41] On the other hand, in towns, such as Hebron, that had static population growth, the traditional forces were not threatened by any new social agitation.[42] This process was replicated throughout Jordan as populations gradually moved toward the city centers for the jobs and the services offered. They upset the traditional political balance by organizing into political parties and demonstrating to demand a voice in the governmental process.

John H. Kautsky has analyzed this process of urbanization and has reported that it brings peasants into the cities and forces them to work in factories; "thrown into the anonymity of life in an industrial plant and an urban slum, where not only the physical surroundings, but also many values and behavior patterns, are utterly alien, the worker is bound to be subject to maladjustments, tensions, and frustrations of various kinds."[43] Additionally, moving into the city did not necessarily mean people disconnected themselves from their village lives.[44] People maintained their ties to the village and used them to find jobs, houses, and spouses. However, when these village connections did not provide enough support, the urban network systems that had worked for centuries to organize events in the city quarters stepped in to help. Such informal networks typically were based on religious, ethnic, occupational, and residential ties and provided, over the centuries, vital links between the people of the city quarters and the government and its proffered social services.[45] As Guilain Denoeux notes, "although they provide some of the economic, social, and psychological support needed to absorb the tensions associated with rapid socioeconomic change, informal networks also offer channels for the articulation of grievances and for the mobilization of the poor into destabilizing political activities."[46] Thus, they serve the dual purpose of providing services and succor to new residents of the cities, and then catalyzing these newcomers to protest against the government. Alongside them and sometimes in competition, new kinds of agencies and leaders were also required in the burgeoning cities. Denoeux theorizes further that

> More generally, the configuration of Middle East urban protest movements has been greatly affected by the ever-increasing integration of the Middle East into the world economy, the centralization of authority, the processes of industrialization, secularization, Westernization, and modernization, and the cities' rapidly changing infrastructure, economy, and social structures. Such processes led to the marginalization or disappearance of some of the actors who had played a prominent role in urban uprisings until the nineteenth century (notables, guild leaders, Sufi shaykhs, lower-ranking ulama, *tullab*, *lutes*, and *futuwwat*, to name just a few).[47]

In their place came a new kind of za'im, who organized the residents via new programs of patronage. The doctors treated the sick, the journalists defined the political debates, and the lawyers defended those the government punished. Muhammad Bajis al-Majali used his position as a government official to exploit his contacts throughout the city. He called upon them whenever the parties needed participants for their many demonstrations. The urban professional leadership of the JNM clearly used its dual role in society to provide new kinds of services and new kinds of political leadership for the urban populations. By using its offices and clinics as political centers, it made the very explicit connection between the new roles. As new kinds of za'ims, they eased the migrants into city life but in return called on them to demonstrate whenever the political parties sent out the call. The reciprocal relationship was not unlike those of old, when city bosses served as middlemen between the government and the masses, but now new kinds of institutions worked to bring people into the process and a new kind of political discourse educated them about the events taking place.

The transition period was eased for many, as demonstrations and events taking place in urban areas typically followed ritualized patterns, often associated with earlier political and religious observances. The new residents could transfer their knowledge of and respect for the older rituals to the new politicized ones. For example, Nabil Haddadin reports that by 1956 all the wedding processions in his small town of Ma'een turned into political events.[48] Tal'at Harb states that once his engagement in 1956 was concluded, Harb then introduced to the thousand invited guests Fayiq Warrad, the party's parliamentary candidate from Ramallah.[49] These events intermingled political ideas with traditional religious and social celebrations and, by so doing, extended new political values.

To spread the National Movement's revolutionary national message to the increasingly educated and urbanized population, the country witnessed an explosion in the number of media outlets. The two most important daily newspapers, *Filastin [Palestine]* and *al-Difa' [Defense]*, had begun publication before and during the British Mandate in Palestine. The third daily, *al-Urdun [Jordan]*, was published out of Amman. The three papers had circulation rates of 2,000, 7,000, and 1,500, respectively, in 1953.[50] Daniel Lerner conducted a survey of mostly male, literate Jordanian and Palestinian readers of newspapers and found that 44 percent read the daily newspapers in the 1950s.[51] The parties issued at least one or more weekly newspapers as well, including the Communist *al-Muqawama al-Sha'biyah [The People's Struggle]*, the Ba'thist *al-Ba'th*, and the National Socialist *al-Mithaq [The Charter]*. Musallam Bseiso opened *al-Hawadath* on January 10, 1951, and it serves as an example of the goals enunciated by so many of the new papers. He describes it as a free paper, saying that "it talks, reflects, talks about the problems of the society, all the problems, starting from the farmers, passing toward students, treating labor's problems, fighting for new laws, to organize society, labor syndicates . . . and I encouraged all the important circles, all the country: intellectuals, writers . . . laborers, farmers, students, women, musicians, artists, and everything and it included all these activities."[52] These papers continually attacked government policy toward Israel and Britain and demanded the creation of a more liberal and inclusive political system. Analyzing his own paper as an example, Bseiso said, "We were not really extreme but we were fair."[53] The population influenced by these papers expanded exponentially as people read articles out loud in coffeeshops and homes.

News was also disseminated via the radio as the number of people owning radio sets increased throughout the 1950s, with 2 sets per 1,000 inhabitants in 1950 and 12 per 1,000 in 1953.[54] In poor villages, radios were often set up in coffeeshops, while in some refugee camps loudspeakers broadcast the news during the day. As Phillips Davison has analyzed, "Radio has been the greatest single instrument for involving people in emerging countries in political activity. Matters that traditionally were almost exclusively the province of a very small group have become subjects of mass attention. . . . People have opinions on issues that did not previously concern them, and the media offer them a range of opinions among which they can choose."[55] The urban populations of Jordan and Palestine acquired the education needed to synthesize this material, and the professional stratum channeled these ideas into support for the political opposition movement.

While the Jordanian government used Ramallah Radio, captured during the 1948 War, and from 1956 Radio Amman, the National Movement relied on outside Arab stations to disseminate information to counter the government's agenda. Egypt's Sawt al-'Arab [Voice of the Arabs] radio station, the most effective in this regard, began broadcasting in 1953. Gamal Abdel Nasser quickly began to use it as a propaganda tool for spreading his opinions around the region. Reports focused on imperialist threats from Israel and the West and the policies instituted by the purportedly reactionary governments ruling Jordan and Iraq.

In the first year of its existence, Sawt al-'Arab's reports focused primarily on the imperialist threats to the Arab world. One such report, on February 23, 1954, stated that "the enemies, O Arabs, are Britain, because she deprives us of livelihood, France because she is spilling our blood and the US because she wants for us enslavement. O Arabs, the enemy is any Eastern or Western state which wants for us enslavement, tyranny and exploitation."[56] In a series of plays broadcast over the service, Sawt al-'Arab illustrated British plans for the Middle East. The following excerpt includes an imaginary discussion among the British officials, Mr. Anthony Eden (foreign minister), Gen. Lord Robertson (military officer for the Middle East), and Mr. Emanuel Shinwell (diplomatic officer for the Middle East).

> *Shinwell:* No use arguing. The crisis in Israel can only be solved by establishing a permanent peace with Israel.
> *Eden:* And how could that come about?
> *Shinwell:* By forcing the Arabs, if possible.
> *Eden:* I wonder is that possible?
> *Robertson:* Don't you know that all the different attempts made by us in this respect have failed?
> *Shinwell:* These attempts which you made were intended to cause the fall of the Revolutionary Government in Egypt.
> *Eden:* That was because Egypt is the main obstacle in our way.
> *Shinwell:* This is true, but we should try what we can do with those subject to our influence. We must work for the fall of the Arab governments one after the other and foster disturbances and disorder in the Arab world.[57]

The play continued with a discussion of which countries should be targeted first and how Israel would ultimately be saved by British actions. In a broadcast on May 25, 1954, Sawt al-'Arab called on the Arab world to unite to fight imperialism, by saying, "O Arabs, while the forces of Arab consciousness unite, the Arabs can rise from Morocco to Iraq, everywhere destroying and sabotaging bases, fortifications and property of the enemy."[58]

These ideas, broadcast for hours every day, to an increasing number of radio listeners in the Arab world, not only made the ideas themselves more popular but made their originator, Nasser, appear as the best possible leader for the Arabs, the only one capable of fighting the West and defeating Israel. In all the broadcasts, Egypt led the way in the struggle to eliminate imperialism in the Arab world, never deviating from the depiction of Egypt's supremacy in the battle. Nasser became a hero to his fellow Arabs in this period as he continually reinforced the image that he, himself, stood in the forefront of the Arab struggle. While the reality of Arab unity had not yet been achieved, the ethos of Arab nationalism and of Nasser's leadership became the dominant philosophy throughout the Arab world in the 1950s. His message tapped into that activist Arab nationalism disseminated out of the schools, universities, and urban areas starting in the late 1940s.

The constant reports of British duplicity and Israeli machinations related in these newspapers and radio broadcasts fueled the growing anti-imperialist sentiment in Jordan. Demonstrators throughout the 1950s called out anti-American and anti-British slogans and demanded that the government actively fight against Israeli infiltrations. Sawt al-'Arab's daily censure of the Iraqi and Jordanian governments echoed statements made by the National Movement and reinforced these ideas in the minds of thousands of listeners. These messages found fertile ground among the increasingly politicized Jordanian and Palestinian populations because of the poor living conditions in the cities and the repressive tactics of the government. Hamad al-Farhan felt that these broadcasts and Nasser's actions had an enormous influence on the people, and as a result they wanted to support those parties they identified as Nasserite, namely those parties that comprised the Jordanian National Movement.[59]

Above and beyond the other changes taking place in Jordan, a large number of specifically Palestinian issues drove this portion of the population into the arms of the Jordanian National Movement, in both leadership and rank-and-file positions. Politically, the system of gerrymandering the districts to reward loyalty and punish political opposition underrepresented the Palestinian population in the Majlis al-Nuwwab. Posts in the national government allotted to loyal Palestinians carried little political power. In general, Palestinians held cabinet posts pertinent only to Palestinian affairs, not national issues. On the local level in the West Bank, the Jordanian regime dissolved many of the political organizations that had been functioning for years and appointed loyal Palestinians to posts in a new government apparatus. Overall, the nature of Jordan's political system, which excluded the majority of the citizenry from its ranks, disaffected the Palestinian population en masse.

Israeli attacks against villages in the West Bank fueled Palestinian distrust of the Hashemite regime as well. While the Palestinians favored escalating the conflict along the border, the government followed a defensive policy to defuse the tension. The Arab Legion served not as an offensive force in this regard but as a police force guaranteeing that no Jordanian or Palestinian infiltrators crossed into Israel. While the government bound the hands of the Arab Legion, only the National Guard stood in each of the border villages ready to battle the Israelis. This force had been formed in 1950 as an answer to Palestinian complaints of constant Israeli attacks. Each village force had an Arab Legion officer commanding it, while Palestinians overwhelmingly filled the lower ranks. By 1956, it contained thirty thousand men, equipped with small weapons and a little training. This force proved incapable of stopping the Israeli attacks in most instances, yet the government ignored the demands for better weapons and more extensive training. The Arab Legion's neglect of the West Bank thus fostered Palestinian distrust toward the British commanders and the Jordanian government. The government's disregard for the National Guard in terms of money and arms further aggravated the situation and made many Palestinians turn toward the National Movement for answers to their demands.

The secondary status of Jerusalem also angered the Palestinians, as the regime essentially ignored the political and economic role the city had occupied in Palestinian life. The Hashemites only highlighted its religious role and its subsequent potential for tourism. To combat this neglect, newspapers published from Jerusalem issued almost daily updates about the city's deteriorating political position.[60] Continually, the Palestinian representatives in the Majlis al-Nuwwab demanded that the prime minister amend the government's policies concerning this issue. However, Amman became the economic and political capital of the country, and no effort by the Palestinian politicians to alter this policy proved successful.

The Jordanian state also consistently neglected the West Bank economically. Since the majority of trade licenses and contracts went to East Bank merchants, their West Bank counterparts had to prove their loyalty to win the few remaining contracts.[61] Many Palestinians found themselves forced to migrate to the East Bank in order to find work. The number of industries present west of the Jordan River remained stagnant, and the number to the east began to grow at a steady rate. Between 1950 and 1967, public investment in West Bank industry totaled just 3.2 percent of all public investment, while the West Bank accounted for 47.9 percent of the population in 1967.[62] Jordan also neglected the West Bank's agricultural sector, with the majority of investment funds allocated to East Bank farmers. In the years immediately before 1967, per capita income in the West Bank was about 75 percent of that in the East Bank.[63]

THE POLITICAL PARTIES OF THE JORDANIAN NATIONAL MOVEMENT (JNM)

Out of this politicization process—for the urban professional strata emerging from the Mandate period in Jordan and Palestine and for the residents of the cities of the 1950s on both banks of the river—came the political parties of the Jordanian National Movement. People, particularly in the urban areas, sought a new kind of leadership that would oppose imperialism and economic inequality. With that new leadership came a new kind of national identity and discourse. Making up this new leadership, as encompassed by the JNM, were the Communist Party, the Ba'th Party, the National Front, the Movement of Arab Nationalists, and the National Socialist Party (NSP).[64] Mahmud al-Mu'ayta and Shahir Abu Shahut established the Free Officers' Movement within the Arab Legion, composed of young Arab officers leaning ideologically toward the Ba'th Party. The parties represented, for a society in flux, a new kind of nationalized solution to not only the boundaries of the region, but also the very real socioeconomic problems present within them. "Everybody belonged to a party in the 1950s" because the parties supplied alternative solutions to the economic problems in the country and the difficulties presented by the Palestinian issue. They promised revolutionary answers to replace the "old" colonially constructed Hashemite state with the "new," more equal Arab union. The leaders of the parties used simple slogans—"Arab unity" and "anti-imperialism"—to tap into people's anger at event after event in the 1950s.

Although all the parties, with the exception of the NSP, served as branches of larger organizations existing outside Jordan, they accepted the realities of political life in the country and worked within the established system to institute political reform there first. The umbrella of Arab nationalism easily allowed this process, because Arab nationalism meant revolution for socioeconomic change. To achieve this, the parties advocated a number of the same positions, including the creation of a liberal, inclusive governmental system in Jordan, guaranteeing natural rights for the citizens, the evacuation of the British forces, militarily and financially, and some form of unity among the Arab states. To establish the level of economic equality the parties desired, all supported various versions of socialism, from the Marxist interpretation to the mixture of publicly owned and privately owned industries and agricultural properties that comprised the particular brand of Arab socialism then current in the region. In respect to the British, the parties particularly targeted John Bagot Glubb, the British chief of staff of the Arab Legion, as the source of innumerable problems within Jordan. He represented for them continuing British control over the state and Hashemite acquiescence to it. If any one issue united the members of the nationalist opposition of Jordanians and Palestinians, it was the need to eliminate this imperialist control over Jordan and the Arab world. The solution to this colonial interference was the unification of the Arab states as an alternative to

Jordan's separate existence as a state. Thus, the anti-imperialist demand simultaneously meant the establishment of Arab unity or, more specifically, the dissolution of the imperialist divisions of the Fertile Crescent. Implicit in this demand was the belief that once unity was achieved, the socioeconomic problems attending imperialism would also be eliminated. The parties also varied in some of their positions, with the Ba'th Party looking to unify with Syria first and the NSP initially calculating that Iraq would be the wiser choice. The Communists officially spent little time focusing on the issue of Arab unity but did not reject it outright. However, the party's members had been immersed in the Arab nationalist influences bombarding them from every direction; the Arab connection was just as natural for them as for the Ba'thists. The Communist Party's views of Arab unity slowly evolved and, by 1956, came more directly into line with those of the other leftist parties in the region. For example, all the Arab Communist parties of the Middle East publicly supported the union of Egypt and Syria in 1958.

The parties left ambiguous in their political platforms the fate of the Hashemite regime. All professed support for it, but then detailed the dramatic means by which they planned to change it. A Communist or a socialist economic system would certainly have overthrown the patronage system the Hashemites had so carefully constructed since 1921. Any such radical change would have necessitated the fall or at least the diminution of the power of the Hashemite leadership. Discussions among the different politicians concerning the overthrow of the king certainly took place in private, but all carefully avoided the subject in public. Jamal al-Sha'ir, in an interview, expressed his belief that Sulayman al-Nabulsi honestly did not want to accomplish his goals in such a fashion. Even when al-Nabulsi headed a nationalist government in 1956 and 1957 and called for the federation of Jordan with the surrounding Arab states, he never explicitly detailed what would happen to King Husayn in such a structure. However, al-Sha'ir also said that

> As soon as you are a member of the Ba'th Party, you are against the king, automatically. Why? They don't explain why. "He's a traitor." "He sold Palestine." "He sold the Arab land to Sykes and Picot, to divide the Arab lands." And all kinds of treason. They were talking about the Hashemite family in general. Although the Ba'th Party—the flag of the Ba'th Party was the same flag of the Greater Arab Revolution led by King Husayn . . . the teaching was that his trust in the British was wrong and his sons all were opportunists. They all wanted to become kings for Syria and Iraq and Jordan and so on. And that's why the Hashemite family should go.[65]

Ahmed Fakher, in an interview, expressed the view that if the nationalist politicians had been able to overthrow the king, they probably would have done so.[66] The parties never succeeded in reaching this level of power, so in the end were never confronted with this dilemma.

The Jordanian Communist Party was born as a result of a merger between the Arab branch of the Palestine Communist Party, working under the name of the Palestinian League of National Liberation, and Jordanian advocates of Marxist ideas. Communist cells existed in many cities of the West and East Banks, with 'Isa Madanat identifying groups in Salt, Amman, and Madaba,[67] and those in Palestine centered on the Old City of Jerusalem, Bethlehem, and, especially, Nablus, a strong Communist stronghold. Tal'at Harb reports small cells spontaneously forming in al-Bira and Ramallah, as well, with him as a member of the latter.[68] *Al-Muqawamah al-Sha'biyah [The People's Resistance]* appeared in 1949 and spread the message of the party. To increase support, Fu'ad Nasser,[69] the leader of the Palestine Communist Party, moved to Amman after the 1948 War to recruit members. There he met with those Jordanian men who had been attracted to Marxist tenets while studying in universities throughout the Arab world. In preparation for this event, these men compiled a report stating their biggest concerns, namely British control over the region and Zionist success.[70] As a result of these efforts the Jordanian Communist Party was formally founded in June 1951, with both Jordanian and Palestinian members. A few months later, Fu'ad Nasser was arrested and sentenced to ten years in prison for antigovernment activities. Despite his incarceration, he remained the head of the party throughout the decade and continued to send orders to the different cells.

The party successfully gained a broad-based appeal by choosing to work under the guise of organizations indirectly associated with Communist ideologies, the most important of which became Ansar al-Salam [Peace Partisans], an organization advocating world peace and a prohibition on nuclear war. In 1951, it launched the "peace campaign," whereby the Partisans gathered thousands of signatures supporting the Stockholm Peace Appeal, prohibiting the use of atomic weapons. By the end of 1951, the organization had collected close to twenty thousand signatures.[71] Or, as Nabih Irsheidat more vividly described it, the paper containing the signatures stretched for more than ten meters.[72] To generate interest in the campaign, Ya'qub Ziyadin spoke to the Federation of Christian Young People [Jam'iyat al-Shubban al-Masihiyin] a couple of times and participated in writing articles for *al-Difa'*, ostensibly about the health dangers resulting from war but carrying on a discussion "between the lines" about the overall perils of war and its lasting results.[73] 'Isa Madanat and others produced a newsletter publicizing the goals of the group, although they quickly found themselves on trial under the provisions of the anti-Communism law. Despite a strong defense led by Ibrahim Bakr, Madanat was sent to prison for more than a year, spending much of that time in al-Jafr prison in the desert.[74] This peace campaign not only recruited new members for the party but also garnered a great deal of sympathy for the Communists, a fact that proved advantageous in later years when the party leaders faced arrest and punishment by the government. At these times, non-Communists rallied around them and demanded that the government ease up on its repressive tactics. The government's warnings of a Communist takeover of Jordan failed to find a receptive audience in part because of the large support the party had generated with its peace campaign.

In recruiting new members, the party focused on urban areas, with particular attention paid to teachers and professionals. For example, Jerusalem, Bethlehem, Baytin, and Nablus served as the main recruitment centers in the West Bank, with Amman and Irbid important on the East Bank. The party's emphasis on the intellectual groups in society to the exclusion of the working classes resulted from a decision within the leadership structure that the best hope for growth lay with the groups who could understand Marxist tenets and then later spread the message to the urban masses. The policy also reflected the fact that the Jordanian economy did not employ enough workers to form the demographic base for a proletarian party. As a result, activists formed cells throughout the major cities and in the upper forms of secondary schools. Teachers played a particularly active role by serving as the centers of the party networks that organized students to distribute leaflets and to participate in street demonstrations.[75] Doctors and lawyers also comprised a large proportion of the leadership of the party. Some of the members of the cadres, such as Amal Nafa', worked in Amman both as agitators during the many demonstrations and as instructors, spreading the message of the party to ever-widening segments of the society.[76] In Karak, in southern Jordan, men of the professional class, who had studied at universities in Syria and Lebanon, established party cells and eventually recruited about 280 of their colleagues.[77] With this foundation, the party began to gradually grow in strength.

Discussions concerning Ba'th ideas took place in various cities and towns around the East Bank in the late 1940s and early 1950s. Many of the participants had joined while at university or had at least become sympathetic to the party's tenets. Al-Sha'ir tells of a meeting he attended in Salt in the summer of 1948 where thirty people sat and listened to the ideas of a new nationalist movement called "Hizb al-Ba'th al-Suri" [the Syrian Ba'th Party]. By the end, a number had pledged their support for it. In Karak, a group of teachers secretly formed a branch of the Ba'th Party in 1951; it ultimately reached a membership of four to five hundred people.[78] Abd al-Rahman Shuqayr joined the party as he continued his political activities in Jordan; his clinic in Amman, located near the center of the town, became a focal point for political activists. In addition, Shuqayr often lectured on political issues at the Arab and Literary Clubs in Amman. Munif al-Razzaz joined the party at this time as well.

In the West Bank, Ba'th Party organization became the most active in Jerusalem and Ramallah. Bahjat Abu Gharbiyah became the first official member of the party from the West Bank and, as such, took on the task of building the party's organizational structure.[79] He, himself, taught at the al-Ibrahimiyah School and gave political lectures at the Arab Cultural Club in Jerusalem. 'Abdullah al-Rimawi and 'Abdullah Na'was began publishing *al-Ba'th*, a political, social, and cultural newspaper, in 1948, although neither had officially joined the party by that time. The Ba'th Party of Jordan held its first organizational conference in the spring of 1951, in al-Rimawi's house. During the meeting, the party laid out its ideological tenets and mapped out plans for the future course of the party. The members met again in 1952, in Na'was's house, and elected a Regional Command, with al-Rimawi as the general secretary.[80] Abu Gharbiyah, Na'was, and Shuqayr agreed to serve on the Central Committee.

From these organizational meetings, the members spread out around Jordan to recruit members to the party. Al-Rimawi and Na'was proved particularly effective in recruiting members and gaining support for Ba'th ideas both on the streets of Jordanian and Palestinian cities and in parliament. They both won seats in the Majlis al-Nuwwab in 1950 and 1951, and al-Rimawi retained his seat in 1956. In the early years, they formed an opposition bloc around themselves.[81] Of the new members of the party, most came from the same groups as the Communist supporters, with teachers, students, and professionals forming the majority of the members. The largest concentrations of Ba'thists lived in Irbid and Amman on the East Bank and Ramallah, Jerusalem, and Nablus on the West Bank.[82] Teacher and student networks were set up in the secondary schools of the West Bank, particularly in the Teacher's Seminary in Beit Hanina and al-Ibrahimiyah School in Jerusalem, where Abu Gharbiyah taught. After the government rejected its application for a license three times, the party appealed the case to the High Court under the name of Hizb al-Ba'th al-'Arabi al-Ishtiraki [Arab Socialist Ba'th Party], in recognition of a similar name change in Syria. On August 28, 1955, the High Court reversed the decision of the cabinet and the Ba'th Party became legal.

To better coordinate their activities, a few members of both the Communist and Ba'th Parties came together to form a National Front. Shuqayr quickly became the leader of this front, and his ideological justification for joining and his activities on behalf of the party illustrate the evolution of the organization. Shuqayr first obtained the chance to study Communist doctrines during a government-imposed exile to southern Jordan at the end of October 1952. Shuqayr had been sent to the area after the government heard that he was planning a strike in Amman against the government of Tawfiq Abu'l-Huda. Once in Tafillah, his first location, Shuqayr immediately began agitating among the inhabitants to convince them to protest against the negligence of the local government. Amman retaliated by moving him a little farther south, to Shobeck. There, he had many discussions with the director of the elementary school and slowly worked his way through a number of Marxist and Leninist books the director owned. Although never officially joining the party, Shuqayr came to support Communist concepts and, more importantly, the reasoning behind the formation of a united front of leftist groups. Shuqayr returned to Amman after the more liberal Fawzi al-Mulqi became prime minister in May 1953, on the accession of King Husayn to the throne.

Upon returning from the south, Shuqayr continued his activities, announcing that his major goal was to "make a front for all the people who are against the imperialists."[83] At one particularly successful lecture, "A New Route in the Struggle," Shuqayr spoke about Zionist and colonial plots to weaken the Arab world.[84] He called this lecture a turning point in the building of the National Front in Jordan and said that more than seventy people, including a number of deputies in the Majlis al-Nuwwab and party figures, rallied to his side.[85]

Shuqayr also lobbied the Ba'th Party to work with him in the National Front. The leaders, including al-Rimawi, Na'was, Abu Gharbiyah, and al-Razzaz, met with Shuqayr and heard his case. Shuqayr emphasized the need "to liberate the house first" and that political "differences could be dealt with later."[86] His Ba'thist colleagues, however, failed to accept his reasoning, so Shuqayr left the meeting in anger and resigned from the party. Thereafter, the National Front, despite its rejection by the Ba'th Party, succeeded in winning the support of a number of leftist politicians on both banks and ran candidates in the 1954 and 1956 elections. The whole story highlights the fact that while the JNM was certainly united around almost all issues, the potential for fragmentation remained ever-present.

The National Socialist Party (NSP), composed of a number of moderate leftist, mostly Jordanian, politicians, was officially founded in July 1954. It stands as the only leftist party in Jordan in the 1950s not affiliated with an outside party, either Arab or foreign. After 1948, the party reached out to prosperous but progressive businessmen, landowners, and professionals.[87] The party also earned adherents from a wide range of people throughout the East Bank because of its relatively conservative platform, in support of the monarchy but against the abuses of government. It opened offices in cities throughout the Kingdom.[88] The party successfully petitioned the government for a license in July 1954. Hazza' al-Majali served as its first leader but resigned from the post when Sulayman al-Nabulsi returned from London in June 1954, having served as Jordanian ambassador there for one year.

Without question, this party was the weakest ideologically; its cohesion relied more on the personality of its leaders than its political positions. As a sign of its ideological weakness, Jamal al-Sha'ir reports that 'Abdullah al-Rimawi actually wrote its constitution.[89] Instead of an ideological appeal, the party primarily revolved around Sulayman al-Nabulsi, a leader of the opposition movement from the mid-1940s, and a rallying point for all political tendencies existing in the country. Ahmed Fakher even called him the "Za'im Watani" [Nationalist Leader] because of his leadership role in the leftist political movement.[90] More importantly, this term can also be applied to him because he combined both the new and older definitions of *za'im* within his own person, serving as the personalized leader of the group, but doing so within an ideological framework. As al-Sha'ir has reported, "When he was a student in the American University of Beirut his room was like a club for Jordanians, Palestinians, Lebanese, Syrians."[91] Back in Amman, his home and his office served as political salons for anyone, in the government or out, who chose to discuss events of the day. Because of the ideological weakness of the party, its importance stems more from its position in society than its political platform. In other words, the party can be seen as a transitional grouping of the traditional village and family collectivities of earlier periods and the types of ideological organizations represented by the Ba'th and Communist Parties. The leaders of the NSP articulated their grievances and demands within a party platform but primarily gathered supporters because of personal alliances. The party would prove to be particularly popular in the voting booths in the 1950s because of its unique place in a changing society.

As for the Movement of Arab Nationalists, a number of groups in Syria and Lebanon have worked under this name, so it is difficult to pinpoint precisely the history of the party that emerged in Jordan and Palestine. Most sources tie the ideology of the movement to the ideas of Constantine Zurayq and the work of the Indissoluble Bond.[92] Munif al-Razzaz, however, questions whether the members of the group who surrounded Zurayq in the 1940s in Beirut went on to form the new Movement of Arab Nationalists or whether completely different men led its revival after World War II. He, himself, remained in Zurayq's circle for a number of years in the late 1930s and believes that little connection existed between the two organizations. Al-Razzaz theorizes that the original Movement of Arab Nationalists was probably weakened, and perhaps disappeared, during the 1948 War, and a new movement, led by men such as George Habash, arose, ideologically swayed by the earlier movement but mostly influenced by the catastrophe in Palestine.[93]

As for its emergence in Jordan and Palestine, the Movement of Arab Nationalists is again shrouded in questions. The written sources generally state that the Palestinians George Habash and his colleague Wadi' Haddad moved from Beirut to Amman, between 1951 and 1953, in order to start the movement. In contrast, Hamad al-Farhan has stated that in 1951 a number of Jordanians came together and formed the Movement of Arab Nationalists and that Habash and Haddad joined a short time later.[94] Regardless of the year, these men and others quickly began to organize a movement including members from both banks of the river. In Amman, Habash and Haddad set up a medical clinic and, as part of their activities, treated refugees and the poor of the city for free.[95] They also initiated literacy campaigns focused on the same groups. Like those of the other parties, these leaders established and then spoke in the political clubs around Jordan to spread their message. The membership of the movement consisted primarily of teachers and students, with doctors at the forefront of the leadership structure. Because of the doctors' work with the Palestinian refugees, both in the clinic and in the educational campaigns, a large number of refugees joined as well. Al-Khatib feels that the presence of so many doctors in the leadership structure played an enormous role in garnering supporters for the movement because they earned the trust of so much of the population with their medical work, above and beyond their political activities.[96]

The platform for the movement stressed "Unity, Liberation, Revenge," because of the Arab defeat in 1948, to be obtained through "Blood, Iron, Fire." According to al-Khatib, "with these slogans, we were in a position to take possession of the hearts and the minds of the large masses migrating from their homes. Revenge for the oppression which enfolded them was the focus of their ideas. Revenge for the Arabs was their biggest issue."[97] They rejected any compromise with Israel and believed that the strength needed to exact this revenge lay in Arab unity. While the movement had a platform outlining various political and socioeconomic positions, the most important aspect of its activities focused on returning Palestine to the Arabs.

The Free Officers' Movement within the Arab Legion emerged out of the defeat in 1948 and the ideas of Arab unity and nationalism that were spreading in the area at the time. A number of graduates of the secondary school in Salt opted to enter the Arab Legion, instead of continuing their education in Damascus or Beirut. This group included Ali Abu Nuwar and Mahmud al-Mu'ayta, along with Shahir Abu Shahut, a graduate of the secondary school in Amman. They, too, absorbed the lessons about imperialist rule and the need for Arab unity and independence that their civilian colleagues had. They continued their politicization process in the army when they had to follow orders given by British officers. When they witnessed the Arab defeat in Palestine in 1948 they were further alienated from the British-controlled state. In particular, they felt that General Glubb had betrayed the Arab cause when he refused to enter the area designated for the Jewish state by the United Nations.

When the Jordanian forces returned to their main military base in Zarqa, on the East Bank, after the 1948 War, a number of the Arab officers began to meet in informal discussion groups to talk about the causes of the defeat and plans for the future liberation of Palestine. Shahir Abu Shahut gleaned from these discussions the planks of the Ba'th Party and, because of his support for them, contacted the leadership and became a member, despite the government's prohibition on political activities for soldiers. After that, he joined a party cell and met with the participants every week to discuss ideological concerns and the activities of the party. After a few months, Abu Shahut convinced a colleague, Mahmud al-Mu'ayta, to join the party as well.

The two then began to spread the message to their fellow officers, unbeknownst to the Ba'th Party leadership. Because of their work, Abu Shahut and al-Mu'ayta managed to convince a number of their colleagues, including Dafi al-Jumani, that they should accept the Ba'thist ideological platform.[98] This movement had two main goals: the withdrawal of British military forces and officers from Jordan and the unity of Jordan and Syria. It favored the former because of its belief that British actions led to the failure in Palestine and the latter because a merger of the Syrian and Jordanian armies would create a new, more powerful military force in the region. The movement then grew in size as Abu Shahut and al-Mu'ayta spread their ideas throughout the army. They began with their own unit, the artillery group, and then extended their reach in 1951 to other units containing the more educated Arab officers, including the engineers, the tank battalions, the mechanized units, and then the infantry. The ideas of the movement proved popular not only because of the military defeat in 1948 but also because of continued British control of the Arab Legion. The British forced most of the Arab officers to remain in the lower ranks of the officer corps while keeping the highest posts for their own officers. Also, by 1950, a new group of young bedouin and peasant officers was starting to gain positions in the military, and its members came equipped with different ideas than their predecessors about the British role in the country. After the Egyptian Free Officers overthrew the government of King Farouk and Gamal Abdel Nasser became popular with the Jordanian population, the officers in Jordan adopted the name of the Free Officers' Movement.[99]

The Muslim Brotherhood also opened a branch in Jordan at this time, but it did not acquire strong influence in the political realm until the 1960s. Its first president, Abdullatif Abu Qourah, inaugurated the movement on November 19, 1945, under the patronage of King 'Abdullah.[100] In the 1950s, as local offices opened in Salt, Karak, and Irbid, the government granted a license to the Muslim Brotherhood as a charitable society under the Ottoman Law of Associations. The Brotherhood also formed a political party, the Tahrir Party, to serve its political goals throughout the 1950s. Sheikh Taqi al-Din al-Nabahani, a Palestinian religious teacher at the Islamic al-'Alamiyah College, established the party in 1952 with a number of his colleagues. Initially, the party retained an affiliation with the Jordanian branch of the Muslim Brotherhood but broke away from it when the two groups failed to agree on a common set of goals. In 1952, the party petitioned the government for a license but was rejected on the grounds that its platform contained tenets contradicting the spirit of the Jordanian constitution. The Party tried to become recognized as an association as defined by the Ottoman Law of Associations, but this action also failed and the Party was forced to work clandestinely. The membership of the Party, as with the others, included a large number of teachers but in this case those who tended to work in Palestinian and Jordanian religious schools rather than the secular public and private ones. Large- and small-scale merchants had a larger representation in the Tahrir Party than in its counterparts in the JNM, and, overall, the Party contained less-educated members than those of the JNM.[101] The Party had few members but did succeed in projecting its opinions onto the national Jordanian political stage through the election of Shaykh Ahmad Da'ur, of Tulkarm, to the Majlis al-Nuwwab in 1954 and 1956. The Party's platform highlighted the members' desire to establish a democratic Islamic government in Jordan.

Occasionally, throughout the decade, the goals of the Muslim Brotherhood, the Tahrir Party, and the Jordanian National Movement coincided, but in most instances differed substantially. In particular, both groups opposed continued Western control over the military, the government, and the finances of the country. As a sign of this agreement, these groups joined in demonstrations to oppose the Baghdad Pact in 1955 and the Eisenhower Doctrine in 1957. However, the ends for which these groups struggled were dramatically different. The JNM sought social justice reform via socialism and Arab political unity; the Brotherhood and the Tahrir Party worked to establish an Islamic system of rule in Jordan. An April 3, 1954, statement by the Muslim Brotherhood read in part, "Jordan is an inseparable part of the Muslim world. Government in accordance with the Shari'ah (law) of Allah is the objective and aspiration of the Ikhwan in this life. The Palestinian issue is an Islamic issue for which all material and moral resources ought to be mobilised so as to liberate Palestine from global Judaism and international crusade [the modern Western Crusaders' Campaign against the Muslim World]."[102] Because of these different goals, the Brotherhood actively opposed many of the policies of the JNM and showed that opposition by supporting the regime whenever the JNM grew strong. While the JNM gained supporters and political clout throughout the 1950s, the Brotherhood attained only minimal influence in national affairs before 1957. The membership of the JNM represented the new strata emerging within Jordan's new state institutions, while the Muslim Brotherhood and the Tahrir Party represented the more traditional middle stratum of merchants and landowners.[103] Accordingly, the Brotherhood and its affiliated party cannot be considered a component within the JNM and were not primary players in the political activities of the country prior to 1957. Their existence and growth do illustrate alternative agencies for mobilization within the society, however.

NUMBERS AND THE JORDANIAN NATIONAL MOVEMENT (JNM)

Because of the changing economic, political, and social scene, the Jordanian National Movement grew dramatically in size in the early 1950s. The exact numbers, however, are difficult to determine.[104] The leaders of the parties naturally exaggerate the numbers. Bahjat Abu Gharbiyah,

Abd al-Rahman Shuqayr, and Ya'qub Ziyadin placed the membership of the parties in the thousands.[105] As Ziyadin said, "Our people are nationalists and we were good agitators. We knew how to get in touch with the people, to defend our liberty, defend our independence . . . and the people listened to us."[106] On the other end of the spectrum stand the historians and the diplomats. According to Shaul Mishal, Peter Gubser, Amnon Cohen, and the British diplomats assigned to Jordan in the 1950s, the parties could count on only a few hundred members.[107]

The answer lies somewhere in between these two extremes and comes down to different definitions of party activist and sympathizer. Clearly, the activist element comprised a small number of people, probably close to the various figures the historians and diplomats calculated. Enormous numbers of people, however, came out in support of the parties' causes, seen in both the demonstrations and the votes in the ballot boxes. Across the board, the small leadership structure of each party was made up of the graduates of the universities of the region, particularly the American University of Beirut and Damascus University. The activist cadres came generally from the teachers, the students, and the professional classes, all with secondary school or university experience. Education had mobilized new classes of the population to consider it their duty to work to better the world around them. With the expansion of educational services in the 1950s came more opportunities for interaction between the party leaders and the student body. Teachers maintained their roles as motivators for the students, urging them to learn skills required for the new political and economic realities, but to think also about possible solutions to regional and national problems. For many of these students, this mobilization continued to mean opposition to Hashemite policies. Tens of thousands more joined in the demonstrations because of their own particular grievances against the state, based on economic and political conditions. As Bseiso analyzes, in any given demonstration, ten or fifteen people might come from the Communist Party, five from the Ba'thists, and ten from the Nationalists, but the vast majority were just "normal people."[108]

Another question that arises is the influence, comparatively, of the parties themselves, versus their leaders. Did people follow a particular leader because of a particular set of political beliefs? Or, did they follow a particular leader because of the promise of goods and services to be delivered? If "everybody" joined, did they all have the same political commitment and understanding of the issues? These questions are difficult to answer because men like 'Abdullah al-Rimawi, Sulayman al-Nabulsi, and Abd al-Rahman Shuqayr were influential and popular in their own right. The doctors in the group, in particular, gained support from the many people they served in their clinics. The mere fact that these men formed a new urban professional intelligentsia put them into a unique category in the society. People admired them for having been educated in a new fashion, just as in the African village Ngugi wa Thiong'o described. They stood as leaders of a new kind of community, a community many clamored to join. They represented a new kind of knowledge and outlook about the world, articulated in a new kind of nationalist message. In demonstrations and lectures throughout the 1950s, people sang songs about men like al-Rimawi, Ziyadin, and Shuqayr, as a sign of the admiration and passion they felt for them. These men took advantage of the personalized political structure that had marked Arab society for so many centuries. Thus, they served as the new middlemen, the new *za'ims*, for the urban areas, because they provided necessary services and articulated grievances to the governing bodies. Through their new offices, they served as the conduits for politicizing whole new segments of the population, particularly the recent urban migrants. In the 1950s, this process meant politicizing people to support the goals of the JNM. Those party leaders fortunate enough to have tribal, village, and family connections tapped into them, convincing their allies to become members of their parties. For example, most of Nabil Haddadin's relatives in Ma'een were Communists.[109] Hamad al-Farhan stated the common opinion that "if I am a Communist, I like my daughter, my wife to become the same."[110]

Party affiliation supplemented the popularity these men acquired on their own. Hamad al-Farhan believes that the parties' platforms proved to be more influential than the standing of their leaders.[111] Ali al-Mahafazah concurs, saying that while al-Rimawi was a popular figure in his own right, he was connected to the Ba'th Party throughout the 1950s; people voted for him precisely because of his Ba'th ideas.[112] For example, the songs sung for al-Rimawi always mentioned the Ba'th. Bseiso feels that the people believed that the individual "should work for the interest of the country and the future so they joined the parties."[113] Overall, as al-Farhan says of the parties, "the parties were kind of the first experiment of political movement, first experiment [in Jordan]. They were not adamantly opposed to the regime. They did not have objections to the behavior of the king. The king was new; he didn't make mistakes [in the first years]. And they wanted more services, basically more services to the people which is [the duty] of the government. Okay? They wanted more links with the Arab world, basically Nasser, which the king did not like."[114] The party leaders spoke about these issues and did so in a dramatic fashion, from the roofs of their clinics and as they led demonstrations through the streets of the cities. The leaders appeared as activists, while the state appeared to plod along behind its British overseers. And that image of the British overseer was reiterated by the party leaders, and Nasser, throughout the decade. As the outsiders, the leaders of the JNM could promise a panacea to their supporters and never seem to fail. The JNM's easy-to-understand slogans—"Arab nationalism" and "anti-imperialism"—generated support for their Movement, albeit uncritical, from enormous numbers of people.[115] People came out to cheer on the group that attacked imperialism the most vociferously. The message disseminated by the parties, and absorbed by much of the urban populace, was that once imperialism was destroyed, all the other problems would disappear quickly thereafter.[116]

Another question thus arises when discussing the JNM: can it be called a unified movement? The answer is, yes, the JNM can be called a unified movement, because the parties advocated so many of the same policies. Few substantive differences existed between the political platforms. On a larger plane, the commitment to revolutionary change, the similarities in social class among the leaders, and the means by which they all recruited supporters are alike enough to put forward a case for unity. The men of all these parties met in the same clubs, gave lectures in the same forums, and read the same newspapers. They attended different universities, but the very act of receiving education gave to them a sense of collegiality. No cadres thus emerged based on educational tracks, as the overall experience gained at institutions of higher education was more important. This unity, however, was not complete, or the JNM would have been a single party and not an umbrella movement of different parties. By the end of the decade, as the JNM grew more successful, unity of action became more difficult. By then, differences over tactics became an individual issue. An inherent contradiction existed in Jordan and within the JNM: realistically, to accomplish the primary goals of the JNM, the Hashemite regime would have to be overthrown; yet most of the leaders of the JNM were reluctant to go that far and most understood that they did not have the power to do so. The king and the "King's men" could not easily be pushed from the political stage, nor would Arab unity be easy to achieve. While out of power, this contradiction could be ignored, but once in power, the JNM's leaders began to differ over the speed with which the move toward Arab unity should be accomplished and the role the king should play in the new regime thus created. For the surviving leaders and members of the JNM, it has become axiomatic to blame 'Abdullah al-Rimawi for the political fragmentation that ultimately beset the JNM, to define him as the most "radical." Without a written record from his side, it is impossible to gauge the truth of these statements. However, this example illustrates a factor important to recognize about the JNM. The JNM's strength always relied on a combination of popular support for the individual leaders themselves and the ideology presented by the parties' platforms. When in power, the new government officials would find their individual preferences becoming more important as they tried to resolve the problems they had always criticized while outside the halls of power. The contradiction between Arab unity and Hashemite power could no longer be ignored. Thus, the JNM proved to be a united movement while in opposition but had problems that kept it from truly maintaining that unity while in power.

CONCLUSION

Whereas the interwar years had seen only a small segment of the population politicized by the new agencies built by the Hashemite state, the British Mandate, and the surrounding Arab countries, the 1950s saw an explosion in these kinds of institutions. In Jordan, the basic pillars of the state held—the "King's men," the merchants, the bedouin, and the peasants—and would prove pivotal in Spring 1957 when the state and opposition came into direct conflict with each other. In the meantime, an increasing number of people began to question the political tenets of the regime. The vast majority of these were the Jordanians and Palestinians exposed to the largest number of new agencies and new stimuli in the cities. The urban areas became the focus of political activism throughout the 1950s precisely because of the concentration of people and agencies inside of them. The Jordanian National Movement, throughout the 1950s, put forward the message that its organizations and its national platform provided the answers more and more people were seeking for the questions posed about socioeconomic change and national identity. By implication, the Hashemites had failed to do so.

OPPOSITION AND COOPERATION: THE STATE AND THE JORDANIAN NATIONAL MOVEMENT (JNM)

1952–1956

. . . a period of tempestuous rebirth among the people.[1]

YAʿQUB ZIYADIN, DESCRIBING
THE POLITICAL SITUATION IN JORDAN
IN 1953

*The Arab people in Jordan in their entirety rose to say
no to imperialism and its underlings. Yes, they said no, while
baring their breasts to the bullets and the threat of the suppression
of their liberties.*[2]

ʿABDULLAH AL-RIMAWI, DISCUSSING
THE BAGHDAD PACT DEMONSTRATIONS
OF 1955–1956

The 1950s witnessed a confluence of events that catapulted the Jordanian National Movement (JNM) to prominence in national affairs. With the assassination of King ʿAbdullah and the ascension to the throne of Talal and then Husayn, the political system became less controlled from the top, less engineered by the Hashemites. This opening allowed the Movement's leaders to find more avenues for political expression. In the early 1950s, the liberalization of the political system under the new kings seemed to presage a peaceful transition from the established political leaders to a "new" generation. The regime granted political parties the right to form, eased censorship rules, and allowed opposition politicians the right to enter parliament. The socioeconomic changes taking place, particularly in the urban areas, were now met by political freedoms granting the National Movement and its followers legal stages from which to work. However, tensions arose between the regime and the leaders of the Jordanian National Movement as the decade progressed because the demand for political access made by the parties implied a wholesale overhaul of the Hashemite regime. As the Jordanian National Movement moved to the political left, closer to Gamal Abdel Nasser's position, and as the urban streets became political battlegrounds, King Husayn clamped down on Movement activities. Thus, cycles of liberalization and repression took place throughout the 1950s. The last liberalization rotation culminated in the period between October 1956 and April 1957, when Sulayman al-Nabulsi served as prime minister of a nationalist government.

Throughout this period, the Hashemite regime represented, for the leaders of the Movement and their expanding cadres of followers, imperialist control and an exclusive political system; or, in other words, the "old" system of governance. The Movement symbolized, in contrast, complete freedom from all outside control, victory over the Israelis—via the agency of Nasser—and the inevitable route toward unity in the Arab world. In the "new" system advocated by the National Movement, new types of collective action—strikes, street demonstrations, boycotts, political party organizing—proved to be the most politically influential and popular. A "new" leadership accompanied them.

As they had been doing since the Mandate period, the National Movement's leaders couched their grievances in a nationalized language. In this political language, anti-imperialism meant anti-Hashemite feeling because of the British role in the state's very creation. No matter how King Husayn professed support for Arab nationalist goals, he could not extricate himself from this historical connection. Every message of the JNM stated the mantra of Arab nationalism, with the implied idea that Arab unity would provide the panacea for all of Jordan's problems. Even though the National Movement worked within the limits of the Jordanian political scene throughout the 1950s, every demand was designed to lead toward eventual Arab unity. Political freedoms in Jordan would allow more voices to be heard, to put forward demands for unity; Palestinian participation presaged greater Arab momentum toward returning the homeland. The JNM may have been working within the Jordanian political body, but the ties of the Arabs provided the ideological and emotional bond. The JNM remained united through this period because of the broad umbrella this Arab nationalism afforded them.

'ABDULLAH'S ASSASSINATION
AND THE NEW KING

A Palestinian tailor's apprentice shot 'Abdullah as he entered the al-Aqsa Mosque in Jerusalem on July 20, 1951. 'Abdullah's bodyguards quickly killed the assailant, and the government subsequently arrested hundreds of Palestinians in order to determine the extent of the conspiracy. In the end, ten people came up for trial, two of them in absentia. Three relatives of the Mufti of Jerusalem were included, and one of them, Dr. Musa al-Husayni, was named the chief conspirator. Of the ten, six, including al-Husayni, were sentenced to death. The other four were acquitted.

'Abdullah's death marked the end of the first period of Jordanian existence. In the vacuum left by 'Abdullah's assassination, the "King's men," who had faithfully executed his policies since the 1920s, now found themselves in decision-making positions. Tawfiq Abu'l-Huda arose as the most powerful of these men in the two years after 'Abdullah's death as he, first, garnered enough support among the other "King's men" to become prime minister and, second, maneuvered, along with Alec Kirkbride, the British ambassador, to have Talal, 'Abdullah's oldest son, chosen as king.[3] With 'Abdullah no longer standing as the most powerful of the politicians in the country, more of an oligarchy emerged during the transition period, wherein the "King's men" accrued far more power than they had ever held before.

Talal became king of Jordan on September 6, 1951, and left his mark on the political system of Jordan by holding new elections and promulgating a new constitution. The people of Jordan viewed Talal as an opponent of Britain and a proponent of democracy and liberalization. As a result, his ascension to the throne generated a great deal of popular support in the country. The subsequent elections of 1951 brought in a number of opposition deputies and solidified the opposition bloc under the Palestinian deputies, 'Abdullah al-Rimawi and 'Abdullah Na'was. Talal's constitution, ratified on January 1, 1952, granted the citizenry key civil rights and opened up the political system to more voices. In its tenets, the constitution guaranteed freedom of opinion in speech, writing, and the press. The opposition forces that had been clamoring to enter the political arena now had official platforms from which to speak and gather supporters.

Talal, however, remained on the throne for less than two years as British and Jordanian officials came to understand the full extent of his mental instability. Led by Prime Minister Tawfiq Abu'l-Huda, the Majlis al-Nuwwab unanimously voted to depose him on August 11, 1952, and replace him with his oldest son, Husayn. This change inaugurated a new period in Jordan's political history, as the young king came to power hoping to build on the work of both his father and his grandfather. His goal was to continue the new liberalization process begun by Talal but to maintain the preeminent position of the Hashemite throne established by 'Abdullah.

COOPERATION AND CONFLICT

Husayn's ascension to the throne on May 2, 1953, marked the beginning of his project to define his monarchy, vis-à-vis his grandfather and the changing social milieu around him. At eighteen, he did not immediately command the respect accorded his grandfather, so had to win the support of the population. To gain that respect, King Husayn had to make his mark on Jordan; he had to show that he was capable of governing the country in accordance with the new realities surrounding him. One step in this regard was to accelerate the process of liberalization begun during his father's reign. Husayn chose to weaken the influence of the "King's men" and promote younger, more liberal-minded politicians to the posts of power, and they, in turn, passed the legislation required to open up Jordan's political arena to more voices and actors. In particular, he pushed from the political scene Tawfiq Abu'l-Huda, the man who had engineered his rise to the throne and who had angered so many of the politicians and activists in the country because of the repressive tactics that accompanied this effort. In his place, the king appointed Fawzi al-Mulqi, the first native-born prime minister, a man who had worked within the administration for years and had become known for his liberal ideas. In key pieces of legislation soon passed, political parties gained the right to form, the press found itself functioning within lighter censorship rules, and groups could publicly assemble. Governments also had to receive an absolute majority of the deputies in a vote of confidence.

However, Husayn's form of liberalization never included instituting a full range of political changes. As Shahid Qadir et al. define the concept, "political liberalisation implies a process of political change controlled from the top down, as a means of preserving most of the *status quo*."[4] Taking al-Mulqi's reforms to their logical end would have meant a dramatic change in the power structure of the country, commensurate with the socioeconomic transformations already reconfiguring people's relationships. The most obvious sign that liberalization would not be al-lowed to grow unhindered was the passage of a new Anti-Communist Law in December 1953. It assigned imprisonment with hard labor for any person who joined a Communist organization, spread Communist propaganda, published Communist documents, or came into possession of Communist literature.

As the state and opposition began to slowly work within this new re-gime, Israeli infiltration into Jordan increased and made al-Mulqi's po-litical position precarious. The worst Israeli incursion occurring during this period targeted the village of Qibya, on the West Bank. In this raid, Ariel Sharon led an Israeli attack against the village on the night of Oc-tober 14–15, 1953. The troop demolished the village and killed sixty-six people in the attack. The Jordanian press and the opposition retaliated with calls for the dismissal of John Bagot Glubb and those British officers in the Arab Legion who had refused to properly protect the frontier vil-lages. The political parties organized demonstrations, filling the streets of Jordan's cities. In Amman, the demonstrators attacked the American Point-IV officers and demanded the ouster of Glubb. On October 18, about twenty opposition leaders held a meeting in Ramallah where a number made speeches denouncing the government for failing to protect the Palestinians from Israeli infiltration and for allowing Glubb to remain at his post.

Al-Mulqi's government then had to ride a fine line between appeas-ing the British, appearing strong against the Israelis, and liberalizing the government. While the British and the "King's men" advocated Jorda-nian nonaggression against these Israeli attacks, a growing percentage of the population demanded swift retaliation. All segments of the politi-cal spectrum—from the "King's men," who felt he was catering to the opposition, to the opposition, who felt he was too weak—came out to denounce al-Mulqi. Liberalization's inherent contradictions quickly led to problems for the state and the opposition, as the former wanted to maintain the power status quo and the latter felt the reforms had not been revolutionary enough. As a sign of the limited nature of the liber-alization program, King Husayn decided that al-Mulqi had failed to rule effectively and opted to return to the "King's men," appointing Tawfiq Abu'l-Huda to the prime ministership in May 1954.

Abu'l-Huda, however, faced a difficult task in gaining a vote of confi-dence from the Majlis al-Nuwwab because of his history of conflict with the opposition. In a telegram to the king, the leaders of the National Movement, including al-Rimawi, Na'was, and Abu Gharbiyah, stated their opposition to Abu'l-Huda's appointment by writing that "Abul

Huda with his terrible history, ideas, dictatorship, and execution of imperialistic plans constitutes a danger to the present and the future of the Arab people of Jordan."[5] To forestall a negative vote, Abu'l-Huda asked the king to dissolve parliament before that session could take place in June 1954. The decree the king subsequently issued declared that the deputies were influenced by personal considerations, many of which conflicted with the best interests of the nation.[6] After the dissolution of parliament, Abu'l-Huda promptly suspended some of the weekly newspapers, including al-Ra'y [The Opinion—Movement of Arab Nationalists], al-Yaqtha [The Awakening—Ba'th Party], al-Jabha [The Front—Communist Party], al-Watan [The Nation], al-Ahd al-Jadid [The New Oath], and Sawt al-Sha'ab [Voice of the People]. During this period, Musallam Bseiso reports of al-Hawadath that "every couple of weeks we [were] closed for two weeks or three weeks. The censorship does not allow [us] to publish."[7] When a particular article was censored, Bseiso would leave the designated area of the paper white to indicate what the government had done.

From that point forward, Abu'l-Huda followed a policy of harsh repression against the political parties and their leaders. As part of his strategy, Abu'l-Huda issued three Defense Regulations, granting the cabinet increased power over public organizations and activities.[8] Given a legal justification by these and similar laws, the government frequently arrested the leaders of the parties because of their activities. When asked about the number of times the police arrested him in the 1950s, Bahjat Abu Gharbiyah stated, "I was put in jail many times. Every year. For two months, six months, something like that. For instance, 1951, in Azraq. In 1952, in Shobeck."[9] Never at any time did he face a court of law.

Al-Jafr prison, located far out in the Jordanian desert, served as the most important prison during the 1950s. Ya'qub Ziyadin took his first trip there in February 1953.[10] That day, he and some other prisoners were shackled and put into jeeps to be transported across the desert. After a few hours of rough riding, he spotted the prison rising from the desert like an ancient castle. Surrounding the main building stood some tents and barbed wire. The weather remained beautiful for the first few days, so Ziyadin began to wonder about the reputedly horrible conditions at the prison. However, one morning, not long after he arrived, the wind began to blow violently and, within minutes, had escalated into a major storm. The wind gathered up rocks and threw them into the men's faces. The intensity of the wind forced them to remain in their places shielding their bodies as much as possible from the storm. When the wind subsided, the administration moved the men into the barracks and crowded them into a space fit for a third the number of prisoners. Food and sanitary conditions were very poor, so to enliven their days the men discussed political topics as well as medical issues and literature. After three months, Ziyadin was released and allowed to return home. Similarly, the Jordanian government sent Tal'at Harb to al-Jafr a number of times. He was first sent there in 1953 because of his participation in a demonstration in Ramallah demanding the establishment of democratic freedoms and an end to Glubb Pasha's interference in domestic affairs.[11] While there, he learned to smoke as a way to offset the pains he felt during the many hunger strikes they held.[12] Despite the conditions, most of the memoirs relate how al-Jafr became something of a cultural and political center because the prisoners contributed their particular skills, be it medicine or language or philosophy, to teach the other prisoners.[13] The incarceration of so many teachers and intellectuals created an atmosphere where prisoners wanted to both teach and learn about new ideas.

Once released, Ziyadin returned to the hospital in Jerusalem to discover that he had been fired, not because of the quality of his work but because of his political activities. To earn a living, he set up a small private clinic specializing in tonsillectomies. He won the admiration of the city because he charged very little for this and other such procedures.[14] As a small country, Jordan has been able to supervise the employment practices of both private and public companies, from the 1950s until the present day. An active member of any of the political parties of the 1950s faced not only imprisonment for his activities but also unemployment, as companies were required to check with the mukhabarat [intelligence service] before hiring any new employees.[15] The penalties also extended to members of the families of activists, as a son or a brother of a party member also faced possible unemployment and persecution for a relative's actions. Since Jordan, in the 1950s, experienced a disproportionately high ratio of dependents to workers, political activity engendered an enormous risk to the participants and their families. Because of this situation, party activists had to have a strong family support system around them.

This era of conflict between the regime and the National Movement came to a climax during the October 16, 1954, elections. All the parties ran candidates as part of the 150 people competing for the forty seats in the Majlis al-Nuwwab.[16] Shuqayr reports that the month before the elections saw a constant stream of visitors to his medical clinic in downtown Amman. He set up a political club at his office and from there sent out flyers and messengers, coaxing the voters into supporting his candidacy. So many people came to the office that one night an impromptu demonstration erupted. Shuqayr and Nabih Irsheidat gave speeches criticizing the government for its repressive tactics during the campaign. When the police broke up the demonstration, participants roamed through the streets singing songs in support of Shuqayr. He also conducted meetings in a number of villages and bedouin campsites around Amman. In the days leading up to the elections, Shuqayr and his party colleagues felt confident that they would be victorious because of the support that had been pledged to them.

On the West Bank, Ziyadin ran for a seat in Jerusalem, organizing his campaign with a group of secondary school students and craftsmen. His program called for the termination of the Anglo-Jordanian Treaty, the guarantee of public freedoms, an end to exceptional laws, and a rejection of all colonial treaties. Driving around to the villages in an old car, he gave speeches denouncing General Glubb and calling for Arabization of the army. By identifying himself as the candidate of the poor, Ziyadin received a warm welcome in all the villages he entered.

Despite the fact that the government announced beforehand that the election would be free, many fraudulent practices occurred. Reports differ as to who led the movement to overturn the results, but most of the leaders and activists of the day pinpoint either Glubb or Prime Minister Abu'l-Huda as the chief culprit. For example, Bahjat Abu Gharbiyah reported that these elections were called "Glubb Pasha's elections" because he played such a large role in manipulating the results.[17] Still others felt that Abu'l-Huda had the upper hand because he controlled more resources in the country.[18] While the cabinet initially informed the British embassy that efforts would only be made to oppose the Communist and Ba'th candidates, the ambassador reported to the London Foreign Office that the government clearly targeted other leftist politicians as well.[19] For example, a month before the elections, the interior minister prohibited the holding of any meetings at night, regardless of the political position of the participants. In addition, the minister of the interior greatly inflated the number of registered voters so that he could manipulate the results later, if needed; the ministry's figure of 445,978 voters represented a 30 percent increase over the 1951 elections.[20] Another way the government manipulated the results was to have General Glubb hand each soldier in the army a government-approved slate of candidates. On election day, regiments of the army were sent to vote in districts where the government feared an opposition candidate might win. Bedouin tribesmen living near Amman reported to Shuqayr that they would not be able to support his candidacy because the authorities had put too much pressure on them not to do so.[21] When the government's actions became apparent on the morning of the election, ten candidates in Amman withdrew their names. Abd al-Rahman Shuqayr joined this boycott because, on the morning of the election, he saw, with his own eyes, ballots being falsified.[22]

Party-led demonstrations erupted throughout the country in reaction to the government's manipulation of the results. After years spent listening to and reading about the National Movement's ideas and goals, the urban population illustrated their support for the Movement in massive numbers. In Amman, demonstrators attacked the United States Information Agency (USIA) building, and many demonstrators were killed and wounded when the city called out the Arab Legion to fight against Jordanian civilians for the first time in its history. In downtown Amman, protesters erected barricades of stones at various places to ward off the army while calling out anti-American and anti-Glubb slogans. The government imposed martial law, but the demonstrations spread to Irbid, Salt, Nablus, Jerusalem, and Ramallah. These demonstrations continued for three days before the army and police managed to disperse the crowds. In the end, the Jordanian Directorate-General of Press and Publications announced that 14 people had been killed during the election demonstrations, with 117 injured, including 75 military personnel and 42 civilians.[23]

Many party leaders were detained during the course of these events. Bahjat Abu Gharbiyah and 'Abdullah Na'was were arrested and imprisoned for months. "The Za'im," Muhammad Bajis al-Majali, was sentenced to al-Jafr for a year. Ziyadin was, yet again, sent to al-Jafr, along with nine other Communists, after failing in his candidacy. Soon after the police arrested Ziyadin, they returned to his home and took his wife, his two sons, and his mother in a car to Ziyadin's hometown outside of Karak as punishment for Ziyadin's political activities. After spending ten months in al-Jafr, Ziyadin was transferred to the central prison in Amman, where he and his colleagues went on a hunger strike to demand better accommodations. In Amman, the guards attempted to intimidate the prisoners into signing petitions pledging to forgo political work in the future. When all refused, a stalemate loomed until Hazza' al-Majali, the interior minister, intervened and allowed the prisoners to leave without signing the pledge.[24] Ziyadin immediately traveled to Karak, where he joined his wife and sons and opened a medical clinic.

For three days, Shuqayr managed to hide from the armed forces in the homes of friends. Before the government discovered his hiding place, Shuqayr escaped to Damascus dressed as a woman. When his car arrived at the Syrian-Jordanian border, the guards looked at the woman's passport proffered to them and completely ignored the "woman" sitting in the front seat. Once in Syria, he changed back into his own clothes and asked the Syrian border authorities for asylum. After two hours the decision arrived from Damascus that Shuqayr could remain in the country under government protection. Leftist and nationalist politicians greeted him warmly. Syrian newspapers published his story of Glubb's activities, the falsification of the election results, and the "bloody battle" that followed during the protest demonstrations.[25] During his subsequent stay in Damascus, Shuqayr opened a clinic to support himself and his family. From there, Shuqayr wrote a number of articles for the Syrian press sharply criticizing Abu'l-Huda's election and his repressive regime. The British disliked Shuqayr's writings, so continually pressured the Syrian government to return him to Jordan for prosecution. The Syrians refused. Only in May 1955, when Sa'id al-Mufti had replaced Abu'l-Huda as prime minister, did the Jordanian government officially welcome Shuqayr back to Jordan. Once Shuqayr crossed the border into Ramtha, a large number of people greeted him, and many cars accompanied him along the route to Amman.

As a result of government manipulation, the newly elected Majlis al-Nuwwab was composed mostly of loyal deputies. Abu'l-Huda could count on at least thirty votes but might have had up to thirty-four seats in the Majlis.[26] The National Socialist Party (NSP) and the National Front each won two seats, with all the Ba'th Party candidates losing their election bids. Abu'l-Huda had succeeded in forming a parliament quiescent to his wishes but at the cost of weakening support throughout the country.[27] The general populace understood what the government had done and forcibly illustrated its opposition in demonstrations and strikes, guided by years of National Movement tutelage and organization.

The cycle of political struggle between 1952 and 1954 had taken the state and opposition from a brief period of cooperation to a potentially stronger period of repression. This "period of tempestuous rebirth among the people" had altered the political balance, however. The government appeared stronger, as it successfully elected a quiescent parliament, but in fact its repressive techniques had proven to much of the population that the National Movement's messages were more suitable for the country than the regime's. As the National Movement gained in popularity after the October 1954 elections, a new cycle emerged, but this time the path went from conflict to cooperation as the streets and the opposition gained prominence in national affairs. The regime had to concede to the opposition's demands to reject the Baghdad Pact and oust General Glubb from power.

BAGHDAD PACT

The British Baghdad Pact[28] plan was designed to create a "northern tier" of states, namely of Turkey, Iraq, Iran, and Pakistan, to ensure that a geographic battle line existed between the Soviet Union and Western interests in the Arab world. To further hamper the Soviet Union's entry into the area via other routes, such as arms sales and financial aid, Britain also tried to entice Egypt and Syria into joining the Pact. Both refused. When Iraqi demands to include at least one other Arab state, to legitimize its own involvement, became more persistent, Britain turned to Jordan as the most likely candidate for membership. However, Britain underestimated the power, strength, and popularity of both the leaders of the Jordanian opposition and the Egyptian-Syrian-Saudi camp's ability to muster forces sufficient to defeat their efforts. While King Husayn and many of his advisors preferred to accept the Pact, in the belief that the additional military materials promised would protect Jordan from an Israeli invasion, the opposition leaders and the majority of the urban population came out in violent protest against the increased imperialist control they feared would result from the Pact.

In addition to highlighting internal rivalries, the Baghdad Pact events illustrated that between 1955 and 1957, Egypt, Syria, Saudi Arabia, and Iraq all became embroiled in domestic Jordanian politics. Egypt and Syria had experienced revolutions to replace postindependence governments, and Cold War politics entered the realm of Arab affairs. After their respective revolutions, Egypt and Syria distanced themselves from their earlier colonizers and looked to alliances within the region and new relationships with the Soviet Union. Saudi Arabia, a much more conservative nation, supported the Egyptian-Syrian camp until mid-1957 because of its opposition to Hashemite rule in Iraq and Jordan. On the other side stood the Iraqis, led in the 1950s by the Hashemite King Faysal II and his aides, Nuri al-Sa'id and Prince Abdul Illah, all of whom openly supported and advocated alliances with the Western powers. As a result of their disparate ideologies and competitive natures, the Egyptians, the Syrians, the Saudis, and the Iraqis all used Jordan as a battlefield to advance their national interests. The leaders of the Jordanian National Movement openly sided with the Egyptians and the Syrians over the other forces and took advantage of the ideological battles waged to increase their own power and influence in Jordan. Surrounding these activities, the circumstances of the Cold War infiltrated the Middle East because the United States and the Soviet Union demanded that the Arab nations choose allies on one side or the other, the West or the East.

Pivotal in this process was Gamal Abdel Nasser, the self-professed leader of the Arab nationalist movement in the 1950s and 1960s. The members of the Jordanian National Movement, however, initially hesitated to select Nasser as their ideological leader because they questioned a number of his methods and policies. The first of which was Nasser's attacks on the Muslim Brotherhood in Egypt, a group that had supported the Revolution of 1952 but which Nasser shunned once in power. When a member of the Brotherhood allegedly attempted to kill Nasser in October 1954, he retaliated by having six of the members hanged as punishment. This act engendered anger throughout the Middle East; in Jordan a group of seven hundred students, led by the leaders of the Jordanian branch of the Muslim Brotherhood, demonstrated in Amman on December 8, 1954,[29] and on December 10 a successful general strike took place in Amman. This event represented one of the few times in the 1950s that the Muslim Brotherhood and the JNM's parties worked together for joint goals. The second reason for Jordanian displeasure with Nasser was the fact that he banned political parties from functioning in Egypt.[30] Nasser had, in place of the Egyptian political parties, created a single political organization, the Liberation Rally, in January 1953. While the government designated it a political party, its primary goal was to elicit support for the new Egyptian leadership, not to lobby the government for change or to field independent candidates for elective office.[31] Jordanian Communist Party literature attacked the Egyptian leadership for disbanding the parties and imprisoning many workers.[32] Munif al-Razzaz of the Jordanian Ba'th Party criticized the Egyptian Revolution for not being a mass-based revolution, but one led by a few military officers.[33] The Free Officers also disliked the new Egyptian leadership because it proffered no help for the officers' burgeoning movement.

This negative view of Nasser changed with the Egyptian leader's rising prestige throughout the Middle East and Third World. According to Abd al-Rahman Shuqayr, the Jordanian people disliked Nasser until the signing of the Czech arms deal in 1955 and the Egyptian extension of diplomatic relations to China in May 1956. At that point, Arab public opinion turned in his favor, and the people admired him because he had become a leader in the fight against colonialism.[34] The newspaper *Filastin*, published out of Jerusalem, defended the arms deal as well, stating that it did not represent a move by Egypt to enter the Soviet bloc; rather it served as a strategic action to build up Egypt's military capacity. The editorial added that "America is anxious lest the rearming of Egypt should disturb stability in the Middle East. But there is no stability to be found in the Middle East, thanks to America's policy which undertook the establishment of the State of Israel in this sensitive spot in the world."[35] The Communist Party looked favorably on Nasser, particularly after the Czech arms deal, because this illustrated Soviet support for the Arab cause and Nasser's commitment to independence from imperialist control. Despite their earlier rejection, the Free Officers also came out in wholehearted support of Nasser after he began to back the cause of Arab unity.

Ba'th and National Socialist Party members also gradually came to support Nasser's activities and ideologies, despite their earlier misgivings. While still critical of Nasser and the "Arab personality" that he had created for himself, al-Razzaz acknowledged that "Nasser entered the heart of every Arab and became, by rights, the leader of the progressive Arab movement and its general inspiration" after negotiating the British evacuation from Egypt, completing the Czech arms deal, and advocating a policy of positive neutrality.[36] The majority of the members of the Ba'th Party and the Movement of Arab Nationalists wholeheartedly supported Nasser's ideology at that point. 'Abdullah al-Rimawi, in particular, came out as a fervent Nasserite. Even the National Socialist Party, which had clung to its view that unity between Iraq and Jordan should be the first step toward complete Arab unity, began to look to Egypt and Syria to fulfill this role after Jordan rejected the Baghdad Pact.[37]

The disaffected Palestinian population proved to be a particularly receptive arena for Nasser's message, because he continually highlighted the need to end their tragedy. Nasser placed himself at the head of the ideological movement fighting to destroy Israel and to push from the Middle East the imperialist nations that had aided in its creation. When the National Movement made statements similar to Nasser's, it increased its support among the Palestinians. The Palestinians would always represent a larger percentage of supporters for the JNM's parties and would often, as illustrated by 'Abdullah al-Rimawi and 'Abdullah Na'was, be more radical politically than their colleagues.

Once the Arab world opened up to Nasser, the Egyptian president sent his military attachés to all the Arab states to make contact with the various nationalist political parties functioning in each country. Shuqayr, personally, met with the Egyptian military attaché for Jordan and maintained extensive relations with the Egyptian journalists of the Middle East News Agency (MENA) stationed in Jordan throughout the 1950s. Other Egyptian representatives served as links to the Jordanian Communists and Ba'thists, and to Sulayman al-Nabulsi and Shafiq Irsheidat of the NSP.

Nasser's growing popularity on the political field meant that his radio broadcasts took on added importance. The Arab cultural, linguistic, and political bond came alive through such broadcasts. An attack against one Arab meant an attack against them all in the vocabulary of Nasser's Arab nationalism. The broadcasts themselves used simplistic language and concepts specifically designed to inflame people, to cater to people's awakening political awareness. These broadcasts were crude propaganda, but they worked because they spoke to the passions spreading throughout the area. They specifically spoke to the listeners, "O Arab," to exhort them to action on behalf of Nasser and, secondarily, the broader goals of Arab nationalism. Schools and political organizing on the local level in Jordan prepared the population to analyze and understand the nationalized vocabulary exploited in these broadcasts. Demonstrations and strikes, equally crude a political tool, were the result. In Shuqayr's opinion, Nasser's speech of July 26, 1956, announcing the nationalization of the Suez Canal, inflamed millions of Arabs from the ocean to the Persian Gulf because he sharply criticized Western colonialism and pushed for positive neutrality as an alternative to Western-dominated alliances.[38]

Nasser promoted a similar campaign for the Baghdad Pact, to guarantee its defeat in Jordan. Egypt's Sawt al-'Arab station kept up a virulent campaign attacking the Pact, Iraq, and Israel. As rumors of the Pact surfaced, Sawt al-'Arab said, in January 1954, that a "dark cloud had started to gather in the sky of the Arab East."[39] Just before Turkey and Iraq signed the first agreement, the broadcaster stated that "every Arab, bewildered by Iraq's action, asks himself: what will be the fate of Arab unity and the 80,000,000 Arabs? Are we heading towards solidarity and strength, or towards discord and disintegration?"[40] Before long, Egyptian radio began to equate the new Pact not only with the disintegration of Arab unity but with the Palestinian issue as well. "Nuri al-Said says strangely that the Iraqi-Turkish alliance would add to the strength of the Arabs and strengthen hope for the salvation of Palestine. But how can it do all this when every word of this agreement is enough to kill any hope for the solution of the Palestine question?"[41] This broadcast resulted from the fact that rumors abounded that Israel would also become a member of the Baghdad Pact and further endanger the lives of the Arabs.

As part of the competition between Nasser and Iraqi political leader Nuri al-Sa'id, the Egyptian radio broadcasts particularly criticized the latter's activities by saying, for example, "today the peoples and States of the Arab League are witnessing a new and barefaced treason, the hero of which is Nuri al-Said."[42] When the British turned their attention to Jordan, Sawt al-'Arab called on the Jordanian people to oppose the Pact, reporting that "the Zionist-imperialist alliance comes out with new plots against the Arabs every day. . . . People of Jordan, hold fast with your

Arab brothers!"[43] The overall message of each of these missives was that
the Arab world faced the greatest imperialist threat it had ever encountered and must unite to successfully defeat it. Constantly, day after day,
for almost a year, these Egyptian broadcasts attacked the Pact. The Jordanians heard these reports and came out en masse in favor of the Egyptian position. Abu Gharbiyah stated that Sawt al-'Arab aided his efforts
enormously, as the whole National Movement was able to benefit from
the messages delivered.[44]

The obvious opposition to the Pact throughout Jordan made British
officials initially reluctant to pressure Jordan too strongly. Starting as
early as March 1955, telegrams from the British embassy in Amman to
the Foreign Office in London spoke of officials' reticence in the face
of this opposition.[45] The campaign waged by the National Movement
proved so successful that the American analysis of the atmosphere stated
that the "government cannot or will not carry through 'unpopular' policies. This weakness [is] growing and mass pressure now so sways Amman authorities [that] they fear mob action if government tries to move
against current Arab thinking."[46] The National Movement raised the
specter of mob action in speech after speech in the months leading up to
the Baghdad Pact debates.

In November 1955, British officials reversed their policy and announced that they planned to initiate a strong effort to persuade Jordan
to enter the Pact.[47] While the cabinet deliberated over the Baghdad Pact,
the National Movement brought people out into the streets to forestall
Jordan's entrance into it. When Turkish President Celal Bayar visited
Jordan on behalf of the Pact, the streets erupted and a commercial strike
paralyzed Amman. Communist-organized student demonstrations broke
out in Jenin, Tulkarm, Salfit, and Nablus in reaction to Jordan's negotiations with both the Turks and the British concerning the Pact. A few days
later, deputies in the Majlis al-Nuwwab protested against the visit and
against Jordan's entrance into the Baghdad Pact. 'Abd al-Qadir al-Salih,
a Communist member of the National Front and a member of the majlis,
called on the government to reject all foreign pacts, but especially the
one headed by Turkey and Pakistan.[48]

Britain took the next step by sending to Amman its Commander of
the General Staff, Sir Gerald Templer, in order to negotiate the details
of the arrangement. Templer, in meetings with government officials,
promised to forward extra military material and financial help to the Jordanian armed forces in return for Jordan's acceptance of the Baghdad
Pact. The prime minister at the time, Sa'id al-Mufti, brought the issue
to the cabinet on December 10. The ministers examined a letter from

the British government granting various increases in aid, both financial and military.[49] Britain also agreed to consider a revision of the Anglo-Jordanian Treaty and to guarantee that the Baghdad Pact alliance would not infringe on Jordan's agreements with other countries. In a night-long meeting on December 12, the cabinet debated the issue. Four Palestinian members of the cabinet emerged from the meeting having resigned; al-Mufti's government subsequently fell. King Husayn then stepped forward and volunteered to sign the Baghdad Pact personally, but British Ambassador Charles Duke persuaded him to wait until a legitimate government could be convinced to do so.[50] King Husayn then asked Hazza' al-Majali to form a government for the express purpose of signing the Baghdad Pact.

With the fall of Sa'id al-Mufti's government and the formation of Hazza' al-Majali's on December 14, 1955, the entire country erupted into the most violent demonstrations the country had ever seen. A year of Sawt al-'Arab broadcasts and years of party organization by the Jordanian National Movement came to fruition in mid-December 1955 to defeat the Baghdad Pact proponents. The urbanization process Jordan experienced in the 1950s placed large proportions of the population within city boundaries in late 1955 and supplied the manpower needed to successfully illustrate the people's opposition to the Baghdad Pact. New kinds of urban networks and collectivized actions, appealing to a much broader segment of the population, organized people around the Movement's nationalized message. Unemployment, life in the refugee camps, and dissatisfaction with government repression generated the necessary passion. Ali Abu Nuwar has stated that Templer's visit "brought the mass of the people to war."[51] Ziyadin added that the masses were mobilized and completely conscious of the dangers of enemy pacts because of the campaign the Communist Party had waged for the two years prior to the crisis.[52] Shuqayr felt that the Egyptian broadcasts were like magic because they made everyone hate the Baghdad Pact.[53] Hazza' al-Majali said that the rumor that Palestine would be lost as a result of the Baghdad Pact came off every tongue and galvanized people to protest.[54]

The leaders of the National Movement were ever-present during the demonstrations. The U.S. embassy in Amman reported that "the regularity of the demonstrations indicates organization. Further indication is given by the fact that secret, mimeographed or printed instructions were distributed to students of the different secondary schools in Amman on December 17."[55] Al-Nabulsi's name appeared throughout the demonstrations, as an indication of his leadership. He acknowledged later that he had, in fact, made a number of speeches during the demonstrations and believed that the "disturbances should not be referred to as mob actions but rather as demonstrations of the will of the people, a will which cannot be expressed through normal democratic channels because of the rigged elections of 1954."[56] Students made up a large bulk of the demonstrators. For example, Nabil Haddadin participated along with his sixth grade class; soon thereafter he joined the Communist Party.[57]

In many of the demonstrations, British, American, French, and Turkish installations came under attack because of the overriding anti-imperialist outrage. The British Chancery in Amman and the Turkish Consulate in Jerusalem became targets as a result. At the British diplomatic offices in Nablus, administrators were forced to take down the Union Jack and the coat of arms. A similar situation occurred at the U.S. Consulate in Jerusalem, where protesters tore down the American flag. The American ambassador, Richard Sanger, watched the demonstrations in Amman on December 17 and reported a large battle in the streets of the city between rock-throwing demonstrators and the Arab Legion.[58] When the soldiers retaliated by shooting into the air above the heads of the crowds and reinforcements arrived, "in that instant the demonstrations changed into riots."[59] Ziyadin led a demonstration through the streets of Karak, followed by hundreds of students, teachers, young men, and, for the first time, many of the *mukhtars*.[60] In front of the local authorities' building, he and others made speeches criticizing the Baghdad Pact and the activities of the imperialist nations dominating the Arab world.

Newspapers railed against the Baghdad Pact in yet another means by which information was disseminated to the population. *Filastin*, in an editorial, said that "the general attitude makes it incumbent upon us to decide that the Jordanians object to the Baghdad Pact. It is in the interest of Jordan to understand that it will suffer more than any other Arab State from the Arab disunity arising from its accession to this Pact."[61] *Al-Jihad* voiced a similar opinion in its editorial when it wrote, "The people of Jordan have proved to be vigilant. They have set an excellent example of their insistence on securing their full rights. They have given sufficient proof that they would remain alive even if they continued to live in camps and caves for ever [sic]."[62] Other newspapers' articles broadcast similar opinions to maintain the high level of political participation.

The government responded by sending out the Arab Legion to suppress the demonstrations and strikes. In the first days of the demonstrations, the Arab Legion was instructed to shoot only over the heads of the crowds. The Arab Legion forces found it difficult to subdue the crowds peacefully, however. One problem the Arab Legion faced was that its soldiers were trained for conventional warfare, not street fighting. Items such as tear gas canisters proved in short supply because no one prepared for demonstrations of this magnitude. Observers of the scenes during December 1955 report that the police and the Arab Legion initially proved incapable of stemming the demonstrations.[63] When peaceful measures proved inefficient, the army began to shoot at the demonstrators directly.[64] Whereas resorting to violence did quell the disturbances, many demonstrators were killed as a result. The Arab Legion arrested hundreds of people for participating in the demonstrations, including Shuqayr, al-Nabulsi, and Irsheidat. However, even as the Arab Legion shot at and arrested demonstrators, groups within the army opposed these measures because they sympathized with the perpetrators.[65] Factions emerged in the army, along the fault lines of the Free Officers' Movement. Those who opposed the Pact did so because they saw Israel as Jordan's enemy, not the Soviet Union.

As a direct result of the massive demonstrations, Hazza' al-Majali resigned from his post after only six days in office, and the king accompanied this resignation with the dismissal of parliament. Calm returned to the country as Ibrahim Hashim formed a caretaker government designed merely to ease the country into the upcoming elections, provisionally set for April 1956.[66] His cabinet included three ex–prime ministers and a number of other Hashemite loyalists. To further quiet the country, Hashim proclaimed that as leader of a caretaker government he lacked the authority to enter into any new pacts, foreign or Arab. As a conciliatory move, Hashim released all the political prisoners on January 1, 1956. Most emerged from al-Jafr and from the central prison in Amman, including, among the latter, al-Nabulsi, Irsheidat, and Shuqayr.[67] Large groups of people massed outside the prison in Amman, singing national songs and ululating, and once the prisoners were released, crowds paraded to each of their homes, shouting slogans against British colonialism and Glubb's leadership.[68]

Early January 1956 saw the country once again rise up, because the Supreme Council announced that King Husayn's dismissal of the parliament had been unconstitutional. Demonstrations erupted across the country as people became aware of the fact that the fraudulently elected parliament had regained power. On the first day of renewed disturbances, police came and arrested Ziyadin and sent him for a third trip to al-Jafr. The police sent so many people to the prison by that time that tents had to be erected to accommodate the large number of prisoners. By the end, more than one hundred Communists alone had been arrested. Many of these prisoners hailed from the Jordanian towns of Karak, Ma'an, Salt, and Madaba, so were not just Palestinians living in the West Bank. Back in Karak, townspeople formed a revolutionary committee to coordinate the strikes and demonstrations, an organizational system that had never been seen before in the town.[69] Students, teachers, party members, urban laborers, and shopkeepers walked side by side down the streets.[70] Throughout the country, demonstrators again attacked foreign institutions, shouted slogans against Glubb, and demanded that the government accept a recently pledged Egyptian-Syrian-Saudi offer to replace the British subsidy with their own aid.

As a result of these demonstrations, Ibrahim Hashim resigned after just seventeen days in office, replaced by Samir al-Rifaʿi, who had a mandate to restore law and order to the country. In his first act, al-Rifaʿi declared that Jordan would not only reject the Baghdad Pact but would also not negotiate any new pacts at that time. In his second act, al-Rifaʿi imposed a nationwide ten-day curfew and, under its provisions, arrested hundreds of people to guarantee that the streets cleared. King Husayn contemplated replacing the civilian government with a military regime because of the intensity of the demonstrations but decided against this move when al-Rifaʿi's mechanisms succeeded in quieting the country.[71] To support the regime, the British government voted to reinforce its armed forces in Cyprus and place its men stationed in Mafraq and Aqaba on alert. In early January 1956, the government received new radio equipment, so began jamming the Sawt al-ʿArab broadcasts.[72] This jamming continued almost nonstop until Husayn dismissed General Glubb on March 1.

The fall of al-Majali's government marked the fall of the Baghdad Pact in Jordan. Through raw street power, the National Movement had finally succeeded in forcing the Jordanian government to accede to its demands. The enormous numbers participating in the demonstrations and strikes in those few weeks reflect the strength of the message the National Movement had spread into the urban populace. The constant organizing efforts, the newspaper articles, and the demonstrations fed on the economic and political dissatisfaction felt by the urban populace. The demonstrations grew dramatically with each day and often grew larger than even the leaders of the Movement could control. The events of mid-December 1955 to early January 1956 changed Jordan's political path for the next year and a half. The National Movement's ideas proved so popular that the government had to incorporate them into its decision-making process for the first time in the country's history. As Hikmat al-Masri, a member of the NSP, stated in parliament on January 31, government policy would hereafter reflect the "intifadeh of the people."[73]

Throughout this *intifadeh*, Nasser exacerbated the emotions pulling people out into the streets. The enormous demonstrations illustrated the power of the Sawt al-'Arab radio broadcasts to disseminate information to a massive number of people. Hamad al-Farhan reported that "Sawt al-Arab was stronger than all the speeches of the Arab Nationalists of which I was a member," and people continually asked of the leaders of the parties, "Are you Nasserite or not? If you are Nasserite, we believe you."[74] Egyptian organizing via the Jerusalem Consulate and the embassy in Amman played a role in the demonstrations. Also, Egyptian military officers secretly met with men like al-Nabulsi throughout the 1950s, to get their support for Nasser's message.[75] Reports of Saudi payments to Jordanian opposition figures have also been recorded.

These efforts by Egypt could not alone have generated the amount of passion seen during the Baghdad Pact demonstrations. 'Abdullah al-Rimawi encapsulated this feeling in a dramatic fashion when he said, "The Arab people in Jordan in their entirety rose to say no to imperialism and its underlings. Yes, they said no, while baring their breasts to the bullets and the threat of the suppression of their liberties."[76] Wahdan Oweis theorizes that, yes, Sawt al-'Arab did prove influential, but only because people already accepted its ideas.[77] Even the British Consul in Jerusalem, T. Wikely, acknowledged that in the Baghdad Pact crisis, "intriguers of various colours had no doubt helped to arouse it and later tried to direct it to their own ends, but the thing was essentially a spontaneous outburst stemming from sentiments of resentment and frustration which have been fermenting under the surface for a long time."[78] The American embassy voiced a similar opinion when it reported that "the bribes which the Egyptians and Saudis may have distributed, and the agitation of political elements could not have produced the results they did had there not been a widespread and genuine discontent and a genuine fear of the Baghdad Pact."[79] Abdul Monem al-Rifa'i, Samir al-Rifa'i's brother and Jordanian ambassador to the United States, asked the Assistant Secretary of State for Near Eastern, South Asian, and African Affairs, if the Saudi king could buy violence in Jordan, "then why didn't Iraq or Britain try to buy domestic tranquility? Britain has experience in distributing money in Jordan."[80]

For the first time in Hashemite Jordanian history, the streets had played a decisive role in policy-making. Socioeconomic change had destabilized the carefully crafted Hashemite-Jordanian structure, and the regime lagged behind the demands of the increasingly urbanized population. The Hashemites failed to respond to the rapidly changing situation. When the National Movement and its followers equated the Pact with imperialism, that idea resonated throughout the urban populations. With this success, the Movement then clamored for General Glubb, yet another symbol of British imperialism, to be removed from the political scene.

THE OUSTER OF GENERAL GLUBB

Members of the National Movement had been demanding the ouster of General Glubb for years, but only with the failure of Britain's campaign to enlist Jordan in the Baghdad Pact did this goal appear feasible. Repeatedly, throughout the demonstrations of December and January, the participants had demanded that the king Arabize the army to make it a truly national force. Jordan's swing to the political left, begun in December 1955, appeared on a steady course on March 1, 1956, the day King Husayn surprised his country and its British officials by dismissing Glubb only a month before his contract was due to expire.

The plan to oust the British officers from the Jordanian army had actually germinated years earlier, just after King Talal had been deposed and as the future King Husayn studied at Sandhurst in England. There, Ali Abu Nuwar, then Jordanian military attaché in Paris, spoke to the new king about his distrust for Glubb and his belief that the Jordanian Arab Legion should be a truly national army.[81] Husayn expressed support for Arabizing the armed forces and promised to fulfill this promise once placed on the throne. Once in power, King Husayn hesitated to do so, however, even with the mounting pressure to remove Glubb. With victory over the Pact completed, the National Movement then set its sights on removing Glubb as the logical next step in its campaign to eradicate imperialism. The Arab Legion's violent suppression of the demonstrations, by Glubb's command, made him a particularly easy target, as the majority of the country distrusted his motives and allegiances.

As March 1 approached, Husayn coordinated his efforts with Abu Nuwar and a group of young officers, to guarantee that Glubb and his loyal followers would not spark a revolt on the day of the dismissal. King Husayn called Abu Nuwar on the night of February 28, 1956, and commanded him to prepare his men.[82] Officers took control of the airport in Amman, surrounded the army base in Zarqa to prevent the British officers living there from leaving, and posted sentries outside Glubb's home.[83] Aware that these maneuvers had been executed, Husayn, on March 1, informed his cabinet that he wished to dismiss Glubb. The cabinet, after some deliberation, passed the decree and sent a messenger to inform Glubb that he must leave Jordan immediately. Glubb followed orders and left that day, accompanied by his two closest officers, Patrick Coghill, head of intelligence, and William Hutton, chief of staff. As Joseph Massad has summarized this event,

> The dismissal of Glubb by King Husayn, although reflective of the king's nationalism and his rivalry with Glubb, was also a political maneuver aimed at silencing the opposition while maintaining the traditional influence that Britain had on the country, as Glubb, contrary to many of his detractors, was not the only conduit for that influence, although he was a central one. His removal did indeed neutralize domestic opponents of government policy as well as criticism from Arab nationalist circles abroad.[84]

As a sign of this change of wind, celebrations raged throughout the country during a government-initiated three-day holiday. For the first time in years, pro-Husayn slogans rang out through the streets of the cities. Abu Nuwar says that drinks and sweets were distributed throughout the towns as the people danced and called out support for their nation and their king.[85] Harb states that when King Husayn toured the West Bank after the expulsion, people warmly welcomed him for the first time.[86] Harb, himself, joined a delegation of the Ramallah National Guidance Committee traveling to the palace in Amman to congratulate the king. In honor of the event, the government released a large number of prisoners, including Ziyadin. Shuqayr drove to the palace and signed his name in the ceremonial register. Jordan's jamming of Egyptian radio broadcasts also ceased for the first time in a month.[87] Egyptian and Syrian broadcasts hailed the dismissal as a victory for the Arabs. "Glubb wanted to make the army the executor of his base schemes, but the army rejected him and the King threw him out," proclaimed Damascus radio.[88] The next few months saw the Arabization of the newly named Jordanian Arab Army as British officials left the country and Arab officers finally found positions in the top ranks. By Summer 1956, Ali Abu Nuwar had been appointed the chief of staff of the army.

With the end of the Baghdad Pact and the dismissal of Glubb, two major demands by the National Movement had been met. Popular opinion had finally swayed the governmental apparatus to change policy. No longer could the king unilaterally steer the country, because the National Movement proved successful in generating the requisite amount of popular opposition to his policies. The next demand, the holding of free elections, was fulfilled in October 1956, when the nationalist parties won a majority of seats in the Majlis al-Nuwwab.

CONCLUSION

In the language of opposition, the National Movement used the analogies of "new" and "old," "state" and "nation," to describe its battle with the Hashemites. It wanted, immediately, more of a voice in the governmental apparatus, to overturn years of Hashemite dominance over the definition of "Jordan" and "Jordanian." In the struggle for control over that definition, the revolutionary tenets of Arab nationalism fought against the Hashemite-Western national regime. In some ways, this movement is not dissimilar in motive to the "Transjordan for the Transjordanians" movement, because this was still a fight against the Hashemite definition of the state and the structure subsequently constructed. Nonetheless, now the grievances were couched in a much broader nationalized vocabulary, and the Palestinians added their own demands. Jordan was just the immediate stage from which to work; the larger Arab world beckoned. The next phase in the political struggle, 1956–1957, would focus specifically on that larger goal: Arab unity. Differences of opinion among the JNM's leadership, while in opposition, would not represent major obstacles to internal unity within the Movement itself. Once this leadership was in power, after the October 1956 elections, these differences would become a deciding factor in the disintegration of the Movement. The larger goal of the opposition was to force out the "old"; in power, the leaders of the parties would find that their differences would make it difficult to define the "new" in practical terms.

SUCCESS AND FAILURE: THE JORDANIAN NATIONAL MOVEMENT (JNM)

1956–1957

People say of his [Nabulsi's] government that there were eleven prime ministers and one minister.

MORAIWID AL-TELL[1]

And I think, now I think, we were—the whole group—the nationalists, at that time, the opposition, at that time, were not wise enough to deal with the matters at that time. You know, that at that time, Nasser was there and everybody was very enthusiastic, very nationalist and so on, and they didn't, this is now, after forty years, I think of it now, we were not wise enough to take things slowly and carefully and step by step.

YA'QUB ZIYADIN[2]

I say today that some of the officials in the period of my government acted rashly and with heedlessness.

SULAYMAN AL-NABULSI, AS REPORTED
BY HISTORIAN SULAYMAN MUSA[3]

The period between October 1956 and April 1957 saw the political climax and then the fall of the Jordanian National Movement (JNM) as a unified political actor on the Jordanian scene.[4] Because of its enormous popularity, King Husayn appointed one of its leaders, Sulayman al-Nabulsi, to serve as prime minister of Jordan's first nationalist government. Sheer momentum had brought the parties to power, riding on the waves of emotions and songs and demonstrations. The "new" had finally arrived to displace the "old." As the JNM's leaders had promised for years, the opportunity now existed to institute the policies of the Arab nationalist and progressive movement in Jordan. The state fought to oppose these measures. The two national identities had now come head-to-head in a struggle to see who could "win," who could control the apparatus of government and the hearts of the citizenry. Those same old questions kept reappearing in new forms and voiced by new people: What nationalism would emerge on the Jordanian political scene? What kind of government would truly represent the new forces in the society?

Once in power, the JNM faced innumerable difficulties, both because of its own inherent weaknesses and the strength represented by the pillars of the Hashemite regime. The JNM, once in power, found that the nationalized solution it had always put forward as the panacea for Jordan's ills proved too simplistic; this solution did not build electricity lines or schools, or employ those alienated urban migrants. The Hashemite national narrative still had not captured the hearts of much of the population, but the Hashemite regime itself had proven that it could spread the largesse if required. The JNM had put forward "new" hopes but then could not fulfill expectations once in power. The state may not have kept pace with the changes so much of the population was experiencing, but many groups in the society had come to expect the steady spread of state services. In a basic way, the Hashemite regime had come to "fulfill the normalizing mission of the modern state" as the population granted it legitimacy. In the surrounding Arab states, compatriots of the JNM's leaders initiated military coups to generate that revolutionary feeling and then found themselves locked in the same bind: how to solve the endemic socioeconomic problems of a changing society. The leaders of the JNM tried to work this revolution from inside the government, but also failed. They did not remain in power long enough to actually initiate many domestic policies, but their previous work had generated such enthusiasm for their rule that their supporters expected miraculous changes.

Simultaneously, outside powers—the United States, Britain, Egypt, Syria—to name just a few, intervened and further weakened the Movement. Jordan does not have the natural resources to survive on its own, unaided by outside powers. From its very inception, the state required a steady infusion of cash and material aid from the British; to continue to exist, the state needed new alliances or unions with the surrounding countries. Egypt and Syria promised that aid and laid open the possibility that union would be the best solution for the country's problems. On the other side, the British and then the United States proffered their support for the Hashemite state structure. In the end, the allies of the Hashemites proved more faithful than the "new" ones aligned behind the JNM.

NATIONALIST ELECTIONS

After the success of the Baghdad Pact demonstrations and the ouster of General Glubb, the JNM became a powerful broker on the Jordanian national stage. King Husayn gave its parties the opportunity to actually run the government by allowing for free and fair elections in October 1956. The elections of October 21, 1956, reflected the power of the National Movement to gain support not only on the streets, but also in the ballot boxes. Earlier elections had shown hints of the Movement's potential electoral power, but only in October 1956, with few governmental restraints, could the leaders of the National Movement use all the forces at their command. When the election results had been tabulated, it was clear that the nationalist movement had won massive support from the populace in predominantly free and fair elections. King Husayn acknowledged this fact and appointed Sulayman al-Nabulsi, leader of the National Socialist Party (NSP), as prime minister.

The electoral campaign took place amidst increasing tension over the fate of the Suez Canal. Gamal Abdel Nasser's popularity soared ever higher as he defied the British, the French, and the Americans to nationalize the Suez Canal Company in July 1956. Political figures throughout Jordan praised Nasser's defiance of imperialist dictates. Large demonstrations broke out throughout Jordan in support of Nasser and in opposition to the nations involved. In Amman, in front of the Husayni Mosque, Abd al-Rahman Shuqayr and Sulayman al-Nabulsi gave speeches about the pivotal role Nasser was playing in driving the Zionists from Palestine and eliminating the borders the Western nations had drawn to divide the Arab world.[5] A large demonstration and then general strike took place on August 14 and 16 to illustrate Jordanian support for Nasser and Egypt. Just about every single business in the country heeded the call for the strike, and thousands, all carrying pictures of Nasser, joined in the demonstrations, organized by the Communists, the NSP, and the Ba'th Party. Another nationwide strike took place on September 29, 1956, involving thousands of demonstrators calling out cheers for Nasser and recriminations against the imperialists.

While Israeli attacks on Jordanian soil had been minimal throughout early 1956, the month before both the elections and the tripartite attack on the Suez Canal saw a massive escalation in these raids in defiance of Jordan's improved military arrangements with Egypt and Syria. In three major Israeli attacks, on the fort at al-Rahwa, the police post at Gharandal in Wadi Araba, and the Husan police post, a total of fifty-six Jordanian soldiers, policemen, and civilians were killed.[6] In the largest such attack in this period, on October 10, the Israelis raided the village of Qalqilya in the West Bank with aircraft, armored cars, field guns, and medium-calibre guns, in retaliation for the recent deaths of Israeli farmers.[7] In that attack, Israeli forces killed forty-eight Jordanians.[8]

As these regional crises impinged on Jordanian life, the candidates went out into the streets to spread their messages. For the first time in Jordanian history, the government declared it would not intervene in the elections and basically kept to its promise. In addition, during the summer, King Husayn declared that soldiers and officers in the army were barred from voting and intervening in the electoral process. This statement came in response to the fraud perpetrated by General Glubb and Tawfiq Abu'l-Huda in 1954 and the ability of the JNM to exploit it to gain supporters. Of the close to 140 candidates vying for the forty seats available, about half ran openly on party tickets, while the other half ran as independents.[9] The National Socialist Party, the Ba'th Party, the National Front, the Muslim Brotherhood, the Arab Constitutional Party,[10] and the Movement of Arab Nationalists all fronted candidates. The primary campaign issues centered on Jordan's position within the Arab world, the fate of the Anglo-Jordanian Treaty, and the deepening Suez crisis.

The Communist Party in Jerusalem asked Ziyadin to return from Karak to campaign for that city's Christian seat. As part of this move, Ziyadin also reestablished his tonsillectomy clinic in one-half of a building, while using the other half for political work. When he traveled around the Jerusalem district, Ziyadin expressed confidence that he would finally win a seat in the Majlis al-Nuwwab because of the signs of support he received along the way. Children sang a song in honor of Ziyadin: "Long live Ziyadin; when he came back from prison; we decorated the city for him."[11] The National Front candidates ran on a platform demanding the establishment of a national government in Jordan, the replacement of the "British Imperialist subsidy with Arab aid," the termination of the Anglo-Jordanian Treaty, recognition of Israel as an illegal state, cooperation with Arab and African states fighting for liberty, establishment of diplomatic relations with Communist states, and the extension of political rights to women.[12]

The Ba'th and National Socialist Parties, favoring similar platforms, also fronted candidates in the elections. Ba'th Party candidates, including al-Rimawi, 'Abdullah Na'was, and Bahjat Abu Gharbiyah, ran on a platform calling for Arab aid to replace the British subsidy, abrogation of the Anglo-Jordanian Treaty, the enactment of positive neutrality, union with Syria and Egypt, rejection of peace with Israel, establishment of political rights for women, and the improvement of working conditions.[13] The NSP candidates, headed by al-Nabulsi, followed a similar line by advocating the liberation of the country from foreign influence; cooperation with free Arab states, politically, economically, and militarily, for the purpose of achieving unity; and aid to the Arab states in their battle against imperialist control.[14]

The final results reflected the leftist-nationalist political tilt of the country, as party candidates and leftist independents won election in large numbers. Between 50 and 60 percent of the 400,000 eligible voters cast their ballots throughout the country.[15] The parties of the Jordanian National Movement together earned 164,195 votes out of the 200,000 to 240,000 votes cast.[16] The National Socialist Party won eleven seats, the National Front three, the Ba'th Party two, and the Muslim Brotherhood four, with the Arab Constitutional Party receiving three seats, independents fifteen, and one deputy unidentified by *al-Jaridah al-Rasmiyah*.[17] As for the division between the East and West Banks, the NSP and independents were essentially evenly divided, while the National Front and the Ba'th Party won only seats on the West Bank, indicating a slant to the left in that area and reflecting the fact that the Palestinians as a whole remained more politicized than their Jordanian counterparts. The effects of urbanization on the election results could also be felt, because the nationalist parties won the vast majority of their seats in the largest and more politicized cities of Jerusalem, Ramallah, Nablus, Salt, and Amman. Also, the rise of the professional, educated classes played a role, as 55 percent of the newly elected *nuwwab* held university degrees and approximately 60 percent were part of the middle class, with farmers making up just 32.5 percent of the total.[18] These numbers indicate how the urban professional stratum had been able to take over leadership positions from the more traditional shaykhs and mukhtars.

The results also highlight signs of disunity among the political parties, as many refused to coordinate their efforts to achieve a larger victory. The Communist, Ba'th, and National Socialist Parties, as well as the National Front, initially agreed on a list of candidates prior to the elections so that left-wing candidates would not cancel each other out in the different districts.[19] However, in the days leading up to the elections, 'Abdullah al-Rimawi accused Sulayman al-Nabulsi of working behind his back to gain votes for himself. Al-Rimawi retaliated by pulling the Ba'th Party out of the coalition.[20] Tal'at Harb reports that the Communist Party also approached al-Rimawi so that Communist and Ba'th candidates could coordinate their efforts in Ramallah, but al-Rimawi rejected that proposal as well.[21] The NSP became the primary beneficiary of these actions, as its leaders used their prominence in the society to win the most seats. This break in the ranks of the leftist parties was the first step toward a weakening of the Movement that would rapidly occur over the next few months. In this atmosphere, the Baʿth Party clearly lost popularity, although many observers considered it the strongest party in the days leading up to the election.[22] Its deputy from Jerusalem, ʿAbdullah Naʿwas, who had won seats in 1950 and 1951, lost in 1956 to Ziyadin. In addition, Abu Gharbiyah lost his bid. These losses can be attributed, in part, to the disunity of the leftist parties and their failure to work together in a united front. In addition, the Baʿth Party appeared so strong before the elections that the other parties worked particularly hard to combat its potential power. Also, a number of the party's key planks, including Arab unity and socialism, had been taken up by the other parties as well, particularly the NSP. This allowed voters to choose the more moderate candidates and still support many of the same ideologies.

Although the elections remain one of the freest of all Jordanian elections, the authorities did not refrain from targeting candidates they particularly feared would disrupt the country. The most blatant case of fraud occurred over Shuqayr's candidacy. After deciding to run for a seat in Amman, Shuqayr visited Damascus to get his platform printed. While there, he heard from Egyptian journalists assigned to the Middle East News Agency that Jordanian security forces planned to arrest him on his return. Despite this threat, Shuqayr returned home and found himself quickly on the way to al-Jafr, just as he had been warned. Undaunted by the administration's action, friends of Shuqayr visited him in jail, obtained his signature, and formally filed his application. Since the Election Law did not forbid candidacies from prison, the authorities allowed Shuqayr to run in this fashion.

Less than a month before the election, the British embassy estimated that Shuqayr would gain an easy victory.[23] Hani Hourani wrote in the foreword to Shuqayr's memoir that he and his fellow classmates in Amman participated in a fictitious election on the day of the actual elections.[24] When the results were tabulated, Hourani proclaimed Shuqayr the most important candidate in those elections, for he had earned a reputation not only for his political work, which ran the gamut of arrests, exile, and legal persecution, but also for his medical work with the poor of Amman. According to Hourani, Shuqayr's speeches had inflamed the nationalist battle raging in Jordan.[25] Despite this enthusiasm, Shuqayr did not win the election.

Even though al-Nabulsi personally lost his bid for a seat in Amman, King Husayn asked him to form a government, based on the NSP's victory.[26] Al-Nabulsi's cabinet reflected the nationalist slant of the country, as it contained a large number of the prime minister's own party colleagues, including Abd al-Halim al-Nimr as the minister of interior and defense, Shafiq Irsheidat as the minister of justice, as well as members of the Ba'th Party, with 'Abdullah al-Rimawi in the new post of minister of state for foreign affairs, and those of the National Front, with 'Abd al-Qadir al-Salih as minister of education, among a coalition of independents. This cabinet was the first in Jordan's history to include primarily members of parliament. All but three ministers had won seats in the Majlis al-Nuwwab. The cabinet stated as its ministerial program the desire to eliminate colonialism, further liberalize Jordan's political life, strengthen Jordan's friendship with countries sympathetic to the Arab cause, improve relations with the liberal Arab states, and terminate the Anglo-Jordanian Treaty.

Before the new majlis could assemble and the government could form, the Suez Crisis intensified. On October 24, the day before the elections, the Jordanian, Egyptian, Syrian, and Saudi Arabian governments signed an agreement uniting the military commands under Egyptian General Abdul Hakim 'Amir. Two days after al-Nabulsi formed his government, on October 29, Israel attacked the Sinai. Britain and France joined the fight the next day. King Husayn immediately declared that Jordan would extend any help it could to support Egypt in its fight. Al-Nabulsi, in contrast, advised delay—paralleling Syria's declaration—to see what would happen. Al-Nabulsi also wanted time to consolidate his new political position. In any event, Nasser declined Husayn's offer and cautioned Jordan to remain outside the battle for fear of endangering the West Bank. To protect Jordan against possible Israeli attack, the Jordanian government asked Syria, Iraq, and Saudi Arabia to move troops into the country; they subsequently did so by the beginning of November. By November 5, Israeli forces occupied all of the Sinai Peninsula except for a small corridor along the Canal. The next day, however, the war was over due to American and Soviet pressure.

October 1956 provided a test for the National Movement, as it faced free elections for the first time and encountered a major regional crisis pitting its ideological hero, Nasser, against the country's financial provider, Britain. In the first test, the National Movement claimed victory, as it won a majority of seats in the Majlis al-Nuwwab and formed a nationalist government mandated to move Jordan away from Britain and toward the Egyptian-Syrian-Saudi camp. In the Suez Crisis, during its second test, the government cautioned delay for fear of an Israeli invasion of the West Bank. The nationalist government's decision proved correct, as

Nasser advised the same tactic and the war ended quickly through American and Soviet intervention. The entire Suez Crisis illustrated that the National Movement's leaders had the ability to keep the country quiet; no violent demonstrations broke out during the crisis. It also proved that Britain's desires for the Middle East conflicted with Arab interests, as the nationalists had been declaring for years; this fact improved the nationalists' popularity at the expense of the king's.

NATIONALIST RULE

The next six months in Jordan's history witnessed a battle between King Husayn and the Jordanian National Movement, a battle essentially fought over two opposing images of the future of Jordan. Key to this debate was the question about whether the JNM could make the transition from an opposition movement into a functioning government. The National Movement favored a state ruled by a representative government and united economically, militarily, and politically with Egypt and Syria. As implied by the spokesmen of this image, future plans for Jordan often excluded the monarchy, and, when the king was included, he held a minimal political role. In contrast, the king and the "King's men" preferred to return to the days when they ruled the country and used the majlis as merely a political tool to force unpopular policies on the people. While al-Nabulsi's government moved Jordan to the left and toward Egypt, signing the Arab Solidarity Agreement with Egypt, Syria, and Saudi Arabia, terminating the Anglo-Jordanian Treaty, and inaugurating relations with the Soviet Bloc, the king and his aides worked to improve relations with the United States and to prevent the nationalist government from treading down the leftward political path. By April 1957, the battle had become a situation where neither side could agree with the other. The question was now which national identity, and its concomitant social and political structure, would "win."

Pushed to the side of the political stage, the king and his advisors could do little at first to combat their loss of power. Al-Nabulsi's government particularly targeted the continued employment of senior officials. In the first half of December 1956, al-Nabulsi retired a few senior government officials, "those who are not sincere nationalists," "those who are corrupt persons," and "those who are not up to standards of efficiency."[27] The king accepted these dismissals and signed the necessary decrees. As Jamal al-Sha'ir states, "So, the people in the country must have felt threatened that they were the ones who had access to the king, they were the ones who were, you know, making money because of contracts with the government. There must have been a number of people in the country at that time who felt threatened that they would lose their position, economic and political position, at that time."[28] Bringing in the "new" threatened those interests inextricably attached to the "old" system of Hashemite rule.

Jordan's status as an independent Arab nation came up for debate during the first months of the new government and further threatened the position of the traditional forces. Al-Nabulsi made a statement to the *New York Times* on December 17, reporting that he felt that "Jordan cannot live forever as Jordan," but must be connected economically, militarily, and politically to one or more Arab states in order to survive.[29] In the new unity he envisaged, Jordan would be part of a federation of countries that coordinated efforts on Arab foreign military issues while local matters remained the domain of each individual country. In the most important step toward achieving this unity and fully integrating Jordan into the pro-Arab camp, the government signed the Arab Solidarity Agreement with Egypt, Syria, and Saudi Arabia on January 19, 1957. In the agreement, the three countries promised to replace the British annual subsidy with Arab aid totaling £12.5 million a year.

Building on his success with the Arab Solidarity Agreement, al-Nabulsi rejected the Eisenhower Doctrine offered by the United States and actually steered his government in the opposite direction by moving closer to the Eastern bloc. The Doctrine promised U.S. aid to any Arab country threatened by Communist infiltration or aggression. Twelve members of the Majlis al-Nuwwab, including Ziyadin, signed a petition attacking the American plan to interfere in the affairs of the Middle East. The discussion in the majlis on January 2, 1957, further criticized U.S. efforts to fill the imperialist position soon to be vacated by the British.[30] In direct violation of the Anti-Communism Law of 1953, al-Nabulsi's government passed a resolution near the end of December allowing the publication in Amman of a Communist newspaper, *al-Jamahir [The Masses]*, and permitted Tass, the Soviet news agency, to open an office in Jordan. *Al-Jamahir* then became a powerful conduit for criticizing many of the issues existing in Jordan. In addition, al-Nabulsi's government released from prison the leader of the party, Fu'ad Nasser, who promptly reestablished his political leadership with a demonstration held under the banner of the hammer and sickle.[31]

Husayn countered al-Nabulsi's leniency toward Communism by issuing, on February 2, a public letter decrying this trend. In his letter, the king warned al-Nabulsi about Communist infiltration by saying, "the

Eastern camp is now trying to entice us with its doctrines . . . But we now detect the danger of Communist infiltration in our Arab homeland, and the threat posed by those who feign loyalty to Arab nationalism" and the threat of a new type of imperialism posed by it, but "we shall not allow our country to become a battlefield for a cold war, to be followed by a destructive shooting war."[32] As Fawas Gerges has analyzed, Husayn played the "Cold War card" to weaken the nationalist government.

> Hussein subsequently capitalized upon it [the Eisenhower Doctrine] to defeat the Jordanian National Movement's opposition to his rule. Throughout the 1957 crisis, Hussein openly accused international communism of attempting to subvert his regime and of fomenting instability in Jordan. His objective was to impress upon US officials the seriousness of the situation and the danger to Western interests if the opposition were to win. In pandering to Washington's anti-communist sentiments, Hussein transformed a local quarrel into an international crisis.[33]

The February 2 letter served as King Husayn's first volley to regain his political position. He now not only worked to reestablish his old power base, but attempted to add the United States as a new, more direct ally. Al-Nabulsi responded to this letter by clamping down on some of the articles appearing in *al-Jamahir;* then, a month later, closing it, shutting down the Tass offices, and confiscating Communist literature sold in bookshops around the country. Communists continued to sell these items under the table, however.[34]

Nonetheless, al-Nabulsi did not completely reject his policy of courting the Eastern bloc, as he made contact with the Soviet ambassador in Damascus concerning establishing diplomatic relations, first sending Ali Abu Nuwar in an informal capacity, and then upgrading the representation by sending Shafiq Irsheidat, the minister of justice. He did not, however, notify the king of these negotiations.[35] In so doing, al-Nabulsi said, "we do not side with the East unless the East sides with us. But we do not side with the West, because the West can never be with us. It wants to colonise and exploit us."[36]

With the Baghdad Pact rejected, Glubb ousted, the Suez Canal attack by Britain foiled, and the Arab Solidarity Agreement signed, the Anglo-Jordanian Treaty had functionally been abrogated, so the two sides agreed to meet to negotiate its official termination in February 1957. Talks opened in Amman on February 4 and came to fruition on March 13 when both sides formally announced the termination of the Anglo-Jordanian Treaty. In the document signed, Britain agreed to remove its troops within six months, while Jordan promised to pay for British facilities in the country in installments over six years. Britain declared it would end its subsidy to Jordan as of April 1, 1957. The Jordanian government then called for a three-day holiday in celebration of the event. Poor weather dampened the spirits of the revelers for the first two days, but on the third the conditions improved enough that thousands poured into the streets for peaceful demonstrations.

With these moves, by the end of March 1957, two major domestic problems had surfaced. On one level, the king and the government no longer favored the same policies. While the king negotiated with the United States concerning aid via the Eisenhower Doctrine, the government made contact with the Soviet Union. In addition, al-Nabulsi implicitly demanded that the king move into the shadows of the political stage, a demand the king refused to accept. Little area for compromise existed between the two sides, as they each refused to listen to the other. The contradiction between the role of the king and the requirements of Arab unity, successfully ignored by the Movement's members while out of power, came into prominence. Now the party leaders were faced with the dilemma of how to push the king from power without alienating his supporters. Inevitably, the new government's policies were bound to anger key members of the society. Just as importantly, on another level, strains appeared as the different groups within the Jordanian National Movement differed over Jordan's next political direction. Even during the October 1956 elections problems had begun to surface among the political parties, as they refused to coordinate their efforts in the different electoral districts. Differences in political opinion among the JNM's leaders remained largely dormant during the opposition phase. Once they were in power, nuanced ideological differences as well as personal conflicts came to the fore.

Al-Nabulsi acknowledged that a number of the members of parliament were not happy with his rule and that the independents and members of his own party who sat in the cabinet disagreed with the policies of the Ba'th and Communist members.[37] Musa reports that "Some of the parties in the country stood against the others, and the animosity came to the point of clashes in the parliament and in the streets and probably the animosity grew in voracity with the passing of days."[38] While this animosity did not lead to an explosion among the parties, Musa theorizes that it led ultimately to the demise of party power in Jordan. As a sign of this rivalry, Musa states that the party partisans arbitrarily identified their supporters and opponents as "progressives" and "reactionaries" to serve their own political ambitions.[39] In other words, Musa feels that the parties did not practice the democracy they preached.[40] In a similar vein, Moraiwid al-Tell says, "People say of his government that there were eleven prime ministers and one minister."[41]

The more moderate voices cautioned al-Nabulsi against moving too quickly to achieve the National Movement's goals. The Ba'th and National Front members of the cabinet, on the other hand, pushed him to pass more radical policies. The biggest conflict within the cabinet occurred between al-Nabulsi and al-Rimawi, as the former advocated a more moderate approach to change and the latter the more radical route.[42] As al-Sha'ir has stated, for example, "'Abdullah Rimawi was not an asset to the government because he was always throwing the government against the king."[43] According to 'Isa Madanat, al-Rimawi came to him during the height of the crisis in 1957 and advocated a coup against the king, but Madanat would not accept it.[44] Even the ruling National Socialists found themselves on different ends of the political spectrum. Naseer Aruri reports, "There were sharp cleavages within the ranks of the Nationalist Socialists in the Cabinet. The left wing faction led by Minister of Justice Shafiq Irsheidat advocated radical change; and the right wing group led by Anwar al-Khatib pursued a conciliatory policy."[45] These divisions would help bring down the nationalist government because the king and the "King's men" would be more successful in maintaining a united front. While party affiliation remained important, individual preferences became more important once the Movement gained access to government power. At the same time, al-Nabulsi's government concentrated solely on political issues and ignored the economic and social problems that had made the urban populations, in particular, look to the National Movement for answers. When this new government also failed to make any headway on these problems, the broad-based coalition previously supporting the National Movement began to unravel and become dissatisfied with the new regime.

To make the situation even more unstable, problems also arose over the payment of the Arab subsidy as the date for the end of British aid approached on April 1, 1957. The Jordanian government faced bankruptcy unless the Arabs fulfilled their promises by that date. Al-Nabulsi sent missives to the three Arab signatories, but all used delaying tactics to postpone their payments. This placed both the national government and the entire state of Jordan in a precarious position because of the lack of financial resources in the country. Since the beginning, Jordan had relied heavily on the British for funds, and al-Nabulsi chose to cut relations with the country's traditional patron based largely on the promise of Arab aid.

Sulayman al-Nabulsi, as prime minister, became the focal point for all these struggles. The parties of the JNM came to power on a platform of Arab unity and socioeconomic change. Arab unity seemed increasingly unattainable as the Movement's Egyptian and Syrian allies appeared to withdraw their support for the nationalist government. The promised socioeconomic benefits to be accrued through Arab unity then seemed equally distant. The king, whose role had never been fully defined by the parties' platforms, refused to move into the shadows and, instead, rallied supporters to oppose the nationalist government's policies. The cabinet continued to fragment throughout the spring as the individual members advocated opposing policies concerning the king and his supporters. Al-Nabulsi was faced with the task of deciding which constituency provided his biggest support. As his subsequent actions illustrate, al-Nabulsi chose to initiate a showdown with the king, hoping that the JNM's hard-earned support on the "streets" would help maintain his power base.

APRIL 1957: THE FALL OF THE NATIONALIST GOVERNMENT AND THE RESTORATION OF THE HASHEMITE REGIME

As a result, al-Nabulsi became bolder in expressing his vision for the future of Jordan and more radical in his approach, advocating both relations with the Communist states and union with the neighboring Arabs. On April 3, al-Nabulsi officially announced that he intended to establish diplomatic relations with the Soviet Union, having promised this a number of times before and having received the sanction of the Majlis al-Nuwwab.[46] This announcement was directly contrary to the expressed views of the king. Al-Nabulsi also publicly announced his desire to put Arab unity into practical effect when he gave a speech in Nablus, stating that "our next step aims at setting up a federal union, preliminary to comprehensive Arab unity . . . Unity in the cultural, economic, military, and foreign political spheres will not be sufficient unless there is real integration and amalgamation [with Egypt and Syria], guided by the interests of liberated Arab nationalism."[47] When al-Nabulsi forced the issue one step further by bringing the king yet another list of senior retirees, the king forced al-Nabulsi's government to resign on April 10, 1957. King Husayn then struggled for the next week to form a new government.

Movements in the military placed Jordan in a yet more precarious political position.[48] On April 8, troops from the First Armoured Regiment, led by Captain Nadhir Rashid, deployed at the major intersections outside Amman, in a mission entitled "Operation Hashim." When King Husayn asked about the maneuver all involved stated that it was a typical training mission to count the number of cars coming into and out of the city, an operation performed many times over the past few years. On Husayn's command, the regiment returned to Zarqa without delay. Some historians site this episode as the beginning of the failed coup attempt against the king, and one which alerted him to the threat posed by the Free Officers.[49] The military officers of the day state that it was merely a training exercise, perpetrated at an inconvenient time in Jordan's political history.[50] It could just as easily have been a prelude to a larger movement. The officers could have been testing the waters to see what they could achieve militarily.

The next step in these military maneuvers occurred in Zarqa, the headquarters for the majority of Jordan's armed forces. Rumors flew that the king had been killed, and, as a result, fighting broke out on the base between bedouin soldiers and those loyal to Chief of Staff Ali Abu Nuwar. During the fighting in Zarqa, a brigade marched to the palace to protect the king. On arriving at the outskirts of Amman, the brigade passed the king traveling to Zarqa with Abu Nuwar. When the soldiers threatened to kill Abu Nuwar as a traitor, the king sent him back to the palace. Husayn drove on to the Khaw camp at Zarqa, waded into the crowd, and then gave a speech calming everyone down. Husayn said that he could hear the bullets whizzing past him as he spoke.[51] Abu Nuwar officially resigned the next day and fled to Syria.

Questions abound about whether this coup attempt originated with the military, led by Abu Nuwar and the Free Officers, or with the king and the Americans, who wanted an excuse to remove the National Movement from Jordan's political scene. According to those who believe that a real coup attempt against the king occurred, the coup faltered because the conspirators failed to gain the support of the bedouin ranks of the Arab Legion, and particularly of the officers who held troop commands.[52] Clinton Bailey feels that the nationalist officers of the Arab Legion feared that they would lose power with al-Nabulsi's dismissal, so quickly plotted a coup.[53] These historians point out that Abu Nuwar had been in contact with Egyptian and Soviet officials in Damascus, so had the opportunity to coordinate his plans with them.[54] Later, when searching Abu Nuwar's office, the army found two samples of new flags for the new Jordanian republic, thus implicating Abu Nuwar in the coup.

On the other side stand a number of political and military figures from the era who discount the official story. They feel governmental forces initiated the plot as a ploy to justify the elimination of the Jordanian

National Movement. Among these are Mahmoud Mu'ayta, Shuqayr, and Abu Gharbiyah. Massad reports that Abu Shahut and the Free Officers knew nothing about plans to overthrow the king.[55] Al-Nabulsi's efforts had altered the balance of power in the country away from the king and the "King's men" and toward a new group of politicians previously excluded from the highest reaches of power. Because of this fact, the "King's men" faced extinction. To forestall this eventuality, the king, with possible help from the United States, commissioned loyal officers of the army, "reactionary officers" from the time of Glubb, to create a disturbance which could then be blamed on the Free Officers, and the National Movement in general.[56]

Regardless of the motivation or originators of the coup attempt, the king and the "King's men" exploited it as an excuse to destroy the National Movement and reinstate their nationalized regime in Jordan. By claiming that the coup posed a real threat to Jordan, Husayn succeeded in gaining the support of the United States, Britain, Iraq, and Saudi Arabia. In particular, the United States and Britain supported Husayn's repressive policies because, while they destroyed Jordan's only representative government, they made Jordan stable enough for the British and the Americans to protect their interests.[57] To keep the West on his side, Husayn spoke of subversive groups in the military and the government trying to create a Jordanian republic. This tactic made the National Movement appear as such a threat to Jordan's existence and the West that it had to be eliminated to restore stability. At the same time, Egyptian and Syrian hesitation to make the promised payments gave the National Movement little leverage against the king and his allies. After repeated requests for the payment, the Syrian prime minister, Sabri al-'Asali, responded that the issue would only be discussed in May as part of the negotiations for the 1957 budget. The Egyptians informed the Jordanian government that the first installment would be forthcoming after arrangements had been made to open credits for Jordan in European countries.[58] In the end, neither country made any of the promised installments.

In the midst of this chaos, the king struggled to form a government acceptable to his supporters and those of the nationalists. On April 15, Husayn Fakhri al-Khalidi, a Palestinian, proved successful in forming a government, one that included Sulayman al-Nabulsi as the foreign minister, in violation of his own party's dictate to boycott the cabinet. Awni Fakher reports that people viewed this government as a "bridge" to the "black" one that would inevitably be formed soon thereafter.[59] As a result, during both the deliberations over the new government and the Zarqa events, demonstrations broke out throughout the country, occurring especially in Nablus, the Old City of Jerusalem, Ramallah, and Amman. In Jerusalem, demonstrations broke out every day at the Haram al-Sharif, and the National Guidance Committee met constantly, including among its ranks the muhafath [mayor] of Jerusalem, party leaders, organizations, and the nuwwab from Jerusalem. In Nablus, demonstrations took place for a week after al-Nabulsi's dismissal. To quell the demonstrations in Amman, loyal bedouin soldiers, with blackened faces and heavy armor, to avoid being recognized and sparking tribal feuds, patrolled the streets. A large demonstration broke out in Jericho, with both Bahjat Abu Gharbiyah and Amin al-Khatib, among others, speaking to the crowd, focusing specifically on the need for al-Khalidi's resignation.[60]

Throughout these political and military crises, the National Movement tried to regroup and reorganize its forces. On April 23, a National Congress convened in Nablus, with representatives from all the opposition parties and groups associated with al-Nabulsi's government, including twenty-three members of the Majlis al-Nuwwab. Resolutions passed at the congress included demands for the dissolution of al-Khalidi's government and replacement with a NSP–Ba'th–National Front coalition; rejection of the Eisenhower Doctrine; establishment of a federal union with Egypt and Syria; dismissal of two of the "King's men," Bahjat al-Talhouni and Sharif Nasser; and acceptance of positive neutralism. The congress also called for a general strike and demonstration on April 24 if these demands had not been met. An elected executive committee brought the demands to al-Khalidi, who refused to extend his support. April 24 saw yet another upheaval in Jordan as al-Nabulsi resigned his government post and al-Khalidi's government fell.

King Husayn then began to restore his powers. Quickly, Husayn appointed Ibrahim Hashim as the new prime minister, controlling a conservative and loyal cabinet. This new government imposed martial law and a nationwide curfew, enforced censorship, banned the political parties, and formed a military regime under Sulayman Tuqan. Six military governors were appointed under Tuqan, all given wide latitude to arrest and imprison. These men consequently arrested hundreds of political activists, with the BBC reporting that 964 people had been arrested as of April 27, 1957.[61] All the parties were banned, their offices closed, and their property confiscated. National Guidance Committees were officially dissolved as well. Military courts were set up, and, in Order #9, all writing, speaking, or spreading of rumors harmful to the stability of the country was made punishable by two years in jail, and writing or drawing with an intent to defame the king was made punishable by three years in jail.[62] All forms of political expression were thus prohibited.

The Jordanian National Movement collapsed as many of its leaders fled the country or came under arrest by the Jordanian government. Al-Nabulsi was placed under house arrest for four and a half years, but was never officially charged with a crime. Those activists who escaped capture fled the country, first to Syria and then, often, to Egypt. Abu Nuwar, Shuqayr, al-Rimawi, Naʿwas, Abd al-Halim al-Nimr, and Nabih Irsheidat all fled to Damascus. A number of the alleged participants were put on trial in the military courts. These trials began in April 1957 and continued until early 1958, but sentences for the major conspirators were announced on September 25, 1957. Abu Nuwar, al-Rimawi, and Nadhir Rashid received fifteen years in prison, although the first two were tried in absentia. Abu Shahut and Mahmud al-Muʿayta, with ten others, including most of the Free Officers' executive committee, got ten years in prison. Others received five-year sentences. Twenty men had their cases dropped for lack of evidence. Ziyadin eluded the police by fleeing Jerusalem and hiding in the hills around Ramallah. When the police finally captured him, they returned him to al-Jafr. Ziyadin received nineteen years in jail for his political activities. Talʿat Harb hid near Ramallah for a number of days, but the military eventually found him and sent him to al-Jafr. Abu Gharbiyah was not arrested, so continued to conduct his political work underground. Al-Khatib spent only a brief time in jail but lost his job with United Nations Relief and Works Agency for Palestine Refugees in the Near East (UNRWA), a job he had held for much of the 1950s.

Domestic and regional forces then began to express their support for King Husayn and his throne. On April 16, two hundred bedouin chieftains arrived at the palace and pledged their loyalty to Husayn. The Saudi king, having changed his position concerning the West after a successful trip to Washington in early March, gave Husayn his support and placed Saudi troops in Jordan under Husayn's command. Furthermore, on April 22, Saudi Arabia's first installment of the subsidy arrived into the government's hands. On April 22, Iraqi forces entered Jordan in support of the king.

More importantly for Husayn's plans, the United States pledged its support for his efforts. On April 17, President Eisenhower officially proclaimed that Jordan was of vital interest to the United States, which would help King Husayn in any way it could. In a practical sign of this resolve, the United States moved the Sixth Fleet to the eastern Mediterranean. In addition, the United States quickly agreed to give Jordan $10 million immediately, without any strings attached. This aid came from the United

States under the Mutual Security Act (Point-IV) rather than the Eisenhower Doctrine because of continued opposition to the latter.[63]

On April 24, King Husayn went on the radio to address the Jordanian people concerning the recent upheavals in the country. He called the former government and, by implication, the National Movement, the "minority" and said,

> I gave them power and granted them full confidence, and made myself their hand in government. But they used foul play and exceeded their power, and they claimed credit and pretended to be nationalists, disregarding the great evils which the enemy and the imperialists are reserving for us to engulf the rest of the usurped homeland and disperse the remaining hundreds of thousands of its people.[64]

With such words, the king repositioned himself as both the leader of the country and the "nationalist" supporting its anti-imperialist goals.

Throughout the short tenure of al-Nabulsi's government a number of problems also arose, irrespective of the king's desire to hang on to power. On one level, the nationalist coalition failed to work together as a solid unit. The NSP, the Ba'th, the Communists, and the independents in the cabinet advocated policies in opposition to each other. Sulayman Musa theorizes of al-Nabulsi that "they say that he was not able to restrain the defiance of the extremists inside and outside his government, and that he allowed himself to be carried away by the current, despite the fact that he, in the depths of himself, wanted to be on the side of caution."[65] On another level, as the cabinet faced the realities of power it discovered that street politics did not translate well into the halls of government. Its support lay with groups who lacked independent power and organizational ability. While "the cabinet and the parliament were as one in echoing the dominant political trends,"[66] these demands did not always make for good governance, as the Arabs renounced their promise to grant Jordan a subsidy and as the United States stepped up to the table. The Jordanian nationalist government did not have enough political leverage to force the Arabs to fulfill their promises of aid, while the king could use his power to convince the United States to extend support for him.

On yet a deeper level, the Movement's broad support within the country began to erode as Jordan's myriad problems remained unresolved and appeared to be growing larger as financial support disappeared. Just as the populace had looked to the opposition as an alternative force prior to 1956, a number began to question its ability to govern once in power.

The problem stemmed from the immediacy of the political problems the government faced, and its subsequent neglect of socioeconomic ones. As the quote at the beginning of this chapter indicates, Ziyadin, looking back on this period forty years later, felt that the politicians of the National Movement had been too impulsive and too enthusiastic to seriously face the realities of political life in Jordan. Al-Nabulsi maintained his position as the "Za'im," or facilitator-leader, of the group, when Jordan had typically been run by a "Sayyid," or leader-authoritarian.[67] In summary, the nationalist government had no financial support and had come up against the combined power of the British and the United States, not to mention the king and his allies.[68]

The Palestinian issue also loomed as a separate problem throughout this period. While the Jordanians and the Palestinians belonging to the Movement subsumed their separate desires within a specifically Arab nationalist framework, the two groups did have different goals and aims attached to this framework. By the end of the 1950s, Palestinians in different areas of the Arab world were starting to organize again on a specifically Palestinian basis. The 1960s would be marked by the creation of forces like Fatah that eschewed the Arab nationalist answer and drew activists into new kinds of military organizations. These issues did not specifically rear their heads during al-Nabulsi's government but stood in the background of the larger debate. Men like 'Abdullah al-Rimawi put forward a more radical position, in part because of the threat faced by the Palestinians. Overcoming the Hashemite problem paled in comparison.

In its battle against the king, the National Movement also made a number of miscalculations concerning the leadership structure in the country. Even through all the upheavals of the early-to-mid 1950s, the Hashemite regime maintained the loyalty of key groups in the society, namely the "King's men," the bedouin tribesmen, urban merchants, and the peasants. The productive apparatus of the state could still co-opt supporters because, to this point, only the Hashemites provided the largesse everyone expected from the government. A bargain had been struck between the Hashemites and the population: the Hashemites supplied the services, the population extended a degree of loyalty toward the regime. The National Movement proffered promises and hopes, but only the state actually continued to fulfill this role. Bureaucratic and educational pilgrimages and the slowly growing social welfare state attached more and more people to the Hashemite structure and thus generated a degree of patriotism. When the state came under threat by 1956 and 1957, key groups such as the bedouin jumped in to aid the regime without question. The socioeconomic changes of the 1950s had siphoned off many of the state's supporters from the peasant and bedouin strata, but not enough, in the end, to help overthrow or radically alter the regime.

The power dynamic in Jordan had always passed between the king and the various British officers delegated to Jordan, with the "King's men" appointed to execute their policies. The system of retaining a small number of loyal men in positions of power remained in place throughout the 1950s. Governments formed and fell over the years of Jordan's existence, but members did not initiate serious reform efforts, with the exception of Fawzi al-Mulqi's brief tenure in 1953. One government naturally flowed into the next with little legislative change.[69] Al-Nabulsi's government attempted to negate forty years of this policy and place itself at the pinnacle of power when it targeted the "King's men" for exile from the political stage and dramatically altered Jordan's legislative and national priorities. However, these men had remained in power for years and refused to move quietly into the political shadows. Their policies had created a framework difficult to overturn. Below this level of government, the bureaucracy was filled with loyal members of the ethnic and religious minorities, as well as the sons of the urban merchants. The state built up the bureaucracy to cater to this system of patronage. While in 1936, 683 employees worked in the state civil service, over 20,000 employees held public service jobs in 1956.[70]

The new government also failed to understand that the different kings had spent years cultivating the support of the bedouin tribes, the largest component of the army. Bedouin tribesmen continued to extend their support to the regime because of the largesse they had received. The army expanded throughout the 1950s to include ever greater numbers of bedouin tribesmen. Glubb often promoted bedouin over the more educated officers. As they represented the military base of the country, they had to be appeased by the government, something the National Movement neglected to do. Al-Nabulsi's policies curtailed their connections to the government apparatus, so they reacted by wholeheartedly supporting the return to full Hashemite rule.

The Movement underestimated the influence of the king himself. By now, four years in power had given him political experience: he successfully used his famous charisma to gain supporters. He understood the level of loyalty among the bedouin soldiers, and he knew people's personalities, their families, their names.[71] He had truly started to become the father of the people, just as his grandfather had always been. When the new government forced the king from the center of the political stage, the rank and file of the army immediately came to his defense. As he began the process of reimposing his political control over the country, the army provided the troops necessary for the successful execution of his repressive measures. Without the support of this group, the king would not have been able to destroy the National Movement. King Husayn was no longer the impressionable young man, following the wishes of the "King's men," but someone starting to put his own stamp on the office of the monarchy. He personally made contact with the actors in the country and made it clear that he stood as the most important politician among them.

As al-Nabulsi struggled with events in Jordan, he could not ignore the foreign actors, Egypt, Syria, Saudi Arabia, Iraq, the United States, and Britain, all laying claim to aspects of Jordanian political life. Egypt and Syria kept pushing the government to move more toward the political left, while Iraq, Britain, and the United States wanted Jordan to stay on the right. In the end, Egypt and Syria did not do enough to support the National Movement, most notably in their refusal to pay the promised Arab subsidy. On the other hand, the United States proved its loyalty to the king by quickly sending money to him and by moving ships into the vicinity to forestall any potential problems. While the United States had only granted Jordan $37.9 million prior to 1957, it handed over $283.3 million between 1957 and 1962.[72] At the same time this struggle was taking place, the king was lining up Arab support for his cause. The Jordanian branch of the Muslim Brotherhood rallied to his side by April 1957, as seen in the fact that its leadership openly sided with the king against al-Nabulsi and organized mass rallies in support of this position.[73] The Saudi king was now determined to promote American policies in Jordan. The restoration of the Hashemite throne fit these policies.

CONCLUSION

The Jordanian National Movement rode a wave of popularity into power and then was expelled from office when it threatened to destroy the traditional structure of the Hashemite state. Effective political organizing allowed the National Movement to gain the support of the majority of the urban population. Arab nationalism proved to be a successful framework for political opposition in Jordan because it encompassed domestic and regional demands of both its Jordanian and Palestinian enthusiasts. The leaders of the National Movement first made their mark on Jordanian politics by using the brute force of street politics to compel the government to veer away from the Baghdad Pact. Recognizing the level of the Movement's popularity, the king allowed free elections to bring the nationalist leaders into the halls of government. They quickly limited his power and attempted to alter Jordan's political framework. This action threatened the "King's men" and the king sufficiently that they retaliated by destroying the National Movement. No compromise could be reached between the two groups. The Jordanian National Movement failed because of disunity within its own ranks but also because it tried to fight against the combined effects of forty years of Hashemite rule, a lack of natural resources, and a king and his allies with too firm a grip on Jordanian political life. The Hashemite state had successfully fulfilled its normalizing mission. "He wanted to satisfy a number of sides at once: King Husayn and President Abdul Nasser and Syria and the Ba'thists and the Communists."[74] As Musa concludes, al-Nabulsi set out on an impossible task.

The Jordanian National Movement, thus, succeeded in gaining support of the majority of the population but failed to win the power game with the king that resulted from its efforts. The Hashemites understood that legitimacy rested on their ability to spread their largesse to key elements in the population. Their example serves as a model for how a colonialist-designed state can generate support and garner a degree of legitimacy from a population. The National Movement ultimately lacked the resources to successfully change this aspect of Jordan's history and orient it away from this pole. The JNM could not overcome the "alienness of the ruling group" because the Hashemites proved to the population that they were the "nationalists" serving their needs. With the JNM's fall, the Hashemite historical narrative held more resonance for the population; power and success helped breed support.

NINE

THE HASHEMITES ASCENDANT

We Win Transjordan.

KING ʿABDULLAH, TITLE OF CHAPTER 7 OF HIS MEMOIRS[1]

I started understanding how much Jordan is attached—Jordan as a
country and people, especially Transjordanians—how much the future
of these people and the whole country is connected with the Hashemite
throne. If the Hashemite throne goes, Jordan goes. I started believing
this only in the last ten years. But many people believed it before us.
But we rejected it when we were young.

JAMAL AL-SHAʿIR, IN LOOKING BACK ON HIS LIFE[2]

How could Jamal al-Shaʿir, a member of the Baʿth Party, say by 1998
that "If the Hashemite throne goes, Jordan goes"? Are the Hashemites
Jordan and Jordan the Hashemite family? Had the Hashemites "won,"
as King ʿAbdullah declared in his memoirs? Is this a pragmatic recognition of political reality? To achieve this status after 1957, the Hashemites had to work harder to improve the economic and social conditions
in the country. In 1957, the Jordanian National Movement (JNM) had
been physically destroyed, but its demands still remained; its supporters
still clamored for better conditions. Arab nationalist goals were just as
popular in May 1957 as in the days of Sulayman al-Nabulsi's government.
And Arab nationalism seemed to be moving apace, with the unification
of Syria and Egypt in 1958. The Hashemite form of territorial nationalism remained under threat from both domestic and regional forces, as a
result. Information gleaned from the Jordanian security files, seized by

Israel in 1967, indicates that at least two political parties made preparations for an armed overthrow of the Jordanian regime between 1957 and 1959.[3] In these files, reports show that Communists stockpiled weapons, smuggled in from the Gaza Strip. The Ba'th Party trained military cadres at bases in Syria to prepare for a military coup d'état, tentatively planned for 1958 or 1959.[4]

The problem King Husayn faced in 1957 was to find a way to widen Homi Bhabha's "circle of growing national subjects," but without appreciably altering the pillars of his state. The Hashemites had always garnered support from the population by "working" to service their needs. The events of April 1957 had shown that the Hashemites had acquired a large well of support among the populace. To expand that power base, they needed to extend services even more widely than they had ever done before. They needed to improve the lives of the urban residents and provide avenues for governmental decision-making for the professional intelligentsia. They also had to appease or subdue the Palestinian population growing in numbers and starting to form specifically Palestinian political and military organizations throughout the 1960s. The Hashemites needed to co-opt these groups into their sphere or permanently negate their influence. But merely extending services would no longer satisfy the politicized population; the state would also have to actively struggle to gain the loyalty of the population. The historical narrative of the Hashemite state would have to be accepted by the bulk of the population for the Hashemites to survive.

The Hashemites had to conduct this new campaign amidst continuing opposition at home and in the region. For example, when the Iraqi military overthrew the Hashemite regime in 1958, King Husayn requested the return of the British military to help protect his throne. Gamal Abdel Nasser's Sawt al-'Arab radio station kept up a barrage of attacks against this act. According to Naseer Aruri, Egyptian radio was so successful the Jordanian security forces confiscated radios in coffeehouses and arrested anyone caught listening to it.[5] Even more distressing for the government, "With the presence of British troops on Jordanian soil, it could no longer boast about having liberated the country from British domination. The ouster of General Glubb and the abrogation of the Anglo-Jordanian agreement gave much-needed popularity to the King."[6] Within a few months, Britain withdrew its troops, but not before the throne uncovered a plot against the regime. Threats to the king and the Hashemite regime itself continued throughout the 1960s. In the most dramatic event, Prime Minister Hazza' al-Majali was assassinated on August 29, 1960. King Husayn accused the Egyptians of perpetrating the act. The next parliament, led by Samir al-Rifaʿi, proved to be far more reactionary as a consequence.

THE HASHEMITE COUNTEROFFENSIVE

To forestall a coup, the Hashemite state waged a multipronged campaign to win the hearts of the populace. From the creation of a comprehensive social safety net, to the writing of school textbooks, to the opening of museums of "national heritage," the state brought people under its wings, both physically and ideologically. Jordan did not witness a revolution or a military coup, as its neighbors did, in part because the regime supplied the services the people wanted and a national story giving it the legitimacy to do so, not to mention the fact that its intelligence organization grew competent enough to uncover antagonistic plots. The myriad institutions now affecting, and often improving, people's everyday lives came via the agency of the Hashemite state—and the state continually made that connection clear.[7] The work the Hashemites began in 1921 was accelerated in the 1960s and 1970s.

In the early 1960s, the chief proponents of these changes were King Husayn and his political ally, Wasfi al-Tell. On January 27, 1962, King Husayn appointed Wasfi al-Tell as the prime minister of a government dedicated to expanding social services and improving the economic situation in the country. Al-Tell formed a second government on December 2, 1962, after the parliamentary elections, and remained in office until March 27, 1963. He returned again from 1965 to 1967 and was assassinated in Cairo in 1971, during his final tenure. As Asher Susser analyzes this new tack, "Husayn sought to accord the new government an innovative image. He wanted to portray Jordan as standing on the threshold of a new era—a period of concentration on domestic affairs, political liberalization and economic development. Jordan, the King said in his letter of appointment to Tall, was to become a 'model homeland.'"[8] Paul Kingston concurs when he says that King Husayn, with a measure of political stability achieved, wanted to "broaden the domestic bases of support for and legitimacy of the Hashemite State. The key groups in this regard were the young, educated, technocratic classes, many of them of Palestinian origin."[9] As a symbol of this new direction, all twelve members of al-Tell's first cabinet were new to their government positions, with the median age forty-three. All of them held college degrees and three had doctorates.[10] Al-Tell specifically chose professionals because so many had been involved in the different political parties of the 1950s.

This meant that they were disciplined and organized.[11] By promoting these men, the al-Tell government finally pushed from positions of influence the old "King's men" who had ruled the country since the Mandate period.[12] To further incorporate the urban professional intelligentsia and to exclude the old political appointees, al-Tell also introduced an examination system for the Ministries of Foreign Affairs and the Interior, thus instituting the rudiments of a meritocracy.[13] From March to May 1962, al-Tell purged the bureaucracy of many political appointees, with members of influential families losing their posts.[14] The government also announced a general amnesty in honor of the birth of the king's first son, 'Abdullah, on January 30, 1962. All political prisoners, with the exception of the Communists, were allowed to leave prison or return to the country if they had fled in 1957. The Communists received the same rights in 1965.

The special focus of al-Tell's successive governments was the economic situation in the country and the need to create a stable social safety net. As Susser says,

> Husayn believed in the possibility of transforming Jordan into a sort of success story, and so did Tall. This was to be achieved by means of economic development, efficient administration and the enhancement of the regime's legitimacy—not by the cultivation of an ideology, but by ensuring "a better life"; not socialism, but pragmatism, and the implementation of a policy the prime objective of which was to establish a socio-economically contented community of citizens, not unduly harassed or oppressed by government.[15]

Many of the same activists of the Ministry of Economy of the 1950s found voice in the 1960s under Wasfi al-Tell. "These ideas were not al-Tall's invention; indeed, their pedigree extended back to the 1950s where they had been cultivated and acted upon by a group of technocrats congregated in the MNE [Ministry of National Economy] under the leadership of Hamad al-Farhan. After the period of drift in the late 1950s and early 1960s, al-Tall provided these ideas with renewed energy and political clout and seemed to offer hope to the more progressive classes that the Hashemite State could be reformed from within."[16] As Kingston states, particular focus was placed on extending services into the rural areas, with agricultural assistance and the building of new schools.[17] By recognizing both the need to service the rural areas of the country and the necessity of advertising those reforms, al-Tell highlighted the connection between the state and the improvements appearing in people's lives. In just two examples, in the early 1960s, the regime built the East Ghor Canal to extend irrigation by tens of thousands of acres and the oil refinery in Zarqa to more efficiently provide oil to the population. Stable prices, expansion in tourism, and the availability of foreign products all created an atmosphere of growth and support for the regime in the first half of the 1960s.[18]

Alongside these changes, the army and the government continued to provide jobs for a growing number of citizens. For example, reform did not mean curtailing the power and size of the Jordanian Arab Army (JAA). "The expenditure of the JAA clearly needed reining in, yet, as Husayn himself recognized in private talks with Americans, to attack this pillar of the Hashemite State threatened to alienate his traditional basis of support within the various tribal elements of the country and precipitate the downfall of his regime."[19] In fact, recruitment actually increased in the early 1960s.[20] In the mid-1960s, the army employed about 15 percent of the labor force.[21] In 1965, the Jordanian government employed 20,550 civilian officials and 15,000 unskilled daily wage workers.[22]

Education, in the late 1960s and 1970s, became compulsory for all children; between 1961 and 1966, for example, total enrollment in all Jordanian schools increased by about 45 percent, while the population increased by only 3 percent.[23] The state opened the University of Jordan in 1962, which, in 1967, had a student body of 2,176.[24] Educational expansion clearly provided the Jordanian state with the opportunity to spread the Hashemite-Arab national narrative to larger groups of students. The overall goal was to develop "Jordanian society in the context of an integrated Arab nation," by, among other things, "fusing together the different population groups into a harmonious and cohesive Arab Jordanian society, through pride in Arab values and spiritual ideals, and the fostering of sound social traditions in a manner consistent with continuous cultural development."[25] To nullify the role of the Jordanian National Movement in the push for Arab unity, the state reiterated the Hashemite place in that Arab history. The Hashemites placed themselves, yet again, at the center of Arab history, the Hashemites serving as the bridge between that history and the current state of Jordan.

Harking back to the discussion in Chapter 1, the cornerstone of this Hashemite nationalization process was the production of textbooks laying out the national narrative the Hashemites wanted the students to imbibe.[26] The Hashemites produced a small number of textbooks in the mid-1950s, but accelerated the process in 1959. Nineteen fifty-nine appears to be a key date, because after the physical destruction of the National Movement, the state clearly wanted to produce a more multidimensional campaign to control the students' nationalized vocabulary. In so doing, the Hashemites specifically co-opted the goals and messages of the JNM, acknowledging the worthiness of them and the passion with which they were put forward. However, all the goals and victories are couched as Hashemite ones. No leader of the JNM is ever mentioned, nor are the parties identified.

The Arab Revolt provides the vital link among the earlier march of Arab history, the articulation of Arab nationalism, and Hashemite rule over Jordan. The Arab Revolt of World War I, led by Sharif Husayn and his sons, played a prominent role in all the Arab history textbooks published throughout the region prior to the independence of Jordan. In Jordan's own textbooks, starting in the 1950s, the Arab Revolt takes on a much more important role, not only for the Hashemite family but for all of Arab history. Throughout all the textbooks, Sharif Husayn's fight to protect and expand the rights of the Arabs is reiterated, starting with his concern as early as 1908 that Young Turk policies would turn out to be hostile to the Arabs.[27] As "leader of the Arab rebirth," he called on the Arabs to "Come to the Jihad, Come to the Jihad."[28] With this call, Sharif Husayn combined allegiances to both Islam and the Arab world, tying together the Hashemite family's descent from the Prophet and its current political activities. As the textbook further states, "Sharif Husayn had three sons and they were emirs: Ali, 'Abdullah and Faysal shared in their father's feelings of nationalism and in his battle to free the Arab umma and [achieve] its unity. There is no doubt that you remember that the late Emir Faysal was the most distinguished member of the secret Young Arab Society which was established in Paris to oppose the Movement to Turkify the Arabs inside the Ottoman Empire."[29] In this way, the movements of Arab nationalism and Sharif Husayn's Arab Revolt merged together, forming part of the natural progression from the Arab Awakening of the nineteenth century to its culmination in the events of World War I, all via the agency of the Hashemite family. "His grave today [on the Haram al-Sharif in Jerusalem] still provokes the Arabs and Muslims to work hard to rescue the holy country from the Zionists and colonialism."[30] According to the narrative presented in these texts, the British government understood the exalted position Sharif Husayn held in the Arab nationalist movement, so looked to him to lead the Revolt.[31] While all the texts published throughout the Arab world make some connection between the Arab Revolt and the earlier movement of Arab nationalism, textbooks published in Jordan go even further and state that the Arab Revolt, personified in the image of Sharif Husayn, made the Hashemites the unquestioned leaders of the Arab nationalist movement. This served as a pointed critique of the Arab nationalist narrative so influential for the leaders of the Jordanian National Movement.

The textbooks of the late 1950s straightforwardly describe 'Abdullah's march into Ma'an in April 1920 and his stated intention that he planned to liberate Syria from French rule. The British then accepted him as a potential leader and requested that he rule over the new Emirate of Transjordan.[32] By the 1960s, his march had taken on a new importance. In the newer version, 'Abdullah's army posed such a threat to stability in the region that the British colonial secretary, Winston Churchill, hurried to Jerusalem to forestall the possibility.[33] Starting with the 1969 textbook, the narrative adds a new component, stressing the fact that the people of Transjordan gave 'Abdullah the title of "savior of Syria," in recognition of the importance of his act.[34]

To downplay the power presented by the JNM, and to stake a stronger claim for national legitimacy in the country, the textbooks excessively praise King Husayn's style of government. Nineteen fifty-nine serves as the turning point for this narrative, as all textbooks published in that year and afterward take on the form of hagiographies of King Husayn. According to the textbooks published throughout the 1960s and 1970s, King Husayn led a constitutional monarchy, unifying the Palestinian and Jordanian people. He won the hearts of all the people in the country and the region when he ousted John Bagot Glubb as leader of the Jordanian Arab Army on March 1, 1956, and, by so doing, Arabized the nation's military. This is the only time Glubb's name is ever revealed in the texts; his importance lies merely in his departure, not in his work for the country. Along this same line, the textbooks credit King Husayn with signing the Arab Solidarity Pact with Egypt, Syria, and Saudi Arabia in January 1957 and abrogating the 1948 Anglo-Jordanian Treaty. By so doing, King Husayn thus takes credit for Jordanian independence from foreign entanglements.

The attempted coup of April 1957, whoever the actors involved, could not be ignored in the narrative, so appears as yet another opportunity for King Husayn to protect the people and wage the fight against imperialism. "Among the distressing things that occurred after [the abrogation of the Anglo-Jordanian Treaty in March] was not what the Arabs wanted. Civil strife broke out in Jordan, which was ended quickly, and there occurred a problem in the understanding between Jordan and Egypt and Syria as a result of foreign efforts among them. Egypt and Syria did not pay their installments, according to the Arab Solidarity Agreement, and this act cut into the soul of Jordan."[35] No mention is made of the fact that

King Husayn then turned to the United States for help in destroying the National Movement.

The Hashemite kings also present themselves as the strongest, and often the sole, protectors of the Palestinian people. For example, the textbooks credit 'Abdullah with leading the interwar and post–World War II movement to protect the area from Zionism and colonialism. "The Palestinian Arabs could not ignore the services King 'Abdullah had offered to the Arabs of Palestine in their struggle which continued for thirty years against the British and the Zionists. ['Abdullah] used his country as a center for sending weapons, supplies and volunteers for the Arab struggles in Palestine, especially during the Great Palestinian Revolt of 1936."[36] In a clear omission, the Mufti of Jerusalem, Hajj Amin al-Husayni, is mentioned for the first time in 1969's *al-Tarikh al-Hadith [Modern History]*, and then only among a list of Palestinian officials who had to flee the country during the 1936–1939 Palestinian Revolt. He is accorded no other respect, and his role as a political leader in Palestine is never mentioned because of the historic rivalry between the Hashemite and Husayni families. This omission fits the pattern in all the textbooks of neglecting to mention political figures who posed a threat to the Hashemite leadership. In contrast, in a number of books on Palestine the exploits of numerous "heroes" are detailed; none of these men is a well-known political or national figure. They are regular people fighting on behalf of their Arab-Palestinian nation and thus do not represent a real threat to the Hashemite position.

During the 1948 War, the Jordanian army, its leadership under John Bagot Glubb going unmentioned, succeeded in protecting East Jerusalem and the West Bank. Then, because of the praise and respect accorded to King 'Abdullah by the Palestinians, they voted, "entirely of their own accord," to unite the West Bank with the East Bank of the Jordan River in 1950.[37] King 'Abdullah's assassination in Jerusalem in 1951 is mentioned in every textbook; however, the perpetrator of the crime, a Palestinian, is never identified, either by name or nationality. 'Abdullah is just declared a martyr to the Arab cause as a result of his death.

Throughout King Husayn's reign, according to the textbooks' explicit message, the Hashemite role as protectors of the Palestinian people and the Hashemite leadership position in the Arab nationalist movement are one. In essence, Husayn is ready to sacrifice his life in order to return Palestine to the Palestinians. "The goal for which all the Arabs were striving was the return of Palestine, and our beloved King Husayn dedicated the greatest part of his thoughts and concerns to this goal and he knew, under the protection of God, with his wisdom and well-known sagacity, that the one route to return the stolen part of Palestine was through power, and so he began to strengthen the Jordanian Arab Army."[38] In addition, sufficient power would only be achieved through the unity of the Arabs, an end that King Husayn continually tried to accomplish. "His Majesty is still drawing up clever plans to achieve the Arab unity which all the Arabs seek. We have pride in the exalted role which His Majesty has established in mending the relationships between the Arab nations and in uniting the forces to facilitate complete Arab unity."[39] In uniting Jordan with Iraq, albeit briefly, in 1957, he further proved his credentials as an Arab leader.

With inspectors and tight control over the syllabi and textbooks, the Ministry of Education was able, to a far greater extent than in the Mandate period and in the 1950s, to dictate a national message to the students. As Husni Ayesh, a longtime educator, has pointed out, teachers had a certain leeway in the 1950s to express their own political views, but those openings have been progressively closed by action of the state since that time.[40] The message disseminated to thousands of students was that the Hashemites are the state's leaders, the sole givers of largesse, and also the national liberators of the Arabs. This story leaves no room for an alternative national message, of Arab, Palestinian, or even subaltern Jordanian tribal or regional nationalism. Students are bombarded by the Hashemites, in these texts, in pictures on the wall, on holidays commemorating great events in Hashemite-Jordanian history. Reinforcing these messages is an awareness that the state serves as the largest employer in the country; opposition means unemployment. Thus, when the messages of affirmation do not work, the repressive apparatus complements them.

Museums and exhibits have opened to display Jordan's cultural heritage, as defined by the Hashemite state. "Traditional" costumes have appeared since the 1970s and 1980s in museums and on television shows. According to Linda Layne, "Alia, the Jordanian airline, has sponsored a number of fashion shows of women modeling traditional dresses and/or new high-fashion versions of the same."[41] She also reports that Queen Noor opened the first Jerash Festival in 1981, "wearing a beautifully embroidered gown, one that did not represent any single tribe or village but was an exquisitely fine example of the combined traditions of the area."[42] The goal was to locate the popular components of the primordial nation. "The folklore section worked from the middle of 1968 on collecting samples illustrating popular traditions. These samples took the form of clothes, some of the tools used in daily life in rural areas, popular songs and the sayings and recollections of elderly people, Bedouin and popular poetry, etc."[43] The Jordanian Folklore Museum and the Jordanian Museum of Popular Traditions, often called the Costume and Jewelry Museum, located in opposite wings of the Roman Amphitheater in Amman, display the costumes of Jordan's different tribal and religious groupings. By presenting these instruments, clothes, and activities in a national museum, the Hashemites included them as intrinsic components of Hashemite-Jordanian society. No names are given, no individuals are identified, but the society presented is all part of the Hashemite project. The Hashemites are co-opting these aspects of culture to fill out their society, to give at least a two-dimensional view of it. They are also implicitly calling on people to move on from these practices, as these exist in the past; the Hashemite future has no place for them.

Complementing this process is the state's emphasis on the bedouin nature of the society, particularly in tourist literature and promotions. The kings appear in bedouin garb in thousands of pictures posted around the country, and tourist books extol bedouin customs. As Layne reports, "In fact in both government- and privately produced touristic materials Bedouin (usually in full regalia) appear to be the only people of Jordan."[44] Before 1967, tourist imagery focused on the biblical sites of the West Bank, changing afterward to the Nabatean sites at Petra. Distinctive tribes do not appear in this literature, just their generalized existence is recognized. The clothing and customs of the bedouin have been co-opted by the Hashemite state as part of its program to fill out the national narrative and give it grounding in the Jordanian—nonurban—experience. In glorifying this indigenous Jordanian culture, the regime is delineating the difference between Jordanians and the majority Palestinian population, solidifying the former's loyalty.[45]

In the 1960s, the king also supported the Muslim Brotherhood as a counterweight to the continuing popularity of the JNM's parties and leaders. As a result, the state granted the Muslim Brotherhood the right to lead and influence many of the legal and cultural institutions of the state. For example, religious courts retained jurisdiction over personal status laws and Islamic waqfs, the religious endowments.[46] Leaders of the Brotherhood, such as Ishaq Farhan and Abdul Latif 'Arabiyyat, held high positions within the Ministry of Education throughout the 1970s and 1980s and had "something of a watchdog role over the content of school curricula and television programmes."[47] Occasionally, problems occurred in the relationship between the Brotherhood and the state. In 1963, Brotherhood members in parliament refused to grant Wasfi al-Tell a vote of confidence because his government did not plan to implement the Shari'ah effectively enough. However, this act did not cause a breach in the relationship between the state and the Brotherhood. As Ali Abdul Kazem has theorized, "Reconciliation followed every misunderstanding between the two, not only because the particulars of Brotherhood meetings were in the open and did not have to be monitored, or because Brotherhood activists and followers were more than welcome to enter parliament or to sit in government, but mainly because the group rushed to offer support to the regime in times of need and crucial crises (the 1950s and early 1960s)."[48] Through this relationship, the Hashemites confirmed their religious legitimacy and gained a large body of supporters at the same time.

As a result of these reforms and this support, the Hashemite national project generated allegiance from many of the JNM's own leaders. As Uriel Dann analyzes, "by 1967, there was hardly a malcontent who had made a name for himself as an enemy of the Hashemite Entity and who had not returned to the king's peace and been given, as often as not, a lucrative position."[49] The Hashemites proved to be geniuses at co-optation, as even the most hardened opposition figures found solace in their institutions. Ali Abu Nuwar lived primarily in Egypt while in exile. After his return to Jordan in 1964, he slowly worked his way back into the regime, eventually serving in the upper house of the majlis. Even Subhi Abu Ghunaymah, exiled to Syria for thirty years, was allowed to return in the 1960s; he was then appointed Jordan's ambassador to Syria.[50] Sulayman al-Nabulsi found an ambiguous position in the country after being released from house arrest in the 1960s, taking positions in the government but constantly serving as a focus for political opposition. As part of his political rehabilitation, he served in the appointed Majlis al-A'yan in the mid-1960s, and the government honored his life's work by naming a major street in Amman after him.[51] At the same time, his home became, yet again, a center for political discussions. Just as in the 1950s, people across the entire political spectrum congregated at his home to debate events of the day.

RESISTANCE CONTINUES

Still others chose to continue their oppositional activities within new kinds of political organizations. The Jordanian leaders of the National Movement, in large part, remained within the Jordanian sphere of political action. Abd al-Rahman Shuqayr fled to Syria soon after the government crackdown in April 1957. Shuqayr returned to Jordan in 1965 as a result of the amnesty granted by King Husayn. Ya'qub Ziyadin found himself, after being captured, imprisoned in al-Jafr. Ziyadin was released as a result of the 1965 amnesty and immediately moved to East Germany, where he worked and studied until 1968. He then returned to Jordan to reestablish his medical practice and his political activities.

A few of the Jordanian members of the National Movement became actively involved in military activities in Palestine during the 1960s. Mahmud al-Mu'ayta remained in al-Jafr prison for five years and then helped lead a Ba'th fedayeen movement, entitled Sa'iqa, after 1968. It included members from the Golan Heights and southern Lebanon, but mostly involved participants from Jordan.[52] During the 1960s and early 1970s, Sa'iqa commandos perpetrated a number of raids against Israeli targets.

The Ba'th Party structure became divided in the 1960s as splits occurred that have never been repaired. In particular, the Jordanian and Palestinian members battled over the role Nasser would play in their future activities. 'Abdullah al-Rimawi particularly favored supporting Nasser and ended up forming his own, independent Ba'th Party in May 1960, officially entitled Hizb al-Ba'th al-'Arabi al-Thawri al-Ishtiraki [Arab Socialist Revolutionary Ba'th Party], when many other members would not follow his lead. This party remained active until 1962 or 1963.[53] Bahjat Abu Gharbiyah kept up his political work, becoming a member of the Palestine Liberation Organization's executive council in 1964 and founding the Palestinian Popular Struggle Front (PPSF) in 1968. As a result of his activities, he found himself in Jordanian jails a number of times throughout the 1970s.

Munif al-Razzaz joined an Iraqi-aligned Ba'thist guerrilla movement, the Arab Liberation Front, in 1966.[54] Al-Razzaz arose within the leadership of the Iraqi Ba'th structure, becoming a member of the National Committee in 1977 and moving to Baghdad about the same time. He later died there under house arrest. Shahir Abu Shahut also joined the Iraqi branch of the Ba'th Party and became the head of the Jordanian section after being released from al-Jafr in 1962 at the time of a government amnesty. He lived in Baghdad from 1970 to 1975 while he led the Palestinian office of the Ba'th Party in that city.

As these continuing activities demonstrate, the actions of King Husayn and the Hashemite regime did not completely wipe out the opposition. Nor did they eliminate all criticism of the regime's practices. Many periods of martial law followed the destruction of the JNM in 1957, and political parties continued to function underground throughout the 1970s and 1980s. Palestinian military groups increasingly used Jordanian soil to attack Israel and, simultaneously, to weaken Hashemite control in areas of

Jordan itself. The popular support shown during the liberalization period of the early 1990s illustrates that the Jordanian population desired a more participatory governmental structure than the Hashemites have typically allowed. However, the Hashemite national project has been successful in gathering enough support to counteract any opposition activities or views and thus has survived far longer than any neighboring regime.

CONCLUSION

This multipronged approach by the Hashemites made people beholden to the state for their survival and livelihood and then loyal to its continued rule. Institutions formed the superstructure of the state; the people gradually granted it support. The Hashemite national narrative now had bodies inside of it, giving it life. The Jordanian example illustrates how a colonial state, with a foreign leadership, can be transformed into a nation. As the Hashemites have shown, if the leadership makes itself indispensable because of the services it offers, it can slowly gain support for its activities. A national narrative must be written along the way that holds resonance with the "traditions" of the area and the new institutions being forged on the ground.

The Hashemite example also shows that the leadership must take into account the desires of the population. The very existence and expansion of the Hashemite state structure meant that lives were changed throughout the country, through the emergence of new agencies of change. No state can control all the information disseminated in these agencies nor can it direct the participants toward skills and ideas needed only to address the state's concerns. In most postcolonial nations, the resulting clash has led to revolutions and coups when the postindependence governments could not fulfill the demands of the rising social strata. In the Hashemite case, the Jordanian National Movement leaders presented themselves as the "nationalists" bent on overthrowing the "alienness of the ruling group." Via the agency of Arab nationalism they stood as the vanguard of change, the only force capable of overthrowing the "old" for the "new." Yet they failed; they could not overcome the support the Hashemite regime generated. The Hashemites had taken on the roles in people's lives of shaykhs of the tribe, as fathers of the family, as leaders of the modern state. By the 1960s, the Hashemites backed this claim up with a new social safety net that gradually encompassed much of the population. In the end, the Hashemites succeeded in convincing much of this population that they were the true "nationalists," by co-opting the goals, symbols, and messages of the JNM. It did not matter that the historical narrative omitted the actions of the Jordanian populace; the Hashemites stood in as their representatives. The ever-expanding "traditions" of the Hashemite state—in the museums and the tourist sites of Jordan—provided visceral connections to the narrative the ruling family disseminated. Is Jordan the Hashemite family and is the Hashemite family Jordan? Yes and no. Indigenously and internationally, the Hashemites are the accepted standard-bearers of the nation, but behind them stands a population that has demanded that its concerns be addressed. Jordan was not a blank slate in 1921, and the Hashemites succeeded because they recognized that.

NOTES

CHAPTER 1

1. Yahya Tahir al-Hijawi, Sadi Murad al-Khayat, and Adnan Lutfi Uthman, *Tarikhuna al-Hadith [Our Modern History]*, Sixth Grade Reader (Nablus: Wizarat al-Tarbiyah wa-al-Taʿlim al-Urduniyah, 1959), 4.

2. See Saʿid al-Dura, Abdul-Rahim Murʿib, Sadiq Uda, and Abd al-Bari al-Shaykh Dura, *al-Tarikh al-ʿArabi al-Hadith [Modern Arab History]* (Amman: Wizarat al-Tarbiyah wa-al-Taʿlim al-Urduniyah, 1975), 174.

3. Saʿid al-Dura, Abdul-Rahim Murʿib, Sadiq Uda, and Abdul-Bari al-Shaykh Dura, *al-Tarikh al-ʿArabi al-Hadith [Modern Arab History]*, Third Secondary Level (Amman: Wizarat al-Tarbiyah wa-al-Taʿlim al-Urduniyah, 1969), 147.

4. al-Dura et al. (1975), 171.

5. See Benedict Anderson, *Imagined Communities: Reflections on the Origin and Spread of Nationalism*, rev. ed. (London and New York: Verso, 1991), for the use of this term. The Hijaz region contains the Muslim holy cities of Mecca and Medina. The Hashemite family, as descendants of the Prophet, traditionally controlled the holy sites located in these cities. Husayn, ʿAbdullah's father, served as the Sharif of Mecca, an Ottoman government post, starting in 1908. ʿAbdullah spent his life shuttling between the Hijaz and the Ottoman capital, Istanbul. For a period before World War I, he served as the Hijazi representative to the Ottoman parliament. Before the establishment of Transjordan, none of the Hashemites had ever lived in the area. Since 1924, the Hijaz has been controlled by the Saudi family and, since 1930, by the Kingdom of Saudi Arabia.

6. See Andrew Shryock, *Nationalism and Genealogical Imagination: Oral History and Textual Authority in Tribal Jordan* (Berkeley and Los Angeles: University of California Press, 1997), 222, for a discussion of this phenomenon.

7. al-Hijawi et al., 108.

8. For examples of how these terms are used, see Saif al-Din Zaid al-Kaylani and Abbas Ahmad al-Kurd, *al-Mujtamaʿ al-Urduni [Jordanian Society]* (Amman: Wizarat al-Tarbiyah wa-al-Taʿlim al-Urduniyah, 1964), 6–12.

9. With British aid, the Hashemite family led the Arab Revolt against the Ottoman Empire during World War I. Sharif Husayn, the father, organized the Revolt from the family's stronghold in the Hijaz. After World War I, he proclaimed himself King Husayn, King of the Arabs, although few Arabs—or the British—recognized this designation. In 1924, the Saudi-Wahhabi alliance conquered the Hijaz, and King Husayn was forced to flee to Cyprus. As commander of the Arab Army, the youngest son, Faysal, successfully liberated Damascus from Ottoman rule in October 1918 and set up an Arab government. In March 1920, the Syrian Arab Congress declared him King of Syria. The French did not recognize this decision, so militarily ousted Faysal in December 1920. The British government then arranged for him to rule as King of Iraq.

10. The "King's men" were originally Palestinians seconded from the Palestine Mandate in the 1920s and 1930s. Robert Satloff describes their position by saying, "Abdullah built up a circle of non-Transjordanians who attained power and privilege solely because they had thrown in their lot with his. Loyalty to the monarchy was the only guarantee of their status; their vested interest in the survival and prosperity of Hashemite Jordan was almost as great as that of the Hashemites themselves. It was a mutually beneficial relationship, so much so that the partnership of Hashemite kings and an expatriate elite of 'king's men' survived well beyond Abdullah's demise." Robert B. Satloff, *From Abdullah to Hussein: Jordan in Transition* (New York: Oxford University Press, 1994), 7. By the 1950s, Jordanian politicians had also joined the ranks of the "King's men."

11. The Palestinians of the West Bank and East Jerusalem came under Jordanian control from 1948 until 1967.

12. Amnon Cohen, *Political Parties in the West Bank under the Jordanian Regime, 1949–1967* (Ithaca, N.Y.: Cornell University Press, 1980), 20 and 251. The terms "West Bank" and "East Bank" refer to the areas to the west and east of the Jordan River. "West Bank" means Palestine and "East Bank" means Jordan. The terms came into regular parlance by the late 1960s.

13. For the use of this term, see Linda L. Layne, *Home and Homeland: The Dialogics of Tribal and National Identities in Jordan* (Princeton, N.J.: Princeton University Press, 1994).

14. Benjamin Shwadran, *Jordan: A State of Tension* (New York: Council for Middle Eastern Affairs, 1959), 392. General John Bagot Glubb created the Desert Mobile Force in the 1930s and from 1939 to 1956 served as the chief of staff of the Jordanian Arab Legion.

15. Uriel Dann, *King Hussein and the Challenge of Arab Radicalism: Jordan, 1955–1967* (New York: Oxford University Press, 1989), 169.

16. Satloff, 175. Alec Kirkbride served as the last British Advisor to the Emirate of Transjordan and the first British ambassador to the Hashemite Kingdom of Jordan after independence.

17. Partha Chatterjee, *The Nation and Its Fragments: Colonial and Postcolonial Histories* (Princeton, N.J.: Princeton University Press, 1993), 10.

18. Ibid.

19. Shryock, *Nationalism and Genealogical Imagination;* Michael R. Fischbach, *State, Society, and Land in Jordan* (Leiden, the Netherlands: Brill, 2000); and

Joseph A. Massad, *Colonial Effects: The Making of National Identity in Jordan* (New York: Columbia University Press, 2001).

20. Sulayman al-Nabulsi recorded his memoirs before his death, but his family and the interviewer have not made them available to Western researchers. Many people in Jordan report having listened to portions of the tapes but none has used them to conduct a research project on Jordan and its political parties.

21. In the 1950s, both men worked within the leadership of the Ba'th Party and led an opposition bloc in parliament for much of the decade.

22. Author interview with Jamal al-Sha'ir, Amman, Jordan, June 24, 1998.

23. The phrase "professional intelligentsia" has been taken from Anthony D. Smith. In defining the concept of a professional intelligentsia, Anthony Smith has stated that "To be a member of the professional intelligentsia is to have a vocation, but also to engage in a certain kind of occupation in order to gain a livelihood; it is to live off one's education and become a member of a particular 'guild' or profession, and accept its code of conduct." *The Ethnic Revival* (Cambridge: Cambridge University Press, 1981), 108–109.

CHAPTER 2

1. *Arar: The Poet and Lover of Jordan*, selected by Abdullah Radwa, translated by Sadik I. Odeh (Amman: National Library, 1999), 65.

2. Author interview with Hamad al-Farhan, Amman, Jordan, June 23, 1998. He was a Jordanian leader of the Movement of Arab Nationalists in the 1950s.

3. Bahjat Abu Gharbiyah, *Fi Khidham al-Nidhal al-'Arabi al-Filastini: Mudhakkirat al-Munadil Bahjat Abu Gharbiyah, 1916–1949 [In the Roar of the Palestinian Struggle: Memoirs of the Fighter Bahjat Abu Gharbiyah, 1916–1949]* (Beirut: Mu'assasat al-Dirasat al-Filastiniyah, 1993), 25. He was a Palestinian leader of the Ba'th Party in the 1950s.

4. In Chatterjee's analysis, "By my reading, anticolonial nationalism creates its own domain of sovereignty within colonial society well before it begins its political battle with the imperial power. It does this by dividing the world of social institutions and practices into two domains—the material and the spiritual. The material is the domain of the 'outside,' of the economy and of statecraft, of science and technology, a domain where the West had proved its superiority and the East had succumbed. In this domain, then, Western superiority had to be acknowledged and its accomplishments carefully studied and replicated. The spiritual, on the other hand, is an 'inner' domain bearing the 'essential' marks of cultural identity. The greater one's success in imitating Western skills in the material domain, therefore, the greater the need to preserve the distinctness of one's spiritual culture." Partha Chatterjee, *The Nation and Its Fragments: Colonial and Postcolonial Histories* (Princeton, N.J.: Princeton University Press, 1993), 6.

5. Benedict Anderson, *Imagined Communities: Reflections on the Origin and Spread of Nationalism*, rev. ed. (London and New York: Verso, 1991), 7.

6. Homi K. Bhabha, *The Location of Culture* (London: Routledge, 1994), 145.

7. Fatma Müge Göçek, "Introduction: Narrative, Gender, and Cultural

Representation in the Constructions of Nationalism in the Middle East," in *Social Constructions of Nationalism in the Middle East*, ed. Fatma Müge Göçek (Albany: State University of New York Press, 2002), 4.

8. Göçek, "The Decline of the Ottoman Empire and the Emergence of Greek, Armenian, Turkish, and Arab Nationalisms," in *Social Constructions of Nationalism in the Middle East*, ed. Fatma Müge Göçek (Albany: State University of New York Press, 2002), 30.

9. Kamal Salibi, *The Modern History of Jordan* (London: I. B. Tauris & Co., 1993), 6.

10. Thongchai Winichakul, *Siam Mapped: A History of the Geo-Body of a Nation* (Honolulu: University of Hawaii Press, 1994), 54.

11. Alec S. Kirkbride, *A Crackle of Thorns: Experiences in the Middle East* (London: John Murray, 1956), 83–84. When Kirkbride and a Jordanian-Syrian team arrived in 1932 to officially demarcate the line on the ground they discovered that the instructions given to them from the committee actually resulted in a number of homes being bisected. At the time, Kirkbride joked that "I suggested that it would not really matter if a villager and his wife had supper in one country and went to bed in another." In the end, the participants on the ground decided that the instructions concerning the angle of the boundary could be modified by five degrees to allow houses to stand completely on one side of the line or the other (Kirkbride, 84–85).

12. Thongchai, 55–56.

13. Ibid., 53–54.

14. al-Farhan interview.

15. See Joseph A. Massad, *Colonial Effects: The Making of National Identity in Jordan* (New York: Columbia University Press, 2001).

16. John M. Roberts, "The Political Economy of Identity: State and Society in Jordan" (Ph.D. diss., University of Chicago, 1994), 35.

17. Ibid., 40.

18. Michael R. Fischbach, *State, Society, and Land in Jordan* (Leiden, the Netherlands: Brill, 2000), 1.

19. See Ibid., 5, for his explanation of this term.

20. Chatterjee, 10.

21. Fischbach, 177–178.

22. Anderson, 114.

23. Ibid.

24. Chatterjee, 10.

25. Abdullah, *Memoirs of King Abdullah of Transjordan*, ed. Philip P. Graves (London: Jonathan Cape, 1950), 208.

26. Mustafa Wahbah al-Tell ('Arar) was born in Irbid in 1899 and can be considered Jordan's uncrowned "poet laureate" for the interwar years. Richard Loring Taylor, *Mustafa's Journey: Verse of 'Arar, Poet of Jordan* (Irbid, Jordan: Yarmouk University, 1988), 1. He took the pen name of 'Arar in homage to 'Arar ibn 'Amr ibn Sha's al-Asadi, a man "who had an emaciated body and a wretched appearance that you despise when you look at him, but he reveals his true mettle when he speaks, and then we find ourselves facing a man endowed with a good

deal of sagacity, a great soul and considerable vigour." Because of these characteristics and other aspects of his own life, al-Tell felt that he resembled 'Arar. *Arar: The Poet and Lover of Jordan*, 25.

27. Andrew Shryock, *Nationalism and Genealogical Imagination: Oral History and Textual Authority in Tribal Jordan* (Berkeley and Los Angeles: University of California Press, 1997), 40.

28. Ibid., 71 n. 4.

29. Ibid., 303. The emphasis is Shryock's. Muhammad Hamdan al-'Adwan is an historiographer of the 'Adwan tribe.

30. Ibid.

31. See Ibid., 303–304, for more information on this transformation.

32. Rashid Khalidi, *Palestinian Identity: The Construction of Modern National Consciousness* (New York: Columbia University Press, 1997), 150–153.

33. Rashid Khalidi, "The Palestinians and 1948: The Underlying Causes of Failure," in *The War for Palestine: Rewriting the History of 1948*, ed. Eugene L. Rogan and Avi Shlaim (Cambridge: Cambridge University Press, 2001), 19.

34. 'Arif al-'Arif, *Tarikh al-Quds [History of Jerusalem]* (Egypt: Dar al-Ma'arif, 1951), 155.

35. Ylana N. Miller, *Government and Society in Rural Palestine: 1920–1948*, Modern Middle East Series, No. 9 (Austin: University of Texas Press, 1985), 117.

36. Sulayman Musa, *A'lam min al-Urdun: Hazza' al-Majali, Sulayman al-Nabulsi, Wasfi al-Tell [Distinguished Men of Jordan: Hazza' al-Majali, Sulayman al-Nabulsi, Wasfi al-Tell]* (Amman: al-Mamlakah al-Urduniyah al-Hashimiyah, 1986), 71.

37. United Kingdom, Colonial Office, *Palestine Royal Commission: Minutes of Evidence Heard at Public Sessions*, Colonial No. 134 (London: His Majesty's Stationery Office, 1937), 365. Hereafter *Minutes of Evidence*. George Antonius, a Lebanese man, served as the highest-ranking Arab in the Palestine Department of Education in the 1920s, but resigned in the 1930s because of frustration with British control over the Department. He wrote the famous book of Arab nationalism *The Arab Awakening* (Philadelphia: J. B. Lippincott, 1939).

38. Ngugi wa Thiong'o, *Decolonising the Mind: The Politics of Language in African Literature* (London: James Currey, 1997), 13. He is specifically addressing the displacement of indigenous languages in Africa by European ones.

39. Ibid., 14–15.

40. *Minutes of Evidence*, 365.

41. Ngugi, 14.

42. Gregory Starrett, *Putting Islam to Work: Education, Politics, and Religious Transformation in Egypt* (Berkeley and Los Angeles: University of California Press, 1998), 11.

43. An earlier version of this section appeared in Betty S. Anderson, "The Duality of National Identity in the Middle East: A Critical Review," *Critique* 11, no. 2 (Fall 2002): 229–250.

44. See Muhammad al-Qaymari, Abbas al-Kurd, and Abd al-Muhaysin Jabir, *Tarikh al-'Arab: Min al-'Ahd al-'Uthmani hata al-Waqt al-Hadith [History*

of the Arabs: From the Ottoman Era to the Present Time], 9th ed., commissioned by Wizarat al-Tarbiyah wa-al-Ta'lim al-Urduniyah (Amman: Matb'at Dar al-Aytam al-Islamiyah al-Sina'yah bi al-Quds, 1959), 46.

45. Muhammad Aza Druza, *Durus al-Tarikh al-'Arabi min Aqdam al-Azmanah ila Alan [Studies of Arab History from the Oldest of Times to Today]* (Damascus: al-Maktabah al-Wataniyah al-'Arabiyah bi Haifa, 1934), 322.

46. Ibid., 330–331.

47. Peter Gubser, *Politics and Change in al-Karak, Jordan: A Study of a Small Arab Town and Its District* (London: Oxford University Press, 1973), 131–132.

48. To give just one illustration of the "unique position" of this new group, A. Konikoff reports that the Emirate of Transjordan issued only 252 licenses to physicians between 1928 and 1943. In 1943, only 30 physicians and 10 dentists held licenses. A. Konikoff, *Transjordan: An Economic Survey* (Jerusalem: Economic Research Institute of the Jewish Agency for Palestine, 1946), 120 and 23.

49. Starrett, 63.

50. Guilain Denoeux, *Urban Unrest in the Middle East: A Comparative Study of Informal Networks in Egypt, Iran, and Lebanon* (Albany: State University of New York Press, 1993), 88.

51. Ibid.

52. Israel Gershoni, "Rethinking the Formation of Arab Nationalism in the Middle East, 1920–1945: Old and New Narratives," in *Rethinking Nationalism in the Arab Middle East*, ed. James Jankowski and Israel Gershoni (New York: Columbia University Press, 1997), 16.

53. Ibid.

54. Musa, *A'lam min al-Urdun*, 78.

CHAPTER 3

1. *Arar: The Poet and Lover of Jordan*, selected by Abdullah Radwa, translated by Sadik I. Odeh (Amman: National Library, 1999), 77–78.

2. Ibid., 160.

3. Richard Loring Taylor, *Mustafa's Journey: Verse of 'Arar, Poet of Jordan* (Irbid, Jordan: Yarmouk University, 1988), 3.

4. Eugene L. Rogan, *Frontiers of the State in the Late Ottoman Empire: Transjordan, 1850–1921*, Cambridge Middle East Studies 12 (Cambridge: Cambridge University Press, 1999), 1.

5. Ibid.

6. Ibid., 227. Cemal *Pasha* was the Ottoman governor of Damascus and then general of the Ottoman army during World War I.

7. Ibid., 228.

8. United Kingdom, Colonial Office, *An Interim Report on the Civil Administration of Palestine during the Period 1st July, 1920–30th June, 1921* (London: Her Majesty's Stationery Office, August 1921), 21.

9. Sulayman Musa, *Awraq min Dafter al-Ayyam Dhikrayat al-Ra'il al-Awal*

[Papers from a Daily Journal] (Amman: al-Mamlakah al-Urduniyah al-Hashimiyah, with support from Amanat Amman al-Kubra, 2000), 77.

10. The historical sources differ on the number of tribesmen who accompanied 'Abdullah. Mary C. Wilson, *King Abdullah, Britain and the Making of Jordan* (Cambridge: Cambridge University Press, 1990), reports on page 44 that five hundred to a thousand men came with him, and then states on page 48 that three hundred men were there. Ma'an Abu Nowar, *The History of the Hashemite Kingdom of Jordan*, Vol. 1, *The Creation and Development of Transjordan: 1920–1929* (Oxford: Middle East Centre, St. Antony's College, 1989), 40, places the number at five hundred. Ali al-Mahafazah, *al-'Alaqat al-Urduniyah al-Baritaniyah: min Ta'sis al-Imarah Hatta Ilgha' al-Muh'ahadah (1921–1957) [Jordanian and British Relations—From the Establishment of the Emirate to the End of the Treaty (1921–1957)]* (Beirut: Dar al-Nahar lil-Nashr, 1973), 33, favors the larger number, one thousand. The town of Ma'an was, at that time, part of the Hijaz, and came within the Emirate of Transjordan only in 1925.

11. Taylor, 4.

12. Ibid., 6.

13. Eugene L. Rogan, "The Making of a Capital: Amman, 1918–1928," in *Amman: Ville et Société—The City and Its Society*, ed. Jean Hannoyer and Seteney Shami (Beirut: Centre d'Études et de Recherches sur le Moyen-Orient Contemporain, 1996), 97.

14. Ibid., 101–103.

15. Ibid., 103.

16. Ibid., 103–104.

17. Michael R. Fischbach, *State, Society, and Land in Jordan* (Leiden, the Netherlands: Brill, 2000), 197.

18. Joseph A. Massad, *Colonial Effects: The Making of National Identity in Jordan* (New York: Columbia University Press, 2001), 36.

19. Fischbach, 4.

20. Ibid.

21. Thongchai Winichakul, *Siam Mapped: A History of the Geo-Body of a Nation* (Honolulu: University of Hawaii Press, 1994), 55.

22. Fischbach, 196.

23. Uriel Dann, *Studies in the History of Transjordan, 1920–1949: The Making of a State* (Boulder, Colo.: Westview Press, 1984), 5.

24. Taylor, 6.

25. In the first years after the establishment of the Emirate of Transjordan, the Saudis and the Transjordanians continually fought over the area of Wadi Jauf. For more information, see Wilson, 71–73.

26. Andrew Shryock, *Nationalism and Genealogical Imagination: Oral History and Textual Authority in Tribal Jordan* (Berkeley and Los Angeles: University of California Press, 1997), 88.

27. Abla Mohamed Amawi, "State and Class in Transjordan: A Study of State Autonomy. (Volumes I and II)" (Ph.D. diss., Georgetown University, 1993), 206. The Bani Sakhr claimed that Mithqal al-Fayiz was merely reclaiming the

lands the Ottomans had taken from them. I want to thank Michael Fischbach for pointing this out.

28. Massad, 247.

29. Taylor, 1.

30. Ibid., 5.

31. *Arar: The Poet and Lover of Jordan*, 64. ʿArar is referring to the Arab Revolt of World War I when discussing the "revolution."

32. Ibid., 157.

33. Taylor, 9. The official's name was C. A. Hooper. Taylor's text misspells his name.

34. Ibid.

35. *Arar: The Poet and Lover of Jordan*, 144. Joseph Massad explains that the title means "Father of Little-Jaw," because of a wound he received in World War I. Massad, 124.

36. *Arar: The Poet and Lover of Jordan*, 63. Raghadan Palace was the Emir's palace.

37. Ibid., 24.

38. Taylor, 1.

39. *Arar: The Poet and Lover of Jordan*, 59.

40. Ibid., 65. The Zamzam Spring is in Mecca and serves as an important component of the annual pilgrimage [hajj].

41. Ibid., 67–68.

42. Taylor, 1.

43. Ibid., 2.

44. Ibid.

45. Acting British Resident, "Report on the Political Situation for the Month of July 1931," United Kingdom, *Political Diaries of the Arab World: Palestine & Jordan, 1924–1936*, ed. Robert L. Jarman, Vol. 2. (Slough, UK: Archive Editions, 2001), 314. Hereafter *Political Diaries: Vol. 2*.

46. Many Syrians who came to Transjordan after the fall of Faysal's government settled in as merchants in the cities. Some chose to work within the "Transjordan for the Transjordanians" movement because they wanted more of a voice in this new government. The episode illustrates the shifting national allegiances taking place within the Fertile Crescent, as "migrants" naturally became citizens and national supporters of their adopted homelands. The many Palestinian officials seconded from the Mandate government served as loyal members of the Hashemite regime, gradually becoming "true" Jordanians in the process.

47. Werner Ernst Goldner, "The Role of Abdullah Ibn Husain, King of Jordan, in Arab Politics, 1914–1951: Critical Analysis of His Political Activities" (Ph.D. diss., Stanford University, 1954), 161.

48. "Transjordan," *Near East and India* (November 19, 1928): 639.

49. In 1939, the Legislative Council voted to change the name of the Executive Council to the Council of Ministers.

50. Sulayman Musa and Munib al-Madi, *Tarikh al-Urdun fi al-Qarn al-'Ishrin [The History of Jordan in the Twentieth Century]* (Amman: Maktabah al-Muhtasib, 1988), 280.

51. Goldner, 162–163.

52. Wilson, 238 n. 47.

53. Abu Nowar, 198–199.

54. Goldner, 162.

55. Kamel S. Abu Jaber, "The Legislature of the Hashemite Kingdom of Jordan: A Study in Political Development," *Muslim World* 59, nos. 3–4 (July–October 1969): 224.

56. Massad, 30–31.

57. The Electoral Law was drafted in the summer of 1928. The Electoral Law followed a pattern whereby ethnic and religious minorities received a certain number of guaranteed seats in the Legislative Council. This system benefited the minorities, deemed loyal to the state, and has remained a feature of Jordanian politics until the present day. The elections followed a two-tiered system wherein all male Transjordanians at the age of eighteen could vote in the primary election. Those elected in the primary then served as electors in the secondary elections. Two seats were also reserved for the northern and southern bedouin tribes, respectively, but the representatives were appointed, not elected.

58. United Kingdom, Colonial Office, "Report by His Majesty's Government in the United Kingdom of Great Britain and Northern Ireland to the Council of the League of Nations on the Administration of Palestine and Trans-Jordan for the Year 1929," in *Palestine and Transjordan Administration Reports, 1918–1948*, (Oxford: Archive Editions, 1995), 2:139.

59. Chief British Representative, "Report on Trans-Jordan by Chief British Representative: Period 1-3-1925 to 1-6-1925," *Political Diaries: Vol. 2*, 187–188. Rikabi Pasha, a Syrian, served as Chief Minister from March 1922 to February 1923 and from April 1924 to June 1926. Wilson, 217.

60. See Massad for a discussion of the intersection between laws and nation-building.

61. al-Mahafazah, 95.

62. United Kingdom, Colonial Office, "Report by His Britannic Majesty's Government to the Council of the League of Nations on the Administration of Palestine and Transjordan for the Year 1925," in *Palestine and Transjordan Administration Reports, 1918–1948* (Oxford: Archive Editions, 1995), 2:121.

63. Lars Wahlin, "Diffusion and Acceptance of Modern Schooling in Rural Jordan," in *The Middle Eastern Village: Changing Economic and Social Relations*, ed. Richard Lawless (London: Croom Helm, 1987), 152.

64. A. Konikoff, *Transjordan: An Economic Survey* (Jerusalem: Economic Research Institute of the Jewish Agency for Palestine, 1946), 27.

65. Hani al-Amad, *Cultural Policy in Jordan* (Paris: UNESCO, 1981), 62. Al-Amad's publication was published by UNESCO but reads like a government propaganda pamphlet.

66. Ibid., 62.

67. *Arar: The Poet and Lover of Jordan*, 95–96. 'Arar frequently equated drinking with freedom and happiness. As Taylor writes, "Arar seems to have held the curious notion that it was some kind of civic duty to appear inebriated on formal or state occasions as an expression of his opinion of the proceedings." Taylor, 1.

68. Taylor, 9.

69. Alec S. Kirkbride, *A Crackle of Thorns: Experiences in the Middle East* (London: John Murray, 1956), 62.

70. Riccardo Bocco and Tariq M. M. Tell, "*Pax Britannica* in the Steppe: British Policy and the Transjordanian Bedouin, 1923–39," in *Village, Steppe and State: The Social Origins of Modern Jordan*, ed. Eugene L. Rogan and Tariq Tell (London: British Academic Press, 1994), 127.

71. Massad, 110–111.

72. John Bagot Glubb, *A Soldier with the Arabs* (London: Hodder and Stoughton, 1957), 263.

73. Fischbach, 3.

74. Ibid., 198–199.

75. See Ibid., 170–178, for a more comprehensive discussion of this relationship.

76. Ibid., 77.

77. Ibid., 175.

78. Hani Hourani, *al-Tarkib al-Iqtisadi al-Ijtima'i li-Sharq al-Urdun (1921–1950) [The Socio-Economic Structure of Transjordan (1921–1950)]* (Beirut: Munazzamat al-Tahrir al-Filastiniyah, Markaz al-Abhath, n.d.), 91–92.

79. Amawi, 385.

80. See Amawi for a discussion of this development.

81. Fischbach, 176.

CHAPTER 4

1. Nabil Irsheidat, *Awraq Laysat Shakhsiyah: Mudhakkirat Nabil Irsheidat [Non-Personal Papers: Memoirs of Nabil Irsheidat]* (Damascus: Dar al-Yanabi', 2001), 14. Just as "Sham" means both Syria and Greater Syria, "Baghdan" includes both the city of Baghdad and the surrounding area.

2. Munif al-Razzaz, "Munif al-Razzaz Yatadhakkar: Sanawat al-Jami'ah" ["Munif al-Razzaz Remembers: The University Years"] *Akhar Khabar* 73 (January 3–4, 1994): 10.

3. Gabriel Almond and Sidney Verba, *The Civic Culture: Political Attitudes and Democracy in Five Nations* (Boston: Little, Brown and Co., 1965), 277.

4. Ibid., 286–287.

5. Abd al-Rahman Shuqayr, *Min Qasiyun . . . ila Rabbat 'Ammun: Rihlat al-'Umr [From Qasiyun . . . to Rabbat 'Ammun: A Stage of Life]*, Silsilat Ihya' al-Dhakirah al-Tarikhiyah (Amman: Kitab al-Urdun al-Jadid, 1991), 26.

6. The Balfour Declaration was issued on November 2, 1917. In it, the British government pledged its support for a Jewish homeland in Palestine.

7. Irsheidat, 8.

8. Ibid., 11.

9. Ibid., 12.

10. Ibid., 23.

11. Ibid., 25–26. Muhammad Bajis al-Majali would later be called "The

Za'im" because of his role in organizing the many street demonstrations in Amman during the 1950s. Author interview with Muhammad Bajis al-Majali, Amman, Jordan, July 11, 2000. "Za'im" technically means just leader in English, but the term also implies that the person holding the title has a mediating role between the populace and the governing authorities. The twentieth century witnessed a changing role for the za'ims of the urban centers as new types of leaders, particularly of the professional stratum, took over these positions. See Chapter 6 for more information on this point.

12. Ahmad Yousef al-Tall, "Education in Jordan: Being a Survey of the Political, Economic and Social Conditions Affecting the Development of the System of Education in Jordan, 1921–1977" (Ph.D. diss., Sind University, Hyderabad, Pakistan, 1978), 47.

13. Najati al-Bukhari, *Education in Jordan* (Amman: Ministry of Culture, n.d.), 8.

14. Abd al-Rahman Munif, *Story of a City: A Childhood in Amman*, trans. Samira Kawar (London: Quartet Books, 1996), 54.

15. Irsheidat, 15.

16. For example, Ya'qub Ziyadin was only the third person from his village to receive a secondary diploma. Ya'qub Ziyadin, *al-Bidayah: Sirah Dhatiyah . . . Arba'un Sanah fi al-Harakah al-Wataniyah al-Urduniyah [The Beginnings: A Personal Biographical History . . . Forty Years in the Jordanian National Movement]* (Beirut: House of Ibn Khaldun Printing, 1981), 22.

17. Gregory Starrett, *Putting Islam to Work: Education, Politics, and Religious Transformation in Egypt* (Berkeley and Los Angeles: University of California Press, 1998), 24.

18. Ibid., 57.

19. Throughout the 1930s and 1940s, instances did occur when the state punished teachers for disseminating political information to their students. A typical punishment would be transfer to another school district within the country.

20. Ziyadin, 17–18.

21. Author interview with Hamad al-Farhan, Amman, Jordan, June 23, 1998.

22. Shuqayr, 29.

23. Ibid., 31.

24. C. H. F. Cox, British Resident, "Report on the Political Situation for the Month of May 1936," United Kingdom, *Political Diaries of the Arab World: Palestine & Jordan, 1924–1936*, ed. Robert L. Jarman, Vol. 2 (Slough, UK: Archive Editions, 2001), 720. Hereafter *Political Diaries: Vol. 2.*

25. C. H. F. Cox, "Report on the Political Situation for the Month of June, 1936," *Political Diaries: Vol. 2*, 725.

26. Ngugi wa Thiong'o, *Writers in Politics: A Re-Engagement with Issues of Literature & Society* (Oxford: James Currey, 1997), 142–143.

27. Sulayman Musa, *A'lam min al-Urdun: Hazza' al-Majali, Sulayman al-Nabulsi, Wasfi al-Tell [Distinguished Men of Jordan: Hazza' al-Majali, Sulayman al-Nabulsi, Wasfi al-Tell]* (Amman: al-Mamlakah al-Urduniyah al-Hashimiyah, 1986), 59.

28. Hazza' al-Majali, *Mudhakkirati [My Memoirs]* (n.p.: n.p., 1960), 18. Hazza' al-Majali initially supported the opposition movement, serving as the first leader of the National Socialist Party (NSP). He stepped down in favor of Sulayman al-Nabulsi and then worked in positions in the government. He held the prime ministership in 1955, for six days, and then in 1960 when he was assassinated in office.

29. Irsheidat, 17.

30. Ibid., 20.

31. Asher Susser, *On Both Banks of the Jordan: A Political Biography of Wasfi al-Tall* (London: Frank Cass, 1994), 10. Wasfi al-Tell was 'Arar's son. He graduated from the American University of Beirut in 1941, fought with the British army in World War II, and then served in a number of government positions throughout the 1950s and 1960s. He held the position of prime minister three times in the 1960s and was assassinated by a Palestinian in Cairo in 1971.

32. Ibid., 12.

33. Ziyadin, 17.

34. Ali Abu Nuwar, *Huna Talashat al-'Arab: Mudhakkirat fi al-Siyasah al-'Arabiyah (1948–1964) [A Time of Arab Decline: Memoirs of Arab Politics (1948–1964)]* (London: Dar al-Saqi, 1990), 11.

35. Munif, 258.

36. Ibid.

37. British Resident, "Report on the Political Situation for the Month of March, 1938," United Kingdom, *Political Diaries of the Arab World: Palestine & Jordan, 1937–1938*, ed. Robert L. Jarman (Slough, UK: Archive Editions, 2001), 3:496.

38. Philip G. Altbach, *Higher Education in the Third World: Themes and Variations* (New York: Advent Books, 1987), 110.

39. Ibid., 123–124.

40. The National Bloc (al-Kutla al-wataniyah) steered Syria's political struggle from 1927 to independence in 1946. It emerged over a period of time in the late 1920s, formed by nationalists who had managed to remain in Syria after the Druze Revolt of 1925–1927. As Philip Khoury reports, by 1930, al-Kutla al-wataniyah was a "household name" (248) throughout the country. It held the most influence in the early 1930s, and then circumstances at home and the French refusal to ratify the 1936 constitution weakened its power. See Philip S. Khoury, *Syria and the French Mandate: The Politics of Arab Nationalism, 1920–1945* (Princeton, N.J.: Princeton University Press, 1987).

41. Ibid., 401.

42. John F. Devlin, *The Baath Party: A History from Its Origins to 1966* (Stanford, Calif.: Hoover Institute Press, Stanford University, 1976), 345.

43. As translated in Sami Hanna and George H. Gardner, *Arab Socialism: A Documentary Study* (Salt Lake City: University of Utah Press, 1969), 301.

44. Sulayman Musa and Munib al-Madi, *Tarikh al-Urdun fi al-Qarn al-'Ishrin [The History of Jordan in the Twentieth Century]* (Amman: Maktabah al-Muhtasib, 1988), 428.

45. A series of articles concerning King 'Abdullah's offer of the prime min-

istership to Subhi Abu Ghunaymah appears in the latter's collected papers. All discuss the fact that King 'Abdullah rejected the conditions Abu Ghunaymah placed upon his acceptance. Only one article, in *al-Bardi*, mentions any of the specifics concerning these conditions, highlighting Abu Ghunaymah's demand that the government amend the constitution. No other specifics are included in this volume. See *al-Bardi*, July 28, 1946, as reprinted in Muhammad Subhi Abu Ghunaymah, *Sirah Manfiyah: Min Awraq al-Duktur Muhammad Subhi Abu Ghunaymah [Exile Biography: From the Papers of Dr. Muhammad Subhi Abu Ghunaymah]*, Vol. 2 (Beirut: al-Mu'assasah al-'Arabiyah lil-Dirasat wa-al-Nashr; Amman: Dar al-Faris lil-Nashr wa-al-Tawzi, 2001), 87.

46. Irsheidat, 45.

47. Ibid., 48 and 50.

48. *American University of Beirut: Description of Its Organization and Work* (n.p.: n.p., 1934), 6.

49. Musa, *A'lam min al-Urdun*, 58.

50. Ibid., 59.

51. Ibid.

52. Albert Hourani, *Arabic Thought in the Liberal Age, 1798–1939* (Cambridge: Cambridge University Press, 1988), 311.

53. Donald Malcolm Reid, *Cairo University and the Making of Modern Egypt* (Cairo: American University in Cairo Press, 1990), 120.

54. Author interview with 'Isa Madanat, Amman, Jordan, June 20, 1998.

55. Author interview with Wahdan Oweis, Amman, Jordan, July 5, 2000.

56. Ibid.

57. Partha Chatterjee, *The Nation and Its Fragments: Colonial and Postcolonial Histories* (Princeton, N.J.: Princeton University Press, 1993), 6.

58. Irsheidat, 41.

59. Musa, *A'lam min al-Urdun*, 62.

60. al-Majali interview.

61. Author interview with Musallam Bseiso, Amman, Jordan, July 13, 2000.

62. Munif, 249.

63. Irsheidat, 121.

64. Peter Gubser, *Politics and Change in al-Karak, Jordan: A Study of a Small Arab Town and Its District* (London: Oxford University Press, 1973), 132.

65. S. H. Amin, *Middle East Legal Systems* (Glascow, Scotland: Royston Ltd., 1985), 252.

66. Kamal Salibi, *The Modern History of Jordan* (London: I. B. Tauris & Co., 1993), 153.

67. "Law of Elections to the Majlis al-Nuwwab," *al-Jaridah al-Rasmiyah*, April 16, 1947.

68. Mary C. Wilson, *King Abdullah, Britain and the Making of Transjordan* (Cambridge: Cambridge University Press, 1990), 165.

69. Shuqayr, 68. In the same vein, Subhi Abu Ghunaymah sent a letter to King 'Abdullah on November 26, 1946, imploring him not to "inflict upon the country a constitution that is a joke on world constitutions." Muhammad Subhi

Abu Ghunaymah, *Sirah Manfiyah: Min Awraq al-Duktur Muhammad Subhi Abu Ghunaymah [Exile Biography: From the Papers of Dr. Muhammad Subhi Abu Ghunaymah]*, Vol. 1 (Beirut: al-Mu'assasah al-'Arabiyah lil-Dirasat wa-al-Nashr; Amman: Dar al-Faris lil-Nashr wa-al-Tawzi, 2001), 482.

70. See "Mithaq al-Urduniyin al-Ahrar al-Qawmi," *al-Yaum*, as reprinted in Abu Ghunaymah, *Sirah Manfiyah*, 2:783.

71. Sulayman Musa, *Awraq min Dafter al-Ayyam Dhikrayat al-Ra'il al-Awal [Papers from a Daily Journal]* (Amman: al-Mamlakah al-Urduniyah al-Hashimiyah, with support from Amanat Amman al-Kubra, 2000), 82.

72. Ibid.

73. Abla Amawi, "Jordan," in *The Political Parties in the Middle East and North Africa*, ed. Frank Tachau (Westport, Conn.: Greenwood Press, 1994), 280. In a statement issued on December 6, 1946, the Party declared, "The struggle imposed upon us is for the sake of our freedoms and to obtain a free, parliamentary, democratic life." "Nad' al-Hizb al-'Arabi al-Urduni lil-Sha'b," *al-Nasr*, as reprinted in Abu Ghunaymah, *Sirah Manfiyah*, 2:729.

74. Uriel Dann, *Studies in the History of Transjordan, 1920–1949: The Making of a State* (Boulder, Colo.: Westview Press, 1984), 14.

75. Hani Hourani, *Tarikh al-Hayat al-Niyabiyah fi al-Urdun [The History of Parliamentary Life in Jordan, 1929–1957]* (Nicosia, Cyprus: Sharq Press Ltd., September 1989), 38.

CHAPTER 5

1. Khalid A. Sulaiman, *Palestine and Modern Arab Poetry* (London: Zed Books, Ltd., 1984), 21.

2. United Kingdom, Colonial Office, *Palestine Royal Commission: Minutes of Evidence Heard at Public Sessions*, Colonial No. 134 (London: His Majesty's Stationery Office, 1937), 314. Hereafter *Minutes of Evidence*. Izzat Darwazah was a key participant in the movement for Arab nationalism in Damascus prior to World War I and served on the Arab Higher Committee in Palestine in the 1930s.

3. Humphrey Bowman, *Middle-East Window* (London: Longmans, Green and Co., 1942), 311–312. Humphrey Bowman was director of education in Palestine in the Mandate period. Sa'ad Zaghlul led the nationalist Wafd Party in Egypt, from 1919 until his death in 1927, briefly serving as prime minister in 1924.

4. See Rashid Khalidi, "The Palestinians and 1948: The Underlying Causes of Failure," in *The War for Palestine: Rewriting the History of 1948*, ed. Eugene L. Rogan and Avi Shlaim (Cambridge: Cambridge University Press, 2001), 19.

5. Rashid Khalidi, *Palestinian Identity: The Construction of Modern National Consciousness* (New York: Columbia University Press, 1997), 10.

6. Khalidi, "The Palestinians and 1948," 20. The "Yishuv" was the Jewish community in Palestine.

7. As quoted in Ibid., 20–21.

8. Khalidi, *Palestinian Identity*, 115. A fellah is a peasant. The plural is fellaheen.

9. Ibid., 57.

10. Rosemary Sayigh, *Palestinians: From Peasants to Revolutionaries* (London: Zed Press, 1979), 57. A story related by nineteenth-century travelers to the Middle East can illustrate something about this social divide. Rosemary Sayigh says that travelers reported that a common fellaheen phrase was: "City people are the lords of the world. Peasants are the donkeys of the world." Sayigh analyzes the feeling behind it by saying, "Self-belittlement is common to most peasantries. But it is particularly deep-rooted in the Arab area, with its ancient cities as the centres of trade, power and Islamic doctrine" (6). From the urban perspective, Karmi reports that "there was a persistent snobbery amongst the better-off classes which relegated the peasants to a lowly and despised position. Even the word for peasant was used as a term of denigration. To call someone a fellah or a fellaha—the feminine form—was to imply that he or she was primitive and uncivilised." Ghada Karmi, *In Search of Fatima: A Palestinian Story* (London: Verso, 2002), 18.

11. A comprehensive analysis of all aspects of Palestinian national development in the Mandate period is beyond the scope of this chapter. This chapter will focus, instead, on the agencies most important to the articulation of the Palestinian nation itself and the reasons why people became activated around its ideas. Those agencies comparable to the ones already discussed for Transjordan—the schools, the media, and the governmental structure itself—will be highlighted, along with institutions specific to the Palestinian experience. For more information, see Samih K. Farsoun, *Palestine and the Palestinians*, with Christina E. Zacharia (Boulder, Colo.: Westview Press, 1997); Sami Hadawi, *Palestine: Loss of a Heritage* (San Antonio, Tex.: Naylor Co., 1963); Issa Khalaf, *Politics in Palestine: Arab Factionalism and Social Disintegration, 1939–1948* (Albany: State University of New York Press, 1991); Khalidi, *Palestinian Identity*; A. W. Khayyali, *Palestine: A Modern History* (London: Croom Helm, 1978); Ann Mosely Lesch, *Arab Politics in Palestine, 1917–1939: The Frustration of a National Movement* (Ithaca, N.Y.: Cornell University Press, 1979); and Charles D. Smith, *Palestine and the Arab-Israeli Conflict* (New York: St. Martin's Press, 1988).

12. Bahjat Abu Gharbiyah, *Fi Khidham al-Nidhal al-'Arabi al-Filastini: Mudhakkirat al-Munadil Bahjat Abu Gharbiyah, 1916–1949 [In the Roar of the Palestinian Struggle: Memoirs of the Fighter Bahjat Abu Gharbiyah, 1916–1949]* (Beirut: Mu'assasat al-Dirasat al-Filastiniyah, 1993), 20.

13. Hala Sakakini, *Jerusalem and I: A Personal Record* (Amman: Economic Press Co., 1990), 49.

14. Abdulla M. Lutfiyya, *Baytin, a Jordanian Village; a Study of Social Institutions and Social Change in a Folk Community* (The Hague: Morton, 1966), 61. Hajj Amin al-Husayni was the Mufti of Jerusalem.

15. Abu Gharbiyah, 20.

16. Sakakini, *Jerusalem and I*, 49.

17. Adnan Abu-Ghazaleh, "Arab Cultural Nationalism in Palestine during the British Mandate," *Journal of Palestine Studies* 1, no. 3 (Spring 1972): 43.

18. Christel Lane, *The Rites of Rulers: Ritual in Industrial Society—The Soviet Case* (Cambridge: Cambridge University Press, 1981), 61.

19. Ibid., 264.

20. Ibid., 263.

21. Gregory Starrett, *Putting Islam to Work: Education, Politics, and Religious Transformation in Egypt* (Berkeley and Los Angeles: University of California Press, 1998), 79.

22. Abu-Ghazaleh, 44.

23. Ibid., 49.

24. Salma Khadra Jayyusi, ed., *Anthology of Modern Palestinian Literature* (New York: Columbia University Press, 1992), 7.

25. Ibid.

26. Sulaiman, 27.

27. Karmi, 39–40. Karmi's uncle was the poet 'Abd al-Karim Karmi.

28. Sakakini, *Jerusalem and I*, 50.

29. Amin al-Khatib, *Tadhakkurat Amin al-Khatib [Memoirs of Amin al-Khatib]*, ed. Salih Abd al-Jawad and Mu'awiyah Tahbub, no. 2 (Bir Zayt: Markaz Dirasat wa-Tawthiq al-Mujtama' al-Filastini, Jami'at Bir Zayt, 1992), 7.

30. Ibid., 13.

31. See Ibid., 13–14.

32. Abu Gharbiyah, 18.

33. Ibid., 41.

34. A. L. Tibawi, *Arab Education in Mandatory Palestine: A Study of Three Decades of British Administration* (London: Luzac & Company, Ltd., 1956), 29. A. L. Tibawi was the inspector for the Southern District of Palestine during the Mandate period.

35. Ibid., 30. The discussion that follows focuses exclusively on the Palestinian Arab school system because the Jewish community in Palestine built and ran its own schools.

36. *Minutes of Evidence*, 351, according to Khalil Totah.

37. Tibawi, 20.

38. Ibid. Kuttab schools primarily taught students to memorize the Quran.

39. United Kingdom, Government of Palestine, "Report on Palestine Administration, 1922," in *Palestine and Transjordan Administration Reports, 1918–1948* (Oxford: Archive Editions, 1995), 1:364.

40. United Kingdom, Government of Palestine, "Supplementary Memorandum by the Government of Palestine, Including Notes on Evidence Given to the United Nations' Special Committee on Palestine up to the 12th July, 1947," in *Palestine and Transjordan Administration Reports, 1918–1948* (Oxford: Archive Editions, 1995), 15:598.

41. Roderic D. Matthews and Matta Akrawi, *Education in Arab Countries in the Near East* (Washington, D.C.: American Council on Education, 1949), 237.

42. Jibrail Katul, *al-Ta'lim fi Filastin [Education in Palestine]* (Beirut: n.p., 1950), 125–130, as quoted in Abu-Ghazaleh, 39; and Naomi Shepherd, *Ploughing Sand: British Rule in Palestine 1917–1948* (London: John Murray, 1999), 157.

43. Tibawi, 42.

44. Only seventy-six privileged few attended the Men's Training College and sixty-four the Women's Training College in the 1927–1928 academic year. United Kingdom, Colonial Office, "Report by His Majesty's Government in the

United Kingdom of Great Britain and Northern Ireland to the Council of the League of Nations on the Administration of Palestine and Trans-Jordan for the Year 1928," in *Palestine and Transjordan Administration Reports, 1918–1948* (Oxford: Archive Editions, 1995), 2:537–538.

45. Tibawi, 50.

46. Amin Hafiz Dajani, *al-Intidab al-Baritani, 1918–1948 [The British Mandate, 1918–1948]*, Vol. 1, *Jabhat al-Tarbiyah wa-al-Ta'lim wa-Nidaliha Dhidda al-Isti'mar: al-Baramij wa-al-Manahij wa-al-Mu'allumun wa-al-Tullab 'Abra 'Arb'a 'Uhud [The Education Front and Its Struggle against Colonialism: The Programs, Curricula, Teachers and Students across Four Eras]* (n.p.: n.p., 199-), 76.

47. Tibawi, 95.

48. Ibid., 86.

49. Ibid., 90.

50. Ibid., 88.

51. Wasfi Anabtawi and Sa'id al-Sabagh, *Jugrafiyat Filastin wa-al-Bilad al-'Arabiyah [Geography of Palestine and the Arab Countries]* (Jaffa: Maktabah al-Tahir Ikhwan, 1946), 81.

52. Khalil Totah, "Education in Palestine," *Annals of the American Academy of Political and Social Science* 164 (November 1932): 162.

53. Author interview with Husni Ayesh, Amman, Jordan, May 20, 2002.

54. Dajani, 56.

55. Ibid., 99.

56. Tibawi, 89.

57. *Minutes of Evidence*, 352.

58. Sa'id al-Dura, *al-Hilal al-Khasib [The Fertile Crescent]* (Cairo: Sharia Faruq, 1946), 55.

59. *Minutes of Evidence*, 351.

60. Ibid., 352–353.

61. Khalil al-Sakakini, *Kadha Ana ya Dunya [As I Am, O World]*, Silsilat Ihya al-Turath al-Thaqafi al-Filastini (Beirut: Al-Ittihad al-'Amm lil-Kuttab wa-al-Suhufiyin al-Filastiniyin, al-Amanah al-Amman, 1982), 264–265.

62. *Minutes of Evidence*, 352.

63. Ibid.

64. Tibawi, 65.

65. United Kingdom, Colonial Office, "Report by His Britannic Majesty's Government to the Council of the League of Nations on the Administration of Palestine and Transjordan for the Year 1926," in *Palestine and Transjordan Administration Reports, 1918–1948* (Oxford: Archive Editions, 1995), 2:259.

66. Tibawi, 59, places the opening in 1918, while Abu-Ghazaleh, 41, places it in 1920.

67. Abu-Ghazaleh, 41.

68. Sadiq Ibrahim 'Oda, "al-Kuliyah al-'Arabiyah fi-il-Quds 1918–1948: Ma'lumat wa-Dhikrayat" ["The Arab College in Jerusalem 1918–1948: Facts and Remembrances"], *Majalat al-Dirasat al-Filastiniyah [Journal of Palestinian Studies]* 40 (Fall 1999): 188.

69. United Kingdom, Colonial Office, *Palestine Royal Commission Report*

(London: His Majesty's Stationery Office, July 1937), 134. Hereafter *Royal Commission*.

70. Karmi, 40.

71. Tibawi, 197.

72. Bowman, 311.

73. Ylana N. Miller, *Government and Society in Rural Palestine: 1920–1948*, Modern Middle East Series, No. 9 (Austin: University of Texas Press, 1985), 69.

74. Author interview with Mahmoud Zeitoun, Amman, Jordan, July 16, 2002.

75. Tibawi, 200.

76. Ronald Storrs, District Governor, Jerusalem-Jaffa District, "Secret Political Resume for Jerusalem-Jaffa District for Period March 1st to April 9th Inclusive," United Kingdom, *Political Diaries of the Arab World: Palestine & Jordan, 1924–1936*, ed. Robert L. Jarman, Vol. 2 (Slough, UK: Archive Editions, 2001), 156. Hereafter *Political Diaries: Vol. 2*.

77. Ibid.

78. Tibawi, 198 and 200. This information is confirmed by Storrs, "Secret Political Resume," *Political Diaries: Vol. 2*, 156.

79. Abu-Ghazaleh, 40.

80. Ibid., 40 n. 9.

81. al-Khatib, 15.

82. Dajani, 93.

83. Tibawi, 198.

84. Abu-Ghazaleh, 42.

85. Hatim Kamal, *Tadhakkurat Hatim Kamal [Memoirs of Hatim Kamal]*, ed. Salih Abd al-Jawad, no. 6 (Bir Zayt: Markaz Dirasat wa-Tawthiq al-Mujtama' al-Filastini, Jami'at Bir Zayt, 1995), 24. However, the students did not always understand what issues they were protesting. One year, Kamal remembers running down the streets calling for the fall of "Falfour." Kamal, 23.

86. Author interview with Musallam Bseiso, Amman, Jordan, July 13, 2000.

87. Tibawi, 201–202.

88. Bowman, 310.

89. Shepherd, 167.

90. United Kingdom, Government of Palestine, "Report on Palestine Administration, 1923," in *Palestine and Transjordan Administration Reports, 1918–1948* (Oxford: Archive Editions, 1995), 1:415; and United Kingdom, Colonial Office, "Report by His Britannic Majesty's Government to the Council of the League of Nations on the Administration of Palestine and Trans-Jordan for the Year 1927," in *Palestine and Transjordan Administration Reports, 1918–1948* (Oxford: Archive Editions, 1995), 2:395.

91. Miller, 115.

92. *Royal Commission*, 134.

93. Shepherd, 167.

94. Bseiso interview.

95. Sakakini, *Jerusalem and I*, 96–97.

96. Ibid., 97.

97. Ibid.

98. Tibawi, 244–245.

99. Abu-Ghazaleh, 43.

100. Ibid., 44.

101. Ibid., 43–44. The three "heroes" were Palestinian men executed by the British authorities for their participation in Arab demonstrations. Ibid., 49.

102. Karmi, 40.

103. Tal'at Harb, *Tadhakkurat Tal'at Harb [Memoirs of Tal'at Harb]*, ed. Salih 'Abd al-Jawad, no. 5 (Bir Zayt: Markaz Dirasat wa-Tawthiq al-Mujtama' al-Filastini, Jami'at Bir Zayt, 1994), 26.

104. For more information on the Arab Revolt, see Ted Swedenburg, *Memories of Revolt: The 1936–1939 Rebellion and the Palestinian National Past* (Minneapolis: University of Minnesota Press, 1995).

105. High Commissioner for Palestine, "Secret Reference No. 3?/472/38," October 24, 1938, in United Kingdom, *Political Diaries of the Arab World: Palestine & Jordan, 1937–1938*, ed. Robert L. Jarman, Vol. 3 (Slough, UK: Archive Editions, 2001), 220. Hereafter *Political Diaries: Vol. 3*.

106. Ibid., 219.

107. *Royal Commission*, 132.

108. Ibid.

109. Ibid., 133.

110. Sakakini, *Jerusalem and I*, 57.

111. Ibid.

112. Yusrah Salah, *Tadhakkurat Yusrah Salah [Memoirs of Yusrah Salah]*, ed. Ali Jarbawi and Lubna 'Abd al-Hadi, no. 3 (Bir Zayt: Markaz Dirasat wa-Tawthiq al-Mujtama' al-Filastini, Jami'at Bir Zayt, 1992), 13.

113. United Kingdom, Colonial Office, "Report by His Majesty's Government in the United Kingdom of Great Britain and Northern Ireland to the Council of the League of Nations on the Administration of Palestine and Trans-Jordan for the Year 1936," in *Palestine and Transjordan Administration Reports, 1918–1948* (Oxford: Archive Editions, 1995), 6:166.

114. al-Khatib, 13.

115. Bseiso interview.

116. Ibid.

117. Miller, 166.

118. Michael J. Cohen, *The Origins and Evolution of the Arab-Zionist Conflict* (Berkeley and Los Angeles: University of California Press, 1987), 74.

119. Zev Abromowitz, "Social-Economic Structure of Arab Palestine," in *Jews and Arabs in Palestine: Studies in a National and a Colonial Problem*, ed. Enzo Sereni and R. E. Ashery (New York: Hechalutz Press, 1936), 60.

120. Ibid., 61.

121. Ibid., 68.

122. United Kingdom, Colonial Office, *Palestine: Report on Immigration, Land Settlement and Development* (London: His Majesty's Stationery Office, October 1930), 54. Hereafter *Palestine: Report on Immigration*.

123. Ibid., 64.

124. A. Granott, *The Land System in Palestine: History and Structure*, trans. M. Simon (London: Eyre & Spottiswoode, 1952), 41 and 183.

125. *Palestine: Report on Immigration*, 61–62.

126. Kenneth Stein, "Palestine's Rural Economy, 1917–1939," *Studies in Zionism* 8 (Spring 1987): 40.

127. United Kingdom, Colonial Office, *Report of the Commission on the Palestine Disturbances of August, 1929* (London: His Majesty's Stationery Office, March 1930), 162. Hereafter *Report of the Commission*.

128. Ibid., 113.

129. Although many more villages had schools by 1948 than they had had at the beginning of the Mandate period, half still had no schools, and even those that did had programs lasting only until the fourth or fifth grade. Sayigh, 6.

130. Saïd K. Aburish, *Children of Bethany: The Story of a Palestinian Family* (London: Tauris, 1988), 34 and 35.

131. Ibid., 35.

132. Ibid., 36–37. Political newspapers began circulating in Palestine earlier than 1929, but Bethany must not have come into contact with them until that year.

133. Ibid., 42.

134. Ibid., 45–46.

135. Ibid., 92.

136. al-Khatib, 19.

137. Bseiso interview.

138. Aburish, 104.

139. 'Abdullah arranged the conference, along with his Palestinian allies, to gain support for his plan to annex the West Bank and East Jerusalem and to make it appear as if the Palestinians were "voting" for the union. He had already held a conference in Amman a couple of months earlier, but few Palestinians considered it representative of their concerns. To drum up support for the Jericho conference, Ramallah Radio, controlled by the Jordanian Arab Legion, broadcast advertisements about it, and 'Abdullah's allies traveled around the villages spreading his message. On the day of the conference, the government supplied military cars and buses to transport the delegates.

140. Despite the fact that the Palestinians at Jericho agreed to unite with Jordan, they harbored hostility toward 'Abdullah himself. Soon after the war ended, reports surfaced about 'Abdullah's dealings with the Zionist leadership prior to the 1947–1948 War concerning a postwar land settlement. While no formal agreement was ever signed between 'Abdullah and the Zionist leadership, 'Abdullah's prime minister, Tawfiq Abu'l-Huda, reported to the British government in February 1948 that the Jordanian Arab Legion would not invade any areas allotted to the Jewish state by the UN Partition Plan. The Jordanian army, led by the British General John Bagot Glubb, held to this promise, leaving the area allotted to Palestinians only to fight in East Jerusalem, an area designated as an international zone by the Partition Plan. For more information about these events, see Sir John Bagot Glubb, *A Soldier with the Arabs* (London: Hodder and

Stoughton, 1957); 'Abdullah al-Tell, *Karithat Filastin: Mudhakkirat 'Abdullah al-Tell [The Catastrophe of Palestine: Memoirs of 'Abdullah al-Tell]* (Cairo: Dar al-Qalam, 1959); and Avi Shlaim, *The Politics of Partition: King Abdullah, the Zionists, and Palestine, 1921–1951* (New York: Oxford University Press, 1998).

141. *Filastin*, April 6, 1950.

142. Aqil Hyder Hasan Abidi, *Jordan: A Political Study, 1948–1957* (New York: Asia Publishing House, 1965), 67 n. 17.

143. Kamel S. Abu Jaber, "The Legislature of the Hashemite Kingdom of Jordan: A Study in Political Development," *Muslim World* 59, nos. 3–4 (July–October 1969): 229.

144. Mary C. Wilson, *King Abdullah, Britain and the Making of Jordan* (Cambridge: Cambridge University Press, 1990), 197.

145. Miller, 170.

146. The Palestinians "who came under Jordanian control" were those who had remained in their homes in the West Bank and East Jerusalem and those who moved as refugees to those areas during the course of the 1947–1948 War.

147. Farsoun, 14.

148. Ann Mosely Lesch, *Arab Politics in Palestine, 1917–1939: The Frustration of a National Movement* (Ithaca, N.Y.: Cornell University Press, 1979), 82.

149. Abu Gharbiyah, 19.

150. Sulayman Musa, *A'lam min al-Urdun: Hazza' al-Majali, Sulayman al-Nabulsi, Wasfi al-Tell [Distinguished Men of Jordan: Hazza' al-Majali, Sulayman al-Nabulsi, Wasfi al-Tell]* (Amman: al-Mamlakah al-Urduniyah al-Hashimiyah, 1986), 61.

CHAPTER 6

Author's Note: An earlier version of this chapter appeared in Betty S. Anderson, "Domestic Influences on Policy-Making: The History of the Jordanian National Movement, 1946–1957," in *The Resilience of Hashemite Rule: Politics and State in Jordan, 1946–67*, ed. Tariq Tell, pp. 37–87 (Amman: CERMOC, 2001).

1. Duke to Eden, August 27, 1954, FO 371.110876/VJ 1015/29, Public Record Office, London. Hereafter, PRO.

2. Robert C. Hayes, *Labor Law and Practice in the Hashemite Kingdom of Jordan*, BLS Report no. 322 (Washington, D.C.: U.S. Department of Labor, U.S. Bureau of Labor Statistics, 1967), 13.

3. Munif al-Razzaz, "Munif al-Razzaz Yatadhakkar: Mu'allim fi Amman" ["Munif al-Razzaz Remembers: A Teacher in Amman"], *Akhar Khabar* 77 (January 8–9, 1994): 13.

4. Author interview with Mahmoud Zeitoun, Amman, Jordan, July 16, 2002. He was so well-known as a political activist that one student tried to join the Ba'th Party in order to receive a better grade in class. Zeitoun refused to go along with this scheme.

5. Samir Khrainou, *al-Harakat al-Tullabiyah al-Urduniyah 1948–1998 [The*

Jordanian Student Movement 1948–1998] (Amman: Al-Urdun al-Jadid Research Center, 2000), 15.

6. Ibid., 47.

7. Ibid.

8. Ibid., 48.

9. Ibid., 153.

10. Ibid., 195.

11. Anan Ameri, "Socioeconomic Development in Jordan (1950–1980): An Application of Dependency Theory" (Ph.D. diss., Wayne State University, 1981), 146.

12. World Bank, *The Economic Development of Jordan: Report of a Mission Organized by the International Bank for Reconstruction and Development at the Request of the Government of Jordan* (Baltimore: Johns Hopkins University Press, 1957), 5.

13. Michael P. Mazur, *Economic Growth and Development in Jordan* (Boulder, Colo.: Westview Press, 1979), 273.

14. Naseer H. Aruri, *Jordan: A Study in Political Development, 1921–1965* (The Hague: Martinus Nijhoff, 1972), 54.

15. Michael R. Fischbach, *State, Society, and Land in Jordan* (Leiden, the Netherlands: Brill, 2000), 135.

16. Ibid.

17. Ibid., 136.

18. Oddvar Aresvik, *The Agricultural Development of Jordan* (New York: Praeger Publishers, 1976), 264.

19. Michael Mazur, "Economic Development in Jordan," in *Economic Development and Population Growth in the Middle East,* ed. Charles Cooper and Sidney S. Alexander (New York: American Elsevier Pub. Co., 1972), 219.

20. Paul Grounds Phillips, *The Hashemite Kingdom of Jordan: Prolegomena to a Technical Assistance Program,* Research Paper #34 (Ph.D. diss., University of Chicago, 1954), 71; and World Bank, 41.

21. World Bank, 441–444; and Mazur, *Economic Growth and Development in Jordan,* 30.

22. United Nations, Department of Economic and Social Affairs, *Organization and Administration of Welfare Programs: A Series of Country Studies, Jordan* (New York: United Nations, 1968), 3.

23. Hayes, 20.

24. Author interview with Hamad al-Farhan, Amman, Jordan, June 23, 1998.

25. Paul Kingston, "Breaking the Patterns of Mandate: Economic Nationalism and State Formation in Jordan, 1951–1957," in *Village, Steppe and State: The Social Origins of Modern Jordan,* ed. Eugene L. Rogan and Tariq Tell (London: British Academic Press, 1994), 190.

26. Ibid., 192.

27. Ibid., 202.

28. Ibid., 205.

29. Ian Seccombe, "Labour Migration and the Transformation of a Vil-

lage Economy: A Case Study from Northwest Jordan," in *The Middle Eastern Village: Changing Economic and Social Relations*, ed. Richard Lawless (London: Croom Helm, 1987), 116.

30. Ibid., 117–118.

31. al-Farhan interview.

32. Jane M. Hacker, *Modern 'Amman: A Social Study*, Research Paper Series, ed. John I. Clarke, no. 3 (Durham, N.C.: Department of Geography, Durham Colleges in the University of Durham, 1960), 64.

33. L. W. Jones, "Demographic Review: Rapid Population Growth in Baghdad and Amman," *Middle East Journal* 23, no. 2 (Spring 1969): 211.

34. Hayes, 17. The numbers cited in the Hayes text add up to 100.1 percent.

35. Hacker, 89.

36. Ibid., 128. The emphasis is hers.

37. Ibid., 129.

38. Jamal al-Sha'ir, *Siyasi Yatadhakkar: Tajribah fi al-'Amal al-Siyasi [A Politician Remembers: Commentary on My Political Experience]* (London: Riad El-Rayyes Books, Ltd., 1987), 154.

39. al-Farhan interview.

40. Lucian Pye, "The Non-Western Political Process," in *Politics in Transitional Societies: The Challenge of Change in Asia, Africa, and Latin America*, ed. Harvey G. Kebschull (New York: Appleton-Century-Crofts, 1968), 53.

41. Moshe Ma'oz, *Palestinian Leadership on the West Bank: The Changing Role of the Arab Mayors under Jordan and Israel* (London: Frank Cass, 1984), 49.

42. Ibid., 49–50.

43. John H. Kautsky, ed., *Political Change in Underdeveloped Countries: Nationalism and Communism* (New York: John Wiley and Sons, 1962), 43.

44. Author interview with Ali al-Mahafazah, Amman, Jordan, July 10, 2000.

45. Guilain Denoeux, *Urban Unrest in the Middle East: A Comparative Study of Informal Networks in Egypt, Iran, and Lebanon* (Albany: State University of New York Press, 1993), 22.

46. Ibid.

47. Ibid., 87–88.

48. Author interview with Nabil Haddadin, Amman, Jordan, July 21, 2000. Nabil Haddadin was a member of the Communist Party in the 1950s.

49. Tal'at Harb, *Tadhakkurat Tal'at Harb [Memoirs of Tal'at Harb]*, ed. Salih 'Abd al-Jawad, no. 5 (Bir Zayt: Markaz Dirasat wa-Tawthiq al-Mujtama' al-Filastini, Jami'at Bir Zayt, 1994), 54.

50. Daniel Lerner, *The Passing of Traditional Society: Modernizing the Middle East* (New York: Free Press of Glencoe, 1958), 198.

51. Ibid., 309–310.

52. Author interview with Musallam Bseiso, Amman, Jordan, July 13, 2000.

53. Ibid.

54. Raphael Patai, ed., *Jordan* (New Haven, Conn.: Human Relations Area Files, 1957), 87.

55. W. Phillips Davison, *International Political Communication* (New York: Frederick A. Praeger, Pub., 1965), 148.

56. *Summary of World Broadcasts—Part IV. The Arab World, Israel, Greece, Turkey and Persia* (Caversham Park, Reading, UK: Monitoring Service of the British Broadcasting Corporation), March 2, 1954. Hereafter *SWB*. All translations that appear were prepared by the British Broadcasting Service.

57. Ibid., March 26, 1954.

58. Ibid., June 4, 1954.

59. al-Farhan interview.

60. Naim Sofer, "The Political Status of Jerusalem in the Hashemite Kingdom of Jordan, 1948–1967," *Middle Eastern Studies* 12, no. 1 (January 1976): 80.

61. Avi Plascov, *The Palestinian Refugees in Jordan: 1948–1957* (London: Frank Cass, 1981), 31.

62. Ameri, 194–195.

63. Mazur, "Economic Development in Jordan," 240.

64. More parties formed in this period, including the Syrian Qawmiyyun [Nationalist] and a number of proregime parties, but they will not be covered in this study. The Syrian Qawmiyyun was not as influential as the parties discussed in the chapter, and the various pro-regime parties that emerged served merely as gambits by the regime to compete against the popularity of the JNM's parties.

65. Author interview with Jamal al-Sha'ir, Amman, Jordan, June 24, 1998.

66. Author interview with Ahmad Fakher, Amman, Jordan, July 7, 2000.

67. Author interview with 'Isa Madanat, Amman, Jordan, June 20, 1998.

68. Harb, 34.

69. Fu'ad Nasser, a Christian, was born in Bludan in Syria in 1914, to Palestinian parents from al-Nasarah. Six years later, the family returned to Palestine, where Nasser attended school. *Fu'ad Nasser: Al-Rajul . . . wa-al-Qadhiyah [Fu'ad Nasser: The Man . . . and the Issue]* (Jerusalem: Manshurat Salah al-Din, 1977), 13. He reached the sixth year of school and then dropped out to enter political work. He led an armed gang during the 1936-1939 Revolt in Palestine in the Jerusalem-Hebron-Jericho area and then went to Iraq to participate in the Rashid Ali coup of 1941. He returned to Palestine in 1943 to become the leader of the League for National Liberation. Walter Z. Laqueur, *Communism and Nationalism in the Middle East* (London: Routledge & Keegan Paul, 1956), 325 n. 2.

70. Madanat interview.

71. Laqueur, 129.

72. Nabil Irsheidat, *Awraq Laysat Shakhsiyah: Mudhakkirat Nabil Irsheidat [Non-Personal Papers: Memoirs of Nabil Irsheidat]* (Damascus: Dar al-Yanabi', 2001), 121.

73. Ya'qub Ziyadin, *al-Bidayah: Sirah Dhatiyah . . . Arba'un Sanah fi al-Harakah al-Wataniyah al-Urduniyah [The Beginnings: A Personal Biographical History . . . Forty Years in the Jordanian National Movement]* (Beirut: House of Ibn Khaldun Printing, 1981), 46.

74. Ibrahim Bakr was a Communist lawyer who frequently defended the leaders of the JNM.

75. Shaul Mishal, *West Bank/East Bank: The Palestinians in Jordan, 1949–1967* (New Haven, Conn.: Yale University Press, 1978), 97.

76. Author interview with Amal Nafa', Amman, Jordan, June 21, 1995.

77. Peter Gubser, *Politics and Change in al-Karak, Jordan: A Study of a Small Arab Town and Its District* (London: Oxford University Press, 1973), 136.

78. Ibid.

79. Muhammad al-Misri, "al-Urdun 1953–1957: Darasat Siyasiyah" ["Jordan 1953–1957: A Political Study"] (Master's thesis, University of Jordan, 1995), 50–51.

80. Both al-Rimawi and Na'was were elected to the National Command in Damascus during the Second National Congress in June 1954.

81. British Ambassador Geoffrey Furlonge reported in 1953 that "the main threat to internal security and our own position is provided by a small group of deputies, of whom the ringleaders are Abdullah al-Rimawi and Abdullah Nawas." Furlonge to Allen, October 21, 1953, FO 371.104890/ET 1017/24, PRO.

82. Author interview with Bahjat Abu Gharbiyah, Amman, Jordan, June 19, 1995.

83. Author interview with Abd al-Rahman Shuqayr, Amman, Jordan, June 21, 1995.

84. Abd al-Rahman Shuqayr, *Min Qasiyun . . . ila Rabbat 'Ammun: Rihlat al-'Umr [From Qasiyun . . . to Rabbat 'Ammun: A Stage of Life]*, Silsilat Ihya' al-Dhakirah al-Tarikhiyah (Amman: Kitab al-Urdun al-Jadid, 1991), 97.

85. Ibid. The British embassy confirms that in June 1954 seventy-two "patriots" signed the National Front manifesto, which blamed Anglo-American imperialism for the continuation of Jordan's poverty and backwardness. June 8, 1954, FO 371.110879/VJ 1018/3, PRO.

86. Shuqayr, 97.

87. Aruri, 96.

88. Sulayman Musa, *A'lam min al-Urdun: Hazza' al-Majali, Sulayman al-Nabulsi, Wasfi al-Tell [Distinguished Men of Jordan: Hazza' al-Majali, Sulayman al-Nabulsi, Wasfi al-Tell]* (Amman: al-Mamlakah al-Urduniyah al-Hashimiyah, 1986), 64.

89. al-Sha'ir interview.

90. Fakher interview.

91. al-Sha'ir interview.

92. See al-Misri, 57; Kamal Salibi, *The Modern History of Jordan* (London: I. B. Tauris & Co., 1993), 173–174; 'Abdullah Naqrash, *al-Tajribah al-Hizbiyah fi al-Urdun [Party Experience in Jordan]* (Amman: Lajnah Tarikh al-Urdun, 1991), 65.

93. Munif al-Razzaz, "Munif al-Razzaz Yatadhakkar: Silah fi al-Awza'i" ["Munif al-Razzaz Remembers: Weapons in al-Awza'i"], *Akhar Khabar* 75 (January 5–6, 1994).

94. al-Farhan interview.

95. al-Misri, 57.

96. Amin al-Khatib, *Tadhakkurat Amin al-Khatib [Memoirs of Amin al-Khatib]*,

ed. Salih Abd al-Jawad and Mu'awiyah Tahbub, no. 2 (Bir Zayt: Markaz Dirasat wa-Tawthiq al-Mujtama' al-Filastini, Jami'at Bir Zayt, 1992), 32.

97. Ibid.

98. Dafi al-Jumani is a Jordanian who spent many years in jail in Jordan and then twenty-four years imprisoned in Syria because of his political activities.

99. Contrary to many sources who discuss this period of time in Jordan, Ali Abu Nuwar, the chief of staff of the Arab Legion between 1956 and 1957, did not lead the Free Officers' Movement, nor, for that matter, even join it. He was aware of the movement and supported its actions but never became a member. For more information, see Ali Abu Nuwar, *Huna Talashat al-'Arab: Mudhakkirat fi al-Siyasah al-'Arabiyah (1948–1964) [A Time of Arab Decline: Memoirs in Arab Politics (1948–1964)]* (London: Dar al-Saqi, 1990).

100. Beverley Milton-Edwards states that Brotherhood activities began in Jordan as early as 1934, but most sources agree that activities began in Jordan and Palestine only in the 1940s. See Beverley Milton-Edwards, "A Temporary Alliance with the Crown: The Islamic Response in Jordan," in *Islamic Fundamentalisms and the Gulf Crisis*, ed. James Piscatori (Chicago: American Academy of Arts and Sciences, 1991), 89.

101. Amnon Cohen, "Political Parties in the West Bank under the Hashemite Regime," in *Palestinian Arab Politics*, ed. Moshe Ma'oz (Jerusalem: Jerusalem Academic Press, 1975), 39.

102. As reprinted in Azzam Tamimi, *Islam and Democracy: Jordan and the Muslim Brotherhood*, Islamic Area Studies Working Paper Series, no. 18 (Tokyo: Islamic Area Studies Project, 2000), 3–4.

103. Gubser, 135–136.

104. See Ellen M. Lust-Okar, "The Decline of Jordanian Political Parties: Myth or Reality?" *International Journal of Middle East Studies* 33, no. 4 (November 2001): 545–569, for a comparison of the strengths and weaknesses of the Jordanian political parties in the 1950s and 1990s.

105. Abu Gharbiyah and Shuqayr interviews; and author interview with Ya'qub Ziyadin, Amman, Jordan, June 25, 1995.

106. Ziyadin interview.

107. Mishal, 98; Duke to Ross, August 23, 1956, FO 371.121469/VJ 1015/246, and Amman to Levant Department, August 4, 1956, FO 371.121468/VJ 1015/236, PRO; Gubser, 136; and Amnon Cohen, "The Jordanian Communist Party in the West Bank, 1950–1960," in *The U.S.S.R. and the Middle East*, ed. Michael Confino and Shimon Shamir (Jerusalem: Israel Universities Press, 1973), 432. The Mishal and Cohen sources covered primarily the West Bank.

108. Bseiso interview.

109. Haddadin interview.

110. al-Farhan interview.

111. Ibid.

112. al-Mahafazah interview.

113. Bseiso interview.

114. al-Farhan interview.

115. al-Mahafazah interview.
116. Ibid.

CHAPTER 7

1. Ya'qub Ziyadin, *al-Bidayah: Sirah Dhatiyah . . . Arba'un Sanah fi al-Harakah al-Wataniyah al-Urduniyah [The Beginnings: A Personal Biographical History . . . Forty Years in the Jordanian National Movement]* (Beirut: House of Ibn Khaldun Printing, 1981), 56.

2. *Summary of World Broadcasts—Part IV. The Arab World, Israel, Greece, Turkey and Persia* (Caversham Park, Reading, UK: Monitoring Service of the British Broadcasting Corporation), December 27, 1956. Hereafter *SWB*.

3. For more information on Talal's ascension to the throne and his subsequent deposition, see Robert B. Satloff, *From Abdullah to Hussein: Jordan in Transition* (New York: Oxford University Press, 1994).

4. Shahid Qadir, Christopher Clapham, and Barry Gills, "Sustainable Democracy: Formalism vs. Substance," *Third World Quarterly* 14, no. 3 (1993): 417.

5. Included in the British embassy's dispatch to the Foreign Office, November 6, 1954, FO 371.110875/VJ 1015/13, Public Record Office, London. Hereafter, PRO.

6. Duke to FO, June 22, 1954, FO 371.110876/VJ 1015/22, PRO.

7. Author interview with Musallam Bseiso, Amman, Jordan, July 13, 2000.

8. All appeared in *al-Jaridah al-Rasmiyah*, August 18, 1954.

9. Author interview with Bahjat Abu Gharbiyah, Amman, Jordan, June 19, 1995.

10. Ziyadin, 54–55.

11. Tal'at Harb, *Tadhakkurat Tal'at Harb [Memoirs of Tal'at Harb]*, ed. Salih 'Abd al-Jawad, no. 5 (Bir Zayt: Markaz Dirasat wa-Tawthiq al-Mujtama' al-Filastini, Jami'at Bir Zayt, 1994), 49.

12. Ibid., 22.

13. See, for example, Ibid., 62.

14. Ziyadin, 59.

15. Amal Nafa' reported in an interview that he experienced this discrimination in the 1950s. His work with the Communist Party became known to the government, and he could not find a job because the mukhabarat would not issue a note of "good behavior" for him. He stated that many other party activists faced the same situation. Author interview with Amal Nafa', Amman, Jordan, June 21, 1995. Bahjat Abu Gharbiyah related in an interview two similar instances where the mukhabarat refused to accept job applications because of the applicants' actions and also, in one case, the father's actions. Abu Gharbiyah interview.

16. *Filastin*, September 28, 1954.

17. Abu Gharbiyah interview.

18. For example, Musallam Bseiso feels that Tawfiq Abu'l-Huda controlled the situation because it was his duty and in his interest to do so. Bseiso interview.

19. Duke to Falla, October 23, 1954, FO 371.110876/VJ 1015/47, PRO.

20. Satloff, 96, and 207 n. 32.

21. Nabil Irsheidat, *Awraq Laysat Shakhsiyah: Mudhakkirat Nabil Irsheidat [Non-Personal Papers: Memoirs of Nabil Irsheidat]* (Damascus: Dar al-Yanabi', 2001), 124.

22. Abd al-Rahman Shuqayr, *Min Qasiyun . . . ila Rabbat 'Ammun: Rihlat al-'Umr [From Qasiyun . . . to Rabbat 'Ammun: A Stage of Life]*, Silsilat Ihya' al-Dhakirah al-Tarikhiyah (Amman: Kitab al-Urdun al-Jadid, 1991), 103, and corroborated by Irsheidat, 124.

23. *SWB*, November 12, 1954.

24. Geren to DOS, August 15, 1955, DOS 785.000/8-1555, U.S. Department of State, *Confidential U.S. State Department Central Files: Jordan: 1955–1959* (Bethesda, Md.: University Publications of America, 1990). Hereafter *Confidential U.S. State Department Central Files.* This report states that Hazza' al-Majali allowed two Communists, Ibrahim Bakr and Abdul Rahman al-Kurdi, to leave al-Jafr, in August 1955, in the hopes of bolstering his reputation as a liberal.

25. Shuqayr, 105–106.

26. Satloff, 97, says the government could count on twenty-eight to thirty-four deputies; "Jordanie," *Cahiers de L'Orient Contemporain*, no. 30 (2e Semestre 1954), 173, reports that Abu'l-Huda could count on 75 percent of the deputies supporting his ministry and policies; and Duke to FO, October 19, 1954, FO 371.110876/VJ 1015/39, PRO, stated that the British ambassador reported that Abu'l-Huda had told him that he could count on the support of thirty deputies.

27. The British embassy termed the government's tactics "clumsy" because they succeeded in creating a parliament beholden to the prime minister but, at the same time, drove the political moderates in the country into the hands of the extremists. "Annual Review for 1954," Richmond to Eden, FO 371.115635/VJ 1101/1, PRO.

28. For more information on Jordan and the Baghdad Pact, see Naseer H. Aruri, *Jordan: A Study in Political Development (1921–1965)* (The Hague: Martinus Nihoff, 1972); Uriel Dann, *King Hussein and the Challenge of Arab Radicalism: Jordan, 1955–1967* (New York: Oxford University Press, 1989); and Satloff.

29. *SWB*, December 14, 1954.

30. Shuqayr, 109.

31. Derek Hopwood, *Egypt: Politics and Society 1945–1984* (Boston: Allen & Unwin, 1985), 87.

32. Amnon Cohen, *Political Parties in the West Bank under the Jordanian Regime, 1949–1967* (Ithaca, N.Y.: Cornell University Press, 1980), 85.

33. Munif al-Razzaz, *al-A'mal al-Fikriyah wa-al-Siyasiyah [Political and Intellectual Actions]*, Part 2 (n.p.: n.p., n.d.), 50.

34. Shuqayr, 109 and 117.

35. *SWB*, October 7, 1955.

36. Al-Razzaz, 51–52.

37. Jamal al-Sha'ir, *Siyasi Yatadhakkar: Tajribah fi al-'Amal al-Siyasi [A Politician Remembers: Commentary on My Political Experience]* (London: Riad El-Rayyes Books, Ltd., 1987), 166.

38. Shuqayr, 117.

39. *SWB*, January 15, 1954.

40. Ibid., January 21, 1955.

41. Ibid., February 1, 1955.

42. Ibid., February 4, 1955.

43. Ibid., December 20, 1955.

44. Abu Gharbiyah interview.

45. See Duke to FO, March 3, 1955, FO 371.115495/VJ 1073/381, PRO.

46. Mallory to DOS, October 23, 1955, DOS 785.00/10-2255, *Confidential U.S. State Department Central Files.*

47. Duke to FO, November 7, 1955, FO 371.115527/VJ 1073/1221, and Commonwealth Relations Office to High Commissioner in Pakistan, November 7, 1955, FO 371.115527/1223A, PRO.

48. "Mudhakkirat Majlis al-Ummah" ["Reports of the Majlis al-Ummah"], *Supplement to al-Jaridah al-Rasmiyah*, November 8, 1955.

49. Hazza' al-Majali, *Hadha Bayani lil-Nas: Qissat Muhadathat Templer [This Is My Statement to the People: The Story of the Discussions of Templer]* (n.p.: n.p., n.d.), 7.

50. Satloff, 119–120.

51. Ali Abu Nuwar, *Huna Talashat al-'Arab: Mudhakkirat fi al-Siyasah al-'Arabiyah (1948–1964) [A Time of Arab Decline: Memoirs in Arab Politics (1948–1964)]* (London: Dar al-Saqi, 1990), 160.

52. Ziyadin, 67.

53. Shuqayr, 112.

54. al-Majali, 171.

55. Parker to DOS, December 31, 1955, DOS 785.00/12-3155, *Confidential U.S. State Department Central Files.*

56. "Memo of Conversation," Amman to DOS, March 19, 1956, DOS 785.00/3-1956, *Confidential U.S. State Department Central Files.*

57. Author interview with Nabil Haddadin, Amman, Jordan, July 21, 2000.

58. Richard H. Sanger, *Where the Jordan Flows* (Washington, D.C.: Middle East Institute, 1963), 372.

59. Ibid.

60. Ziyadin, 67–68.

61. Added to Fouracres to FO, December 29, 1955, FO 371.121241/VJ 1071/8, PRO.

62. Added to Ibid.

63. See, for example, Memorandum of a Telephone Conversation between the Secretary of State and the Assistant Secretary of State for Near Eastern, South Asian, and African Affairs (Allen), Washington, January 8, 1956, 12:50 P.M., in *Foreign Relations of the United States, 1955–1957: Near East: Jordan-Yemen*, Vol. 8, Editor in Chief John P. Glennon, ed. Will Klingaman, Aaron D. Miller, and Nina J. Noring (Washington, D.C.: U.S. Government Printing Office, 1988), 15. Hereafter *U.S. Foreign Relations, 1955–1957*. Wikely to FO, January 7, 1956, FO 371.121462/VJ 1015/23, PRO.

64. A number of the British officials advocated firing on the crowds. Wikely,

in Jerusalem, has said, "authorities had great difficulty in controlling the situation and, in my opinion, should have fired on the crowds earlier than they did." Wikely to FO, December 19, 1955, FO 371.115640/VJ 1015/52, PRO.

65. Wikely, in Jerusalem, reported that the police were particularly unreliable and allowed busloads of demonstrators through the road blocks so they could participate in demonstrations. Wikely to FO, December 19, 1955, FO 371.115640/VJ 1015/52, PRO. Parker at the American embassy in Amman stated that Arab Legion soldiers frequently stood back and watched the demonstrators destroy property. Parker to DOS, December 31, 1955, DOS 785.00/12-3155, *Confidential U.S. State Department Central Files.*

66. The elections were actually held on October 21, 1956.

67. *al-Difaʿ*, December 23, 1955.

68. Shuqayr, 112.

69. Ziyadin, 71.

70. Peter Gubser, *Politics and Change in al-Karak, Jordan: A Study of a Small Arab Town and Its Districts* (London: Oxford University Press, 1973), 137.

71. Mason to FO, January 9, 1956, FO 371.121462/VJ 1015/27, PRO.

72. John Bagot Glubb, *A Soldier with the Arabs* (New York: Hodder and Stoughton, 1957), 405.

73. "Mudhakkirat Majlis al-Ummah" ["Reports of the Majlis al-Ummah"], *Supplement to al-Jaridah al-Rasmiyah*, January 31, 1956.

74. al-Farhan interview.

75. Author interview with Jamal al-Shaʿir, Amman, Jordan, June 24, 1998.

76. *SWB*, December 27, 1956.

77. Author interview with Wahdan Oweis, Amman, Jordan, July 5, 2000.

78. Wikely to FO, January 3, 1956, FO 371.121464/VJ 1051/9, PRO.

79. Parker to DOS, December 31, 1955, DOS 785.00/12-3155, *Confidential U.S. State Department Central Files.*

80. Memorandum of a Conversation between the Assistant Secretary of State for Near Eastern, South Asian, and African Affairs (Allen) and the Jordanian Ambassador (Rifaʿi), Department of State, Washington, January 28, 1956, *U.S. Foreign Relations, 1955–1957*. Ambassador Rifaʿi discounted all reports of Saudi and Egyptian bribes to Jordanian political figures, but as the brother of Samir Rifaʿi might have had a political reason for denying their existence.

81. Abu Nuwar, 145–146. See Joseph A. Massad, *Colonial Effects: The Making of National Identity in Jordan* (New York: Columbia University Press, 2001), 171–176, for a discussion of Shahir Abu Shahut's participation in the ouster of John Bagot Glubb.

82. Abu Nuwar, 171.

83. Author interview with Mahmud al-Muʿayta, Amman, Jordan, June 30, 1995.

84. Massad, 189. Soon after Glubb's dismissal, the government, as part of its process of Arabizing the armed forces, renamed the Jordanian Arab Legion, the Jordanian Arab Army (JAA).

85. Abu Nuwar, 180.

86. Harb, 51.

87. *SWB*, March 6, 1956.
88. Ibid., March 13, 1956.

CHAPTER 8

1. Author interview with Moraiwid al-Tell, Amman, Jordan, July 7, 2000. Al-Tell worked in the Ministry of the Economy in the 1950s.

2. Author interview with Ya'qub Ziyadin, Amman, Jordan, June 25, 1995.

3. Sulayman Musa, *A'lam min al-Urdun: Hazza' al-Majali, Sulayman al-Nabulsi, Wasfi al-Tell [Distinguished Men of Jordan: Hazza' al-Majali, Sulayman al-Nabulsi, Wasfi al-Tell]* (Amman: al-Mamlakah al-Urduniyah al-Hashimiyah, 1986), 88.

4. For additional information on the political events discussed in this chapter, see Naseer H. Aruri, *Jordan: A Study in Political Development, 1921–1965* (The Hague: Martinus Nijhoff, 1972); Uriel Dann, *King Hussein and the Challenge of Arab Radicalism: Jordan, 1955–1967* (New York: Oxford University Press, 1989); and Robert B. Satloff, *From Abdullah to Hussein: Jordan in Transition* (New York: Oxford University Press, 1994).

5. Abd al-Rahman Shuqayr, *Min Qasiyun ... ila Rabbat 'Ammun: Rihlat al-'Umr [From Qasiyun ... to Rabbat 'Ammun: A Stage of Life]*, Silsilat Ihya' al-Dhakirah al-Tarikhiyah (Amman: Kitab al-Urdun al-Jadid, 1991), 117–118.

6. Sulayman Musa and Munib al-Madi, *Tarikh al-Urdun fi al-Qarn al-'Ishrin [The History of Jordan in the Twentieth Century]* (Amman: Maktabah al-Muhtasib, 1988), 589; and *Summary of World Broadcasts—Part IV. The Arab World, Israel, Greece, Turkey and Persia* (Caversham Park, Reading, UK: Monitoring Service of the British Broadcasting Corporation), September 28, 1956. Hereafter, *SWB*.

7. *SWB*, October 12, 1956.

8. Peter Snow, *Hussein: A Biography* (London: Barrie & Jenkins, 1972), 97.

9. For example, 'Abd al-Qadir al-Salih and Abd al-Rahman Shuqayr ran advertisements in *Filastin* proclaiming their candidacies and their membership in the National Front. *Filastin*, October 19, 1956, and *Filastin*, October 20, 1956. Sulayman al-Hadidi, in his ad, announced his membership in the NSP. *Filastin*, October 21, 1956.

10. Supporters of Tawfiq Abu'l-Huda formed al-Hizb al-'Arabi al-Dusturi [Arab Constitutional Party] in April 1956, calling for the liberation of Palestine and cooperation with Arab countries. This party supported the regime and consisted primarily of the "King's men."

11. Ya'qub Ziyadin, *al-Bidayah: Sirah Dhatiyah ... Arba'un Sanah fi al-Harakah al-Wataniyah al-Urduniyah [The Beginnings: A Personal Biographical History ... Forty Years in the Jordanian National Movement]* (Beirut: House of Ibn Khaldun Printing, 1981), 74.

12. The official party platform was included in Amman to FO, September 29, 1956, FO 371.121469/VJ 1015/260, Public Record Office, London. Hereafter, PRO.

13. Amman to FO, October 14, 1956, FO 371.121469/VJ 1015/262. The

official party platform was included in Amman to FO, September 29, 1956, FO 371.121469/VJ 1015/260, PRO.

14. The official party platform was included in Amman to FO, September 29, 1956, FO 371.121469/VJ 1015/260, PRO.

15. *al-Difaʿ*, October 22, 1956.

16. Aqil Hyder Hasan Abidi, *Jordan: A Political Study, 1948–1957* (New York: Asia Publishing House, 1965), 209. In total, 50 to 60 percent of the registered voters cast their ballots in this election. Under the electoral law, the system of proportional voting existed, so that each person voted as many times as there were nuwwab assigned to his district. Ibrahim Hajazin calculates that the NSP won 72,000 votes, the Baʿth 34,000, and the Communists and their sympathizers 51,000. Ibrahim Hajazin, "al-Hizb al-Shuyuʿi wa-al-Jabhah al-Wataniyah wa Hukumat al-Nabulsi" ["The Communist Party, the National Front, and the Government of Nabulsi"], in *Hukumat Sulayman al-Nabulsi: 1956/1957 [The Government of Sulayman al-Nabulsi: 1956/1957]*, supervised by Hani Hourani (Amman: Dar Sindibad lil-Nashr, 1999), 127.

17. "Mudhakkirat Majlis al-Ummah" ["Reports of the Majlis al-Ummah"], *Supplement to al-Jaridah al-Rasmiyah*, October 25, 1956. The unidentified deputy is Abdul Khalek Yaghmour from Hebron. The American embassy classified him as an independent deputy, but one who extended his support to the National Socialist Party. See Sabini, Jerusalem, to DOS, October 24, 1956, DOS 785.00/10-2456, U.S. Department of State, *Confidential U.S. State Department Central Files: Jordan: 1955–1959* (Bethesda, Md.: University Publications of America, 1990). Hereafter *Confidential U.S. State Department Central Files.*

18. Hani Hourani, "Intakhabat Tashrin al-Awal 1956 wa-al-Majlis al-Niyabi al-Khamisa" ["The Elections of October 1956 and the Fifth Legislative Majlis"], in *Hukumat Sulayman al-Nabulsi: 1956/1957 [The Government of Sulayman al-Nabulsi: 1956/1957]*, supervised by Hani Hourani (Amman: Dar Sindibad lil-Nashr, 1999), 34.

19. Hajazin, 126, feels that the NSP and Baʿth initially worked together, but excluded the Communists because they felt the government would attack them for such an alliance.

20. Author interview with ʿIsa Madanat, Amman, Jordan, June 20, 1998. This statement and the many that follow concerning ʿAbdullah al-Rimawi's activities in 1956 and 1957 illustrate the commonly held view that al-Rimawi helped fragment the JNM once in power. Without memoirs from al-Rimawi, this view is impossible to refute or to reexamine.

21. Talʿat Harb, *Tadhakkurat Talʿat Harb [Memoirs of Talʿat Harb]*, ed. Salih ʿAbd al-Jawad, no. 5 (Bir Zayt: Markaz Dirasat wa-Tawthiq al-Mujtamaʿ al-Filastini, Jamiʿat Bir Zayt, 1994), 54.

22. See, for example, Amman to DOS, September 1, 1956, DOS 785.00/9-156, *Confidential U.S. State Department Central Files.*

23. Amman to FO, September 29, 1956, FO 371.121469/VJ 1015/260, PRO.

24. Hani Hourani is the director of the al-Urdun al-Jadid Research Center in Amman.

25. Shuqayr, 8.

26. Sources differ over the reasons why al-Nabulsi lost his bid. Some feel that he was not popular enough in Amman to garner sufficient numbers of votes, while others feel that the government rigged the results against him. For example, Sulayman Musa reports that al-Nabulsi personally felt that the government had interfered in his election, giving as evidence the fact that many of his supporters could not find their names on the voting registers. Musa, himself, adds that some analysts at the time felt that al-Nabulsi's personal popularity was limited to a group of leftists and Nasserites and was not wide enough to wage a successful electoral campaign. Musa cites as another reason the breakdown of the alliance system among the leftist parties. See Musa, *A'lam min al-Urdun*, 70.

27. *New York Times*, December 17, 1956.

28. Author interview with Jamal al-Sha'ir, Amman, Jordan, June 24, 1998.

29. *New York Times*, December 17, 1956.

30. "Mudhakkirat Majlis al-Ummah" ["Reports of the Majlis al-Ummah"], *Supplement to al-Jaridah al-Rasmiyah*, January 6, 1957.

31. Musa, *A'lam min al-Urdun*, 80.

32. *SWB*, February 4, 1957.

33. Fawaz A. Gerges, "In the Shadow of Nasser: Jordan in the Arab Cold War, 1955–65," in *The Resilience of the Hashemite Rule: Politics and the State in Jordan, 1946–67*, ed. Tariq Tell (Amman: Centre d'études et de recherches sur le Moyen-Orient Contemporain, 2001), 102.

34. Amman to Information Research Department, FO, March 5, 1957, FO 371.127979/VJ 1671/3, PRO.

35. Hajazin, 130.

36. *SWB*, April 8, 1957.

37. Jamal al-Sha'ir, *Siyasi Yatadhakkar: Tajribah fi al-'Amal al-Siyasi [A Politician Remembers: Commentary on My Political Experience]* (London: Riad El-Rayyes Books, Ltd., 1987), 200.

38. Musa, *A'lam min al-Urdun*, 77.

39. Ibid., 78.

40. Ibid.

41. Moraiwid al-Tell interview.

42. Author interview with Ali al-Mahafazah, Amman, Jordan, July 10, 2000.

43. al-Sha'ir interview.

44. Madanat interview.

45. Aruri, 140.

46. *Filastin*, April 4, 1957.

47. *SWB*, April 8, 1957.

48. For more information on the "coup" of 1957, see Joseph A. Massad, *Colonial Effects: The Making of National Identity in Jordan* (New York: Columbia University Press, 2001).

49. Satloff, 165; and Dann, 57.

50. Ali Abu Nuwar, *Huna Talashat al-'Arab: Mudhakkirat fi al-Siyasah al-'Arabiyah (1948–1964) [A Time of Arab Decline: Memoirs of Arab Politics (1948–*

1964)] (London: Dar al-Saqi, 1990), 317; and author interview with Mahmoud al-Mu'ayta, Amman, Jordan, June 30, 1995. The only question everyone seems to have is why Rashid chose to use armored cars instead of the usual jeeps and small cars used in previous operations.

51. King Hussein of Jordan, *Uneasy Lies the Head: The Autobiography of His Majesty King Hussein I of the Hashemite Kingdom of Jordan* (n.p.: Bernard Geis Associates, 1962), 176.

52. P. J. Vatikiotis, *Politics and the Military in Jordan: A Study of the Arab Legion 1921–1957* (London: Frank Cass & Co., Ltd., 1967), 130.

53. Clinton Bailey, *Jordan's Palestinian Challenge, 1948–1983: A Political History* (Boulder, Colo.: Westview Press, 1984), 13.

54. Hussein, 168.

55. Massad, 195.

56. Author interview with Bahjat Abu Gharbiyah, Amman, Jordan, June 19, 1995; and Hani Hourani, *Tarikh al-Hayat al-Niyabiyah fi al-Urdun [The History of Parliamentary Life in Jordan]* (Nicosia, Cyprus: Sharq Press Ltd., September 1989), 89–90.

57. See Johnston to FO, May 11, 1957, FO 371.127880/VJ 1015/112, Johnston to FO, October 9, 1957, FO 371.127887/VJ 10110/7, PRO; and Memorandum of a Conversation, Department of State, Washington, April 24, 1957, in *Foreign Relations of the United States, 1955-1957*, Vol. 8, *Near East: Jordan-Yemen*, Editor in Chief John P. Glennon, ed. Will Klingaman, Aaron D. Miller, and Nina J. Noring (Washington, D.C.: U.S. Government Printing Office, 1988). As a sign that U.S. support of repressive policies had existed for years, Parker to DOS, April 3, 1956, DOS 785.00/4-356 criticizes the Jordanian government for releasing prisoners in the aftermath of Glubb's ouster because these "destructive elements" were dangerous for the country. As a possible solution, the document states, "it has been suggested that weighted sacks dropped into the Gulf of Aqaba would be more efficient than detention in Jafr." *Confidential U.S. State Department Central Files.*

58. Dann, 185 n. 22.

59. Author interview with Awni Fakher, Amman, Jordan, July 14, 2000. Awni Fakher belonged to the Communist Party in the 1950s.

60. Amin al-Khatib, *Tadhakkurat Amin al-Khatib [Memoirs of Amin al-Khatib]*, ed. Salih Abd al-Jawad and Mu'awiyah Tahbub, no. 2 (Bir Zayt: Markaz Dirasat wa-Tawthiq al-Mujtama' al-Filastini, Jami'at Bir Zayt, 1992), 33–34.

61. BBC Monitoring, April 27, 1957, FO 371.127879/VJ 1015/93, PRO.

62. Aruri, 147.

63. Dann, 71. King Husayn also began receiving payments from the CIA in 1957, under the project name "No Beef." This money came outside the conventional channels of military and economic aid to Jordan. In return for these annual cash payments, Husayn allowed American intelligence agencies to operate freely in Jordan, and he personally provided information to the CIA. *Washington Post*, February 18, 1977.

64. *SWB*, April 26, 1957.

65. Musa, *A'lam min al-Urdun*, 87.

66. Abidi, 184.

67. The different political terms come from Musa, *Aʿlam min al-Urdun*, 87.

68. Author interview with Husni Shiyab, Amman, Jordan, July 13, 2000.

69. Musa, *Aʿlam min al-Urdun*, 79.

70. Ali al-Mahafazah, *al-ʿAlaqat al-Urduniyah al-Baritaniyah: min Taʾsis al-Imarah Hatta Ilghaʾ al-muʿahadah (1921–1957) [Jordanian and British Relations— From the Establishment of the Emirate to the End of the Treaty (1921–1957)]* (Beirut: Dar al-Nahar lil-Nashr, 1973), 95; and Joel S. Migdal, *Palestinian Society and Politics* (Princeton, N.J.: Princeton University Press, 1980), 177.

71. Shiyab interview.

72. U.S. Congress, House Committee on Government Operations, *Report of a Study of United States Foreign Aid in Ten Middle Eastern and African Countries: Turkey, Iran, Syria, Lebanon, Jordan, Israel, Greece, Tunisia, Libya, Egypt*, 88th Cong., 1st session, 1963, 63.

73. Ali Abdul Kazem, "The Muslim Brotherhood: The Historic Background and the Ideological Origins," in *Islamic Movements in Jordan*, ed. Jillian Schwedler, trans. George A. Musleh (Amman: al-Urdun al-Jadid Research Center, 1997), 20.

74. Musa, *Aʿlam min al-Urdun*, 87.

CHAPTER 9

1. Abdullah, *Memoirs of King Abdullah of Transjordan*, ed. Philip P. Graves (London: Jonathan Cape, 1950), 199.

2. Author interview with Jamal al-Shaʿir, Amman, Jordan, June 24, 1998.

3. Amnon Cohen, *Political Parties in the West Bank under the Jordanian Regime, 1949–1967* (Ithaca, N.Y.: Cornell University Press, 1980), 237–238.

4. Author interview with Bahjat Abu Gharbiyah, Amman, Jordan, June 19, 1995, confirms that the Baʿth Party prepared to overthrow the king in the period after April 1957.

5. Naseer H. Aruri, *Jordan: A Study in Political Development, 1921–1965* (The Hague: Martinus Nijhoff, 1972), 157.

6. Ibid.

7. To give some idea of how successful the Hashemites actually were in bringing people into the state structure via such agencies, some of the teachers who taught the future leaders of the Jordanian National Movement about Arab nationalist politics in the 1930s and 1940s found their way onto the textbook-writing committees in the 1950s and 1960s. The most glaring example is Husni Fariz, who influenced Yaʿqub Ziyadin and Nabih Irsheidat and faced periods of time in political exile because of his activities. Starting in the late 1950s, he wrote a number of the historical texts that negate, by omission, the very message the National Movement tried to disseminate.

8. Asher Susser, *On Both Banks of the Jordan: A Political Biography of Wasfi al-Tall* (London: Frank Cass, 1994), 36.

9. Paul Kingston, "Rationalizing Patrimonialism: Wasfi al-Tall and Eco-

nomic Reform in Jordan, 1962–67," in *The Resilience of the Hashemite Rule: Politics and State in Jordan, 1946–67*, ed. Tariq Tell, Les Cahiers du CERMOC, no. 25 (Amman: Centre d'études et de recherches sur le Moyen-Orient Contemporain, 2001), 120.

10. Aruri, 177.

11. Author interview with Ali al-Mahafazah, Amman, Jordan, July 20, 2000.

12. Aruri, 179.

13. al-Mahafazah interview.

14. Susser, 40.

15. Ibid., 37.

16. Kingston, 142.

17. Ibid., 129.

18. Clinton Bailey, *Jordan's Palestinian Challenge, 1948–1983: A Political History* (Boulder, Colo.: Westview Press, 1984), 17–18.

19. Kingston, 118.

20. Ibid., 123.

21. Robert C. Hayes, *Labor Law and Practice in the Hashemite Kingdom of Jordan*, BLS Report no. 322 (Washington, D.C.: U.S. Department of Labor, U.S. Bureau of Labor Statistics, 1967), 21.

22. Ibid., 23.

23. Ibid., 10.

24. Ibid., 13.

25. Hani al-Amad, *Cultural Policy in Jordan* (Paris: UNESCO, 1981), 35.

26. An earlier version of this section appeared in Betty S. Anderson, "Writing the Nation: Textbooks of the Hashemite Kingdom of Jordan," *Comparative Studies of South Asia, Africa and the Middle East* 21, nos. 1–2 (2001): 5–14.

27. Thuqan al-Hindawi, *al-Qathiyah al-Filastiniyah [The Palestinian Issue]*, Third Secondary Level (Amman: Wizarat al-Tarbiyah wa-al-Ta'lim al-Urduniyah, 1964), 21.

28. Yahya Tahir al-Hijawi, Sadi Murad al-Khayat, and Adnan Lutfi Uthman, *Tarikhuna al-Hadith [Our Modern History]*, Sixth Grade Reader (Nablus: Wizarat al-Tarbiyah wa-al-Ta'lim al-Urduniyah, 1959), 71.

29. Ibid., 75.

30. Sa'id al-Dura, Abdul-Rahim Mur'ib, Sadiq Uda, and Abdul-Bari al-Shaykh Dura, *al-Tarikh al-'Arabi al-Hadith [Modern Arab History]*, Third Secondary Level (Amman: Wizarat al-Tarbiyah wa-al-Ta'lim al-Urduniyah, 1969), 128.

31. See al-Hijawi et al., 76.

32. See Ibid., 106–107.

33. al-Dura et al. (1969), 146.

34. Ibid., 147.

35. Said al-Dura, Abdul-Rahim Mur'ib, Sadiq Uda, and Abd al-Bari al-Shaykh Dura, *al-Tarikh al-'Arabi al-Hadith [Modern Arab History]* (Amman: Wizarat al-Tarbiyah wa-al-Ta'lim al-Urduniyah, 1975), 175.

36. al-Hijawi et al., 109.

37. Ibid., 110.

38. Ibid., 113.

39. Ibid., 114.

40. Author interview with Husni Ayesh, Amman, Jordan, May 29, 2002.

41. Linda L. Layne, *Home and Homeland: The Dialogics of Tribal and National Identities in Jordan* (Princeton, N.J.: Princeton University Press, 1994), 130.

42. Ibid.

43. Al-Amad, 23.

44. Layne, 102.

45. See Joseph A. Massad, *Colonial Effects: The Making of National Identity in Jordan* (New York: Columbia University Press, 2001), for a more comprehensive discussion of this campaign.

46. Mansoor Moaddel, *Jordanian Exceptionalism: A Comparative Analysis of State-Religion Relationships in Egypt, Iran, Jordan, and Syria* (New York: Palgrave, 2002), 36.

47. Valerie Yorke, *Domestic Politics and Regional Security: Jordan, Syria and Israel: The End of an Era?* (Aldershot, England: International Institute for Strategic Studies, Gower, 1998), 50.

48. Ali Abdul Kazem, "The Muslim Brotherhood: The Historic Background and the Ideological Origins," in *Islamic Movements in Jordan*, ed. Jillian Schwedler, trans. George A. Musleh (Amman: al-Urdun al-Jadid Research Center, 1997), 21–22.

49. Uriel Dann, *King Hussein and the Challenge of Arab Radicalism: Jordan, 1955–1967* (New York: Oxford University Press, 1989), 117.

50. Bailey, 17–18.

51. The street runs between the old mukhabarat building and the Abdali bus station.

52. Author interview with Mahmud al-Mu'ayta, Amman, Jordan, June 30, 1995.

53. John F. Devlin, *The Baath Party: A History from Its Origins to 1966* (Stanford, Calif.: Hoover Institute Press, 1976), 176.

54. Author interview with Mu'nis al-Razzaz, Amman, Jordan, June 20, 1995; and William B. Quandt, "Political and Military Dimensions of Contemporary Palestinian Nationalism," in *The Politics of Palestinian Nationalism*, ed. William B. Quandt, Fuad Jabber, and Ann Mosely Lesch (Berkeley and Los Angeles: University of California Press, 1974), 90.

BIBLIOGRAPHY

GOVERNMENT DOCUMENTS: JORDAN

The Constitution of the Hashemite Kingdom of Jordan. Amman: Hashemite Kingdom of Jordan, 1952.

Currency Control Department. *Balance of Payments: 1958.* March 1959.

———. *Balance of Payments for the Year 1959.* May 30, 1964.

Department of Statistics. *The Jordan Economy in Figures.* August 1968.

———. *The Jordan Economy in Figures: 1964–1966.*

———. *The National Income, 1959–1960.*

———. *Statistical Guide to Jordan: 1965.*

Hashemite Kingdom of Jordan, 1953–1957. *Mudhakkirat Majlis al-Ummah [Reports of the Majlis al-Ummah].*

GOVERNMENT DOCUMENTS: UNITED KINGDOM

Summary of World Broadcasts—Part IV. The Arab World, Israel, Greece, Turkey and Persia. Caversham Park, Reading, UK: Monitoring Service of the British Broadcasting Company, 1954–1957.

United Kingdom. "Exchange of Notes between the Government of the United Kingdom of Great Britain and Northern Ireland and the Government of the Hashemite Kingdom of Jordan Modifying the Annex to the Exchange of Notes of March 13, 1957, Terminating the Treaty of Alliance of March 15, 1948." *Treaty Series* no. 106. London: H. M. Stationery Office, 1961.

———. *Parliamentary Debates,* Commons, 5th ser., vol. 143 (1921), cols. 265–334. London: Her Majesty's Stationery Office, 1921.

———. *Parliamentary Debates,* Commons, 5th ser., vol. 151 (1922), cols. 1536–1602. London: Her Majesty's Stationery Office, 1922.

————. *Parliamentary Debates*, Commons, 5th ser., vol. 450 (1947–1948), cols. 373–377. London: Her Majesty's Stationery Office, 1948.

————. *Parliamentary Debates*, 5th ser., vol. 451 (1947–1948), cols. 999–1002. London: Her Majesty's Stationery Office, 1948.

————. *Parliamentary Debates*, 5th ser., vol. 453 (1947–1948), cols. 355–358. London: Her Majesty's Stationery Office, 1948.

————. *Political Diaries of the Arab World: Palestine & Jordan, 1924–1936*, ed. Robert L. Jarman. Vol. 2. Slough, UK: Archive Editions, 2001.

————. *Political Diaries of the Arab World: Palestine & Jordan, 1937–1938*, ed. Robert L. Jarman. Vol. 3. Slough, UK: Archive Editions, 2001.

United Kingdom. Colonial Office. *An Interim Report on the Civil Administration of Palestine during the Period 1st July, 1920–30th June, 1921.* London: Her Majesty's Stationery Office, August 1921.

————. Colonial Office. *Palestine: Report on Immigration, Land Settlement and Development.* London: His Majesty's Stationery Office, October 1930.

————. Colonial Office. *Palestine Royal Commission: Minutes of Evidence Heard at Public Sessions.* Colonial No. 134. London: His Majesty's Stationery Office, 1937.

————. Colonial Office. *Palestine Royal Commission Report.* London: His Majesty's Stationery Office, July 1937.

————. Colonial Office. "Report by His Britannic Majesty's Government to the Council of the League of Nations on the Administration of Palestine and Transjordan for the Year 1925." In *Palestine and Transjordan Administration Reports, 1918–1948*, pp. 2:61–226. Oxford: Archive Editions, 1995.

————. Colonial Office. "Report by His Britannic Majesty's Government to the Council of the League of Nations on the Administration of Palestine and Trans-Jordan for the Year 1926." In *Palestine and Transjordan Administration Reports, 1918–1948*, pp. 2:227–329. Oxford: Archive Editions, 1995.

————. Colonial Office. "Report by His Britannic Majesty's Government to the Council of the League of Nations on the Administration of Palestine and Trans-Jordan for the Year 1927." In *Palestine and Transjordan Administration Reports, 1918–1948*, pp. 2:363–492. Oxford: Archive Editions, 1995.

————. Colonial Office. "Report by His Majesty's Government in the United Kingdom of Great Britain and Northern Ireland to the Council of the League of Nations on the Administration of Palestine and Trans-Jordan for the Year 1928." In *Palestine and Transjordan Administration Reports, 1918–1948*, pp. 2:493–627. Oxford: Archive Editions, 1995.

————. Colonial Office. "Report by His Majesty's Government in the United Kingdom of Great Britain and Northern Ireland to the Council of the League of Nations on the Administration of Palestine and Trans-Jordan for the Year 1929." In *Palestine and Transjordan Administration Reports, 1918–1948*, pp. 3:1–228. Oxford: Archive Editions, 1995.

————. Colonial Office. "Report by His Majesty's Government in the United Kingdom of Great Britain and Northern Ireland to the Council of the League of Nations on the Administration of Palestine and Trans-Jordan for the Year

1930." In *Palestine and Transjordan Administration Reports, 1918–1948*, pp. 3:229–499. Oxford: Archive Editions, 1995.

———. Colonial Office. "Report by His Majesty's Government in the United Kingdom of Great Britain and Northern Ireland to the Council of the League of Nations on the Administration of Palestine and Trans-Jordan for the Year 1931." In *Palestine and Transjordan Administration Reports, 1918–1948*, pp. 3:599–776. Oxford: Archive Editions, 1995.

———. Colonial Office. "Report by His Majesty's Government in the United Kingdom of Great Britain and Northern Ireland to the Council of the League of Nations on the Administration of Palestine and Trans-Jordan for the Year 1932." In *Palestine and Transjordan Administration Reports, 1918–1948*, pp. 4:1–283. Oxford: Archive Editions, 1995.

———. Colonial Office. "Report by His Majesty's Government in the United Kingdom of Great Britain and Northern Ireland to the Council of the League of Nations on the Administration of Palestine and Trans-Jordan for the Year 1933." In *Palestine and Transjordan Administration Reports, 1918–1948*, pp. 4:287–619. Oxford: Archive Editions, 1995.

———. Colonial Office. "Report by His Majesty's Government in the United Kingdom of Great Britain and Northern Ireland to the Council of the League of Nations on the Administration of Palestine and Trans-Jordan for the Year 1934." In *Palestine and Transjordan Administration Reports, 1918–1948*, pp. 5:1–323. Oxford: Archive Editions, 1995.

———. Colonial Office. "Report by His Majesty's Government in the United Kingdom of Great Britain and Northern Ireland to the Council of the League of Nations on the Administration of Palestine and Trans-Jordan for the Year 1935." In *Palestine and Transjordan Administration Reports, 1918–1948*, pp. 5:431–831. Oxford: Archive Editions, 1995.

———. Colonial Office. "Report by His Majesty's Government in the United Kingdom of Great Britain and Northern Ireland to the Council of the League of Nations on the Administration of Palestine and Trans-Jordan for the Year 1936." In *Palestine and Transjordan Administration Reports, 1918–1948*, pp. 6:1–431. Oxford: Archive Editions, 1995.

———. Colonial Office. "Report by His Majesty's Government in the United Kingdom of Great Britain and Northern Ireland to the Council of the League of Nations on the Administration of Palestine and Trans-Jordan for the Year 1937." In *Palestine and Transjordan Administration Reports, 1918–1948*, pp. 7:1–425. Oxford: Archive Editions, 1995.

———. Colonial Office. "Report by His Majesty's Government in the United Kingdom of Great Britain and Northern Ireland to the Council of the League of Nations on the Administration of Palestine and Trans-Jordan for the Year 1938." In *Palestine and Transjordan Administration Reports, 1918–1948*, pp. 7:427–867. Oxford: Archive Editions, 1995.

———. Colonial Office. *Report of the Commission on the Palestine Disturbances of August, 1929.* London: His Majesty's Stationery Office, March 1930.

———. Colonial Office. "Report of the High Commissioner on the Administration of Palestine, 1920–1925." In *Palestine and Transjordan Administration Reports, 1918–1948*, pp. 2:1–59. Oxford: Archive Editions, 1995.

———. Colonial Office. "Reports of the Mandate Period 1922–1924." In *Palestine and Transjordan Administration Reports, 1918–1948*, pp. 1:443–627. Oxford: Archive Editions, 1995.

———. Foreign Office. "Agreement between the Arab League States Concerning the Nationality of Arabs Resident in Countries to Which They Are Not Related by Origin—Opened for Signature at Cairo on 12th November, 1952." *British and Foreign State Papers, 1952*. London: Her Majesty's Stationery Office, 1952.

———. Government of Palestine. "Reports of the Civil Government 1920–1923." In *Palestine and Transjordan Administration Reports, 1918–1948*, pp. 1:137–442. Oxford: Archive Editions, 1995.

———. Government of Palestine. "Unpublished Supplement to the Survey of Palestine Prepared in June 1947 for the Information of the Anglo-American Committee of Inquiry." In *Palestine and Transjordan Administration Reports, 1918–1948*, pp. 15:607–767. Oxford: Archive Editions, 1995.

———. Public Record Office, London. File FO 371: Political.

GOVERNMENT DOCUMENTS: UNITED STATES

Foreign Relations of the United States, 1946: The Near East and Africa. Vol. 7. Washington, D.C.: U.S. Government Printing Office, 1969.

Foreign Relations of the United States, 1952–1954: The Near and Middle East. Vol. 9, part 1. Editor in Chief John P. Glennon. Edited by Paul Claussen, Joan M. Lee, and Carl N. Raether. Washington, D.C.: U.S. Government Printing Office, 1986.

Foreign Relations of the United States, 1955–1957: Near East: Jordan-Yemen. Vol. 8. Editor in Chief John P. Glennon. Edited by Will Klingaman, Aaron D. Miller, and Nina J. Noring. Washington, D.C.: U.S. Government Printing Office, 1988.

Hayes, Robert C. *Labor Law and Practice in the Hashemite Kingdom of Jordan*. BLS Report no. 322. Washington, D.C.: U.S. Department of Labor, U.S. Bureau of Labor Statistics, 1967.

U.S. Congress. House Committee on Government Operations. *Report of a Study of United States Foreign Aid in Ten Middle Eastern and African Countries: Turkey, Iran, Syria, Lebanon, Jordan, Israel, Greece, Tunisia, Libya, Egypt*. 88th Cong., 1st sess., 1963.

U.S. Department of State. *American Foreign Policy, 1950–1955: Basic Documents*. General Foreign Policy Series 117, Vol. 1. Washington, D.C.: U.S. Government Printing Office, 1957.

———. *American Foreign Policy, 1950–1955: Basic Documents*. General Foreign Policy Series 117, Vol. 2. Washington, D.C.: U.S. Government Printing Office, 1957.

———. *Confidential U.S. State Department Central Files: Jordan: 1955–1959.* Bethesda, Md.: University Publications of America, 1990.

———. "Mob Violence in Amman and Jerusalem." *Bulletin* 34, no. 864 (January 16, 1956): 85.

———. Historical Office. Bureau of Public Affairs. *American Foreign Policy: Current Documents, 1957.* No. 7101. Washington, D.C.: Historical Division, Bureau of Public Affairs, 1961.

———. Office of Media Services. *Fact Sheet: Jordan.* Washington, D.C.: U.S. Government Printing Office, 1963.

LEAGUE OF NATIONS AND UNITED NATIONS

League of Nations. "Mandate for Palestine Together with a Note by the Secretary-General Relating to Its Application to the Territory Known as Trans-Jordan under the Provisions of Article 25." In *Palestine and Transjordan Administration Reports, 1918–1948,* Vol. 1, pp. 485–495. London: His Majesty's Stationery Office, 1995.

United Nations. *Laws Concerning Nationality.* United Nations Legislative Series. ST/LEG/SER.B/4. New York: United Nations, July 1954.

———. Department of Economic and Social Affairs. *Organization and Administration of Welfare Programs: A Series of Country Studies, Jordan.* ST.SOA/78. New York: United Nations, 1968.

———. Educational, Scientific and Cultural Organization. *World Radio and Television.* New York: United Nations, 1965.

UN General Assembly. Seventh Session. Official Records, Supplement 14. *Annual Report of the Commissioner-General of the United Nations Relief and Works Agency for Palestine Refugees: 1 July 1961–30 June 1962.* A/5214. New York: United Nations, 1962.

United Nations Relief and Works Agency for Palestine Refugees in the Near East. *Palestine Refugees in Jordan.* PL 12 J. New York: United Nations, October 1984.

INTERVIEWS

Abu Gharbiyah, Bahjat, Amman, Jordan, June 19, 1995. (Leader of the Ba'th Party, 1950s.)

Ayesh, Husni, Amman, Jordan, May 29, 2002. (Educator, 1950s.)

Barghouti, Jawdat J., Amman, Jordan, July 11, 2000. (Member of the Ba'th Party, 1950s.)

Bseiso, Musallam, Amman, Jordan, July 13, 2000. (Journalist, 1950s.)

Fakher, Ahmad, Amman, Jordan, July 7, 2000. (Member of the Communist Party, 1950s.)

Fakher, Awni, Amman, Jordan, July 14, 2000. (Member of the Communist Party, 1950s.)

al-Farhan, Hamad, Amman, Jordan, June 23, 1998. (Member of the Movement of Arab Nationalists and undersecretary in the Ministry of the Economy, 1950s.)

Haddad, George, Amman, Jordan, July 12, 2000. (Member of the Syrian Nationalists Movement, 1950s.)

Haddadin, Nabil, Amman, Jordan, July 21, 2000. (Member of the Communist Party, 1950s.)

Madanat, 'Isa, Amman, Jordan, June 20, 1998. (Leader of the Communist Party, 1950s.)

al-Mahafazah, Ali, Amman, Jordan, July 10, 2000. (Historian, University of Jordan, starting 1971.)

al-Majali, Muhammad Bajis, Amman, Jordan, July 11, 2000. (Known as the "Za'im" for his control over the streets of Amman, 1950s.)

al-Mu'ayta, Mahmud, Amman, Jordan, June 30, 1995. (Leader of the Free Officers' Movement, 1950s.)

Nafa', Amal, Amman, Jordan, June 21, 1995. (Member of the Communist Party, 1950s.)

Oweis, Wahdan, Amman, Jordan, July 5, 2000. (Member of the Ba'th Party, 1950s.)

al-Razzaz, Mu'nis, Amman, Jordan, June 20, 1995. (Son of Munif al-Razzaz, Employee, Culture Department, Jordan, 1990s.)

al-Sha'ir, Jamal, Amman, Jordan, June 24, 1998. (Member of the Ba'th Party, 1950s.)

Shiyab, Husni, Amman, Jordan, July 13, 2000. (Political scientist, al-Isra University, 1990s.)

Shuqayr, Abd al-Rahman, Amman, Jordan, June 21, 1995. (Leader of the National Front, 1950s.)

al-Tell, Moraiwid, Amman, Jordan, July 7, 2000, and July 21, 2000. (Employee, Ministry of the Economy, 1950s.)

al-Tell, Salty, Ajlun, Jordan, July 22, 2000. (Member of the Communist Party, 1950s.)

Zeitoun, Mahmoud, Amman, Jordan, July 16, 2002. (Member of the Ba'th Party, 1950s.)

Ziyadin, Ya'qub, Amman, Jordan, June 25, 1995. (Leader of the Communist Party, 1950s.)

MEMOIRS: ARABIC AND ENGLISH

Abdullah. *Memoirs of King Abdullah of Transjordan.* Edited by Philip P. Graves. London: Jonathan Cape, 1950.

Abu Gharbiyah, Bahjat. *Fi Khidham al-Nidhal al-'Arabi al-Filastini: Mudhakkirat al-Munadil Bahjat Abu Gharbiyah, 1916–1949 [In the Roar of the Palestinian Struggle: Memoirs of the Fighter Bahjat Abu Gharbiyah, 1916–1949].* Beirut: Mu'assasat al-Dirasat al-Filastiniyah, 1993.

Abu Ghunaymah, Muhammad Subhi. *Sirah Manfiyah: Min Awraq al-Duktur Mu-*

hammad Subhi Abu Ghunaymah [Exile Biography: From the Papers of Dr. Mu-hammad Subhi Abu Ghunaymah]. Volume 1. Beirut: al-Mu'assasah al-'Arabiyah lil-Dirasat wa-al-Nashr; Amman: Dar al-Faris lil-Nashr wa-al-Tawzi, 2001.

———. *Sirah Manfiyah: Min Awraq al-Duktur Muhammad Subhi Abu Ghunaymah [Exile Biography: From the Papers of Dr. Muhammad Subhi Abu Ghunaymah]*. Volume 2. Beirut: al-Mu'assasah al-'Arabiyah lil-Dirasat wa-al-Nashr; Amman: Dar al-Faris lil-Nashr wa-al-Tawzi, 2001.

Abu Nuwar, Ali. *Huna Talashat al-'Arab: Mudhakkirat fi al-Siyasah al-'Arabiyah (1948–1964) [A Time of Arab Decline: Memoirs of Arab Politics (1948–1964)]*. London: Dar al-Saqi, 1990.

Aburish, Saïd K. *Children of Bethany: The Story of a Palestinian Family*. London: Tauris, 1988.

Bowman, Humphrey. *Middle-East Window*. London: Longmans, Green and Co., 1942.

Glubb, Sir John Bagot. *A Soldier with the Arabs*. London: Hodder and Stoughton, 1957.

Harb, Tal'at. *Tadhakkurat Tal'at Harb [Memoirs of Tal'at Harb]*. Edited by Salih 'Abd al-Jawad. No. 5. Bir Zayt: Markaz Dirasat wa-Tawthiq al-Mujtama' al-Filastini, Jami'at Bir Zayt, 1994.

Hussein, King of Jordan. *Uneasy Lies the Head: The Autobiography of His Majesty King Hussein I of the Hashemite Kingdom of Jordan*. n.p.: Bernard Geis Associates, 1962.

Irsheidat, Nabil. *Awraq Laysat Shakhsiyah: Mudhakkirat Nabil Irsheidat [Non-Personal Papers: Memoirs of Nabil Irsheidat]*. Damascus: Dar al-Yanabi', 2001.

Johnston, Charles. *The Brink of Jordan*. London: Hamish Hamilton, 1972.

Kamal, Hatim. *Tadhakkurat Hatim Kamal [Memoirs of Hatim Kamal]*. Edited by Salih Abd al-Jawad. No. 6. Bir Zayt: Markaz Dirasat wa-Tawthiq al-Mujtama' al-Filastini, Jami'at Bir Zayt, 1995.

Karmi, Ghada. *In Search of Fatima: A Palestinian Story*. London: Verso, 2002.

al-Khatib, Amin. *Tadhakkurat Amin al-Khatib [Memoirs of Amin al-Khatib]*. Edited by Salih Abd al-Jawad and Mu'awiyah Tahbub. No. 2. Bir Zayt: Markaz Dirasat wa-Tawthiq al-Mujtama' al-Filastini, Jami'at Bir Zayt, 1992.

Kirkbride, Alec S. *A Crackle of Thorns: Experiences in the Middle East*. London: John Murray, 1956.

———. *From the Wings: Amman Memoirs 1947–1951*. London: Frank Cass, 1976.

al-Majali, Hazza'. *Hadha Bayani lil-Nas: Qissat Muhadathat Templer [This Is My Statement to the People: The Story of the Discussions of Templer]*. n.p.: n.p., n.d.

———. *Mudhakkirati [My Memoirs]*. n.p.: n.p., 1960.

Munif, Abd al-Rahman. *Story of a City: A Childhood in Amman*. Translated by Samira Kawar. London: Quartet Books, 1996.

al-Razzaz, Munif. *al-A'mal al-Fikriyah wa-al-Siyasiyah [Political and Intellectual Actions]*. Part 2. n.p.: n.p., n.d.

———. "Munif al-Razzaz Yatadhakkar: 'A'ilat 'Sirbitar' al-Jaysh" ["Munif al-Razzaz Remembers: The Family of the 'Commander of the Vets' of the Army"]. *Akhar Khabar* 70 (December 30–31, 1993): 10.

———. "Munif al-Razzaz Yatadhakkar: Hama . . . Taʿni Suriya" ["Munif al-Razzaz Remembers: Hama . . . Means all Syria"]. *Akhar Khabar* 69 (December 29–30, 1993): 10.

———. "Munif al-Razzaz Yatadhakkar: Al-Hanin ila al-Judhur" ["Munif al-Razzaz Remembers: The Desire for Roots"]. *Akhar Khabar* 68 (December 28–29, 1993): 8.

———. "Munif al-Razzaz Yatadhakkar: Al-Jamiʿah al-Amrikiyah" ["Munif al-Razzaz Remembers: American University"]. *Akhar Khabar* 72 (January 2–3, 1994): 10.

———. "Munif al-Razzaz Yatadhakkar: Kalam ʿan al-Burjuwaziyah al-Saghirah" ["Munif al-Razzaz Remembers: Discourse on the Petty Bourgeoisie"]. *Akhar Khabar* 71 (January 1–2, 1994): 7.

———. "Munif al-Razzaz Yatadhakkar: Mawqif Muzdawaj min Hitler" ["Munif al-Razzaz Remembers: A Double-Standard Regarding Hitler"]. *Akhar Khabar* 76 (January 6–7, 1994): 10.

———. "Munif al-Razzaz Yatadhakkar: Muʿallim fi Amman" ["Munif al-Razzaz Remembers: A Teacher in Amman"]. *Akhar Khabar* 77 (January 8–9, 1994): 12–13.

———. "Munif al-Razzaz Yatadhakkar: Sanawat al-Jamiʿah" ["Munif al-Razzaz Remembers: The University Years"]. *Akhar Khabar* 73 (January 3–4, 1994): 10.

———. "Munif al-Razzaz Yatadhakkar: Silah fi al-Awzaʿi" ["Munif al-Razzaz Remembers: Weapons in al-Awzaʿi"]. *Akhar Khabar* 75 (January 5–6, 1994): 10.

———. "Munif al-Razzaz Yatadhakkar: ʿUsbat al-ʿAmal al-Qawmi" ["Munif al-Razzaz Remembers: The League of National Action"]. *Akhar Khabar* 74 (January 4–5, 1994): 8.

Sakakini, Hala. *Jerusalem and I: A Personal Record.* Amman: Economic Press Co., 1990.

al-Sakakini, Khalil. *Kadha Ana ya Dunya [As I Am, O World].* Silsilat Ihya al-Turath al-Thaqafi al-Filastini. Beirut: Al-Ittihad al-ʿAmm lil-Kuttab wa-al-Suhufiyin al-Filastiniyin, al-Amanah al-Amman, 1982.

Salah, Yusrah. *Tadhakkurat Yusrah Salah [Memoirs of Yusrah Salah].* Edited by Ali Jarbawi and Lubna ʿAbd al-Hadi. No. 3. Bir Zayt: Markaz Dirasat wa-Tawthiq al-Mujtamaʿ al-Filastini, Jamiʿat Bir Zayt, 1992.

Sanger, Richard H. *Where the Jordan Flows.* Washington, D.C.: Middle East Institute, 1963.

al-Shaʾir, Jamal. *Khamsun ʿAman wa-Nayyif [Fifty Years and a Little Bit More].* Amman: Maktab al-Raʾy, 1995.

———. *Siyasi Yatadhakkar: Tajribah fi al-ʿAmal al-Siyasi [A Politician Remembers: Commentary on My Political Experience].* London: Riad El-Rayyes Books, Ltd., 1987.

al-Sharaʿ, Salih. *Filastin: Al-Haqiqah wa-al-Tarikh: Mudhakkirat Jundi. [Palestine, The Facts and History: Memoirs of a Soldier]* Part 2. n.p.: n.p., 1989.

———. *Mudhakkirat Jundi [Memoirs of a Soldier].* Part 1. n.p.: n.p., 1985.

Shuqayr, Abd al-Rahman. *Min Qasiyun . . . ila Rabbat ʿAmmun: Rihlat al-ʿUmr [From Qasiyun . . . to Rabbat ʿAmmun: A Stage of Life].* Silsilat Ihyaʾ al-Dhakirah al-Tarikhiyah. Amman: Kitab al-Urdun al-Jadid, 1991.

al-Tell, 'Abdullah. *Karithat Filastin: Mudhakkirat 'Abdullah al-Tell [The Catastrophe of Palestine: Memoirs of 'Abdullah al-Tell].* Cairo: Dar al-Qalam, 1959.
al-Tell, Wasfi. *Fi Mujabahat al-Ghazw al-Sihyuni [Confronting the Zionist Invasion].* Prepared and edited by Nahid Hatr, Sultan Hatr, and 'Abdullah Abu Raman. Amman: Amanat Amman al-Kubra, 1997.
Ziyadin, Ya'qub. *al-Bidayah: Sirah Dhatiyah . . . Arba'un Sanah fi al-Harakah al-Wataniyah al-Urduniyah [The Beginnings: A Personal Biographical History . . . Forty Years in the Jordanian National Movement].* Beirut: House of Ibn Khaldun Printing, 1981.

NEWSPAPERS: ENGLISH AND ARABIC

al-Difa' (Jerusalem).
Economist (London).
Filastin (Jerusalem).
al-Jaridah al-Rasmiyah (Amman).
London Times (Jerusalem).
Mideast Mirror (Beirut).
al-Muqawamah al-Sha'biyah (Amman).
The Near East and India (London).
New York Times (New York).
Supplement to al-Jaridah al-Rasmiyah (Amman).
The Times (London).
Washington Post (Washington, D.C.).

PUBLISHED SOURCES:
ENGLISH AND FRENCH

Abidi, Aqil Hyder Hasan. *Jordan: A Political Study, 1948–1957.* New York: Asia Publishing House, 1965.
Abromowitz, Zev. "Social-Economic Structure of Arab Palestine." In *Jews and Arabs in Palestine: Studies in a National and a Colonial Problem,* ed. Enzo Sereni and R. E. Ashery, pp. 29–47. New York: Hechalutz Press, 1936.
Abu-Ghazaleh, Adnan. "Arab Cultural Nationalism in Palestine during the British Mandate." *Journal of Palestine Studies* 1, no. 3 (Spring 1972): 37–63.
Abu Jaber, Kamel S. *The Arab Ba'th Socialist Party: History, Ideology, and Organization.* Syracuse, N.Y.: Syracuse University Press, 1966.
———. "The Legislature of the Hashemite Kingdom of Jordan: A Study in Political Development." *Muslim World* 59, nos. 3–4 (July–October 1969): 220–250.
Abu Nowar, Ma'an. *The History of the Hashemite Kingdom of Jordan.* Vol. 1. *The Creation and Development of Transjordan: 1920–1929.* Oxford: Middle East Centre, St. Anthony's College, 1989.
Aflaq, Michel. "Nationalism and Revolution." In *Arab Nationalism: An Anthology,*

ed. Sylvia G. Haim, pp. 242–249. Berkeley and Los Angeles: University of California Press, 1962.

Agwani, M. S. *Communism in the Arab East.* Bombay: Asia Publishing House, 1969.

Almond, Gabriel A., and Sidney Verba. *The Civic Culture: Political Attitudes and Democracy in Five Nations.* Boston: Little, Brown and Co., 1965.

Altbach, Philip G. *Higher Education in the Third World: Themes and Variations.* New York: Advent Books, 1987.

al-Amad, Hani. *Cultural Policy in Jordan.* Paris: UNESCO, 1981.

Amadouny, Vartan M. "Infrastructural Development under the British Mandate." In *Village, Steppe and State: The Social Origins of Modern Jordan,* ed. Eugene L. Rogan and Tariq Tell, pp. 128–161. London: British Academic Press, 1994.

Amawi, Abla. "Jordan." In *The Political Parties in the Middle East and North Africa,* ed. Frank Tachau, pp. 259–296. Westport, Conn.: Greenwood Press, 1994.

American University of Beirut: Description of Its Organization and Work. n.p.: n.p., 1934.

Amin, S. H. *Middle East Legal Systems.* Glascow, Scotland: Royston Ltd., 1985.

Anderson, Benedict. *Imagined Communities: Reflections on the Origin and Spread of Nationalism.* Revised Edition. London and New York: Verso, 1991.

Anderson, Betty S. "Domestic Influences on Policy-Making: The History of the Jordanian National Movement, 1946–1957." In *The Resilience of Hashemite Rule: Politics and State in Jordan, 1946–67,* ed. Tariq Tell, pp. 37–87. Amman: CERMOC, 2001.

———. "The Duality of National Identity in the Middle East: A Critical Review." *Critique* 11, no. 2 (Fall 2002): 229–250.

———. "Writing the Nation: Textbooks of the Hashemite Kingdom of Jordan." *Comparative Studies of South Asia, Africa and the Middle East* 21, nos. 1–2 (2001): 5–14.

Antonius, George. *The Arab Awakening.* Philadelphia: J. B. Lippincott, 1939.

———. "The Machinery of Government in Palestine." *The Annals of the American Academy of Political and Social Science* 164 (November 1932): 55–61.

Apple, Michael W., and Linda K. Christian-Smith. "The Politics of the Textbook." In *The Politics of the Textbook,* ed. Michael W. Apple and Linda K. Christian-Smith, pp. 1–21. London: Routledge, 1991.

Arar: The Poet and Lover of Jordan. Selected by Abdullah Radwa. Translated by Sadik I. Odeh. Amman: National Library, 1999.

Aresvik, Oddvar. *The Agricultural Development of Jordan.* New York: Praeger Publishers, 1976.

Aruri, Naseer H. *Jordan: A Study in Political Development, 1921–1965.* The Hague: Martinus Nijhoff, 1972.

Bailey, Clinton. "Cabinet Formation in Jordan, 1950–1970." *Middle East Outlook* 13, no. 8 (November 1970): 11–23.

———. *Jordan's Palestinian Challenge, 1948–1983: A Political History.* Boulder, Colo.: Westview Press, 1984.

Be'eri, Eliezer. *Army Officers in Arab Politics and Society.* London: Praeger, 1970.

Bhabha, Homi K. *The Location of Culture.* London: Routledge, 1994.

Bill, James A., and Carl Leiden. *The Middle East: Politics and Power*. Boston: Allyn and Bacon, 1974.

Bocco, Riccardo, and Tariq M. M. Tell. *"Pax Britannica* in the Steppe: British Policy and the Transjordanian Bedouin, 1923–39." In *Village, Steppe and State: The Social Origins of Modern Jordan*, ed. Eugene L. Rogan and Tariq Tell, pp. 108–127. London: British Academic Press, 1994.

Bottomore, T. B. *Elites and Society*. New York: Basic Books, 1964.

Boyd, Douglas A. *Broadcasting in the Arab World: A Survey of Radio and Television in the Middle East*. Philadelphia: Temple University Press, 1982.

Brand, Laurie. "'In the Beginning Was the State . . .': The Quest for Civil Society in Jordan." In *Civil Society in the Middle East*, ed. Richard Augustus Norton, pp. 148–185. Leiden, the Netherlands: E. J. Brill, 1995.

———. *Jordan's Inter-Arab Relations*. New York: Columbia University Press, 1994.

———. *Palestinians in the Arab World: Institution Building and the Search for State*. New York: Columbia University Press, 1988.

———. "The Politics of Passports: Palestinian Legal Status in Arab Host States, 1948–86." In *The Middle East and North Africa: Essays in Honor of J. C. Hurewitz*, ed. Reeva S. Simon, pp. 26–42. New York: Columbia University Press, 1990.

al-Bukhari, Najati. *Education in Jordan*. Amman: Ministry of Culture, n.d.

Certeau, Michel de. *The Writing of History*. New York: Columbia University Press, 1988.

Chatterjee, Partha. *The Nation and Its Fragments: Colonial and Postcolonial Histories*. Princeton, N.J.: Princeton University Press, 1993.

Chizik, I. "The Political Parties in Trans-Jordan." *Journal of the Royal Central Asian Society* 22, part 1 (January 1935): 96–99.

Clancy-Smith, Julia A. *Rebel and Saint: Muslim Notables, Populist Protest, Colonial Encounters (Algeria and Tunisia, 1800–1904)*. Berkeley and Los Angeles: University of California Press, 1994.

Cohen, Amnon. "The Jordanian Communist Party in the West Bank, 1950–1960." In *The U.S.S.R. and the Middle East*, ed. Michael Confino and Shimon Shamir, pp. 419–436. Jerusalem: Israel Universities Press, 1973.

———. "Political Parties in the West Bank under the Hashemite Regime." In *Palestinian Arab Politics*, ed. Moshe Ma'oz, pp. 21–49. Jerusalem: Jerusalem Academic Press, 1975.

———. *Political Parties in the West Bank under the Jordanian Regime, 1949–1967*. Ithaca, N.Y.: Cornell University Press, 1980.

Cohen, Michael J. *The Origins and Evolution of the Arab-Zionist Conflict*. Berkeley and Los Angeles: University of California Press, 1987.

"Communism and the Problems of the Arab World." In *Political and Social Thought in the Contemporary Middle East*, ed. Kemal H. Karpat, pp. 262–268. New York: Frederick A. Praeger, Pub., 1968.

Dann, Uriel. "Glubb and the Politicization of the Arab Legion: An Annotated Document." *Asian and African Studies* 21, no. 2 (July 1987): 213–220.

———. "The Hashemite Monarchy 1948–88: The Constant and the Changing—An Integration." In *Jordan in the Middle East: The Making of a Pivotal State, 1948–1988,* ed. Joseph Nevo and Ilan Pappé, pp. 15–25. Newbury Park, Ilford, Essex, England: Frank Cass, 1994.

———. *King Hussein and the Challenge of Arab Radicalism: Jordan, 1955–1967.* New York: Oxford University Press, 1989.

———. "The National Government: Processes and Forces." In *The Hashemite Kingdom of Jordan and the West Bank: A Handbook,* ed. Anne Sinai and Allen Pollack, pp. 89–101. Middle East Confrontation Series. New York: American Academic Association for Peace in the Middle East, 1977.

———. *Studies in the History of Transjordan, 1920–1949: The Making of a State.* Boulder, Colo.: Westview Press, 1984.

Davis, Helen Miller. *Constitutions, Electoral Laws, Treaties of States in the Near and Middle East.* Durham, N.C.: Duke University Press, 1953.

Davison, W. Phillips. *International Political Communication.* New York: Frederick A. Praeger, Pub., 1965.

Dawisha, Adeed. "Jordan in the Middle East: The Art of Survival." In *The Shaping of an Arab Statesman: Sharif Abd al-Hamid Sharaf and the Modern Arab World,* ed. Patrick Seale, pp. 61–74. London: Quartet Books, 1983.

Day, Arthur R. *East Bank/West Bank: Jordan and the Prospects for Peace.* New York: Council on Foreign Relations, 1986.

Dearden, Ann. *Jordan.* London: Robert Hale Ltd., 1958.

Denoeux, Guilain. *Urban Unrest in the Middle East: A Comparative Study of Informal Networks in Egypt, Iran, and Lebanon.* Albany: State University of New York Press, 1993.

Devlin, John F. *The Baath Party: A History from Its Origins to 1966.* Stanford, Calif.: Hoover Institute Press, 1976.

Diamond, Larry, ed. *Political Culture and Democracy in Developing Countries.* Boulder, Colo.: Lynne Rienner Publishers, 1993.

Dorr, Steven R. "Democratization in the Middle East." In *Global Transformation and the Third World,* ed. Robert O. Slater, Barry M. Schutz, and Steven R. Dorr, pp. 131–157. Boulder, Colo.: Lynne Rienner Pub., 1993.

Drysdale, Alasdair, and Gerald H. Blake. *The Middle East and North Africa.* New York: Oxford University Press, 1985.

"Education in Palestine." *Great Britain and the East: Middle East Issue* 62, no. 1769 (February 1947): 52.

El-Edroos, Syed Ali. *The Hashemite Arab Army 1908–1979.* Amman, Jordan: Publishing Committee, 1980.

Faddah, Mohammad Ibrahim. *The Middle East in Transition: A Study in Jordan's Foreign Policy.* London: Asia Publishing House, 1974.

Farrag, Amina. "The *Wastah* among Jordanian Villagers." In *Patrons and Clients in Mediterranean Societies,* ed. Ernest Gellner and John Waterbury, pp. 225–238. London: Gerald Duckworth & Co., Ltd., 1977.

Farsoun, Samih K. *Palestine and the Palestinians.* With Christina E. Zacharia. Boulder, Colo.: Westview Press, 1997.

Fischbach, Michael R. "The Implications of Jordanian Land Policy for the West Bank." *Middle East Journal* 48, no. 3 (Summer 1994): 492–509.

————. *State, Society, and Land in Jordan.* Leiden, the Netherlands: Brill, 2000.

Garfinkle, Adam. "The Nine Lives of Hashemite Jordan." In *The Politics of Change in the Middle East*, ed. Robert B. Satloff, pp. 85–118. Boulder, Colo.: Westview Press, 1993.

Gellner, Ernest. *Nations and Nationalism.* Ithaca, N.Y.: Cornell University Press, 1993.

————. "Patrons and Clients." In *Patrons and Clients in Mediterranean Societies*, ed. Ernest Gellner and John Waterbury, pp. 1–6. London: Gerald Duckworth & Co., Ltd., 1977.

————. *Thought and Change.* London: Weidenfeld and Nicolson, 1964.

Gerges, Fawaz A. "In the Shadow of Nasser: Jordan in the Arab Cold War, 1955–65." In *The Resilience of the Hashemite Rule: Politics and the State in Jordan, 1946–67*, ed. Tariq Tell, pp. 89–114. Amman: Centre d'études et de recherches sur le Moyen-Orient Contemporain, 2001.

Gershoni, Israel. "Rethinking the Formation of Arab Nationalism in the Middle East, 1920–1945: Old and New Narratives." In *Rethinking Nationalism in the Arab Middle East*, ed. James Jankowski and Israel Gershoni, pp. 3–25, 291–296. New York: Columbia University Press, 1997.

Gilbar, Gad G. "The Economy of Nablus and the Hashemites: The Early Years, 1949–56." *Middle Eastern Studies* 25, no. 1 (January 1989): 51–63.

Gilbert, Martin. *Winston S. Churchill: Documents July 1919–March 1921.* Vol. 4. Companion, Part 2. London: Heinemann, 1977.

Göçek, Fatma Müge. "The Decline of the Ottoman Empire and the Emergence of Greek, Armenian, Turkish, and Arab Nationalisms." In *Social Constructions of Nationalism in the Middle East*, ed. Fatma Müge Göçek, pp. 15–83. Albany: State University of New York Press, 2002.

————. "Introduction: Narrative, Gender, and Cultural Representation in the Constructions of Nationalism in the Middle East." In *Social Constructions of Nationalism in the Middle East*, ed. Fatma Müge Göçek, pp. 1–12. Albany: State University of New York Press, 2002.

Göçek, Fatma Müge, ed. *Social Constructions of Nationalism in the Middle East.* Albany: State University of New York Press, 2002.

Granott, A. *The Land System in Palestine: History and Structure.* Translated by M. Simon. London: Eyre & Spottiswoode, 1952.

Gubser, Peter. *Jordan: Crossroads of Middle Eastern Events.* Boulder, Colo.: Westview Press, 1983.

————. *Politics and Change in al-Karak, Jordan: A Study of a Small Arab Town and Its District.* London: Oxford University Press, 1973.

Hacker, Jane M. *Modern 'Amman: A Social Study.* Research Paper Series, ed. John I. Clarke, no. 3. Durham, N.C.: Department of Geography, Durham Colleges in the University of Durham, 1960.

Hadawi, Sami. *Palestine: Loss of a Heritage.* San Antonio, Tex.: Naylor Co., 1963.

Hale, Julian. *Radio Power: Propaganda and International Broadcasting.* London: Paul Elek, 1975.

Halpern, Manfred. *The Politics of Social Change in the Middle East and North Africa.* Princeton, N.J.: Princeton University Press, 1963.

Hamarneh, Mustafa B. "Jordan's Political Developments and Foreign Policy: A Brief Historical Overview." *Al-Nadwah* 7, no. 1 (July 1993): 13–23.

Hanna, Sami, and George H. Gardner. *Arab Socialism: A Documentary Study.* Salt Lake City: University of Utah Press, 1969.

Harkabi, Yehoshafat. "The Palestinians in the Fifties and Their Awakening as Reflected in Their Literature." In *Palestinian Arab Politics,* ed. Moshe Ma'oz, pp. 51–90. Jerusalem: Jerusalem Academic Press, 1975.

Harris, George L. *Jordan: Its People, Its Society, Its Culture.* New Haven, Conn.: Hraf Press, 1958.

Hatem, M. Abdel-Kader. *Information and the Arab Cause.* London: Longman Group, Ltd., 1974.

Hinnebusch, Raymond A. *Authoritarian Power and State Formation in Ba'thist Syria: Army, Party, and Peasant.* Boulder, Colo.: Westview Press, 1990.

Hobsbawm, E. J. *Nations and Nationalism since 1780: Programme, Myth, Reality.* Cambridge: Cambridge University Press, 1993.

Hopwood, Derek. *Egypt: Politics and Society 1945–1984.* Boston: Allen & Unwin, 1985.

Hourani, Albert. *Arabic Thought in the Liberal Age, 1798–1939.* Cambridge: Cambridge University Press, 1988.

———. *Syria and Lebanon: A Political Essay.* London: Oxford University Press, 1954.

Hudson, Michael C. *Arab Politics: The Search for Legitimacy.* New Haven, Conn.: Yale University Press, 1977.

Huntington, Samuel P. "Political Development and Political Decay." In *Politics in Transitional Societies: The Challenge of Change in Asia, Africa, and Latin America,* ed. Harvey G. Kebschull, pp. 288–296. New York: Appleton-Century-Crofts, 1968.

———. *Political Order in Changing Societies.* New Haven, Conn.: Yale University Press, 1969.

———. *The Third Wave: Democratization in the Late Twentieth Century.* Norman: University of Oklahoma Press, 1991.

Hyman, Herbert H. *Political Socialization: A Study in the Psychology of Political Behavior.* Glencoe, Ill.: Free Press, 1959.

Ismael, Tareq Y. *The Arab Left.* Syracuse, N.Y.: Syracuse University Press, 1976.

Jayyusi, Salma Khadra, ed. *Anthology of Modern Palestinian Literature.* New York: Columbia University Press, 1992.

Jones, L. W. "Demographic Review: Rapid Population Growth in Baghdad and Amman." *Middle East Journal* 23, no. 2 (Spring 1969): 209–215.

"Jordanie." *Cahiers de L'Orient Contemporain,* no. 21 (1er Semestre 1950): 85–88.

———. *Cahiers de L'Orient Contemporain,* no. 30 (2e Semestre 1954): 171–173.

———. *Cahiers de L'Orient Contemporain,* nos. 33–34 (Année 1956): 154–162.

———. *Cahiers de L'Orient Contemporain,* no. 37 (Année 1957): 98–109.

Jreisat, Jamil E. "Bureaucracy and Development in Jordan." In *Bureaucracy and Development in the Arab World,* ed. Joseph G. Jabbra, pp. 94–105. Leiden, the Netherlands: E. J. Brill, 1989.

Jureidini, Paul A., and William E. Hazen. *The Palestinian Movement in Politics.* Lexington, Mass.: Lexington Books, D. C. Heath and Co., 1976.

Kautsky, John H., ed. *Political Change in Underdeveloped Countries: Nationalism and Communism.* New York: John Wiley and Sons, 1962.

Kazem, Ali Abdul. "The Muslim Brotherhood: The Historic Background and the Ideological Origins." In *Islamic Movements in Jordan,* ed. Jillian Schwedler, trans. George A. Musleh, pp. 13–43. Amman: al-Urdun al-Jadid Research Center, 1997.

Kazziha, Walid. "The Political Evolution of Transjordan." *Middle Eastern Studies* 15, no. 2 (May 1979): 239–257.

———. *The Social History of Southern Syria (Trans-Jordan) in the 19th and Early 20th Century.* Beirut: Beirut Arab University, 1972.

Khalaf, Issa. *Politics in Palestine: Arab Factionalism and Social Disintegration, 1939–1948.* Albany: State University of New York Press, 1991.

Khalidi, Rashid. *Palestinian Identity: The Construction of Modern National Consciousness.* New York: Columbia University Press, 1997.

———. "The Palestinians and 1948: The Underlying Causes of Failure." In *The War for Palestine: Rewriting the History of 1948,* ed. Eugene L. Rogan and Avi Shlaim, pp. 12–36. Cambridge: Cambridge University Press, 2001.

Khayyali, A. W. *Palestine: A Modern History.* London: Croom Helm, 1978.

Khoury, Philip S. *Syria and the French Mandate: The Politics of Arab Nationalism, 1920–1945.* Princeton, N.J.: Princeton University Press, 1987.

———. *Urban Notables and Arab Nationalism: The Politics of Damascus 1860–1920.* Cambridge: Cambridge University Press, 1983.

Kimmerling, Baruch, and Joel S. Migdal. *Palestinians: The Making of a People.* Cambridge, Mass.: Harvard University Press, 1994.

Kingston, Paul. "Breaking the Patterns of Mandate: Economic Nationalism and State Formation in Jordan, 1951–1957." In *Village, Steppe and State: The Social Origins of Modern Jordan,* ed. Eugene L. Rogan and Tariq Tell, pp. 187–216. London: British Academic Press, 1994.

———. "Rationalizing Patrimonialism: Wasfi al-Tall and Economic Reform in Jordan, 1962–67." In *The Resilience of the Hashemite Rule: Politics and State in Jordan, 1946–67,* ed. Tariq Tell, pp. 115–144. Les Cahiers du CERMOC. No. 25. Amman: Centre d'études et de recherches sur le Moyen-Orient Contemporain, 2001.

Kirk, George E. *Contemporary Arab Politics: A Concise History.* London: Methuen & Co., 1961.

Kliot, Nurit, and Arnon Soffer. "The Emergence of a Metropolitan Core Area in a New State—The Case of Jordan." *Asian and African Studies* 20, no. 2 (July 1986): 217–232.

Konikoff, A. *Transjordan: An Economic Survey.* Jerusalem: Economic Research Institute of the Jewish Agency for Palestine, 1946.

Kornhauser, William. *The Politics of Mass Society.* Glencoe, Ill.: Free Press, 1959.

Kuroda, Alice K., and Yasumasa Kuroda. *Palestinians without Palestine: A Study of Political Socialization among Palestinian Youths.* Washington, D.C.: University Press of America, 1978.

L., J. D. "The Jordan Coup D'Etat: March 1st, 1956." *History Today* 7, no. 1 (January 1957): 3–10.

Landau, Jacob M., trans. "Political Tenets of the Liberation Party in Jordan." In *Man, State, and Society in the Contemporary Middle East*, ed. Jacob M. Landau, pp. 183–188. New York: Praeger, 1972.

Lane, Christel. *The Rites of Rulers: Ritual in Industrial Society—The Soviet Case.* Cambridge: Cambridge University Press, 1981.

Laqueur, Walter Z. *Communism and Nationalism in the Middle East.* London: Routledge & Keegan Paul, 1956.

———. "Communism in Jordan." *World Today* 12, no. 3 (March 1956): 109–119.

———. *Nasser's Egypt.* London: Weidenfeld and Nicolson, n.d.

Layne, Linda L. *Home and Homeland: The Dialogics of Tribal and National Identities in Jordan.* Princeton, N.J.: Princeton University Press, 1994.

———. "'Tribalism': National Representations of Life in Jordan." *Urban Anthology* 2 (Summer 1987): 183–203.

———. "Tribesmen as Citizens: 'Primordial Ties' and Democracy in Rural Jordan." In *Elections in the Middle East: Implications of Recent Trends*, ed. Linda L. Layne, pp. 113–151. Boulder, Colo.: Westview Press, 1987.

Lerner, Daniel. *The Passing of Traditional Society: Modernizing the Middle East.* New York: Free Press of Glencoe, 1958.

Lesch, Ann Mosely. *Arab Politics in Palestine, 1917–1939: The Frustration of a National Movement.* Ithaca, N.Y.: Cornell University Press, 1979.

Lewis, Norman N. *Nomads and Settlers in Syria and Jordan, 1800–1980.* Cambridge, Cambridge University Press, 1987.

Longrigg, Stephen Hemsley. *Syria and Lebanon under French Mandate.* London: Oxford University Press, 1958.

Louis, Wm. Roger, and Roger Owen. *The British Empire in the Middle East, 1945–1951: Arab Nationalism, the United States, and Postwar Imperialism.* Oxford: Clarendon Press, 1984.

———. *Suez 1956: The Crisis and Its Consequences.* Oxford: Clarendon Press, 1989.

Luciani, Giacomo, ed. *The Arab State.* London: Routledge, 1990.

Luke, Harry, and Edward Keith-Roach, eds. *The Handbook of Palestine and Trans-Jordan.* London: MacMillan and Co., 1934.

Lunt, James. *Hussein of Jordan: A Political Biography.* London: MacMillan, 1989.

Lust-Okar, Ellen M. "The Decline of Jordanian Political Parties: Myth or Reality?" *International Journal of Middle East Studies* 33, no. 4 (November 2001): 545–569.

Lutfiyya, Abdulla M. *Baytin, a Jordanian Village; a Study of Social Institutions and Social Change in a Folk Community.* The Hague: Morton, 1966.

McFadden, Tom J. *Daily Journalism in the Arab States.* Journalism Series, no. 15. Columbus: Ohio State University Press, 1953.

Mansfield, Peter. "Jordan and Palestine." In *The Shaping of an Arab Statesman: Sharif Abd al-Hamid Sharaf and the Modern Arab World*, ed. Patrick Seale, pp. 21–38. London: Quartet Books, 1983.

Ma'oz, Moshe. *Palestinian Leadership on the West Bank: The Changing Role of the Arab Mayors under Jordan and Israel.* London: Frank Cass, 1984.

Marayati, Abid A. *Middle Eastern Constitutions and Electoral Laws.* New York: Frederick A. Praeger, Pub., 1968.

Marlowe, John. *Arab Nationalism and British Imperialism: A Study in Power Politics.* London: Cresset Press, 1961.

Massad, Joseph A. *Colonial Effects: The Making of National Identity in Jordan.* New York: Columbia University Press, 2001.

Matthews, Roderic D., and Matta Akrawi. *Education in Arab Countries in the Near East.* Washington, D.C.: American Council on Education, 1949.

Mazur, Michael. "Economic Development in Jordan." In *Economic Development and Population Growth in the Middle East,* ed. Charles Cooper and Sidney S. Alexander, pp. 211–279. New York: American Elsevier Pub. Co., 1972.

———. *Economic Growth and Development in Jordan.* Boulder, Colo.: Westview Press, 1979.

The Middle East: 1950. London: Europa Pub., Ltd., 1950.

The Middle East: 1953. 3rd ed. London: Europa Pub., Ltd., 1953.

The Middle East: 1955. 4th ed. London: Europa Pub., Ltd., 1955.

The Middle East: 1957. 5th ed. London: Europa Pub., Ltd., 1957.

The Middle East: 1958. 6th ed. London: Europa Pub., Ltd., 1958.

The Middle East and the Refugees: A Program to Counter the Soviet Menace in the Middle East. Washington, D.C.: Public Affairs Institute, December 1958.

Migdal, Joel S. *Palestinian Society and Politics.* Princeton, N.J.: Princeton University Press, 1980.

———. *Strong Societies and Weak States: State-Society Relations and State Capabilities in the Third World.* Princeton, N.J.: Princeton University Press, 1988.

Miller, Ylana N. *Government and Society in Rural Palestine: 1920–1948.* Modern Middle East Series, No. 9. Austin: University of Texas Press, 1985.

Milton-Edwards, Beverley. "A Temporary Alliance with the Crown: The Islamic Response in Jordan." In *Islamic Fundamentalisms and the Gulf Crisis,* ed. James Piscatori, pp. 88–108. Chicago: American Academy of Arts and Sciences, 1991.

Mishal, Shaul. "Jordanian and Israeli Policy on the West Bank." In *The Hashemite Kingdom of Jordan and the West Bank: A Handbook,* ed. Anne Sinai and Allen Pollack, pp. 210–221. Middle East Confrontation Series. New York: American Academic Association for Peace in the Middle East, 1977.

———. *West Bank/East Bank: The Palestinians in Jordan, 1949–1967.* New Haven, Conn.: Yale University Press, 1978.

Moaddel, Mansoor. *Jordanian Exceptionalism: A Comparative Analysis of State-Religion Relationships in Egypt, Iran, Jordan, and Syria.* New York: Palgrave, 2002.

Neumann, Sigmund, ed. *Modern Political Parties: Approaches to Comparative Politics.* Chicago: University of Chicago Press, 1956.

Nevo, Joseph, and Ilan Pappé, eds. *Jordan in the Middle East: The Making of a Pivotal State, 1948–1988.* Newbury Park, Ilford, Essex, England: Frank Cass, 1994.

Ngugi wa Thiong'o. *Decolonising the Mind: The Politics of Language in African Literature*. London: James Currey, 1986.

———. *Writers in Politics: A Re-Engagement with Issues of Literature & Society*. Oxford: James Currey, 1997.

Norton, Augustus Richard, ed. *Civil Society in the Middle East*. Leiden, the Netherlands: E. J. Brill, 1995.

Ochsenwald, William. "Ironic Origins: Arab Nationalism in the Hijaz, 1882–1914." In *The Origins of Arab Nationalism*, ed. Rashid Khalidi, Lisa Anderson, Muhammad Muslih, and Reeva S. Simon, pp. 189–203. New York: Columbia University Press, 1991.

Olson, Robert W. *The Ba'th and Syria, 1947 to 1982: The Evolution of Ideology, Party, and State: From the French Mandate to the Era of Hafiz al-Asad*. Princeton, N.J.: Kingston Press, 1982.

Oren, Michael B. "A Winter of Discontent: Britain's Crisis in Jordan, December 1955–March 1956." *International Journal of Middle East Studies* 22, no. 2 (May 1990): 171–184.

Osseiran, Sanàa. "The Democratization Process in the Arab-Islamic States of the Middle East." In *Building Peace in the Middle East: Challenges for States and Civil Society*, ed. Elise Boulding, pp. 79–90. Boulder, Colo.: Lynne Rienner Publishers, 1994.

Owen, Roger. "The Practice of Electoral Democracy in the Arab East and North Africa." In *Rules and Rights in the Middle East: Democracy, Law, and Society*, ed. Ellis Goldberg, Resat Kasaba, and Joel Migdal, pp. 17–40. Seattle: University of Washington Press, 1993.

Pappé, Ilan. "Jordan between Hashemite and Palestinian Identity." In *Jordan in the Middle East: The Making of a Pivotal State, 1948–1988*, ed. Joseph Nevo and Ilan Pappé, pp. 61–91. Newbury Park, Ilford, Essex, England: Frank Cass, 1994.

———. "The State and the Tribe: Egypt and Jordan, 1948–88." In *Jordan in the Middle East: The Making of a Pivotal State, 1948–1988*, ed. Joseph Nevo and Ilan Pappé, pp. 161–188. Newbury Park, Ilford, Essex, England: Frank Cass, 1994.

Partner, Peter. *Arab Voices: The BBC Arabic Service 1938–1988*. London: British Broadcasting Corp., 1988.

Patai, Raphael. *The Kingdom of Jordan*. Princeton, N.J.: Princeton University Press, 1958.

Patai, Raphael, ed. *Jordan*. Country Survey Series. New Haven, Conn.: Human Relations Area Files, 1957.

Plascov, Avi. *The Palestinian Refugees in Jordan: 1948–1957*. London: Frank Cass, 1981.

Pye, Lucian W. "The Non-Western Political Process." In *Politics in Transitional Societies: The Challenge of Change in Asia, Africa, and Latin America*, ed. Harvey G. Kebschull, pp. 49–59. New York: Appleton-Century-Crofts, 1968.

Pye, Lucian W., and Sidney Verba, eds. *Political Culture and Political Development*. Princeton, N.J.: Princeton University Press, 1972.

Qadir, Shahid, Christopher Clapham, and Barry Gills. "Sustainable Democracy: Formalism vs. Substance." *Third World Quarterly* 14, no. 3 (1993): 415–422.

Quandt, William B. "Political and Military Dimensions of Contemporary Palestinian Nationalism." In *The Politics of Palestinian Nationalism*, ed. William B. Quandt, Fuad Jabber, and Ann Mosely Lesch, pp. 43–153. Berkeley and Los Angeles: University of California Press, 1973.

Rabinovich, Itamar. "Arab Political Parties: Ideology and Ethnicity." In *Ethnicity, Pluralism, and the State in the Middle East*, ed. Milton J. Esman and Itamar Rabinovich, pp. 155–172. Ithaca, N.Y.: Cornell University Press, 1988.

———. "The Suez-Sinai Campaign: The Regional Dimension." In *The Suez-Sinai Crisis, 1956: Retrospective and Reappraisal*, ed. Selwyn Ilan Troen and Moshe Shemesh, pp. 162–171. New York: Columbia University Press, 1990.

"Régime Représentatif Jordanien, Le." In *Etudes Tribu et Citoyennete*, no. 114, pp. 7–29. Maghreb: Machrek, October–November–December 1986.

Reid, Donald Malcolm. *Cairo University and the Making of Modern Egypt*. Cairo: American University in Cairo Press, 1990.

Al-Rimawi, ʿAbdullah. "Nationalism and Unity in the Modern Arab Movement." In *Political and Social Thought in the Contemporary Middle East*, ed. Kemal H. Karpat, pp. 147–153. New York: Frederick A. Praeger, Pub., 1968.

Roberts, David. *The Baʿth and the Creation of Modern Syria*. London: Croom Helm, 1987.

Rogan, Eugene L. *Frontiers of the State in the Late Ottoman Empire: Transjordan, 1850–1921*. Cambridge Middle East Studies 12. Cambridge: Cambridge University Press, 1999.

———. "The Making of a Capital: Amman, 1918–1928." In *Amman: Ville et Société—The City and Its Society*, ed. Jean Hannoyer and Seteney Shami, pp. 89–107. Beirut: Centre d'Études et de Recherches sur le Moyen-Orient Contemporain, 1996.

Rudé, George. *The Crowd in History: A Study of Popular Disturbances in France and England, 1730–1848*. London: Lawrence and Wishart, 1981.

Safran, Nadav. *From War to War: The Arab-Israeli Confrontation, 1948–1967*. New York: Pegasus, 1969.

Salibi, Kamal. *The Modern History of Jordan*. London: I. B. Tauris & Co., 1993.

Satloff, Robert B. *From Abdullah to Hussein: Jordan in Transition*. New York: Oxford University Press, 1994.

Sayigh, Rosemary. *Palestinians: From Peasants to Revolutionaries*. London: Zed Press, 1979.

Schiff, Zeev, and Raphael Rothstein. *Fedayeen: The Story of the Palestinian Guerrillas*. London: Vallentine, Mitchell, 1972.

Schleifer, Abdullah. "Izz al-Din al-Qassam: Preacher and *Mujahid*." In *Struggle and Survival in the Modern Middle East*, ed. Edmund Burke III, pp. 164–178. Berkeley and Los Angeles: University of California Press, 1993.

Schueftan, Dan. "Jordan's 'Israel Option.'" In *Jordan in the Middle East: The Making of a Pivotal State, 1948–1988*, ed. Joseph Nevo and Ilan Pappé, pp. 254–282. Newbury Park, Ilford, Essex, England: Frank Cass, 1994.

Scott, James. "Patronage or Exploitation?" In *Patrons and Clients in Mediterranean Societies*, ed. Ernest Gellner and John Waterbury, pp. 21–39. London: Gerald Duckworth & Co., Ltd., 1977.

Seale, Patrick. *The Struggle for Syria: A Study of Post-War Arab Politics, 1945–1958.* London: I. B. Tauris & Co., Ltd., 1986.

Seccombe, Ian. "Labour Migration and the Transformation of a Village Economy: A Case Study from Northwest Jordan." In *The Middle Eastern Village: Changing Economic and Social Relations*, ed. Richard Lawless, pp. 115–144. London: Croom Helm, 1987.

Seton, C. R. W. *Legislation of Transjordan, 1918–1930.* London: William Clowes & Sons, Ltd., n.d.

Shepherd, Naomi. *Ploughing Sand: British Rule in Palestine 1917–1948.* London: John Murray, 1999.

Shlaim, Avi. *Collusion across the Jordan: King Abdullah, the Zionist Movement, and the Partition of Palestine.* Oxford: Clarendon Press, 1988.

———. "Conflicting Approaches to Israel's Relations with the Arab: Ben Gurion and Sharett." *Middle East Journal* 37, no. 2 (Spring 1983): 180–201.

———. "The Debate about 1948." *International Journal of Middle East Studies* 27, no. 3 (August 1995): 287–304.

———. *The Politics of Partition: King Abdullah, the Zionists, and Palestine, 1921–1951.* New York: Oxford University Press, 1998.

Shryock, Andrew. *Nationalism and Genealogical Imagination: Oral History and Textual Authority in Tribal Jordan.* Berkeley and Los Angeles: University of California Press, 1997.

Shwadran, Benjamin. *Jordan: A State of Tension.* New York: Council for Middle Eastern Affairs, 1959.

———. "The Kingdom of Jordan: To Be or Not to Be." *Middle Eastern Affairs* 8, nos. 6–7 (June–July 1957): 206–225.

———. "The Kingdom of Jordan: To Be or Not to Be—II." *Middle Eastern Affairs* 8, nos. 8–9 (August–September 1957): 270–288.

Simon, Reeva. "The Imposition of Nationalism on a Non-Nation State: The Case of Iraq during the Interwar Period, 1921–1941." In *Rethinking Nationalism in the Arab Middle East*, ed. James Jankowski and Israel Gershoni. New York: Columbia University Press, 1997.

Sinai, Anne, and Allen Pollack, eds. *The Hashemite Kingdom of Jordan and the West Bank: A Handbook.* Middle East Confrontation Series. New York: American Academic Association for Peace in the Middle East, 1977.

Smith, Anthony. *The Ethnic Revival.* Cambridge: Cambridge University Press, 1981.

Smith, Charles D. *Palestine and the Arab-Israeli Conflict.* New York: St. Martin's Press, 1988.

Snow, Peter. *Hussein: A Biography.* London: Barrie & Jenkins, 1972.

Sofer, Naim. "The Political Status of Jerusalem in the Hashemite Kingdom of Jordan, 1948–1967." *Middle Eastern Studies* 12, no. 1 (January 1976): 73–94.

Sparrow, Gerald. *Modern Jordan.* London: George Allen and Unwin Ltd., 1961.

Starrett, Gregory. *Putting Islam to Work: Education, Politics, and Religious Transformation in Egypt*. Berkeley and Los Angeles: University of California Press, 1998.

Stein, Kenneth. "Palestine's Rural Economy, 1917–1939." *Studies in Zionism* 8 (Spring 1987): 25–49.

Sulaiman, Khalid A. *Palestine and Modern Arab Poetry*. London: Zed Books, Ltd., 1984.

Sullivan, Michael B. "Industrial Development in Jordan." In *The Economic Development of Jordan*, ed. Bichara Khader and Adnan Badran, pp. 133–142. London: Croom Helm, 1987.

Susser, Asher. *On Both Banks of the Jordan: A Political Biography of Wasfi al-Tall*. London: Frank Cass, 1994.

Swedenburg, Ted. *Memories of Revolt: The 1936–1939 Rebellion and the Palestinian National Past*. Minneapolis: University of Minnesota Press, 1995.

Tamimi, Azzam. *Islam and Democracy: Jordan and the Muslim Brotherhood*. Islamic Area Studies Working Paper Series, No. 18. Tokyo: Islamic Area Studies Project, 2000.

Taylor, Richard Loring. *Mustafa's Journey: Verse of 'Arar, Poet of Jordan*. Irbid, Jordan: Yarmouk University, 1988.

Thongchai Winichakul. *Siam Mapped: A History of the Geo-Body of a Nation*. Honolulu: University of Hawaii Press, 1994.

Tibawi, A. L. *Arab Education in Mandatory Palestine: A Study of Three Decades of British Administration*. London: Luzac & Company, Ltd., 1956.

———. *A Modern History of Syria, Including Lebanon and Palestine*. London: Macmillan & Co., Ltd., 1969.

Torrey, Gordon H., and John F. Devlin. "Arab Socialism." In *Politics in Transitional Societies: The Challenge of Change in Asia, Africa, and Latin America*, ed. Harvey G. Kebschull, pp. 137–141. New York: Appleton-Century-Crofts, 1968.

Totah, Khalil. "Education in Palestine." *Annals of the American Academy of Political and Social Science* 164 (November 1932): 155–166.

Vatikiotis, P. J. *Arab and Regional Politics in the Middle East*. London: Croom Helm, 1984.

———. *Politics and the Military in Jordan: A Study of the Arab Legion 1921–1957*. London: Frank Cass & Co., Ltd., 1967.

———. "The Politics of the Fertile Crescent." In *Political Dynamics in the Middle East*, ed. Paul Y. Hammond and Sidney S. Alexander, pp. 225–268. New York: American Elsevier Pub. Co., 1972.

Wahlin, Lars. "Diffusion and Acceptance of Modern Schooling in Rural Jordan." In *The Middle Eastern Village: Changing Economic and Social Relations*, ed. Richard Lawless, pp. 145–174. London: Croom Helm, 1987.

Wilson, Mary C. "The Hashemites, the Arab Revolt, and Arab Nationalism." In *The Origins of Arab Nationalism*, ed. Rashid Khalidi, Lisa Anderson, Muhammad Muslih, and Reeva S. Simon, pp. 204–221. New York: Columbia University Press, 1991.

———. *King Abdullah, Britain and the Making of Jordan*. Cambridge: Cambridge University Press, 1990.

World Bank. *The Economic Development of Jordan: Report of a Mission Organized by the International Bank for Reconstruction and Development at the Request of the Government of Jordan.* Baltimore: Johns Hopkins University Press, 1957.

Yorke, Valerie. *Domestic Politics and Regional Security: Jordan, Syria and Israel: The End of an Era?* Aldershot, England: International Institute for Strategic Studies, Gower, 1988.

PUBLISHED SOURCES: ARABIC

al-'Arif, 'Arif. *Tarikh al-Quds [History of Jerusalem].* Egypt: Dar al-Ma'arif, 1951.

Dajani, Amin Hafiz. *al-Intidab al-Baritani, 1918–1948 [The British Mandate, 1918–1948].* Vol. 1, *Jabhat al-Tarbiyah wa-al-Ta'lim wa-Nidaliha Dhidda al-Isti'mar: al-Baramij wa-al-Manahij wa-al-Mu'allumun wa-al-Tullab 'Abra 'Arba'a 'Uhud [The Education Front and Its Struggle against Colonialism: The Programs, Curricula, Teachers and Students across Four Eras].* n.p.: n.p., 199- .

al-Falhut, Sabar. *Tatawwur Tarikh al-Sihafah al-Suriyah wa-al-Urduniyah [Development of the History of the Syrian and Jordanian Presses].* Qism al-Dirasat fi al-Wakalah al-'Arabiyah al-Suriyah lil-Anba' wa-Wizarat al-Thaqafah wa-al-I'lam, Mudiriyat al-Dirasat wa-al-Buhuth. Damascus: n.p., 1976.

Fu'ad Nasser: al-Rajul . . . wa-al-Qadhiyah [Fu'ad Nasser: The Man . . . and the Issue]. Jerusalem: Manshurat Salah al-Din, 1977.

Haikal, Yusuf. *Filastin: Qabla wa-Ba'd [Palestine: Before and After].* Beirut: Dar al-'Ilm lil-Malayin, 1971.

Hajazin, Ibrahim. "al-Hizb al-Shuyu'i wa-al-Jabhah al-Wataniyah wa Hukumat al-Nabulsi" ["The Communist Party, the National Front, and the Government of Nabulsi"]. In *Hukumat Sulayman al-Nabulsi: 1956/1957 [The Government of Sulayman al-Nabulsi: 1956/1957]*, supervised by Hani Hourani, pp. 121–137. Amman: Dar Sindibad lil-Nashr, 1999.

Hourani, Hani. "Intakhabat Tashrin al-Awal 1956 wa-al-Majlis al-Niyabi al-Khamisa" ["The Elections of October 1956 and the Fifth Legislative Majlis"]. In *Hukumat Sulayman al-Nabulsi: 1956/1957 [The Government of Sulayman al-Nabulsi: 1956/1957]*, supervised by Hani Hourani, pp. 21–39. Amman: Dar Sindibad lil-Nashr, 1999.

———. *al-Iqtisad al-Urduni [The Jordanian Economy].* Cyprus: T. H. O. Publishers Co., Ltd., 1989.

———. *Tarikh al-Hayat al-Niyabiyah fi al-Urdun [The History of Parliamentary Life in Jordan, 1929–1957].* Nicosia, Cyprus: Sharq Press Ltd., September 1989.

———. *al-Tarkib al-Iqtisadi al-Ijtima'i li-Sharq al-Urdun (1921–1950) [The Socio-Economic Structure of Trans-Jordan (1921–1950)].* Beirut: Munazzamat al-Tahrir al-Filastiniyah, Markaz al-Abhath, n.d.

Khrainou, Samir. *al-Harakat al-Tullabiyah al-Urduniyah 1948–1998 [The Jordanian Student Movement 1948–1998].* Amman: Al-Urdun al-Jadid Research Center, 2000.

al-Khufash, Husni Salih. *Hawla Tarikh al-Harakah al-'Ummaliyah al-'Arabiyah al-Filastiniyah: Mudhakkirat [The Arab Palestine Labour Movements: Memoirs].*

Silsilat Kutub, no. 2. Beirut: Munazzamat al-Tahrir al-Filastiniyah, Markaz al-Abhath, May 1973.

al-Mahafazah, Ali. *al-ʿAlaqat al-Urduniyah al-Baritaniyah: min Taʾsis al-Imarah Hatta Ilghaʾ al-Muʿahadah (1921–1957) [Jordanian and British Relations—From the Establishment of the Emirate to the End of the Treaty (1921–1957)]*. Beirut: Dar al-Nahar lil-Nashr, 1973.

Muhadin, Mufaq. *al-Ahzab wa-al-Quwa al-Siyasiyah fi al-Urdun [Political Parties and Forces in Jordan 1927–1987: A Bibliography]*. Beirut: Dar al-Sidaq lil-Tibaʿah wa-al-Nashr, 1988.

Murad, Abbas. *al-Dawr al-Siyasi lil-Jaysh al-Urduni (1921–1973) [The Political Role of the Jordanian Army (1921–1973)]*. Silsilat Kutub, no. 48. Beirut: Munazzamat al-Tahrir al-Filastiniyah, Markaz al-Abhath, December 1973.

Musa, Sulayman. *Aʿlam min al-Urdun: Hazzaʿ al-Majali, Sulayman al-Nabulsi, Wasfi al-Tell [Distinguished Men of Jordan: Hazzaʿ al-Majali, Sulayman al-Nabulsi, Wasfi al-Tell]*. Amman: al-Mamlakah al-Urduniyah al-Hashimiyah, 1986.

———. *Awraq min Dafter al-Ayyam: Dhikrayat al-Raʿil al-Awal [Papers from a Daily Journal: Memoirs of the First Contingent]*. Amman: al-Mamlakah al-Urduniyah al-Hashimiyah, with support from Amanat Amman al-Kubra, 2000.

Musa, Sulayman, and Munib al-Madi. *Tarikh al-Urdun fi al-Qarn al-ʿIshrin [The History of Jordan in the Twentieth Century]*. Amman: Maktabah al-Muhtasib, 1988.

Naqrash, ʿAbdullah. *al-Tajribah al-Hizbiyah fi al-Urdun [Party Experience in Jordan]*. Amman: Lajnah Tarikh al-Urdun, 1991.

ʿOda, Sadiq Ibrahim. "al-Kuliyah al-ʿArabiyah fi-il-Quds 1918–1948: Maʿlumat wa-Dhikrayat" ["The Arab College in Jerusalem 1918–1948: Facts and Remembrances"]. *Majalat al-Dirasat al-Filastiniyah [Journal of Palestinian Studies]* 40 (Fall 1999): 170–188.

al-Qaymari, Muhammad Sulayman. *al-Harakah al-ʿUmmaliyah al-Niqabiyah fi al-Urdun (1950–1970) [The Trade-Unionist Movement in Jordan 1950–1970]*. n.p.: n.p., 1982.

Shardan, Musa ʿAdil Bikamarza. *al-Urdun bayna ʿAhdayn [Jordan between Two Periods]*. n.p.: n.p., n.d.

Susser, Asher. *al-Khatt al-Akhdar bayna al-Urdun wa-Filastin: Sirat Wasfi al-Tell al-Siyasiyah [The Green Line between Jordan and Palestine: The Political Story of Wasfi al-Tell]*. Translated by Jawdat al-Saʾd. Amman: Dar Azminah lil-Nashr, 1994.

al-Tell, Bilal Hasan. *al-Urdun: Muhawalah lil-Fahm [Jordan: An Attempt to Understand]*. Amman: al-Muʾassasah al-Sahifiyah al-Urduniyah—al-Raʾy, 1976.

al-Tell, Saʿid. *al-Urdun wa-Filastin: Wijhat Nazar ʿArabiyah [Jordan and Palestine: An Arab Point of View]*. Amman: Dar al-Jalil lil-Nashr, 1984.

DISSERTATIONS AND THESES: ENGLISH AND ARABIC

Amawi, Abla Mohamed. "State and Class in Transjordan: A Study of State Autonomy. (Volumes I and II)." Ph.D. diss., Georgetown University, 1993.

Ameri, Anan. "Socioeconomic Development in Jordan (1950–1980): An Application of Dependency Theory." Ph.D. diss., Wayne State University, 1981.

Goldner, Werner Ernst. "The Role of Abdullah Ibn Husain, King of Jordan, in Arab Politics, 1914–1951: Critical Analysis of His Political Activities." Ph.D. diss., Stanford University, 1954.

al-Misri, Muhammad. "al-Urdun 1953–1957: Darasat Siyasiyah" ["Jordan 1953–1957: A Political Study"]. Master's thesis, University of Jordan, 1995.

Phillips, Paul Grounds. *The Hashemite Kingdom of Jordan: Prolegomena to a Technical Assistance Program.* Research Paper #34. Ph.D. diss., University of Chicago, 1954.

Roberts, John M. "The Political Economy of Identity: State and Society in Jordan." Ph.D. diss., University of Chicago, 1994.

al-Tall, Ahmad Yousef. "Education in Jordan: Being a Survey of the Political, Economic and Social Conditions Affecting the Development of the System of Education in Jordan, 1921–1977." Ph.D. diss., Sind University, Hyderabad, Pakistan, 1978.

TEXTBOOKS

al-Alami, Akram Sa'id. *Watanuna al-'Arabi al-Kabir [Our Great Arab Nation].* Fifth Elementary Level. Jerusalem: Wizarat al-Tarbiyah wa-al-Ta'lim al-Urduniyah, 1965.

Anabtawi, Wasfi, and Sa'id al-Sabagh. *Jugrafiyat Filastin wa-al-Bilad al-'Arabiyah [Geography of Palestine and the Arab Countries].* Jaffa: Maktabah al-Tahir Ikhwan, 1946.

Ayesh, Husni, Watfa al-Jabi, and Yusif Jum'a. *al-Tarikh al-'Arabi al-Hadith wa-al-Mu'asir [Modern and Contemporary Arab History].* Sixth Grade Reader. Amman: Wizarat al-Tarbiyah wa-al-Ta'lim al-Urduniyah, 1971.

al-Dabagh, Mustafa Murad. *Tarikh al-Filastin.* Sixth Grade Reader. Commissioned by Wizarat al-Tarbiyah wa-al-Ta'lim al-Urduniyah. Amman: Matb'at al-Istiqlal, 1956.

Druza, Muhammad Aza. *Durus al-Tarikh al-'Arabi min Aqdam al-Azmanah ila Alan [Studies of Arab History from the Oldest of Times to Today].* Damascus: al-Maktabah al-Wataniyah al-'Arabiyah bi Haifa, 1934.

al-Dura, Sa'id. *al-Hilal al-Khasib [The Fertile Crescent].* Cairo: Sharia Faruq, 1946.

al-Dura, Sa'id, Abdul-Rahim Mur'ib, Sadiq Uda, and Abd al-Bari al-Shaykh Dura. *al-Tarikh al-'Arabi al-Hadith [Modern Arab History].* Amman: Wizarat al-Tarbiyah wa-al-Ta'lim al-Urduniyah, 1975.

al-Dura, Sa'id, Abdul-Rahim Mur'ib, Sadiq Uda, and Abdul-Bari al-Shaykh Dura. *al-Tarikh al-'Arabi al-Hadith [Modern Arab History].* Third Secondary Level. Amman: Wizarat al-Tarbiyah wa-al-Ta'lim al-Urduniyah, 1969.

Ghahnawi, Wasfi, Sa'id Dura, Sa'id al-Sabagh, and Husni Fariz. *al-Watan al-'Arabi [The Arab Nation].* Fourth Elementary Level. Amman: Wizarat al-Tarbiyah wa-al-Ta'lim al-Urduniyah, n.d.

al-Hijawi, Yahya Tahir, Sadi Murad al-Khayat, and Adnan Lutfi Uthman. *Tarik-huna al-Hadith [Our Modern History]*. Sixth Grade Reader. Nablus: Wizarat al-Tarbiyah wa-al-Taʿlim al-Urduniyah, 1959.

al-Hindawi, Thuqan. *al-Qathiyah al-Filastiniyah [The Palestinian Issue]*. Third Secondary Level. Amman: Wizarat al-Tarbiyah wa-al-Taʿlim al-Urduniyah, 1964.

al-Kaylani, Saif al-Din Zaid, and Abbas Ahmad al-Kurd. *al-Mujtamaʿ al-Urduni [Jordanian Society]*. Amman: Wizarat al-Tarbiyah wa-al-Taʿlim al-Urduniyah, 1964.

al-Qaymari, Muhammad, Abbas al-Kurd, and Abd al-Muhaysin Jabir. *Tarikh al-ʿArab: Min al-ʿAbd al-ʿUthmani hata al-Waqt al-Hadith [History of the Arabs: From the Ottoman Era to the Present Time]*. 9th ed. Commissioned by Wizarat al-Tarbiyah wa-al-Taʿlim al-Urduniyah. Amman: Matbʿat Dar al-Aytam al-Islamiyah al-Sinaʿyah bi al-Quds, 1959.

INDEX

JNM in the index refers to Jordanian National Movement (JNM).

Abdul Illah, Prince, 157
'Abdullah, King: and Abu Ghu-
    naymah, 74, 218–219n.45, 219–
    220n.69; and Arab nationalism,
    20, 197; assassination of, 147, 149,
    199; compared with King Husayn,
    5; criticisms of, 46, 50; and end of
    British Mandate in Jordan, 1–2;
    as head of Hashemite Kingdom of
    Jordan, 79, 82; as head of Trans-
    jordan government, 15, 17, 18, 19,
    33–34, 38–60, 66; and King's men,
    53, 59, 145, 149, 208n.10; and
    Muslim Brotherhood, 117, 141;
    and al-Nabulsi, 77; non-
    Jordanians in government and
    army under, 42–43, 53–54;
    number of tribesmen accompa-
    nying, 213n.10; and Ottoman
    Empire, 207n.5; and Palestine's
    union with Jordan, 114–115, 199,
    226nn.139,140; and pan-Arabism,
    37–39; and religious rituals, 90;
    textbooks on, 1–2, 198; and Zion-
    ism, 199, 226n.140
Abu Gharbiyah, Bahjat: as ambassador
    to Syria, 202; and Arab-Israeli War

(1948), 113; on Arab nationalism,
    12, 13; arrests and imprisonment
    of, 152, 155; and Baghdad Pact,
    161; and Ba'th Party, 87, 92, 136,
    137, 209n.3; on elections of 1954,
    154; in elections of 1956, 173, 175;
    exile of, 202; and job discrimina-
    tion against Communists, 233n.15;
    memoirs by, 87; on 1957 coup
    attempt against King Husayn, 184;
    after 1957 coup attempt against
    King Husayn, 186; opposition of,
    to Abu'l-Huda as prime minister,
    151–152; and Palestinian issues,
    203; return of, to Jordan in 1960s,
    202; in scout troop, 103; on size of
    JNM, 142–143; youth of, 92–93,
    103
Abu-Ghazaleh, Adnan, 90–91, 100,
    223n.66
Abu Ghunaymah, Subhi, 74, 77, 81,
    218–219n.45, 219–220n.69
Abu'l-Huda, Hasan Khalid, 48, 50
Abu'l-Huda, Tawfiq: arrests under,
    82, 152; and assassination of King
    'Abdullah, 149; Bseiso on, 233n.18;
    and deposing of King Talal, 150;
    and elections of 1954, 154, 175;
    and al-Hizb al 'Arabi al-Dusturi
    [Arab Constitutional Party],

of, 15–18, 40–42; British Mandate in, 1–2, 4, 15–16, 38–60, 117; constitutions of, 79–80, 149; Defense Law in, 82; economy of, during 1950s-1960s, 121–124, 131, 162, 195–196; employment and unemployment in, 122–123, 162, 189, 196; establishment of, 2; Hashemite-Jordanian nationalism in, 15–22, 32, 196–200; Hashemite Kingdom of, 79–80; independence for, in 1946, 79; Israeli attacks against West Bank, 130–131, 151, 172–173; land reform in, 122; martial law in, 185, 203; nationalist rule of, in 1956-1957, 177–182, 187–191; 1957 coup attempt against King Husayn in, 62, 182–184, 198–199, 240n.50; Palestine's union with, 114–115, 199, 208n.11, 226nn.139,140, 227n.146; Palestinians as government officials in, 130, 194; population of, 122; scholarship on, 4–6; termination of Anglo-Jordanian Treaty, 179–180, 193, 198; textbooks on, 1–4, 67–68, 194, 196–200, 241n.7; tribal names on maps of, 21; urban areas and urbanization in, 2–3, 6–8, 124–127, 162, 174; writing national narrative for, 1–11, 196–200, 204–205. *See also* 'Abdullah, King; Anglo-Jordanian Treaty; Arab Legion; Elections; Husayn, King; Parliament, Jordanian; Transjordan; *and headings beginning with Jordanian, specific cities*

Jordanian Arab Army (JAA), 168, 173, 196, 200, 236n.84. *See also* Arab Legion

Jordanian Arab Legion. *See* Arab Legion

Jordanian Arab Party, 81, 220n.73

Jordanian Folklore Museum, 201

Jordanian Free Youth Association, 74

Jordanian Museum of Popular Traditions, 201

Jordanian National Guard, 130, 131

Jordanian National Movement (JNM): and assassination of King 'Abdullah, 147, 149; and Baghdad Pact (1955), 161–167, 190; compared with "Transjordan for the Transjordanians" movement, 169; destruction of, by Hashemites, 4, 5, 8, 11, 182–191; and economic change, 121–127; and education, 119–121; and Eisenhower Doctrine, 185; and elections of 1954, 153–156; and elections of 1956, 168, 172–177, 190–191, 238n.16; fragmentation of and conflicts within, 145, 180–182, 187, 238n.20; and Glubb's dismissal, 167–168; goals of, 7, 117–119, 142, 148, 169, 204; influence of parties versus leaders in, 143–145; and King Husayn, 4, 148, 150–156, 177–182, 187, 189–191, 202; leaders of, 7, 8–10, 24, 62–65, 83, 119, 143–145; motivations for joining, 9–10; and Muslim Brotherhood, 142, 158; and Nasser, 144, 145, 148, 158–160, 191; National Congress of, in 1957, 185; and nationalist rule in 1956-1957, 170–171, 177–182, 187–191; and news media, 127–130; and Palestinian issues, 130–131, 159, 188; Palestinians in, 4, 7–10, 24, 87, 118, 159; and political freedoms of 1950s, 147–148; political parties of, 4, 11, 131–145; size of, 142–146; slogans of, 145; and Suez Crisis, 176–177; support for, 119–131; and Talal, 147–150; as unified movement, 145–146

Jordanian National Party, 74

Jordanian People's Party, 81

Jordanian Student Union, 120–121

Jumani, Dafi al-, 140, 232n.98

Kamal, Asaf, 101
Kamal, Hatim, 88, 101, 224n.85
Karim, Abd al-Karim, 98
Karmi, Ghada, 88, 91, 106, 221n.10
Kautsky, John H., 126
Kazem, Ali Abdul, 202
Khalaf, Issa, 86
Khalidi, Husayn Fakhri al-, 184–185
Khalidi, Rashid, 22, 23, 85, 86
Khalil, Muhammad, 112
Khatib, Amin al-: and Arab-Israeli War (1948), 113; on Arab Revolt (1936–1939) in Palestine, 109; and Ba'th Party, 88; education and student political activism of, 100, 103; imprisonment of, 186; and Movement of Arab Nationalists, 139–140; and UNRWA, 186; youth of, 92
Khatib, Anwar al-, 181
Khiza'i, Rashid al-, 50
Khoury, Philip, 218n.40
Khrainou, Samir, 121
King's men: and Arab Constitutional Party, 237n.10; after assassination of King 'Abdullah, 149; decline in influence of, 195; and JNM, 185, 189; and King 'Abdullah, 53, 59, 145, 149, 208n.10; and King Husayn, 4, 150, 151, 177, 181, 184, 185, 188, 189, 190; and al-Tell government, 195
Kingston, Paul, 194, 195
Kirkbride, Alec, 5, 16, 41, 57, 79, 208n.16, 210n.11
Konikoff, A., 212n.48
al-Kura rebellion, 44
Kurdi, Abdul Rahman al-, 234n.24
Al-Kutla al-wataniyah [National Bloc in Syria], 72, 74, 218n.40

Land Law (1858), 34
Land reform, 19, 58–59, 122

Land rights and land ownership, 41–42, 45
Lane, Christel, 89–90
Language and culture, 25–26
Layne, Linda, 200, 201
League of National Action, 72–73, 75
League of National Liberation, 106, 134, 230n.69
League of Nations, 51, 110
Lebanon, 17, 26, 72–76, 94, 114, 138, 203
Lerner, Daniel, 127
Liberation Rally, 158

Madanat, 'Isa, 62, 63–64, 76, 77, 134–135, 181
Mahafazah, Ali al-, 144
Mahmud, Abd al-Rahim, 101
Majali, Atawi al-, 45
Majali, Hazza' al-, 70, 138, 155, 162, 164, 165, 193, 218n.28, 234n.24
Majali, Muhammad Bajis al-, 65, 77, 127, 155, 216–217n.11
Majali, Rafiqan al-, 65
Majali, Rufayfan al-, 45, 213–214n.27
Majlis al-A'yan [Chamber of Notables], 80, 115, 202
Majlis al-Nuwwab [Chamber of Deputies]: and Baghdad Pact, 161; creation of, 79–80; and Eisenhower Doctrine, 178; and elections of 1954, 153–154, 156; and elections of 1956, 168, 173–177; King Talal deposed by, 150; and al-Nabulsi government, 182; and National Front, 137; opposition bloc in, 136; Palestinians in, 115, 130, 131; size of, after union of Jordan and Palestine, 115; and Tahrir Party, 141
Majlis al-Ummah [Parliament], 79–80. See also Parliament
Ma'oz, Moshe, 125
Masri, Hikmat al-, 165
Massad, Joseph, 6, 18, 41, 45, 51, 57–58, 168, 184

Milton Keynes UK
Ingram Content Group UK Ltd.
UKHW012106230923
429161UK00016B/402